Journal of Biblical Literature

Volume 137
2018

GENERAL EDITOR
ADELE REINHARTZ
University of Ottawa
Ottawa, ON K1N 6N5

A Quarterly Published by
SBL Press

JOURNAL OF BIBLICAL LITERATURE

EDITORS OF THE JOURNAL
General Editor: ADELE REINHARTZ, University of Ottawa
Managing Editor: JONATHAN M. POTTER, Society of Biblical Literature
Editorial Assistant: JONATHAN C. GROCE, Society of Biblical Literature

EDITORIAL BOARD

ELIZABETH BOASE, Flinders University
HELEN BOND, University of Edinburgh
JO-ANN A. BRANT, Goshen College
TONY BURKE, York University
DAVID M. CARR, Union Theological Seminary
RICHARD J. CLIFFORD, Boston College
KELLEY COBLENTZ BAUTCH, St. Edwards University
COLLEEN CONWAY, Seton Hall University
TOAN DO, Australian Catholic University
KATHY EHRENSPERGER, University of Potsdam
GEORG FISCHER, Leopold-Franzens-Universität Innsbruck
PAULA FREDRIKSEN, Hebrew University of Jerusalem
WIL GAFNEY, Brite Divinity School
FRANCES TAYLOR GENCH, Union Presbyterian Seminary
SHIMON GESUNDHEIT, Hebrew University of Jerusalem
MARK GOODACRE, Duke University
MARTIEN A. HALVORSON-TAYLOR, University of Virginia (Charlottesville)
RACHEL HAVRELOCK, University of Illinois at Chicago
ELSE K. HOLT, Aarhus Universitet
DAVID G. HORRELL, University of Exeter
CAROLINE E. JOHNSON HODGE, College of the Holy Cross
JONATHAN KLAWANS, Boston University
JENNIFER KNUST, Boston University
BRUCE W. LONGENECKER, Baylor University
MICHAEL A. LYONS, Simpson University
DANIEL MACHIELA, McMaster University
JOHN W. MARSHALL, University of Toronto
NAPHTALI MESHEL, Hebrew University of Jerusalem
CHRISTINE MITCHELL, St. Andrew's College, University of Saskatchewan
KENNETH NGWA, Drew University
KEN M. PENNER, St. Francis Xavier University
PIERLUIGI PIOVANELLI, University of Ottawa
MARK REASONER, Marian University
THOMAS RÖMER, Collège de France and University of Lausanne
DALIT ROM-SHILONI, Tel Aviv University
JEAN-PIERRE RUIZ, St. John's University (New York)
SETH L. SANDERS, University of California, Davis
KONRAD SCHMID, University of Zurich
WILLIAM M. SCHNIEDEWIND, University of California, Los Angeles
ABRAHAM SMITH, Perkins School of Theology, Southern Methodist University
JOHANNA STIEBERT, University of Leeds
JOHN T. STRONG, Missouri State University
MATTHEW THIESSEN, McMaster University
STEVEN TUELL, Pittsburgh Theological Seminary
CECILIA WASSEN, Uppsala University
EMMA WASSERMAN, Rutgers University
LAWRENCE M. WILLS, Episcopal Divinity School

The Society of Biblical Literature is a constituent member of the American Council of Learned Societies. *President of the Society:* Brian K. Blount, Union Presbyterian Seminary, Richmond, VA 23227; *Vice President:* Gale A. Yee, Episcopal Divinity School, Cambridge, MA 02138; *Chair, Research and Publications Committee:* M. Patrick Graham, Candler School of Theology, Atlanta, GA 30322; *Executive Director:* John F. Kutsko, Society of Biblical Literature, 825 Houston Mill Road, Suite 350, Atlanta, GA 30329.

The *Journal of Biblical Literature* (ISSN 0021–9231) is published quarterly by the Society of Biblical Literature, 825 Houston Mill Road, Suite 350, Atlanta, GA 30329. The annual subscription price is US$55.00 for members and US$220.00 for nonmembers. Institutional and online rates are also available. For information regarding subscriptions and membership, contact: SBL Press, 825 Houston Mill Road, Suite 350, Atlanta, GA 30329. Phone: 866-727-9955 (toll free) or 404-727-9498. E-mail: sblservices@sbl-site.org. For information concerning permission to quote, editorial and business matters, please see the first issue of the year, p. 2. Periodical postage paid at Atlanta, Georgia, and at additional mailing offices. POSTMASTER: Send address changes to SBL Press, 825 Houston Mill Road, Suite 350, Atlanta, GA 30329. Copyright © 2018 by the SBL Press.

JBL is indexed in the following resources:

Arts and Humanities Citation Index
Scopus
ATLA Religion Database
Religious and Theological Abstracts
New Testament Abstracts (ATLA)
Old Testament Abstracts (ATLA)
Periodicals Index online (Proquest)
European Reference Index for the Humanities

PRINTED IN THE UNITED STATES OF AMERICA

Editor's Foreword

Passing the Torch

ADELE REINHARTZ

This issue of the *Journal of Biblical Literature* marks my last as General Editor. On December 31, 2018, I will conclude a sixteen-year stint with the *Journal*: nine years as an editorial board member, and seven as General Editor. Since 2012, I have spent countless hours reading submissions, assigning them to reviewers, reading the reviews, making decisions, copyediting, and proofreading. No one will be surprised to learn that I look forward, just a bit, to having that time freed up for other tasks and pastimes. Yet as I look back on these years, it is not the time spent that first comes to mind but the satisfaction of being involved in a worthwhile enterprise, and gratitude for the opportunity to learn so much about our field, far beyond the limited areas of my own expertise. It has been a privilege and a pleasure to serve the *Journal* and the Society of Biblical Literature in this way. And it is with confidence that I turn the *Journal* over to the care of Mark Brett, who, I hope, will enjoy his tenure as General Editor much as I have enjoyed mine.

When I first began as General Editor, I aimed above all to continue the fine work of my predecessors, the late Gail O'Day and James VanderKam. Gail and Jim were the General Editors of *JBL* during my years as an editorial board member, and they set a high bar for their successors. In addition, however, I set myself a small number of goals. The first was to move the *Journal* from a paper and snail-mail system to a web-based endeavor. I did not have the time, space, institutional support, or desire to store physical copies of all submissions, to keep manual records, or to send paper copies by mail to reviewers. Our first attempt was via an improvised database and email system that was helpful but cumbersome. We then experimented with and considered other web-based systems until we settled on Scholastica. As our technical issues have been (mostly) ironed out, it has been possible for us to think about how best to use the data that Scholastica provides in order to get a better understanding of how, and how well, *JBL* is serving our community.

My hope was that by moving to a more efficient, web-based system, we would be able to achieve a second goal: to improve our time lines, especially the lengthy time from submission to decision. We have indeed seen some improvement, but there is still more work to be done, especially given the ever-increasing number of submissions. In order to address the problem, while still maintaining our firm commitment to a thorough, double-blind peer review process, I have gradually increased the size of the board; I have also secured more guest reviews by experts outside the editorial board, especially for highly specialized articles. I continue to hope that with such measures our time lines will decrease significantly over the coming years.

Another goal was to maintain and improve the diversity on the editorial board, with the aim of better mirroring the diversity of SBL membership and taking into account the wide range of approaches and methods that are increasingly being deployed in our field. Previous General Editors had already been paying attention to gender diversity as well as to international representation on the board; I have taken care to include African American, Asian/Asian American, and Latino/a scholars, and in the process have come to know the work of many fine scholars whom I had not previously encountered.

On a related note, we continue to monitor the percentage of articles submitted, accepted, and published by women authors. For reasons that I do not entirely understand, the statistics have remained fairly constant over many years. Approximately 20 percent of submitted articles are by women. But it is worth noting that every year starting from 2013 to the present has seen a greater share of manuscript submissions by women compared with the period 2005–2011. It remains my hope that more women will consider *JBL* as a venue for publication. Despite the discrepancy in numbers, we are committed to ensuring that each issue contains at least two and preferably more articles by women authors.[1]

Finally, I aimed to broaden the range and types of articles we publish. I soon learned that the *Journal*'s reputation as a home primarily for historical-critical and philological scholarship discouraged some scholars from submitting other sorts of articles for consideration. As I perused the issues published under my two predecessors, however, it became clear that *JBL* had already been publishing articles using diverse approaches such as literary analysis, social-scientific criticism, and queer theory. Memorable titles include "The Politics of Interpretation: The Rhetoric of Race and Ethnicity in Paul" (2004), "Paul, the Goddess Religions, and Queer Sects: Romans 1:23–28" (2011), "The Man with the Flow of Power: Porous Bodies in Mark 5:25–34 (2010), and "Ideology and Social Context of the Deuteronomic Women's Sex Laws (Deuteronomy 22:13–29)" (2009), addressing issues of race, ethnicity, gender, sexuality, disability, and many others. The obstacle was not, and is not, implicit bias against certain types of articles or authors but outdated

---

[1] For a detailed report on statistics pertaining to *JBL* article submission, review, and publication over the past several years, see the forthcoming *JBL* Analysis posted on the *JBL* webpage (https://www.sbl-site.org/publications/journals_jbl_nologin.aspx).

reputation. My task therefore was to convince scholars whose views of the *Journal* had been shaped in days gone by to take another look.

One way I attempted to do so was via an Occasional Forum series, for which I solicited articles and responses on a particular topic. These invited contributions were not subject to double-blind peer review, though they did undergo the same careful editorial process as did the articles that were accepted via our peer review process. These Forums focused on areas of controversy within the field, such as postmodernism, or areas not often addressed in submissions to the *Journal*, such as African biblical interpretation, and, perhaps most striking in the American context, Black Lives Matter. As for turning around the *Journal*'s reputation, I have begun to see some movement, at least with regard to the articles being submitted, and draw encouragement from the fact that editorial board member Wil Gafney's contribution to the *JBL* Forum on "Black Lives Matter for Critical Biblical Scholarship" is in the list of top five *JBL* articles downloaded from JSTOR.

This is not to say, however, that *JBL* is moving away from historical-critical scholarship or that it should do so. It is certainly important, in my view, for the *Journal* better to reflect the diversity of approaches, topics, and concerns of our field, which will develop and change over time and in response to intellectual, social, and political currents in the United States and globally. Nevertheless, the ongoing major presence in the *Journal* of the sort of scholarship traditionally associated with higher biblical criticism speaks not just to the *Journal*'s long-standing reputation but also to ongoing interest on the part of many biblical scholars, including myself, in historical-critical, philological, and other questions pertaining to the ancient contexts of biblical and related literature. As General Editor, I have found almost every article to be intrinsically interesting. To give but one example, Philip Esler's article, "'All That You Have Done … Has Been Fully Told to Me': The Power of Gossip and the Story of Ruth,'" in the September 2018 issue of *JBL*, was both fascinating and fun. Although I have read Ruth many times, I had simply not paid attention to this element of the book, and, indeed, of numerous other biblical stories, such as 1 Samuel 11, the story of David and Bathsheba, where the plot is propelled by the whispering of information. JSTOR statistics testify clearly to our readers' ongoing fascination with every detail of biblical and extrabiblical literature, from semantics, syntax, and textual variants to rhetoric, social context, and cultural memory.

As General Editor, I have had the pleasure to work with many individuals and groups within the SBL. I have appreciated very much the strong support by the leadership of the Society and the Press, including John Kutsko, Bob Buller, the SBL Council, and the Research and Publications Committee. I am deeply grateful to the hard-working members of the editorial board, all dedicated scholars, who ensure the integrity of the peer review process and the high quality of the *Journal*, and to Maurya Horgan and Paul Kobelski, who copyedit and typeset each issue with consummate skill and commitment to excellence.

The job of *JBL* General Editor would be impossible without the help of the Managing Editor. In seven years I have had the pleasure of working with four Managing Editors: Billie Jean Collins, Christopher Holmes, Christopher Hooker, and Jonathan Potter. Not only did they take the lead in researching and managing our arduous process of technological change, but they also took care of innumerable details, from routine communications with authors to proofreading the final copy. In particular, I wish to mention the present Managing Editor, Jonathan Potter, who came on board less than a year ago and has proven to be a quick study. Although we have rarely met in person, we have developed a wonderful working relationship, thanks in great measure to his tremendous skill set and knowledge, his goodwill, and his sense of humor. Thank you, Jonathan, for everything.

Above all, I wish to thank our authors for the confidence they place in the *Journal* to conduct a fair peer review process, as well as you, the readers, who continue to view *JBL* as a vital resource for your own scholarship. As I edited the articles that make up this present issue, it occurred to me that all of the articles whose publication I oversaw, from the most detailed philological studies to the most socially engaged reflections, testify not only to the ongoing importance of biblical studies writ large but also to the ongoing fascination that the Bible and adjacent areas holds for so many of us. Long may it be so!

… *JBL* 137, no. 4 (2018): 789–819

The Syntax of Complex Adding Numerals and Hebrew Diachrony

JOHN SCRENOCK
john.screnock@orinst.ox.ac.uk
University of Oxford, Oxford, OX1 2HG, UK

The syntax of complex adding numerals and its apparent development in Ancient Hebrew contribute several new pieces to the puzzle of Hebrew diachrony and, consequently, to the dating of biblical texts. I describe undiscussed aspects of the structure of adding numerals and analyze the distribution of structural types according to diachrony. I also provide a diachronic analysis of the order of adding numerals that challenges the traditional position. The syntactical phenomena of adding numerals confirm the idea that the Hebrew in the biblical texts changed over time. Although the diachronic progression of adding-numeral syntax argues against a strict periodization of Hebrew into two stages, the evidence of adding numerals is compatible with the traditional model of Hebrew diachrony.

The syntax of cardinal numerals has received little attention from Hebrew linguists and philologists. With the exception of a handful of studies, the syntax of numbers is discussed only in reference grammars.[1] I offer the following study as part of an attempt to fill this lacuna in Ancient Hebrew scholarship.[2]

My investigation focuses entirely on complex adding numerals (or simply "adding numerals"), in which two or more numerals are used in tandem to convey a value that would otherwise not be possible, specifically by *adding* the value of the component parts. For example, שבעים ושבעה (Gen 4:24) is equal to 70 (שבעים) plus 7 (שבעה), that is, *seventy-seven*. I will admit that when I first began to study numeral syntax, I found the adding numerals quite dull. They seem, on first sight, rather straightforward. How much syntactic complexity could really be involved?

I would like to thank Jan Joosten for feedback on previous drafts of this study.
[1] See John Screnock, "The Syntax of Cardinal Numerals in Judges, Amos, Esther, and 1QM," *JSS* 63 (2018): 125–54, here 125–26.
[2] I use the term *Ancient Hebrew* to refer to all Hebrew before the Mishnah; I avoid the term *Biblical Hebrew* because real language is not defined by its use in texts and because we have evidence of Hebrew at this time that comes from outside the Bible.

I came to see that the matter is much more complicated, and interesting, than meets the eye.

The data suggest diachronic development in numeral syntax when variations are plotted on a text-by-text basis. I suggest an account of change and gradual diffusion for both the *structure* and the *order* of adding numerals. The most plausible scenarios for both areas of syntax show a similar relative dating of the language of texts for which we have a high number of tokens[3]—Genesis, Exodus, Numbers, Joshua–2 Kings, Ezra-Nehemiah, and Chronicles.[4] The language of Genesis, Exodus, and Numbers falls earlier than the language of Joshua–2 Kings, Ezra-Nehemiah, and Chronicles in both diachronic developments.[5] Or, following source-critical distinctions, the language in the Toledoth book is earliest;[6] language in P material falls in a period of transition in adding-numeral syntax; and language in Joshua–2 Kings, Ezra-Nehemiah, and Chronicles comes later.[7] There is not enough evidence to plot J/E material, and the texts falling at the end of the process of diffusion cannot be further distinguished on the basis of adding-numeral syntax.

These models contribute but one piece to the overall picture of Hebrew diachrony. To a certain extent they confirm traditional views of diachrony in the biblical texts, inasmuch as the language of Genesis, Exodus, and Numbers belongs (according to the features in question) to a relatively older stratum. The traditional place of Joshua–2 Kings, in the period of so-called Classical Biblical Hebrew alongside pentateuchal texts, is neither confirmed nor disconfirmed, though for the features in question it falls later than pentateuchal material in the processes of change.

I. Method

Before presenting and analyzing the data of adding numerals, I will briefly outline my framework for approaching numerals in general, my method of diachronic analysis, and my corpus.

---

[3] A "token" is an occurrence of the linguistic feature in question.

[4] The notion of "the language of texts" can be problematized in a variety of ways. There are a number of textual witnesses for each of these texts, which contain different language in particular places; see, e.g., Michael O. Wise, "Accidents and Accidence: A Scribal View of Linguistic Dating of the Aramaic Scrolls from Qumran," in *Studies in Qumran Aramaic*, ed. T. Muraoka, AbrNSup 3 (Louvain: Peeters, 1992), 124–67. Moreover, identifying "Genesis," for example, as a text isolates one main stage of development, whereas we could instead think about various earlier souces or traditions (also conceivable as "texts") that stand behind what today is known as Genesis. I group Joshua–2 Kings together because they are often conceived of as a single "Deuteronomistic History" and because their adding numeral evidence aligns.

[5] Moreover, the language of the Mishnah agrees in both areas with the latter group of texts.

[6] The "Toledoth book" comprises Gen 5:1, 3–32; 9:28–29; 10; 11:10–26; 25:12–26; 36:9–14. I am following Martin Noth for this potential source-critical distinction; see his *Überlieferungsgeschichte des Pentateuch* (Stuttgart: Kohlhammer, 1948). See section IV below.

[7] See section IV below for a discussion of source-critical distinctions.

A. General Framework

My basic framework for approaching cardinal numerals is as follows.[8] A *number phrase* contains a cardinal numeral and the noun that it quantifies.

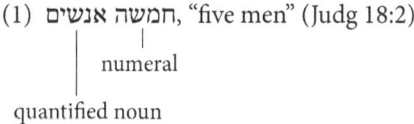

(1) חמשה אנשים, "five men" (Judg 18:2)

There are simple numerals, as in Judg 18:2, and complex numerals, which are made up of two or more simple numerals working together to express a value. In *multiplying numerals*, interior numerals or "members" are multiplied to produce the resulting numeral.

(2) שבע מאות, "seven hundred" (Num 1:39)

- 1s member
- 100s member

Teen numerals express values 11–19 by combining a 1s digit with עשר or עשרה, "teen."

(3) תשע עשרה, "nineteen" (Gen 11:25)

- 1s member
- teen member

In *adding numerals*, the focus of this study, the value of the complex numeral results from addition. Adding numerals can have more than two members, usually one for each digit (1s, 10s, 100s, etc.).

(4) שבע ועשרים ומאה, "a hundred and twenty-seven" (Esth 1:1)

- 1s member
- 10s member
- 100s member

Each member of an adding numeral can be a simple cardinal, as in Esth 1:1, or can itself be a multiplying or teen numeral. Moreover, adding numerals can themselves be embedded within multiplying numerals. For example, Num 2:26:

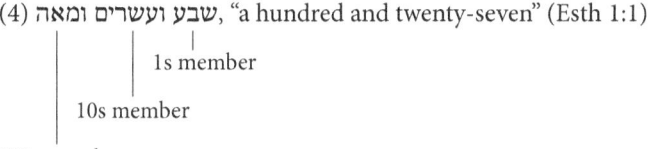

(5) שנים וששים אלף ושבע מאות, "sixty-two thousand seven hundred"

- 100s member is multiplying numeral
- adding numeral w/in multiplying

---

[8] See Screnock, "Syntax of Cardinal Numerals," 127–31.

Using this approach, I have isolated adding numerals and included them in my data whether or not they contain other internal complex numerals or are embedded in a multiplying numeral.

B. *Diachronic Analysis*

In my diachronic analysis of the features under study, I follow the methodology of Robert D. Holmstedt and others who argue that the principles of historical linguistics can be applied successfully to Ancient Hebrew.[9] Diachronic development is but one way to explain variable linguistic evidence. David Crystal identifies several kinds of uncontrollable and controllable features that result in linguistic variation.[10] Uncontrollable features belong to three types of dialect: temporal dialect (diachrony), regional dialect (what we usually mean by "dialect"), and class dialect (register). In other words, distinct varieties of language can arise because of geography, social strata, or the passage of time. Controllable features belong to the stylistic aspects of language and text. Although alternative explanations that draw on register, dialect, and stylistics should always be understood and kept in mind,[11] when a plausible diachronic explanation for language variation exists, the alternative explanations carry the burden of proof.

Language change involves the replacement of an old feature with a new feature. The replacement is not immediate; rather, there is a process of diffusion wherein the new feature gradually replaces the old.[12] To track diachronic change,

---

[9] Robert D. Holmstedt, "Historical Linguistics and Biblical Hebrew," in *Diachrony in Biblical Hebrew*, ed. Cynthia L. Miller-Naudé and Ziony Zevit, LSAWS 8 (Winona Lake, IN: Eisenbrauns, 2012), 97–124; Holmstedt, "Investigating the Possible Verb–Subject to Subject–Verb Shift in Ancient Hebrew: Methodological First Steps," in *"Schrift und Sprache": Papers Read at the 10th Mainz International Colloquium on Ancient Hebrew (MCAH), Mainz, 28–30 October 2011*, ed. Reinhard G. Lehmann and Anna Elise Zernecke, Kleine Untersuchungen zur Sprache des Alten Testaments und seiner Umwelt 15 (Kamen: Spenner, 2013), 3–31; John Screnock and Robert D. Holmstedt, *Esther: A Handbook on the Hebrew Text*, Baylor Handbook on the Hebrew Bible (Waco, TX: Baylor University Press, 2015), 18–23; cf. B. Elan Dresher, "Methodological Issues in the Dating of Linguistic Forms: Considerations from the Perspective of Contemporary Linguistic Theory," in Miller-Naudé and Zevit, *Diachrony in Biblical Hebrew*, 19–38; and, in the same volume, Jacobus A. Naudé, "Diachrony in Biblical Hebrew and a Theory of Language Change and Diffusion," 61–81; and John A. Cook, "Detective Development in Biblical Hebrew Using Diachronic Typology," 83–95.

[10] David Crystal, "New Perspectives for Language Study: 1. Stylistics," *English Language Teaching* 24 (1970): 99–106; see also Crystal, "Style: The Varieties of English," in *The English Language*, ed. W. F. Bolton and David Crystal (London: Penguin, 1987), 199–222.

[11] See, e.g., Robert D. Holmstedt and Alexander T. Kirk, "Subversive Boundary Drawing in Jonah: The Variation of אשר and ש as Literary Code-Switching," *VT* 66 (2016): 542–55.

[12] Naudé, "Diachrony in Biblical Hebrew," 61–81; Naudé, "Qumran Hebrew Syntax in the Perspective of a Theory of Language Change and Diffusion," *JNSL* 26.1 (2000): 105–32; Naudé, "The Transitions of Biblical Hebrew in the Perspective of Language Change and Diffusion," in *Biblical Hebrew: Studies in Chronology and Typology*, ed. Ian Young, JSOTSup 369 (London: T&T

one should ideally use features and corpora containing a large amount of evidence or tokens. An analysis should not lean on texts that have only one or two points of data. Finally, the process of diffusion for a few diachronic changes cannot conclusively speak to the relative time frame of the language of each text. Rather, hundreds of changes should be tracked and then averaged, because individual users of a language adopt different changes at different rates. Thus, when I describe the relative positions occupied by each text in the process of diffusion for two types of change below, these positions do not indicate the overall relative time frame of that text's language.

The process of diffusion is often plotted along a Sigmoid- or S-curve. When the date of language use (whether in a text or spoken) is known, S-curves often, though not always, approximate the distribution of language change. They can therefore serve as a visual model of the process of diffusion. Moreover, we can use S-curves, albeit cautiously, to plot the language of various texts of unknown date[13] within a single sequence; significantly, this sequence is not pegged strictly to temporality, since a language user may be more or less innovative than other users, employing new features before or after the average. Given the potential pitfalls, my use of S-curves in this study is meant strictly to provide heuristically valuable visuals.

In theory, there is the potential for textual "noise," whether text-critical, source-critical, or redaction-critical, to threaten a diachronic analysis. Ancient Hebrew texts are undoubtedly complicated, and wherever reasonable I have accounted for this complexity.[14] Moreover, my impression from working with these data and taking a close look at the potential effect of textual complexity—various sources in the Pentateuch, for example, or text-critical variation in the manuscript evidence—is that such "noise" can change the data slightly but never in a way that fundamentally changes the overall analysis. This is the advantage of working with language features that occur hundreds of times in Ancient Hebrew; one or two odd variants do not make a significant impact.

C. *Corpus*

My corpus consists of every text in Ancient Hebrew before the Mishnah. This includes biblical texts, epigraphic evidence, and the Dead Sea Scrolls. Most of the

---

Clark, 2003), 189–214; Walt Wolfram and Natalie Schilling-Estes, "Dialectology and Linguistic Diffusion," in *The Handbook of Historical Linguistics*, ed. Brian D. Joseph and Richard D. Janda, Blackwell Handbooks in Linguistics (London: Blackwell, 2003), 713–35; Mark Hale, *Historical Linguistics: Theory and Method*, Blackwell Textbooks in Linguistics 21 (London: Blackwell, 2007), 27–47.

[13] We fortunately have some texts for which we have knowledge about dating on non-linguistic grounds; for example, the self-presentation and content of Esther and Ezra-Nehemiah present a postexilic *terminus post quem*.

[14] When, for example, there are textual variants in the manuscript evidence.

evidence comes from biblical texts. In the Dead Sea Scrolls, 1QH and 1QS have no adding numerals; Ben Sira also has no adding numerals, while the Damascus Document has just two adding numerals. Given their lack of evidence, I have not included those texts. The data in the Temple Scroll are problematic, given how thoroughly the Temple Scroll reflects a patchwork of different biblical texts, and as a result I have not included it either.[15] The evidence outside the Bible comes from 1QM and the Copper Scroll, both of which have several adding numerals, and the Siloam Tunnel inscription, which contains one.[16] There is no evidence from the supposedly archaic poetry in the Hebrew Bible. Where there are parallel texts, as in Chronicles, Nehemiah, Isaiah, and Jeremiah, I do not count evidence unless the secondary text is unique in terms of the feature under consideration.[17]

II. The Structure of Complex Adding Numerals

The internal structure of adding numerals seems simple at first glance. Each member of the adding numeral appears to be coordinated by *vav*, similar to lists of coordinated noun phrases. One complexity in the data, however, reveals a deeper structure: the quantified noun is sometimes repeated two or three times in the midst of the adding numeral that quantifies it. A close look at these cases, together with crosslinguistic evidence, tells us more about the structure of adding numerals. Diachronic analysis based on this understanding provides a picture of how Ancient Hebrew developed with respect to the structure of adding numerals.

---

[15] The language used in the Temple Scroll is frequently borrowed directly, with slight changes, from a text in the Hebrew Bible; moreover, a main source and secondary sources are often spliced together. See Dwight D. Swanson, *The Temple Scroll and the Bible: The Methodology of 11QT*, STDJ 14 (Leiden: Brill, 1994). The difficulty of identifying the sources and determining which linguistic aspects belong to the Temple Scroll make using the Temple Scroll highly problematic.

[16] Because the one token occurs in a monumental inscription, it provides more weighty evidence: we have reason to believe that, in an inscription meant to last, the use of particular linguistic features would be careful and deliberate. There are also some adding numerals written in ciphers (e.g., Arad 17.8; 33.2; 34.11; 60.2; 112.1; see Yohanan Aharoni, *Arad Inscriptions*, Judea Desert Studies [Jerusalem: Israel Exploration Society, 1981]), but we should not expect these to transparently reflect the syntax of spoken language any more than Arabic numerals reflect the numeral syntax of any modern language that uses them.

[17] While some cases of semantic variation in parallel texts are interesting—e.g., Ezra 2:12 has 1,222 descendants of Azgad, while Neh 7:17 has 2,322—only *syntactic* changes are relevant to the present study.

A. Distribution of Quantified Noun

The majority of adding numerals in Ancient Hebrew have a surface structure similar to that of modern English adding numerals: the adding numeral appears to stand in for a simple numeral.

(6) twenty-six paperclips

(7) six paperclips

(8) תשעים ותשע שנה
"ninety-nine years" (Gen 17:24)

(9) תשע שנים
"nine years" (2 Kgs 17:1)

In the preceding examples, the numerals *twenty-six*, *six*, תשעים ותשע, and תשע seem to belong in a single position reserved for the numeral, and the nouns *paperclips*, שנה, and שנים in a single position reserved for the noun.

A number of cases in Ancient Hebrew in which the quantified noun is repeated[18] complicate this analysis. In the following example, the noun שנה appears twice, once after each member of the adding numeral.

(10) שלשים שנה וארבע מאות שנה
"four hundred and thirty years" (Gen 11:17)

There are other languages where a noun quantified by an adding numeral can appear multiple times. In Old English, Biblical Welsh,[19] Kalabari, Arabic, and Bantu languages such as Luvale, this is the surface structure of adding numerals.[20]

---

[18] See *IBHS*, §15.2.4b.

[19] Biblical Welsh, an older stage of Welsh, distinct from both Classical Welsh and Modern Welsh, is preserved solely in the Welsh Bible; in the linguistic literature, it is referred to as "Biblical Welsh." See James R. Hurford, *The Linguistic Theory of Numerals*, CSLin 16 (Cambridge: Cambridge University Press, 1975), 136.

[20] On Biblical Welsh and Kalabari, see James R. Hurford, *Language and Number: The Emergence of a Cognitive System* (New York: Blackwell, 1987), 236. On Old English, see Ferdinand von Mengden, *Cardinal Numerals: Old English from a Cross-Linguistic Perspective*, Topics in English Linguistics 67 (Berlin: de Gruyter, 2010), 139–41. On Arabic, see Joshua Blau, "On Some Vestiges of Univerbalization of the Units and Tens of the Cardinalia 21–99 in Arabic and Hebrew," in *Bar-Ilan Departmental Researches: Arabic and Islamic Studies II* (Ramat Gan: Bar Ilan University Press, 1978), 10. On Bantu, see Eytan Zweig, "Nouns and Adjectives in Numeral NPs," in *NELS 35: Proceedings of the Thirty-fifth Annual Meeting of the North East Linguistic Society*, ed. Leah Bateman and Cherlon Ussery (Amherst, MA: Graduate Linguistic Student Association, 2005), 666.

(11) mikoko makumi atanu na-mikoko vatanu
　　 sheep　　 ten　　 five　and-sheep　 five
　　 "fifty-five sheep" (Luvale)

In Old English and Biblical Welsh, the multipliers *þusend* and *mil* (both mean "thousand") can also appear two or more times.[21] Ancient Hebrew, too, can use this sort of distribution at times with the multiplier אלף, "thousand."

(12) twa hund　　 þusend　　 &　 twa　 &　 feowertig þusend
　　 two hundred thousand　 and　 two　 and　 forty　 thousand
　　 "two hundred and forty-two thousand" (Old English)

(13) bedair mil　　 a　　 saithugeinmil
　　 four thousand and seven-twenty-thousand
　　 "one hundred and forty-four thousand" (Biblical Welsh; Rev 14:1)

(14) מאת אלף ושבעה וחמשים אלף
　　 "one hundred and fifty-seven thousand" (Num 2:31)

The evidence suggests that the quantified noun and multiplier "thousand" are not *repeated* in these examples but rather *removed* in examples like (6)–(9) above. In the deep structure, the quantified noun occurs twice, whether the same is true in the surface structure (as in examples 10–14) or not (as in examples 6–9).[22] This is probably the deep structure of adding numerals in the majority of the world's languages, as linguists have argued for similar syntactic structures underneath the surface structure of adding numerals in Modern English, Russian, German, and Inari Sami.[23]

The following tree of the surface structure in Lev 12:14 transparently reflects this deep structure, which lies beneath all adding numerals in Ancient Hebrew.

(15) שלשים יום ושלשת ימים
　　 "thirty-three days" (Lev 12:4)

---

[21] On Old English, see Mengden, *Cardinal Numerals*, 136–39; on Biblical Welsh, see Hurford, *Linguistic Theory of Numerals*, 176. Multipliers behave like quantified nouns in this and several other ways; see Screnock, "Syntax of Cardinal Numerals," 139.

[22] In generative linguistics, "deep structure" is the underlying, basic structure of a syntactical construction, which undergoes transformations that result in the "surface structure" (the structure that most closely resembles the language as spoken or written); see David Crystal, *A Dictionary of Linguistics and Phonetics*, 6th ed. (Oxford: Blackwell, 2008), s.vv. "Deep Structure" and "Surface Structure."

[23] Hurford, *Linguistic Theory of Numerals*, 175–77; Hurford, *Language and Number*, 232–36. Tania Ionin and Ora Matushansky, "The Composition of Complex Cardinals," *Journal of Semantics* 23 (2006): 340–42.

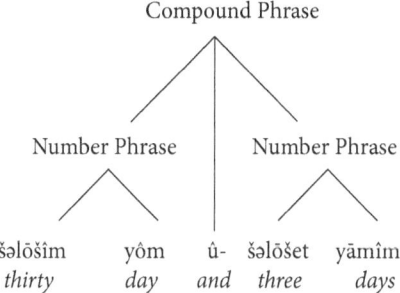

FIGURE 1. Structure of Multiple Distribution (Lev 12:4)

In addition to being the deep structure of all adding numerals, this surface structure (multiple distribution) is found in many numerals in Ancient Hebrew.[24]

Crosslinguistic studies on adding numerals show that this deep structure, besides being manifested transparently in multiple-distribution surface structure, can be transformed in two ways—*right node raising* and *deletion*.[25] Languages can use one, two, or all three of these surface structures in their adding numerals. Though there is insufficient space here, in a future publication I will describe these structures and demonstrate that Ancient Hebrew uses all three. In both right node raising and deletion, the quantified noun appears only once, making it easy to distinguish these from multiple distribution.

B. Diachronic Analysis

Despite the complex nature of adding-numeral structure and its evidence, it is possible to plot some aspects of the syntactic variety along a line of diachronic progression. When the evidence is analyzed diachronically, both node raising and

---

[24] Gen 5:5, 6, 7, 8, 10, 11, 13, 14, 15, 16; 9:28, 29; 11:13, 15, 17, 19, 21, 25, 32; 12:4; 16:16; 17:1; 23:1; 25:7, 17; 35:28; Exod 12:40, 41; 38:26; Lev 12:4, 5; Num 1:46; 2:9, 24, 32; 26:51; 31:32, 36, 43; 1 Sam 6:19; 1 Kgs 6:1; 1 Chr 21:5; 2 Chr 26:13. Multiple distribution is also found in combination with partial deletion in the following cases: Gen 5:17, 18, 20, 23, 25, 26, 27, 28, 30, 31; 47:28; Num 2:16, 31; 2 Chr 2:16. Cf. Eduard König's incomplete list in "Zur Formenlehre der hebräischen Zahlwörter," *ZAW* 16 (1896): 328—based on his tables in *Historisch-kritisches Lehrgebäude der hebräischen Sprache*, 3 vols. (Leipzig: Hinrichs, 1881–1897), 2.1:215–24.

[25] Ionin and Matushansky, "Composition of Complex Cardinals," 340–41; Zweig, "Nouns and Adjectives in Numeral NPs," 666. Right node raising is a common phenomenon in all languages; see Crystal, *Dictionary of Linguistics and Phonetics*, s.v. "Right Node Raising (RNR)." For example, in *I wrote but did not send the e-mail*, the noun phrase *the e-mail* is the complement of the verbs *wrote* and *send* and as such appears twice in the deep structure, but both instances have been moved to a higher point in the structure (right node raising) so that the single phrase *the e-mail* can do "double-duty" for both verbs.

deletion appear to be used at the same time; the use or nonuse of multiple distribution, on the other hand, does exhibit correspondence with diachrony. Multiple distribution appears to be an older feature that was replaced by deletion and node raising.

Beginning with all the adding numerals in pre-Mishnaic Hebrew, we must remove from consideration any adding numerals that are complements in copular clauses (e.g., 1 Kgs 20:15, ויהי מאתים שנים ושלשים, "and they were two hundred and thirty-two"), quantify a null/covert noun (e.g., Ezek 48:17, "the city will have open land to the north, two hundred fifty [חמשים ומאתים] [cubits]"), or put the quantified noun before the numeral (e.g., Josh 19:30, ערים עשרים ושתים, "twenty-two cities").[26] Even so, we are left with a considerable amount of data with which to work. The evidence is as follows.[27]

Multiple Distribution. Gen 5:5, 6, 7, 8, 10, 11, 13, 14, 15, 16, 17, 18, 20, 23, 25, 26, 27, 28, 30, 31; 9:28, 29; 11:13, 15, 17, 19, 21, 25, 32; 12:4; 16:16; 17:1; 23:1; 25:7, 17; 35:28; 47:28; Exod 12:40, 41; 38:26; Lev 12:4, 5; Num 1:46; 2:9, 16, 24, 31, 32; 26:51; 31:32, 36, 43; 1 Sam 6:19; 1 Kgs 6:1; 1 Chr 21:5^; 2 Chr 2:16; 26:13.

Node Raising or Deletion. Siloam Tunnel Inscription line 5; Gen 5:3, 21; 6:3; 7:24; 8:3, 13, 14; 11:12, 16, 20, 24; 17:24; 47:9; 50:22, 26; Exod 6:16, 18, 20; 7:7; 38:24[twice], 25, 29; Lev 25:8; Num 1:21, 23, 25, 27, 29, 31, 35, 37, 39, 41, 43; 2:4, 6, 8, 11, 13, 15, 21, 23, 26, 28, 30; 3:39, 43; 7:88; 8:24; 16:2, 17, 35; 25:9; 26:7, 10, 14, 22, 25, 34, 37, 41, 43, 47, 50, 62; 31:33, 34, 35, 38, 40, 44, 52; 33:39; 35:6, 7; Deut 2:14; 31:2; 34:7; Josh 7:5; 14:10[twice]; 24:49; Judg 2:8; 7:3; 8:10, 14, 26; 10:2, 3; 12:6; 16:5; 17:2, 3; 20:15, 21, 35[twice], 46; 1 Sam 4:15; 22:18; 2 Sam 2:31; 5:5; 8:4, 5; 1 Kgs 2:11; 7:3; 8:63[twice]; 9:14, 28; 10:10, 14, 26; 12:21; 14:20, 21; 15:10, 33; 16:8, 15, 23, 29[twice]; 18:22; 20:1, 16, 30; 22:42[twice]; 2 Kgs 2:24; 8:17, 26; 10:14, 36; 12:7; 13:1, 10; 14:2[twice], 23; 15:1, 2, 8, 13, 17, 27, 33; 18:2[twice]; 19:35; 21:1, 19; 22:1; 23:31, 36; 24:18; 25:27; Isa 7:8; Ezek 4:5, 9; 8:16; 11:1; 29:17; 40:1, 13, 25, 29, 30, 33, 36; 45:1, 3, 5, 6, 12[twice]; 48:8, 9, 10[twice], 13[twice], 15, 20[twice], 21[twice], 30, 33; Job 42:16; Esth 1:1, 4; 8:9; 9:16, 30; Dan 10:13; Ezra 8:9, 10, 11, 12; Neh 5:17; 6:15; 11:6; 1 Chr 2:22; 3:4; 5:18, 21; 7:2, 5, 11, 40; 9:13; 12:25, 31, 35, 36, 38; 19:7*; 21:5*; 23:3, 4; 27:1, 2, 4, 5, 7, 8, 9, 10, 11, 12, 13, 14, 15; 29:7; 2 Chr 11:21; 12:3; 13:21; 14:7; 17:15, 18; 24:15; 28:6; 1QM II, 6, 9, 10; VI, 10; VII, 3; IX, 4–5.

---

[26] Because the quantified noun is null in the first two cases, its distribution cannot be determined. Where the noun precedes the numeral, a significantly different structure is being used, and it is unclear how or whether multiple distribution is possible within such a structure.

[27] I do not include tokens in exact parallels (with Samuel–Kings and Ezra) found in Isaiah, Jeremiah, Nehemiah, and Chronicles. If the texts are parallel but the dependent text is different with regard to structure, I count it as a token. References marked with an asterisk (*) indicate adding numerals that are not found in the parallel source text (whether there is no numeral or whether the counterpart is a simple or multiplying numeral). References marked with a caret (^) are cases where the parallel source text has the adding numeral but its structure has been changed.

Table 1 provides the profiles of texts containing five or more tokens of evidence. Numerous source- and redaction-critical distinctions could be made to complicate the "texts" of table 1, but only two potential distinctions help to make better sense of the data.[28] If we consider the Toledoth book to be a distinct source, it patterns differently from other material in Genesis. Moreover, there is a higher concentration of earlier features in material that is widely understood to belong to P. Nearly all the data in Genesis, Exodus, and Numbers come from P material,[29] with the exception of six adding numerals from J/E material in Genesis. I will therefore include figures for the Toledoth book and the rest of P Genesis ("P Gen" for simplicity) as distinct texts in my analysis here and in section III.B; since there are fewer than five usable tokens from J/E Genesis for the analysis of structure and order, I will not include J/E Genesis.[30] Note that the profiles given for Exodus and Numbers are identical to the profiles of P Exodus and P Numbers, and therefore I will not make any distinction between P and non-P material within these two books.

TABLE 1. Multiple Distribution versus Deletion or Node Raising

	Multiple distribution (old)	Deletion or node raising (new)	% Deletion or node raising
Gen	37	15	29
Exod	3	8	73
2 Chr	2	8	80
Num	10	52	84
Chr	3	40	93
1 Kgs	1	25	96
Josh–2 Kgs (DeutH)	2	78	97
1 Chr	1	32	97
Judg	0	16	100
2 Kgs	0	28	100
Ezek	0	31	100
Esth	0	5	100
Ezra-Neh	0	7	100
1QM	0	6	100

[28] For further discussion of the following summary, see section IV below.
[29] This depends in part on how one analyzes the evidence in Numbers; see section IV.
[30] On J/E versus P and the methodological difficulty of saying anything certain about the language of J/E, see section IV.

TABLE 2. Structure of Adding Numerals in the Toledoth Book and P Genesis

	Multiple distribution (old)	Deletion or node raising (new)	% Deletion or node raising
Toledoth	29	6	17
P Gen	8	5	38

Unfortunately, the earliest stage of the language according to this reconstruction—the stage when multiple distribution was completely dominant—is not evidenced in any of our texts. Although the Toledoth book, at 17 percent, is close to this period, my proposed diachronic interpretation would be more obvious if we had evidence extant from the period before there was change. Using a model of change and diffusion, however, we can discern a direction of change and project backwards to reconstruct the earlier stage. The data, when plugged into an S-curve model, patterns as in fig. 2, where y equals the percentage of uses following the new feature (deletion or node raising) and x equals an arbitrary integer approximating the stage in the process of diffusion.

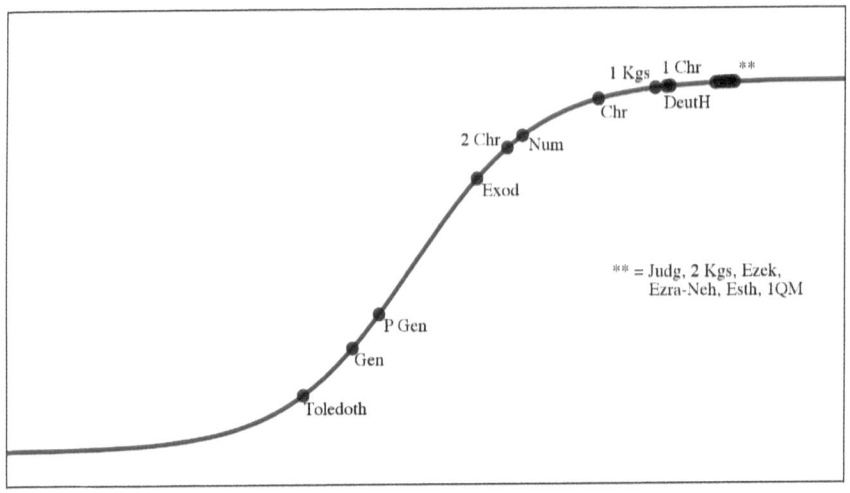

FIGURE 2. S-curve Model of Diachronic Change in Adding-Numeral Structure[31]

As far as I am aware, Mishnaic Hebrew does not employ multiple distribution,[32] confirming the trajectory of this diachronic change and corroborating the hypothesis that multiple distribution is replaced by deletion and node raising.

[31] All graphs were made using Desmos Graphing Calculator (https://www.desmos.com).
[32] I have not undertaken an exhaustive analysis of adding numerals in the Mishnah or related texts.

The evidence from 2 Chronicles is slightly out of place. However, it contains only ten tokens and may be statistically anomalous for this feature. It is reasonable to balance the data from 2 Chronicles with that in 1 Chronicles, considering the language of Chronicles as a whole. It may also be possible that one or two of the cases of multiple distribution are present because of sources older than Samuel–Kings.

Because I use a model of change and diffusion, I do not take the mere presence, however small, of an old or new feature as indicative of old or new language. We see a few cases in Chronicles where multiple distribution is used because the old feature has not completely died out. This does not, however, indicate that Chronicles is earlier than texts not containing multiple distribution. Moreover, this particular diachronic development tells us nothing about the language of Joshua–2 Kings relative to Ezra-Nehemiah and Chronicles, since all of these fall at the end of the process of diffusion.

III. The Order of Complex Adding Numerals

The members within adding numerals can be ordered in several ways. At times they decrease in order:

(16) שלשים ושלש   10s – 1s
"thirty-three" (2 Sam 5:5)

(17) אלפים ושש מאות ושלשים   1000s – 100s – 10s
"two thousand six hundred and thirty" (Num 4:40)

At other times adding numerals increase in order:

(18) תשע ועשרים   1s – 10s
"twenty-nine" (Exod 38:24)

(19) חמשה וששים ושלש מאות ואלף   1s – 10s – 100s – 1000s
"one thousand three hundred and sixty-five" (Num 3:50)

There are even cases in Ancient Hebrew that use *both* orders:[33]

(20) שש מאות חמש ושבעים   100s – 1s – 10s
"six hundred and seventy-five" (Num 31:37)

Although many texts show a clear preference for decreasing (e.g., Ezra) or increasing (e.g., 1QM) order, some texts (e.g., Numbers) exhibit the full variety of options. This variety is reflected in Christo van der Merwe, Jacobus Naudé, and Jan

---

[33] Exod 38:25, 28; Num 2:16, 31; 3:43; 31:37; 1 Kgs 20:15; Ezra 2:5.

Kroeze's statement that "there is no rigid sequence for the different elements within the compound number."[34] Scholars have noted that adding numerals made up of 1s and 10s can be found with both increasing and decreasing order,[35] while other adding numerals are generally thought to prefer decreasing order.[36]

The diversity in the evidence was interpreted by Sven Herner as resulting in part from diachronic development of Hebrew,[37] and subsequent commentary on adding numerals has followed his interpretation.[38] Herner interacted with the reference grammars of Heinrich Ewald and Bernhard Stade, both of whom viewed decreasing order as the dominant order in later texts.[39] He concluded that their claims were flawed because of an outdated view of the provenance of P.[40] Ewald considered P to be older, while Stade appeared to simply follow Ewald's faulty analysis. According to Herner, increasing order is rarely found in preexilic texts, while J, E, D, Judges, Samuel, and Job primarily use decreasing order. On this basis, Herner argues that decreasing order is old and increasing order new.

Although Herner had a large amount of evidence at his disposal, a decreasing-to-increasing model of diachronic development in this area is unlikely given all the data. This is because, as Herner acknowledged, several of our latest texts heavily favor decreasing order, including Ezra-Nehemiah, the unique sections of Chronicles, and most significantly, the Mishnah.[41] As such, a feasible diachronic explanation of the order of adding numerals must see increasing order as earlier, contra

---

[34] Christo H. J. van der Merwe, Jacobus A. Naudé, and Jan H. Kroeze, *A Biblical Hebrew Reference Grammar*, Biblical Languages: Hebrew 3 (Sheffield: Sheffield Academic, 1999), §37.2.1.v. Cf. Robert Hetzron, "Innovations in the Semitic Numeral System," *JSS* 22 (1977): 167–201, here 169 n. 1, on the similar, apparent variety in other Semitic languages.

[35] E.g., *IBHS*, §15.2.4a; van der Merwe, Naudé, and Kroeze, *Biblical Hebrew Reference Grammar*, §37.2.2.v; Joüon, §100m; GKC, §97f.

[36] See *IBHS*, §15.2.5d; GKC, §§97f, 134i. Against this trend, see Screnock, "Syntax of Cardinal Numerals," 147–48.

[37] Sven Herner, *Syntax der Zahlwörter im Alten Testament* (Lund, 1893), 71–75.

[38] S. R. Driver, *Notes on the Hebrew Text and the Topography of the Books of Samuel* (Oxford: Clarendon, 1913), x; J. C. L. Gibson, *Davidson's Introductory Hebrew Grammar: Syntax* (Edinburgh: T&T Clark, 1994), §47c; Joüon, §100m.

[39] Heinrich Ewald, *Ausführliches Lehrbuch der Hebräischen Sprache des alten Bundes* (Göttingen: Dieterich, 1870), §268c; Bernhard Stade, *Lehrbuch der Hebräischen Grammatik* (Leipzig: Vogel, 1879), 218.

[40] Herner, *Syntax der Zahlwörter*, 73. Many of the cases of increasing order occur in the supposed P-source in Genesis and Numbers.

[41] On Ezra-Nehemiah and Chronicles, see Herner, *Syntax der Zahlwörter*, 73, 75. I have not conducted an exhaustive survey of the order of adding numerals in the Mishnah, but an initial survey of the data indicates that the evidence is strongly for decreasing order.

Herner and those who have followed him.[42] Table 3 on the following page provides the profiles of texts containing five or more tokens of evidence.[43]

The language of texts that we know to be late generally falls at the end of the spectrum, along with the texts in Joshua–2 Kings (and related Jer 52). There are a few unexpected points in the data: Esther and 1QM are certainly later than Joshua–2 Kings, yet they fall at the very beginning of the spectrum; Ezekiel, too, we would expect to come at the end, while the unique material in 1 Chronicles falls a little earlier than would be expected. The language of Esther and 1QM can only be explained as classicizing.[44] They in fact contribute important evidence for the existence of an early stage where increasing order was primarily used, without much or any decreasing order, insofar as they show an awareness of this stage through their classicizing. The position of 1 Chronicles, on the other hand, becomes clearer

---

[42] In an article written shortly after his dissertation, Herner criticized König for his work on numerals in his reference grammar (König, *Historisch-kritisches Lehrgebäude der hebräischen Sprache*); see Herner, "Einige Anmerkungen über die Behandlung der Zahlwörter im 'Lehrgebäude der hebräischen Sprache', Zweite Hälfte I. Theil, von Prof Fr. Eduard König," *ZAW* 16 (1896): 123–28. Had König accounted for various sources within the Pentateuch, argued Herner, he would have concluded that decreasing order is the older syntax of adding numerals ("Einige Anmerkungen," 126–27). (König, in his own defense, pointed out that he did not intend to make these sorts of analyses in his reference grammar ["Zur Formenlehre der hebräischen Zahlwörter," 329].) Herner's argument, however, was based on the presupposition that P is postexilic. While it is theoretically possible that the order of adding numerals changed from decreasing to increasing and then back again, it is unlikely; given our knowledge of the date of the Mishnah, I prefer to postulate one model of change and diffusion from increasing to decreasing.

[43] See section III.B for full references to all of the data used here.

[44] The War Scroll's classicizing is perhaps betrayed in the very copying of 1QM, where in col. II, line 10 the scribe began to write ותשע עשרים, "twenty-nine," with decreasing order but stopped short after writing half of the initial ʿayin—catching himself in a slip into vernacular language and then correcting to the language of the *Vorlage*, ותשע ועשרים. The language of Esther has been described as classicizing with other features as well and is known to use language reminiscent of earlier biblical texts (e.g., the Joseph story, 1 Kgs 21). See Steven E. Fassberg, "The Infinitive Absolute as Finite Verb and Standard Literary Hebrew of the Second Temple Period," in *Conservatism and Innovation in the Hebrew Language of the Hellenistic Period: Proceedings of a Fourth International Symposium on the Hebrew of the Dead Sea Scrolls and Ben Sira*, ed. Jan Joosten and Jean-Sébastien Rey, STDJ 73 (Leiden: Brill, 2008), 47–60, here 57–58; Jon D. Levenson, *Esther: A Commentary*, OTL (Louisville: Westminster John Knox, 1997), 54; Joyce G. Baldwin, *Esther: An Introduction and Commentary*, TOTC (Downers Grove, IL: InterVarsity Press, 1984), 26; Michael V. Fox, *Character and Ideology in the Book of Esther* (Grand Rapids: Eerdmans, 2001), 52, 284; Frederic W. Bush, *Ruth, Esther*, WBC 9 (Dallas: Word, 1996), 437; Jonathan Grossman, "'Dynamic Analogies' in the Book of Esther," *VT* 59 (2009): 394–414. Esther's use of differential object marking may also indicate classicizing; Peter Bekins, personal correpondence; see also Bekins, *Transitivity and Object Marking in Biblical Hebrew: An Investigation of the Object Preposition ʾet*, HSS 64 (Winona Lake, IN: Eisenbrauns, 2014), 135–39.

TABLE 3. Increasing Order versus Decreasing Order

	Increasing order (old)	Decreasing order (new)	% Decreasing order
Siloam Tunnel	1	0	0
Esth	6	0	0
1QM	9	1	10
Toledoth[45]	31	4	11
Ezek	34	9	21
Gen	40	17	30
Exod	14	6	30
P Gen	7	8	53
Num	65	72	53
Jer 52	1	5	83
1 Kgs	5	30	86
Josh	1	7	87
1 Chr	8	52	87
Chr	9	77	90
Josh–2 Kgs (DeutH)	8	89	92
Judg	1	15	94
Neh	1	18	95
Ezra-Neh	3	78	96
2 Chr	1	25	96
Ezra	2	60	98
2 Sam	0	6	100
2 Kgs	0	29	100
Hag	0	5	100
Dan	0	7	100
3Q15	0	5	100

when we consider another wrinkle in the evidence in the following section. The remainder of the evidence, it should be noted, is similar to the evidence for multiple distribution, node raising, and deletion, where the best evidence of the earliest stage may be the Toledoth book, and already in Joshua–2 Kings we have the new feature dominating. Note, also, the number of late texts where decreasing order dominates, suggesting that Herner's analysis of decreasing-to-increasing change is

[45] On the inclusion of "Toledoth" and "P Gen," see section II.B.

incorrect. Besides Ezra-Nehemiah and Chronicles, pointed out above, Haggai, Daniel, and 3Q15 (the Copper Scroll) all use decreasing order; although each has a small number of tokens, taken together they are suggestive. Figure 3 below shows an S-curve with these data plotted.

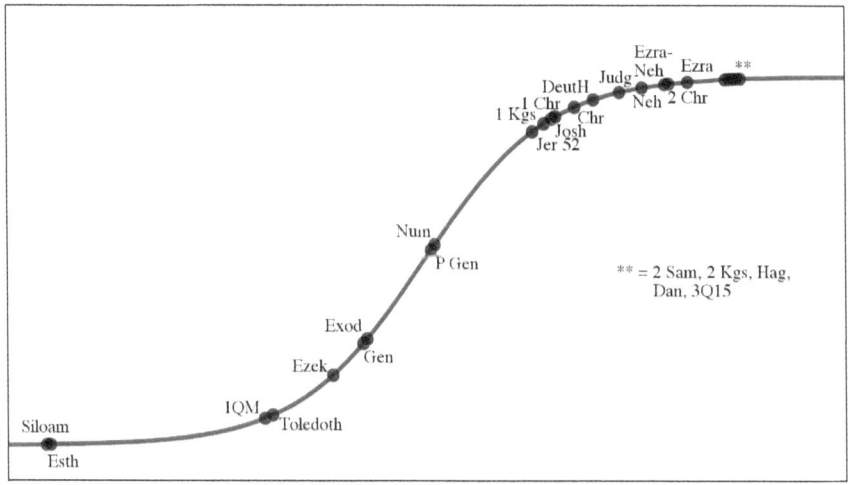

FIGURE 3. S-curve Model of Diachronic Change in Adding-Numeral Order

This preliminary sketch of diachronic change is clarified when we take into account the internal structure of adding numerals.

A. *The 1s/10s Grouping*

Crosslinguistic evidence suggests that in adding numerals of three or more members the 1s and 10s members are more closely related than the rest of the members. In contemporary English, for example, use of coordination "and" between the 10s and 1s digit is ungrammatical, whereas use of "and" between other members is acceptable.

(21) One hundred twenty

(22) One hundred and twenty

(23) Fifty-two

(24) *Fifty and two[46]

---

[46] "Two and fifty" might strike a native speaker as *possibly* grammatical, *via* remembrance of an older order fossilized in some texts, for example, "four and twenty blackbirds."

In German, Dutch, Old English, some dialects of Norwegian, Arabic, and Brythonic languages, the standardized order is decreasing until the end, where the 1s and 10s members are increasing.

(25) tweehonderd vijfendertig
 two-hundred five-and-thirty
 "two hundred and thirty-five" (Dutch)

This same order, though not dominant in any text, can be found in Ancient Hebrew, as in most of the cases of "mixed" order noted above.[47]

(20) שש מאות חמש ושבעים   100s – 1s – 10s
 "six hundred and seventy-five" (Num 31:37)

This evidence suggests both that the 1s and 10s members form a discrete unit *and* that this unit is very capable of taking an order different from the external order of the entire adding numeral.

Finally, the evidence of partial multiple distribution in Ancient Hebrew suggests that the 1s and 10s members form a discrete unit within adding numerals.[48]

(26) חמש ותשעים שנה ושמנה מאות שנה
 "eight hundred and ninety-five years" (Gen 5:17)

On this basis, I suggest that the structure of most adding numerals had the 1s/10s as a compound phrase that itself was compounded with the 100s (and/or 1000s) member.

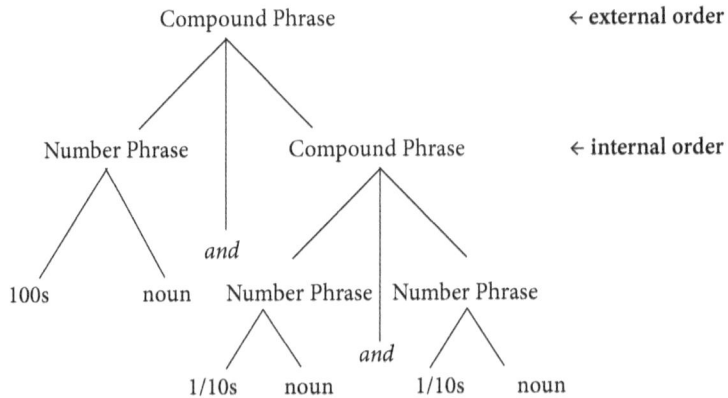

FIGURE 4. Structure of Adding Numerals: Discrete 1s/10s Unit

---

[47] Cf. also modern dialects of Neo-Aramaic, where decreasing order is the standard but mixed order sometimes occurs with the 1s/10s unit taking increasing order. See Geoffrey Khan, *A Grammar of Neo-Aramaic: The Dialect of the Jews of Arbel*, HdO 47 (Leiden: Brill, 1999), §12.1.6.

[48] In the majority of cases, the 1s and 10s members are grouped, as in example (26); cf. Gen 5:17, 18, 20, 23, 25, 26, 27, 28, 30, 31; Num 2:16, 31. The only exceptions are Gen 47:28 and 2 Chr 2:16. Cf. Blau, "On Some Vestiges of Univerbalization," 10–11.

B. Diachronic Analysis

The internal grouping of the 1s and 10s members helps explain why we see cases of mixed order in the data. It also helps to clarify the diachronic development of adding-numeral order. More frequently used lexemes and phrases are known to resist language change.[49] Our evidence suggests that adding numerals consisting of 1s and 10s members were in greater use than other adding numerals; speakers were much more likely to use a numeral with 1s and 10s members as they were to use an adding numeral without both 1s and 10s members.[50] Therefore, we should not be surprised if the 1s/10s unit of adding numerals changes from increasing to decreasing order at a slower pace. When the data are analyzed and a distinction is made between 1s/10s adding numerals—whether as individual adding numerals or as a unit embedded in a larger adding numeral—and other adding numerals (which I term "non-1s/10s" for simplicity), the results are as follows.[51]

Increasing non-1s/10s. Siloam Tunnel line 5; Gen 5:3, 6, 7, 8, 10, 11, 13, 14, 16, 17, 18, 20, 23, 25, 26, 27, 28, 30, 31; 7:24; 8:3, 13; 11:13, 15, 17, 19, 21, 25, 32; 14:14; 47:9, 28; Exod 6:16, 18, 20; 12:40, 41; 30:23^{twice}; Num 3:43, 50; 7:49, 55, 61, 67, 73, 79, 85, 86; 16:2, 17, 35; 26:10; 33:39; 1 Sam 6:19; 1 Kgs 5:12; 6:1; 9:23; 10:29; Ezek 48:16$^{four\ times}$, 17$^{four\ times}$, 30, 32, 33, 34; Esth 1:1, 4; 8:9; 9:30; Neh 7:69*; 1QM VI, 10.

Increasing 1s/10s. Gen 5:15, 17, 18, 20, 21, 23, 25, 26, 27, 28, 30, 31; 8:14; 11:12, 16, 20, 24; 12:4; 47:28; Exod 6:16, 18, 20; 7:7; 12:18; 26:2; 36:9; 38:24, 25, 28; Lev 25:8; Num 1:21, 23, 25, 27, 29, 31, 35, 37, 39, 41, 43; 2:4, 6, 8, 11, 13, 15, 16, 21, 23, 26, 28, 30, 31; 3:39, 43^{twice}, 50; 8:24; 25:9; 26:7, 14, 22, 25, 34, 37, 41, 43, 47, 50, 62; 31:33, 34, 35, 37, 38^{twice}, 39, 40, 44; 33:39; Josh 14:10; Judg 20:21; 1 Kgs 20:15; Jer 25:3; 52:30; Ezek 40:21, 25, 30, 33, 36; 41:6; 45:1, 3, 5, 6, 12; 48:8, 9, 10^{twice}, 13^{twice}, 15, 20^{twice}, 21^{twice}; Esth 1:1; 8:9^{twice}; 9:16, 30; Ezra 1:9; 2:5; 1 Chr

---

[49] See, for example, the high-use verbs in English that form the past tense through ablaut (an older feature of English) instead of suffixed *-ed* (the new feature), e.g., *run*, the past tense of which is *ran*, not **runned*.

[50] In my corpus, 1s and 10s adding numerals appear about 450 times, including 84 times within larger adding numerals; other digits (100s, 1000s, and 10000s) are involved in just over 260 cases, including the 84 that contain an internal 1s/10s unit. Gary Rendsburg has argued that the specific "numeral 75 in ancient Hebrew operated in a unique fashion," because it is found four times with increasing order inside an adding numeral with decreasing order (i.e., 100s-1s-10s), and because it is used in a late text (Esther) with increasing order ("Hebrew Philological Notes (III)," *HS* 43 [2002]: 27–29). Rendsburg's evidence, however, includes too few tokens, and he does not account for numerals with multiple distribution; there are examples of the number 75 with decreasing order in Gen 25:7 and Num 31:32, and examples of 1s-10s increasing order inside decreasing order with numerals *other than* 75 in Num 2:16, 31; 3:43; and 1 Kgs 20:15 (the last of which is noted by Rendsburg).

[51] On my use or nonuse of parallel texts, and the references marked with an asterisk (*) or caret (^), see n. 22.

19:7*[52]; 24:17[twice], 18[twice]; 25:28, 29, 30, 31; 2 Chr 36:2^; 1QM II, 1, 2, 6, 9, 10; VI, 14; VII, 3; IX, 4–5.

Decreasing non-1s/10s. Gen 5:5; 6:3; 9:28, 29; 23:1; 25:7, 17; 35:28; 50:22, 26; Exod 38:24, 25, 26[twice], 28, 29; Num 1:21, 23, 25, 27, 29, 31, 33, 35, 37, 39, 41, 43, 46[twice]; 2:4, 6, 8, 9[twice], 11, 13, 15, 16[twice], 19, 21, 23, 24[twice], 26, 28, 30, 31[twice], 32[twice]; 3:22, 28, 34, 43;[53] 4:36, 40, 44, 48; 7:85; 17:14; 26:7, 14, 18, 22, 25, 27, 34, 37, 41, 43, 47, 50, 51[twice]; 31:32, 36[twice], 37, 39, 43[twice], 45, 52; Deut 31:2; 34:7; Josh 24:49; Judg 2:8; 8:10; 8:26; 16:5; 17:2; 17:3; 20:35; 2 Sam 2:31; 8:4; 1 Kgs 5:30; 8:63; 9:14, 28; 10:10, 14, 26; 12:21; 18:19, 22; 20:15; 2 Kgs 19:35; Jer 52:28, 29, 30[twice]; Ezek 4:5, 9; Job 42:16; Dan 8:14; 12:11, 12; Ezra 1:10, 11; 2:3, 4, 5, 6, 7, 8, 9, 10, 11, 12, 13, 14, 15, 17, 18, 19, 21, 23, 25, 26, 27, 28, 30, 31, 32, 33, 34, 35, 36, 37, 38, 39, 41, 42, 58, 60, 64, 65, 66[twice], 67[twice], 69; 8:3, 9, 10, 12, 20, 26; Neh 5:17; 7:10^, 26^, 67*, 70*; 11:6, 8, 12, 13, 14, 18, 19; 1 Chr 5:18, 21; 7:2, 9, 11; 8:40; 9:6, 9, 13, 22; 12:25, 26, 27, 28, 31, 36, 38; 15:5, 6, 7, 10; 21:5[twice*]; 25:7; 26:30, 32; 29:7; 2 Chr 2:16[twice]; 3:4*; 5:12; 12:3; 14:7; 17:11[twice], 15, 18; 24:15; 26:12, 13[twice]; 28:6; 35:8; 1QM VI, 10; 3Q15 III, 4.

Decreasing 1s/10s. Gen 4:24; 16:16; 17:1, 24; 18:28; 23:1; 25:7, 17; 46:15, 26; Lev 12:4, 5; Num 2:9; 7:88; 31:32, 36, 43; 35:6, 7; Deut 2:14; Josh 7:5; 12:24; 14:10; 15:32; 19:30; 21:41; Judg 7:3; 8:14; 10:2, 3; 12:6; 20:15, 35, 46; 1 Sam 4:15; 22:18; 2 Sam 5:5; 8:5; 21:20; 23:39; 1 Kgs 2:11; 7:3; 8:63; 10:14; 14:20, 21; 15:10, 33; 16:8, 10, 15, 23, 29[twice]; 20:1, 16, 30; 22:31, 42[twice]; 2 Kgs 2:24; 8:17, 26; 10:14, 36; 12:7; 13:1, 10; 14:2, 23; 15:1, 2, 8, 13, 17, 27, 33; 18:2[twice]; 19:35; 21:1, 19; 22:1; 23:31, 36; 24:18; 25:27[twice]; Isa 7:8; Jer 52:23, 28, 29, 30; Ezek 8:16; 11:1; 29:17; 40:1, 13, 29; 45:12;[54] Hag 1:15; 2:1, 10, 18, 20; Zech 1:7; Dan 9:25, 26; 10:4, 13; 12:12; Ezra 2:3, 4, 7, 8, 10, 11, 12, 13, 14, 15, 16, 17, 19, 20, 21, 22, 23, 24, 25, 26, 27, 28, 29, 30, 31, 33, 34, 36, 37, 38, 40, 41, 42, 58, 60, 65, 66[twice], 67; 8:11, 35[twice]; Neh 5:14; 6:15[twice]; 7:10^, 26^, 67*, 71*; 9:1; 11:6, 8[twice], 12, 13, 14, 18, 19; 13:6; 1 Chr 2:22; 3:4; 5:18; 7:2, 4, 5, 40; 9:9; 12:29, 35, 36; 16:38; 23:3, 4; 25:7; 26:8; 27:1, 2, 4, 5, 7, 8, 9, 10, 11, 12, 13, 14, 15; 2 Chr 2:16; 3:15; 7:10*; 11:21; 13:21; 15:19*; 16:1, 12, 13*; 21:20*; 3Q15 II, 4; IV, 4;[55] VII, 6; VIII, 12–13; X, 7.

The distribution of the above data is summarized in table 4.

---

[52] First Chronicles 19:7 is perhaps based on a variant *Vorlage* of Samuel–Kings; see the evidence for 2 Sam 10:6 found in 4QSamuel[a].

[53] Because the numeral in Num 3:43 has the order 1000s–1s–10s–100s, I include it as a token for decreasing non-1s/10s *and* increasing non-1s/10s.

[54] In this instance, the value 15 is created without the use of a teen numeral: עשרה וחמשה שקל ("ten and five shekels"), with two 1s digits. Although עשרה is technically a 1s digit, it is the larger value and thus resembles decreasing order.

[55] The adding numeral in 3Q15 IV, 4 is largely reconstructed (אמות ארבע[ין ואח[ת), "forty-one cubits") and thus uncertain.

TABLE 4. Order of Adding Numerals with 1s/10s Distinguished[56]

	Increasing non-1s/10s	Increasing 1s/10s	Decreasing non-1s/10s	Decreasing 1s/10s
Siloam Tunnel	1	0	0	0
Gen	32	19	10	10
Toledoth	25	16	4	1
P Gen	5	3	3	7
Exod	7	10	6	0
Num	15	51	69	7
Josh	0	1	1	6
Judg	0	1	7	8
2 Sam	0	0	2	4
1 Kgs	4	1	11	20
2 Kgs	0	0	1	29
Josh–2 Kgs	5	3	22	69
Jer 52[57]	0	1	4	4
Ezek	12	21–22	2	6–7
Hag	0	0	0	5
Esth	4	5	0	0
Dan	0	0	3	5
Ezra	0	2	51	42
Neh	1	0	12	17
Ezra-Neh	1	2	63	59
1 Chr	0	9	27	29
2 Chr	0	1	16	10
Chr	0	10	43	39
1QM	1	8	1	0
3Q15	0	0	1	4–5

[56] Where a 1s/10s adding numeral is embedded within a larger adding numeral, there are two tokens although there is only one total adding numeral: one token for the internal 1s/10s order, and one token for the external order.

[57] Though the data that I include from Jer 52 do not come from material that parallels 2 Kgs 24–25 (where it does, I have excluded it), the material is likely to be from a similar source and thus should be distinguished from the rest of Jeremiah. See William L. Holladay, *Jeremiah 2: A Commentary on the Book of the Prophet Jeremiah, Chapters 26–52*, Hermeneia (Minneapolis: Fortress, 1989), 439.

On the one hand, given the resistance to change and thus variant order of 1s/10s adding numerals, we might focus on the order of non-1s/10s adding numerals as better reflecting the process of diffusion.[58] On the other hand, the combination of the two gives strong witness, especially in the case of Numbers, which heavily prefers decreasing order with non-1s/10s, but increasing with 1s/10s, suggesting that the language of Numbers fell somewhere in the middle of the transition. When one considers each type of adding numeral, the texts with five or more tokens pattern as in table 5 and fig. 5.

TABLE 5. Percent of Decreasing Order of Non-1s/10s and 1s/10s

	% Decreasing order non-1s/10s	% Decreasing order 1s/10s
Siloam	0	-
Esth	-	0
1QM	-	0
Toledoth	14	6
Ezek	14	24
Exod	46	0
Gen	24	34
Num	82	12
P Gen	38	70
Jer 52	-	80
1 Kgs	73	95
Josh	-	86
1 Chr	100	76
Josh–2 Kgs (DeutH)	81	96
Chr	100	80
Judg	100	89
Ezra	100	91

[58] In the study of word order, for example, certain clauses are best excluded from consideration for similar reasons; see Anna Siewierska, *Word Order Rules* (London: Croom Helm, 1988), 8; and Robert D. Holmstedt, "Word Order in the Book of Proverbs," in *Seeking Out the Wisdom of the Ancients: Essays Offered to Honor Michael V. Fox on the Occasion of His Sixty-Fifth Birthday*, ed. Ronald L. Troxel, Kelvin G. Friebel, and Dennis R. Magary (Winona Lake, IN: Eisenbrauns, 2005), 135–54.

TABLE 5 (cont.)

	% Decreasing order non-1s/10s	% Decreasing order 1s/10s
2 Chr	100	91
Neh	92	100
Ezra-Neh	98	97
2 Kgs	-	100
Hag	-	100
Dan	-	100

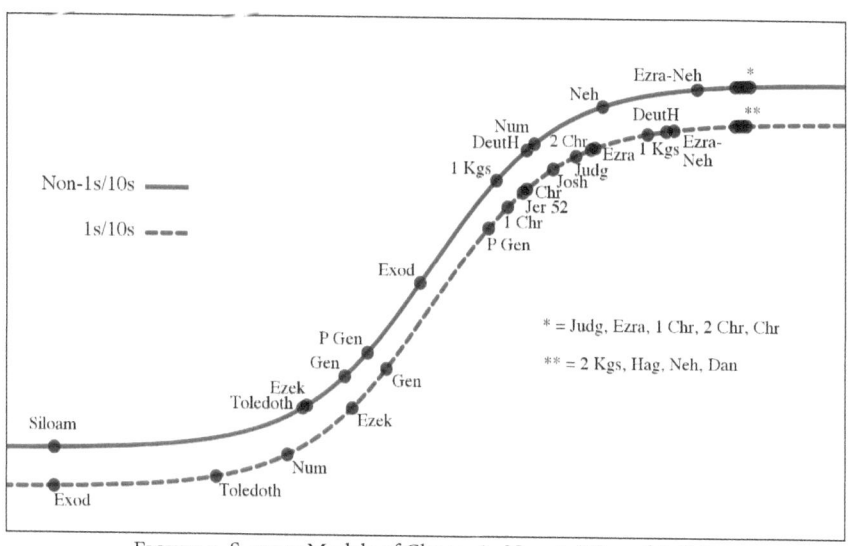

FIGURE 5. S-curve Models of Change in Non-1s/10s and 1s/10s Adding-Numeral Order

Given that two distinct but related processes are involved, the diachronic change of adding-numeral order cannot be pared down to a one-dimensional account of change and diffusion. The book of Numbers, for example, has a high percentage of the new feature in non-1s/10s adding numerals, but a low percentage of the new feature in 1s/10s adding numerals. In this case we need to account for the process of diffusion *and* resistance to that process in particular contexts. The transition between majority use of the old feature and majority use of the new feature is marked both by *mixed use* of both features (20–80 percent new) and by the coexistence of the old feature used in high-use settings and the new feature used elsewhere. When we consider the latter, it is easiest to look again at the actual numbers of occurrences (see table 6). Earlier language should use mostly increasing order in both types of phrase, with the potential for the new feature beginning to creep in. Later language should use mostly decreasing order in both types of phrase, with the old feature never quite disappearing altogether. Transitional language should have a concentration of increasing order in 1s/10s and decreasing order in non-1s/10s.

TABLE 6. Order of Adding Numerals with Three Phases Highlighted

	Increasing non-1s/10s	Increasing 1s/10s	Decreasing non-1s/10s	Decreasing 1s/10s
	EARLIER		LATER	
		TRANSITION		
Gen	32	19	10	10
Toledoth	25	16	4	1
P Gen	5	3	3	7
Exod	7	10	6	0
Num	15	51	69	7
Josh–2 Kgs	5	3	22	69
Ezek	12	21–22	2	6–7
Esth	4	5	0	0
Ezra-Neh	1	2	63	59
Chr	0	10	43	39
1QM	1	8	1	0

In table 6, the high concentration of older order in Genesis is due mostly to evidence in the Toledoth book. The remainder of the P material in Genesis does not pattern neatly, but there is a somewhat low number of tokens. If we combined these data with P Exodus and P Numbers, the language would pattern as transitional. As noted above, Esther and 1QM are classicizing. Ezekiel may be a statistical outlier, or it may be explained in other ways.[59] A small level of idiosyncrasy with individual features is to be expected;[60] this is the very reason we should consider many features and average them, rather than latching onto one or two as independently indicative. Moreover, one statistical outlier does not negate the clear general

---

[59] We could explain Ezekiel's preference for increasing order as imitation of the language of the Pentateuch or of Priestly literature (see section IV). It is also noteworthy that the majority of the evidence from Ezekiel, and all the cases of increasing order, are found in chapters 40–48.

[60] Every language community and even every speaker has their own grammar with unique aspects, particularly if they have interacted with a diverse range of speakers (Hale, *Historical Linguistics*, 3–17).

trend in the evidence. Joshua–2 Kings, Ezra-Nehemiah, and Chronicles fall at the end of the process of diffusion, while Genesis, Exodus, and Numbers fall in the transition. In the case of Chronicles, the recognition that 1s/10s resist the change to decreasing order helps explain the ten occurrences of increasing order. As was the case with the structure of adding numerals, the diachronic development of adding-numeral order tells us nothing about the language of Joshua–2 Kings relative to Ezra-Nehemiah and Chronicles, because Joshua–2 Kings falls at the end of this process of diffusion.

The cause for the change from increasing to decreasing order may well stem from contact with Imperial Aramaic. According to Takamitsu Muraoka and Bezalel Porten, adding numerals in the Old Aramaic material found in Egypt use decreasing order.[61] This could have begun during the Babylonian exile, but not necessarily, since Hebrew speakers came into contact with Aramaic during other periods of history.

IV. The Data according to Source- and Redaction-Critical Distinctions

Modern scholarship recognizes the conglomerate nature of our evidence for each book of the Hebrew Bible. While I do not have space to explore the adding-numeral data in light of every theory of source and redaction criticism for every book, I will briefly address some particular examples. I leave it to redaction and source critics to fully consider the evidence in light of their texts and to use the diachronic development of adding-numeral features as a tool for further analysis. My point here is to demonstrate that the known textual complexities do not undermine the basic model offered above.

Within the Pentateuch, most of our evidence is found in Genesis, Exodus, and Numbers; Leviticus and Deuteronomy contain just three tokens each. If we were to follow Martin Noth's division of sources,[62] most of the adding numerals in the Pentateuch would fall within the P source and related material (the Toledoth book and supplements to P). Six tokens in non-P material (only four of which can be analyzed for structure) do not give enough evidence. Thirty tokens in Numbers 25–31 fall within material that Noth does not think can be identified;[63] others, for

---

[61] Takamitsu Muraoka and Bezalel Porten, *A Grammar of Egyptian Aramaic*, rev. ed., HdO 32 (Leiden: Brill, 2003), §21.b; see also the examples cited in Muraoka, *An Introduction to Egyptian Aramaic*, Lehrbücher orientalischer Sprachen 3.1 (Münster: Ugarit-Verlag, 2012), §12.b.

[62] Noth, *Überlieferungsgeschichte des Pentateuch*, 17–19, 29–35, 38–39. Though dated, I use Noth because he presents a clearly defined analysis that is minimally contentious in the context of today's debates.

[63] Ibid., 35 n. 126.

example, Baruch Levine, consider this material to be P.[64] Given the high proportion of evidence in Genesis, Exodus, and Numbers that stems from Priestly material, the general profile of those three books—that they contain earlier syntax for adding numerals—holds true for P. The data when catalogued according to Noth's sources pattern as follows.

TABLE 7. Structure of Adding Numerals according to Noth's Source Distinctions

	Multiple distribution	Deletion/ node raising	% Deletion/ node raising
P (including Toledoth and supplements)	51	56	52
J	0	1	-
E	0	3	-
Unknown material in Numbers	1	16	94

TABLE 8. Order of Adding Numerals according to Noth's Source Distinctions

	Increasing	Decreasing	% Decreasing
P (including Toledoth and supplements)	102	76	43
J	0	3	-
E	1	2	-
Unknown material in Numbers	14	16	53

Dividing the material in Genesis–Numbers along source-critical lines does not provide a neat solution to the variety of data found therein—it is not as though P clearly favors multiple distribution and increasing order. All eight cases of deletion/ node raising in Exodus are found in P. Similarly, Numbers has a high proportion of deletion/node raising in its P material (thirty-six cases). The undesignated material in Numbers patterns with the rest of (P) Numbers in its use of decreasing order for the larger external numeral and increasing order for internal 1s/10s numerals. In other words, distinguishing P from non-P in these three books does little to change their profile.

[64] Baruch A. Levine, *Numbers 1–20: A New Translation with Introduction and Commentary*, AYB 4A (New York: Doubleday, 1993; repr., New Haven: Yale University Press, 2008), 68–69.

The insufficient data in J/E make it impossible to compare to P; for Driver, the lack of adding numerals in J/E results from J/E's being less concerned with "exact chronological standards" and "statistical data" than P.[65] In some cases the presence of an adding numeral (which is by nature more precise than a simple numeral) may be a determining factor in the material being assigned to P. Since there is essentially nothing *within* Genesis–Deuteronomy with which to compare, we can only compare P to Josh–2 Kings and other later texts—all of which clearly prefer deletion/node raising and decreasing order. The distribution of data in P is certainly different from the distribution found in the rest of the Hebrew Bible. The question remains, however, why this should be the case. I see no literary or stylistic features playing a role in this evidence—with the possible exception of the Toledoth book. Similarly, the distribution of data does not line up with the theory of a distinct northern dialect of Hebrew. The best explanation for the data is diachronic, since P does not clearly favor one structure or one order for adding numerals. Frank Polak has suggested a distinct "priestly sociolect" found in P,[66] but even if this notion were correct, we might appeal to diachronic development as part of this sociolect difference, as it is more likely for a religious class of people to use older features to distinguish their language than to innovate new features. Whether one wants, then, to follow a particular source-critical theory or not, my sense is that diachrony must still be involved as the cause of change.

Within the Priestly material itself, we might ask whether further distinctions correspond with our data. When we distinguish (following Noth) supplementary material and the Toledoth book in Genesis from the rest of P, as well as the legal material in P and H Leviticus, the data are as follows.

TABLE 9. Structure of Adding Numerals within P Material

	Multiple distribution	Deletion/node raising	% Deletion/node raising
Toledoth	29	6	17
P	19	35	65
P supplements	3	15	83
P Leviticus	2	0	-
H Leviticus	0	1	-

---

[65] Samuel R. Driver, *An Introduction to the Literature of the Old Testament* (Edinburgh: T&T Clark, 1950), 126–27.

[66] Frank H. Polak, "Poetic Style and Parallelism in the Creation Account (Genesis 1.1–2.3)," in *Creation in Jewish and Christian Tradition*, ed. Henning Graf Reventlow and Yair Hoffman, JSOTSup 319 (London: Sheffield Academic, 2002), 12, 27. This notion might help to explain Ezekiel's use of increasing order if Ezekiel was aware of a unique P source and meant to imitate Priestly literature and language.

TABLE 10. Order of Adding Numerals within P Material

	Increasing	Decreasing	% Decreasing
Toledoth	31	4	11
P	45	58	56
P supplements	26	14	35
P Leviticus	0	2	-
H Leviticus	1	0	-

If I am correct to see the changes in adding-numeral structure and order as diachronic features of the language, the Toledoth book—when seen as a distinct source that was incorporated into P—would preserve the stage of the language where the older features dominated. These features could also conceivably appear in higher concentration in the Toledoth for literary reasons; if such numeral syntax was characteristic of genealogies, it again could stem ultimately from diachrony (with genealogies preserving/using older features of the language).

Outside the Pentateuch, redaction- and source-critical issues appear to have little effect on my analysis. Taking 1–2 Kings as an example, if we consider the adding-numeral data in light of potential sources, the compilation of those sources, and later redactional stages, the general picture does not change. This is because the evidence is very nearly monolithic, with only a few traces of old features in 1–2 Kings. Following Mordechai Cogan's general outline of the composition history of 1–2 Kings,[67] we find new features—node raising/deletion and decreasing order—dominating in all compositional layers: those that potentially stem directly from an older source, revisions made by the earliest editor(s) (Cogan's "Dtr1"), and later stages of redaction.[68] Old features—multiple distribution and increasing order—are similarly present in multiple compositional layers.[69] Though I have not exhausted this kind of analysis for every proposed composition history of 1–2 Kings, it looks as though all stages of compositional development have the same general character. The widespread presence of new features in earlier compositional stages shows that the latest redactions are not responsible for the new adding-numeral features in 1–2 Kings. I suspect that most, if not all,

---

[67] Mordechai Cogan, *1 Kings: A New Translation with Introduction and Commentary*, AB 10 (New York: Doubleday, 2008), 90–100.

[68] See, e.g., 1 Kgs 7:3 and 2 Kgs 12:7, perhaps reflecting temple sources; and 1 Kgs 8:63, where an editor exaggerates the number of Solomon's offerings.

[69] For example, we see increasing order in 1 Kgs 5:12, possibly stemming from a Solomon source; multiple distribution and increasing order in 1 Kgs 6:1, where the ideologically motivated number 480 may indicate editing; and increasing order in an editorial summary in 1 Kgs 9:23. Old features may be completely absent from the latest stages of redaction; examples of adding numerals with new features include 2 Kgs 23:31, 36; 24:18; 25:27. However, old features in 1–2 Kings are, on the whole, very sparse.

redaction-critical analyses of 1–2 Kings would similarly entail new and old adding-numeral features in all layers of composition. The character of the data in Joshua–2 Kings described in my model above reasonably applies regardless of one's outlook on the development of these texts.

While the texts of the Hebrew Bible have complicated textual histories, the known complexities do not undermine my basic model offered above. Source criticism of the Pentateuch does not explain away the diachronic trend, and potential sources and stages of redaction do not explain away the new features in Joshua–2 Kings. The ways in which diachronic linguistics ought to participate in a conversation with redaction and source criticism is another question altogether, which I cannot address here. To take one example, recent scholarship views the book of Numbers as very late, some seeing Numbers as nearly contemporaneous with Chronicles because of thematic similarities between the two corpora.[70] The linguistic evidence from adding numerals is incongruous with such an analysis. The question, then, is which type of evidence should take precedence, thematic similarities or linguistic evidence. Whatever the answer, I suspect that linguistic evidence has been underappreciated in recent decades.

V. Conclusion

The results of this study impact the ongoing debate about Hebrew diachrony and the dating of texts in three ways. First, the adding-numeral data confirm the idea that the Hebrew found in the biblical texts changed over time, and these changes cannot be adequately explained by recourse to dialect or stylistics alone. Second, the evidence of adding numerals is compatible with the traditional model of Hebrew diachrony. Third, the diachronic progression of adding-numeral syntax argues against a strict periodization of Hebrew into two (or three) stages.

The evidence of adding numerals supports the notion that we can track diachronic developments in Ancient Hebrew. For the two main features I reviewed, diachrony is the most powerful explanation for the variation in the data; stylistics and register may possibly help explain some of the deviation from the overall model, but diachrony is the most likely overarching framework for what is happening. A few things are important to keep in mind on this point. First, the use of an old or new feature once or twice in a text does not necessarily indicate that the language of that text is old or new; rather, it means merely that the old or new feature was an available option. Second, this study thinks in terms of the *process by which a language changes*, not firm time frames. In other words, for a text to be earlier or later on the S-curve means that its language occurs at an earlier or

---

[70] See Hans-Peter Mathys, "Numeri und Chronik: Nahe Verwandte," in *The Books of Leviticus and Numbers*, ed. Thomas Römer, BETL 215 (Leuven: Peeters, 2008), 555–78.

later point in the process. It is *possible* that the tradents behind Genesis, Exodus, and Numbers were language innovators or early adopters of these particular features, making them earlier in the process of diffusion though temporally around the same time as other texts. To sort out whether this was the case would require the addition of many more features tracked in the same way that I have tracked adding-numeral syntax here. What I have sketched here does not, in itself, give the full picture of the relative time frames of the language in each text; what it does, rather, is contribute more pieces of the puzzle that can be combined with others to say something significant about the relative dates of the language in each text.[71]

The results of my study are compatible with the classic approach to Hebrew diachrony to an extent. The data suggest a diachronic distinction between some biblical texts and fit the overall chronology of the traditional approach. The fact that the material in Joshua–2 Kings, Chronicles, and Ezra-Nehemiah has the same profile does not entail that these texts or their language are even roughly contemporaneous, since the last stage of the process of diffusion will always extend for a long time. Moreover, though the two syntactical features discussed here are not sufficient in themselves to *firmly* date texts, the evidence of adding numerals *supports* a view of the pentateuchal material (or P at least) as being earlier than Ezra-Nehemiah, Chronicles, and the Deuteronomistic History (Joshua–2 Kings)[72] —including its sources and subsequent redactional layers. If we follow traditional source-critical distinctions, my analysis suggests that language in the Toledoth book falls near the beginning of the processes of diffusion, language in P material falls within the transitional stages, and language in the remainder of our Ancient Hebrew evidence falls at the end, with the exception of texts that are classicizing.

The evidence of this study runs contrary to a strict periodization of Classical Biblical Hebrew, Late Biblical Hebrew, and Transitional Biblical Hebrew, since some of the Classical Biblical Hebrew texts (Joshua–2 Kings) fall at the end of the process of diffusion for each feature and other Classical Biblical Hebrew texts (P, Genesis, Exodus, Numbers) occur at the beginning or in the transition. I find it likely that diachronic changes to Hebrew occurred at different periods in the history of Hebrew. Many scholars who adhere to the classic model of Hebrew diachrony, of course, agree that not all features would have changed at the same time.[73] In the case of each individual feature, there are early, transitional, and late stages in

---

[71] To be sure, content-based evidence—for example, clear references to corroborated historical events—is often better than linguistic evidence in terms of dating the texts (as opposed to their language).

[72] See Jan Joosten, "Diachronic Linguistics and the Date of the Pentateuch," in *The Formation of the Pentateuch: Bridging the Academic Cultures of Europe, Israel, and North America*, ed. Jan C. Gertz et al., FAT 111 (Tübingen: Mohr Siebeck, 2016), 327–44, here 336–37.

[73] Ibid., 331–32.

the process of diffusion. And though major social upheaval and intense language contact—of the sort that would have resulted from the Babylonian exile—often bring about widespread change to a language,[74] I am not yet convinced that a large number of features, under influence of Aramaic, changed *en masse* over a short period of time, nor that we can properly speak of two (or three) distinct temporal dialects of Ancient Hebrew.

In conclusion, complex adding numerals are valuable objects of study in two regards. On the synchronic level, their syntax is more complicated than is typically assumed. By exploring areas of previously uncharted syntax, this study clarifies the use and shape of adding numerals in their various forms. On the diachronic level, both the structure and order of adding numerals offer ample evidence for tracking development in the history of Ancient Hebrew. Significantly, the relative positions of each text's language in the process of diffusion coincide for both features. Though inconclusive on their own, the diachronic analyses offered here are important evidence to add to the larger conversation about Hebrew diachrony. In addition to the syntactic and diachronic knowledge afforded by study of adding numerals, we also find in adding numerals a suggestive example of the *potential* of the study of numeral syntax. Adding numerals are but one part of numeral syntax. Teen numerals, multiplying numerals, and number phrases may hide similar secrets of syntactic complexity and diachronic development.

---

[74] Compare, for example, the shift from Old English to Middle and Modern English, brought on by the Norman invasion of Britain and increased contact between English and French.

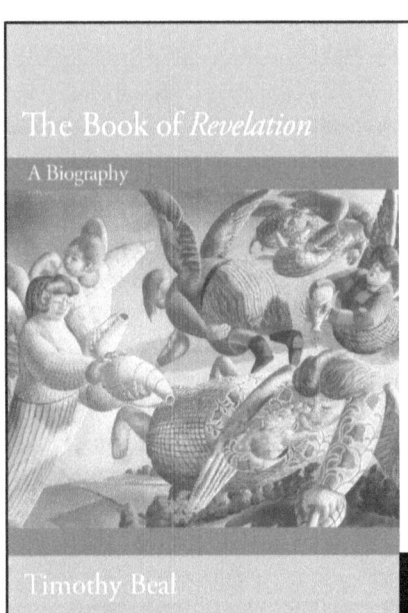

The life and times of the New Testament's most mystifying and incendiary book

"This is perhaps the most engaging, accessible, and thought-provoking book on Revelation that I have ever read."
—Adele Reinhartz,
   author of *Bible and Cinema*

"Beal's reception history captures the diverse uses of Revelation beyond the theological and ecclesiological."
—Amy-Jill Levine,
   author of *Short Stories by Jesus*

Cloth $26.95

PRINCETON UNIVERSITY PRESS

Cambridge Scholars Publishing

Proving Jesus' Authority in Mark and John
Overlooked Evidence of a Synoptic Relationship
Gary Greenberg

"Greenberg offers a fresh and compelling study on the literary relationship between the Gospels of Mark and John. The study offers striking parallels between these two Gospels as well as a comprehensive and compelling explanatory theory for them. This careful and erudite comparison of Mark and John should be read by any engaged in the field of comparative gospel studies."
Adam Winn
Professor of Christian Studies, University of Mary Hardin-Baylor

"In an engaging new approach to these issues, Gary Greenberg explores ways that the Gospel of John may actually represent an augmentation of Mark, with a bit of corrective engagement along the way. And if so, such a thesis has profound implications for understanding more clearly the Jesus of history, not simply the Christ of faith."
Paul N. Anderson
Professor of Biblical and Quaker Studies, George Fox University

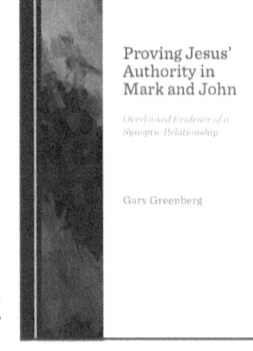

ISBN 978-1-5275-0790-6
Hardback 244pp
£61.99 UK
$99.95 US

20% Discount available
Order online at our website
www.cambridgescholars.com
Discount Code: JESUS20

Our books are also sold worldwide on Amazon, Blackwell and Ingram
www.cambridgescholars.com
orders@cambridgescholars.com

150 Men at Nehemiah's Table? The Role of the Governor's Meals in the Achaemenid Provincial Economy

LISBETH S. FRIED
lizfried@umich.edu
University of Michigan, Ann Arbor, MI 48104

Nehemiah claims that, although he never exacted tribute from the population nor acquired land, he still served 150 people at his table every day at which he provided one ox, six sheep, and an unnumbered amount of birds (5:17–18). In this article, I examine this claim against the background of royal, satrapal, and gubernatorial behavior in the Achaemenid Empire and conclude that Nehemiah, in his role as governor of Yehud, would indeed have hosted 150 nobles and prefects at his table every day, serving the huge amounts that he lists. Archaeological evidence supports the claim that satrapal and gubernatorial courts looked and functioned like small-scale replicas of the royal palace. While the official reason for the banquet may have been sharing wealth, generosity, and conviviality, underneath lay the legitimization of the unequal patron–client relationship between the noble and his host.

Nehemiah states that, during his more than twelve years as governor of Judah, he never exacted tribute from the population nor did he acquire land. Nevertheless, he claims that he served 150 people at his table every day at which he provided one ox, six sheep, and an unnumbered amount of birds (Neh 5:17–18):

17והיהודים והסגנים מאה וחמשים איש והבאים אלינו מן־הגוים אשר־סביבתינו
על־שלחני: 18ואשר היה נעשה ליום אחד שור אחד צאן שש־בררות וצפרים
נעשו־לי ובין עשרת ימים בכל־יין להרבה ועם־זה לחם הפחה לא בקשתי כי־
כבדה העבדה על־העם הזה:

This article was originally presented as "Nehemiah 5 and the Economics of Persian Period Judah" at the 2015 Annual Meeting of the Society of Biblical Literature in Atlanta. I wish to thank the audience at that session for their enthusiastic response as well as Avraham Faust, Margaret Cool Root, and the anonymous *JBL* reviewers of this article for their helpful comments which greatly improved the article.

¹⁷And the Judeans and the prefects—150 men—coming to us from the nations roundabout—were at my table. ¹⁸And that which was prepared for one day was one ox, six picked sheep, and birds were prepared for me, but with this, the bread of the governor I never sought because the labor was heavy upon this people. (my translation)

Are these claims simply hyperbole, and, if not, how did Nehemiah pay for all this food without taxing the populace? Who were they who ate at his table every day, and could a mere 150 people eat all this food? Why did they eat at Nehemiah's table, and why did Nehemiah invite them? What was the rationale behind this practice? I will address each of these issues in turn.

I. The Daily Banquet at the Governor's Table

According to this passage in Nehemiah, one ox and six sheep were served daily. This has been estimated (by my butcher) to be well over eight hundred pounds—and this is in addition to the numerous fowl and the other foods not mentioned. One must ask, therefore, if this is all simply hyperbole. Greek authors describe the banquets of the Persians as offering immense amounts of food (especially meat) and tables set with utensils of gold and silver (Herodotus, *Hist.* 1.133; Xenophon, *Anab.* 4.4.21).[1] Biblical texts such as Esth 1 and Jdt 12:1 and 15:11 make reference to similar banquets and accoutrements. These texts portray the riches and the power of the rulers, and their descriptions reveal the fascination that these meals held for outsiders. This fascination suggests that the description in Nehemiah may be hyperbole.

Yet other texts force reconsideration of this assessment. The inscription of Ashurnaṣirpal II (883–859 BCE) lists the huge amounts of food and the large number of guests (almost 70,000) that participated in a special banquet celebrating the opening of his palace at Nimrud (*ANET*, 558–60). This, however, reports a unique occurrence and is therefore not helpful. More relevant is the witness of Heraclides of Cyme to the daily banquets of Artaxerxes II:

> One thousand animals are served each day which are cut into pieces for the king's dinner. Among these are horses, camels, oxen, donkeys, deer, and especially sheep. They also consume numerous birds, Arabian ostriches (and this is an animal of a very great size), geese, and cocks. (Heraclides of Cyme [350 BCE], quoted in Athenaeus, *Deipn.* F2.4.146a)[2]

This text makes the daily feasts of Nehemiah seem quite modest by comparison.

---

[1] See also Pierre Briant, *From Cyrus to Alexander: A History of the Persian Empire*, trans. Peter T. Daniels (Winona Lake, IN: Eisenbrauns, 2002), 286–97.

[2] My translation of the French translation of Dominique Lenfant, *Les Histoires perses de Dinon et d'Héraclide: Fragments édités, traduits et commentés*, Persika 13 (Paris: de Boccard, 2009), 280.

More compelling is the nonliterary evidence from the Persepolis Fortification Tablets (PF) dated to the reign of Darius I, which suggest the veracity of Heraclides's account.³ There are eighty-two texts from Persepolis that use the phrase "consumed before the king" or "poured before the king," each listing a wide variety of foodstuffs including animals in large numbers that were approved by the royal treasurer there.⁴ There are nineteen additional texts that refer to animals and foods "consumed before" the royal women Irdabama, the king's mother, and Irtaštuna (Artysone), the king's wife, along with their son Iršama (Arsames). The amounts reported in these texts are tremendous. Individual tablets mention *single requisitions* as high as 1,224 head of sheep and goats (PF 0696), 126,100 quarts of flour (PF 0701), 1,044 head of poultry (PF 2034), 5,000 quarts of fruit (NN 0923 [NN designates an unpublished fortification tablet transliterated by R. T. Hallock]), and 12,350 quarts of wine (PF 0728). These quantities were consumed at the courts of the royals named: the king's mother or his wife. Yet the large quantities of cereals, meat, wine, and beer consumed before Irdabama, the queen mother, amount to a mere one-tenth of the quantities consumed before the king.⁵ The huge amounts reported in these texts support the descriptions of royal meals portrayed by the Greek and biblical authors. In fact, Wouter F. M. Henkelman regards the figures from the tablets as too low and the descriptions of the Greek authors as more accurate.⁶ The royal court would have had other sources for foodstuffs besides those requiring requisitions from the royal treasurer at Persepolis. Additional foods could have been obtained from local peasants and farmers or may have been the result of taxes paid in kind.

Also relevant for our purposes are the Persepolis Fortification texts that refer to Karkiš, satrap of Carmania. The huge amounts of food designated to be "consumed before Karkiš" demonstrate that he too had his own house and his own table to provide for, agreeing with the Greek authors that the court of the satrap imitated that of the king.⁷ Provincial governors too evidently had their own houses and tables on the model of the great king and the satraps, as suggested by Neh 5:17–18. Xenophon reports, for example, that the personal wealth of Zenis of Dardanus, a provincial governor of the satrap Pharnabazus, was enough to provide nearly a year's pay to an army of eight thousand men (*Hell.* 3.1.27–28).

---

³ R. T. Hallock, *Persepolis Fortification Tablets*, OIP 92 (Chicago: University of Chicago Press, 1969); Wouter F. M. Henkelman, "'Consumed before the King': The Table of Darius, That of Irdabama and Irtashtuna, and That of the Satrap, Karkish," in *Der Achämenidenhof / The Achaemenid Court: Akten des 2. Internationalen Kolloquiums zum Thema "Vorderasien im Spannungsfeld klassischer und altorientalischer Überlieferungen," Landgut Castelen bei Basel, 23.-25. Mai 2007*, ed. Bruno Jacobs and Robert Rollinger, Classica et Orientalia 2 (Wiesbaden: Harrassowitz, 2010), 667–775; Lenfant, *Les* Histoires perses, 255–315.
⁴ Henkelman, "'Consumed before the King,'" 679.
⁵ Ibid., 695.
⁶ Ibid., 685.
⁷ Ibid., 704–13.

II. Providing Food for 150 Men

If he did not tax the people (5:15), how was Nehemiah able to feed these huge quantities to 150 men every day? He may have supplied them from his gubernatorial estate (5:14). Rather than envisioning a simple house within the city of Jerusalem, perhaps we ought to imagine a huge tract of land in the country with cattle, sheep, and flocks of geese and poultry.[8] The Persian word *ulhi*, usually translated "house," refers not only to a building but to lands and farms, as well as to the ensemble of people who worked on them.[9] Xenophon uses the word βασίλειον ("palace") for the estates of both kings and satraps.[10] Archaeology reveals that the satrapal estate at Daskyleion included παράδεισοι for hunting and fishing which helped to supply the satrap's table.[11] Daskyleion was surrounded by villages that would have provided the satrapal court with produce, which might have been designated as gifts and so not included as part of their tribute or taxes.[12] A string of provincial administrative centers has been identified along the coast of Achaemenid Palestine, for example, each surrounded by agricultural settlements to provide the centers with their needs.[13] Verifying the existence of such estates in the archaeology of Judah is problematic, however, since strata pertaining to the Persian and early Hellenistic periods are meager. Even so, several large agricultural estates have been identified in Persian-period Yehud—Har Adar, Qalandya, and Aderet may be estates that belonged to nobles.[14]

Ramat Raḥel has also been identified as a gubernatorial estate.[15] Located on a

---

[8] For the presence of such estates in Judah, see now Avraham Faust, "Forts or Agricultural Estates? Persian Period Settlement in the Territories of the Former Kingdom of Judah," *PEQ* 150 (2018): 34–59.

[9] Briant, *From Cyrus to Alexander*, 445.

[10] Christopher Tuplin, "Xenophon and Achaemenid Courts: A Survey of Evidence," in Jacobs and Rollinger, *Der Achämenidenhof*, 189–230, esp. 189.

[11] Deniz Kaptan, "From Xenophon to Kritoboulos: Notes on Daskyleion and the Satrapal Court," in Jacobs and Rollinger, *Der Achämenidenhof*, 829–52, esp. 829–31.

[12] Mariano San Nicolò, "Zur Verproviantierung des kgl. Hoflagers in Abanu durch den Eanna-Tempel in Uruk," *AnOr* 17 (1949): 323–30; Briant, *From Cyrus to Alexander*, 394–99, 402–5.

[13] Oren Tal, "Some Remarks on the Coastal Plain of Palestine under Achaemenid Rule: An Archaeological Synopsis," in *L'archéologie de l'empire Achéménide: Nouvelles recherches; Actes du colloque organisé au Collège de France par le "Réseau international d'études et de recherches achéménides," GDR 2538 CNRS, 21–22 novembre 2003*, ed. Pierre Briant and Rémy Boucharlat, Persika 6 (Paris: de Boccard, 2005), 71–96; Kaptan, "From Xenophon to Kritoboulos," 830.

[14] Alexander Fantalkin and Oren Tal, "Judah and Its Neighbors in the Fourth Century," in *From Judah to Judaea: Socio-economic Structures and Processes in the Persian Period*, ed. Johannes Unsok Ro, HBM 43 (Sheffield: Sheffield Phoenix, 2012), 133–96.

[15] Oded Lipschits et al., "A. Palace and Village, Paradise and Oblivion: Unraveling the Riddles of Ramat Raḥel," *NEA* 74 (2011): 2–49; Lipschits et al. "B. The Riddle of Ramat Raḥel: The Archaeology of a Royal Persian Period Edifice," *Transeu* 41 (2012): 57–79.

prominent ridge four kilometers south of Jerusalem, it overlooks the two main roads that connect Jerusalem to the rest of the country: the "King's Road," which leads to Jerusalem to the north, and back to Bethlehem, Hebron, and Beer-Sheva in the south, and a second road leading west to Beth Shemesh through the Rephaim Valley. The palatial architecture of Ramat Raḥel—its pools and gardens revealing pollen of flora from Persia, as well as a profusion of Persian-period artifacts including *yhwd* stamp impressions dated to the sixth–fourth centuries—indicate that Ramat Raḥel was an administrative and tax collection center in the Persian period and may have served as the governor's residence.[16] Further, agricultural data suggest that the Rephaim Valley was dotted with agricultural installations and small farmsteads during this period.[17] Nehemiah and his 150 or more guests could have been amply provided for by the several farmsteads identified in the archaeology of the area, with contributions from these farms being counted as gifts, not taxes.

Besides the provisions from the surrounding farms, guests would have brought other gifts to Nehemiah's table, as they did to that of the great king as shown in the Apadana reliefs.[18] Like the contributions from the villages, such offerings would have been considered not tribute or taxes but gifts. Archaeological evidence suggests a pattern of gift bringing similar to that at Susa and Persepolis, not only at satrapal courts but also at the provincial capitals.[19] Stelae and elite tombs at Ikiztepe, one hundred kilometers east of Sardis, the satrapal capital, portray processions of tribute carriers in emulation of the reliefs at Apadana.[20] Indeed, the reliefs at Ikiztepe display a wide variety of court activities: processions, banquets, and hunts, as well as presentations of gifts. Provincial courts, like those of the satrap, attempted to mimic the court of the great king.

III. The Guests at Nehemiah's Table

Although the text does not provide the names of those who ate daily at Nehemiah's table, the guest list would have included only men. The Greek authors testify that the only women present when the king dined in public were courtesans,

---

[16] Lipschits et al., "Palace and Village," 34, 36; Lipschits et al., "Riddle of Ramat Raḥel," 72.

[17] Oded Lipschits, "The Rural Economy of Judah during the Persian Period and the Settlement History of the District System," *The Economy of Ancient Judah in Its Historical Context*, ed. Marvin Lloyd Miller, Ehud Ben Zvi, and Gary N. Knoppers (Winona Lake, IN: Eisenbrauns, 2015), 237–64.

[18] Heleen Sancisi-Weerdenburg, "Gifts in the Persian Empire," in *Le tribut dans l'Empire perse: Actes de la table ronde de Paris, 12–13 décembre 1986*, ed. Pierre Briant and Clarisse Herrenschmidt, Travaux de l'Institut d'études iraniennes de l'Université de la Sorbonne nouvelle 13 (Paris: Peeters, 1989), 129–46.

[19] Margaret C. Miller, "Luxury Toreutic in the Western Satrapies: Court-Inspired Gift-Exchange Diffusion," in Jacobs and Rollinger, *Der Achämenidenhof*, 853–97, esp. 877.

[20] Ibid., 860–61.

and this was likely the case for satraps and governors as well.[21] The Nehemiah passage reads "Judeans and prefects" (והיהודים והסגנים), but who were these people? The title "prefect" appears regularly among the Aramaic papyri of Elephantine[22] and refers to a Persian satrapal official operating at or just above the level of the provincial governor and just below the level of the satrap (cf. Dan 3:2, 3).[23] We may refer to Xenophon to explain who the other men were who ate at Nehemiah's table:

> He [Cyrus the Great] gave orders to all the satraps he sent out to imitate him in everything that they saw him do: they were, in the first place, to organize companies of cavalry and charioteers from among the Persians who went with them and from the allies; *to require as many as received lands and palaces to attend at the satrap's court* and exercising proper self-restraint to put themselves at his disposal in whatever he demanded; to have the boys that were born to them educated at the local court, just as was done at the royal court; and to take the retinue at his gates out hunting and to exercise himself and them in the arts of war. (Xenophon, *Cyr.* 8.6.10; W. Miller, LCL; emphasis added)

According to Xenophon, those who ate at Nehemiah's table would have been those who received land and palaces in Yehud from the king, satrap, or governor. Thus, they were not hereditary landowners who had received their estates from their fathers or grandfathers. Rather, they would have been Persians, relatives or friends of the king, satrap, or governor, who received landed estates in Judah as rewards for services rendered. Beyond these Persians, local Judean collaborators may also have been recognized and rewarded with grants of land or donations of income from villages and cities (see *TAD* B5.1; as well as the stela of Mnesimachus).[24] The Greek authors, the Elephantine and Bactrian papyri, the Murašû documents, and the stela of Mnesimachus all testify that conquered land was royal land.[25] Plots of

---

[21] Tuplin, "Xenophon and Achaemenid Courts," 206–23, esp. 223

[22] See, e.g., Bezalel Porten and Ada Yardeni, *Textbook of Aramaic Documents from Egypt* [*TAD*], 4 vols. (Winona Lake, IN: Eisenbrauns, 1986–1999), B2.3:13; B3.1:13, 18.

[23] André Lemaire, "Administration in Fourth-Century BCE Judah in Light of Epigraphy and Numismatics," in *Judah and the Judeans in the Fourth Century B.C.E.*, ed. Oded Lipschits, Gary N. Knoppers, and Rainer Albertz (Winona Lake, IN: Eisenbrauns, 2007), 53–74.

[24] M. M. Austin, "Greek Tyrants and the Persians," *ClQ* 40 (1990): 289–306; Frédéric Maffre, "Indigenous Aristocracies in Hellespontine Phrygia," in *Persian Responses: Political and Cultural Interaction with(in) the Achaemenid Empire*, ed. Christopher Tuplin (Swansea: Classical Press of Wales, 2007), 117–41.

[25] Pierre Briant, "Dons de terres et de villes: L'Asie mineure dans le contexte achéménide," *REA* 87.1–2 (1985): 53–71; Briant, *From Cyrus to Alexander*, 326, 413–21; Muhammad A. Dandamayev, "Die Lehnsbeziehungen in Babylonien unter den ersten Achämeniden," in *Festschrift für Wilhelm Eilers: Ein Dokument der internationalen Forschung zum 27. September 1967*, ed. Gernot Wiessner (Wiesbaden: Harrassowitz, 1967), 37–42; Matthew W. Stolper, *Entrepreneurs and Empire: The Murašû Archive, the Murašû Firm, and Persian Rule in Babylonia*, UNHAII 54 (Leiden: Nederlands Instituut voor het Nabije Oosten, 1985); Lisbeth S. Fried, "The Exploitation of Depopulated Land in Achaemenid Judah," in Miller, Ben Zvi, and Knoppers, *Economy of Ancient Judah*, 149–62; Fried, "Implications of 5th and 4th Century Documents for Understanding

this now royal land were allocated as revocable grants to friends and relatives of the king or satrap as well as to foreign military and nonmilitary colonists. These too would have eaten at Nehemiah's table. The men who sat at Nehemiah's table were thus the Persian nobles residing in Judah, holders of estates granted by the king, satrap, or governor to friends and retainers, and the text should be emended to reflect this.[26] This process of land grants illustrates the replacement of a hereditary nobility by a court nobility.[27] Land was no longer obtained by virtue of belonging to a hereditary caste. Rather, conquered land throughout the empire was obtained and retained by virtue of one's friendship with and support of king, satrap, or governor.

IV. Nehemiah's Table and the Redistributive Economy

It is obvious that 150 men could not eat one ox and six sheep every night. I pointed out above that this amount of meat would come to over eight hundred pounds and does not include the meat from the numerous fowl as well as the other foods that Nehemiah does not mention—the wheat and barley flour breads and cakes, as well as the fruits, vegetables, pistachio nuts, and sweets that the Fortification Tablets list. The birds mentioned by Nehemiah would have included, according to the Tablets, fattened geese, ducks, and doves. There may have been wild game as well. Since the 150 men who sat at Nehemiah's table could not eat all this food, who did eat it? The Greek authors affirm that food from banquets was not wasted. According to Heraclides of Cyme, guests were able to take home their uneaten portions to feed their families, their servants, and the families of their servants. Continuing from the passage quoted above, Heraclides affirms:

---

the Role of the Governor in Persian Imperial Administration," in *In the Shadow of Bezalel: Aramaic, Biblical, and Ancient Near Eastern Studies in Honor of Bezalel Porten*, ed. Alejandro F. Botta, CHANE 60 (Leiden: Brill, 2012), 319–31.

[26] The passage is likely corrupt; commentators have had difficulty understanding it. The Greek text reads simply "Judeans," omitting "prefects," while the Syriac reads "nobles and prefects," omitting "Judeans." Of the seven other times that the term סגנים ("prefects") appears in Nehemiah, it is coupled with חרים ("nobles") in five of them; in the other two it is not coupled with anything. This suggests that יהודים ("Judeans") was somehow substituted for חרים here. David J. A. Clines states that "Jews" refers to Jewish officials (*Ezra, Nehemiah, Esther*, NCBC [Grand Rapids: Eerdmans, 1984], 171). Joseph Blenkinsopp suggests that the reference is to "the provincial bureaucracy, native and Persian" (*Ezra-Nehemiah: A Commentary*, OTL [Philadelphia: Westminster, 1988], 265). H. G. M. Williamson" (*Ezra, Nehemiah*, WBC 16 [Waco, TX: Word, 1985], 232) translates "the Jews—150 officials," as does A. H. Gunneweg (*Nehemiah*, KAT 19.2; [Berlin: Gütersloher Verlagshaus Gerd Mohn, 1987], 90), who translates as "The Jews, namely the officials, 150 men." Sigmund Mowinckel reads "nobles" with the Syriac (*Die Nehemia-Denkschrift*, vol. 2 of *Studien zu dem Buche Ezra-Nehemiah*, SNVAO.HF 3 [Oslo: Universitetsforlaget, 1964], 28). See further Fried, *Nehemiah: A Commentary* (London: T&T Clark, forthcoming).

[27] Briant, *From Cyrus to Alexander*, 326.

Only moderate portions are served to each of the king's guests, but *each of them may carry home whatever he leaves untouched at the meal*. The greater part of these meats and other foods are taken out into the courtyard for the body-guard and light-armed troopers maintained by the king; there they divide all the half-eaten remnants of meat and bread and share them in equal portions. Just as hired soldiers in Greece receive their wages in money, so these men receive food from the king in requital for services. Similarly, among other Persians of high rank, all the food is served on the table at one and the same time; but when their guests have done eating, whatever is left from the table, consisting chiefly of meat and bread, is given by the officer in charge of the table to each of the slaves; this they take and so obtain their daily food. Hence the most highly honored of the king's guests go to court only for breakfast; for they beg to be excused in order that they may not be required to go twice, but may be able to entertain their own guests. (Heraclides of Cyme, quoted in Athenaeus, *Deipn.* 4.145; emphasis added)[28]

The guests at Nehemiah's table thus would have taken food home to their families and retainers. Portions not taken home by the guests went to feed Nehemiah's own soldiers and staff. The royal dining table, as well as the tables of satraps and provincial governors, served a redistributive function for the entire economy.[29]

These claims of Heraclides of Cyme (quoted in Athenaeus) are more believable since Athenaeus is intent on demonstrating τρυφή (the extravagant desire for luxury) among the Persians. That the text emphasizes instead the modest amount that each guest ate, and that each took home the uneaten portions to his family and retainers, contradicts the polemical theme of dissolute luxury that characterizes the entire text.[30] Further, the testimony of the Persepolis Fortification Tablets supports the assertion in Athenaeus that the guests took food home. This must be assumed for Nehemiah's table as well.

V. The Power of the Governor's Table

The Greek authors reveal that neither Nehemiah nor his guests had a choice about attending.[31] The 150 men who ate at Nehemiah's table every day were obligated to eat there, and Nehemiah was obligated to invite them. The Greek authors make it clear that those who received lands and palaces from king, satrap, or governor were required to attend the local court. If anyone did not, those lands and palaces were to be taken from him and given to someone who would attend:

> In the first place, if any of those who were able to live by the labors of others failed to attend at court, he [Cyrus] made inquiry after them.... We will describe first

---

[28] My translation of the French translation in Lenfant, *Les* Histoires perses, 280–82.
[29] Henkelman, "'Consumed before the King,'" 685; Briant, *From Cyrus to Alexander*, 326; Sancisi-Weerdenburg, "Gifts in the Persian Empire," 137.
[30] Lenfant, *Les* Histoires perses, 58.
[31] Briant, *From Cyrus to Alexander*, 326.

therefore the manner in which he obliged all such to come; he would direct some one of the best friends he had at court *to seize some of the property of the man who did not present himself* and to declare that he was taking only what was his own.... That was one of his methods of training them to attend.... But the surest way of compulsion was this: *if a man paid no attention to any of these methods, he would take away all that he had and give it to some one else who he thought would present himself [at court] when he was wanted; and thus he would get a useful friend in exchange for a useless one.* (Xenophon, *Cyr.* 8.1.16–20; W. Miller, LCL; emphasis added)

Conversely, satraps and governors were required to invite these nobles and officials to their daily meals. Provincial governors and satraps had to follow the pattern of the great king and hold daily banquets for the landed nobles in their locale.[32] Nehemiah thus testifies in this passage that he has done his duty, that he had indeed served daily at his table the nobles and prefects round about, as well as all those officials en route from one place to another who carried travel orders from the king or satrap.

VI. The System's Rationale

These daily banquets served several purposes. One reason for requiring a noble's daily attendance at the court of his sovereign is clear from the example of Histiaeus. When Histiaeus, tyrant of Miletus, lost Darius's trust, Darius moved him to Susa and had him live with him there and eat daily at his table (Herodotus, *Hist.* 5.23–24). Presumably Darius, and all the kings who followed him, encouraged his satraps and governors to follow that important adage: "Keep your friends close and your enemies closer." Forcing nobles and officials who owned estates and palaces, *and who were thus in control of independent resources*, to be in daily attendance upon their sovereign prevented them from conspiring with others against him. The eyes and ears of their lord were constantly upon them. These daily banquets were thus instruments of control. They established and stabilized local rule in a vast network that spread over the entire empire. That satraps and governors were also required to host at their court and to educate there the sons of the nobles growing up in their jurisdiction (Xenophon, *Cyr.* 8.6.10) means that the sons of these nobles were being held hostage at court. Nobles would not plan rebellions against the very man who held their son's life in his hands.

Second, these dinners established the hierarchical order of the guests, who were seated in order of honor and importance:

"And whoever I find has the largest number of chariots to show and the largest number of the most efficient horsemen in proportion to his power," Cyrus added, "him will I honor as a valuable ally and as a valuable fellow-protector of the

---

[32] Erich Kistler, "Achämenid Becher und die Logik kommensaler Politik im Reich der Achämeniden," in Jacobs and Rollinger, *Der Achämenidenhof,* 411–57, esp. 425–28.

sovereignty of the Persians and of myself. And with you also, just as with me, *let the most deserving be set in the most honorable seats* [at your table]; and *let your table, like mine, feed first your own household and then, too, be bountifully arrayed so as to give a share to your friends* and to confer some distinction day by day upon anyone who does some noble act." (Xenophon, *Cyr.* 8.6.11; W. Miller, LCL; emphasis added)

The ruler's table thus served to create rivalry among the nobles, forcing them to compete in the favors they performed for their host and in the gifts they brought him. In fact, the royal banquet was the primary occasion for gift giving, as is illustrated by the reliefs of the palaces at Apadana.[33]

A third and most important function of these banquets was economic in that they functioned as a mechanism for the redistribution of wealth. Gifts brought to the king or sovereign did not stay with him. The silver and gold dishes and utensils shown being brought to the king on the Apadana reliefs are the same items that appear as valued heirlooms among grave goods of the elites in excavations throughout the empire (Athenaeus, *Deipn.* 4.145b; Plutarch, *Art.* 22.6).[34] The king evidently regifted these items to those attending his banquets. These together with the leftover food from the daily meals that was provided to servants and soldiers confirm a program of redistribution of wealth.

This custom of regifting was an important mechanism of wealth distribution and was practiced throughout the empire.[35] Archaeological evidence shows that satraps and governors mimicked Achaemenid royal behavior in distributing not only the leftover food but also the obligatory gifts to those who attended their table. Persian-looking silver bowls were found in a tomb at Ikiztepe, about one hundred kilometers east of Sardis.[36] These bowls exactly mirrored those carried by the Lydian Delegation (IV) depicted at Persepolis but were locally made. They were intended to be the significant gifts distributed by the provincial governor at Ikiztepe to his guests. This evidence of local imitations in precious metal of Achaemenid royal iconography is apparent also in Egypt and in Beyond-the-River. Petosiris's tomb at Hermopolis, Egypt, contained locally made Persian forms of silver vessels.[37] The local satrapal and provincial courts in Egypt would have been the sources of these gifts.

---

[33] Sancisi-Weerdenburg, "Gifts in the Persian Empire," 136–37; Sancisi-Weerdenburg, "Baji," in *Studies in Persian History: Essays in Memory of David M. Lewis*, ed. Maria Brosius and Amélie Kuhrt, Achaemenid History 11 (Leiden: Nederlands Instituut voor het Nabije Oosten, 1998), 23–34; M. C. Miller, "Luxury Toreutic in the Western Satrapies," 855.

[34] Sancisi-Weerdenburg, "Gifts in the Persian Empire," 134; David M. Lewis, "The King's Dinner (Polyaenus IV 3, 32)," in *The Greek Sources: Proceedings of the Groningen 1984 Achaemenid History Workshop*, ed. Heleen Sancisi-Weerdenburg and Amélie Kuhrt, Achaemenid History 2 (Leiden: Nederlands Instituut voor het Nabije Oosten, 1987), 79–87; M. C. Miller, "Luxury Toreutic in the Western Satrapies," 853–97.

[35] Margaret C. Miller, *Athens and Persia in the Fifth Century B.C.: A Study in Cultural Receptivity* (Cambridge: Cambridge University Press, 1997), esp. 109–33.

[36] M. C. Miller, "Luxury Toreutig in the Western Satrapies," 857–58.

[37] Ibid., 860–61.

VII. Conclusions

It is reasonable to conclude that Nehemiah, as governor of Yehud, did indeed host 150 nobles and prefects of Judah at his table every day, serving the huge amounts that he lists. Archaeological evidence supports the claim that satrapal and gubernatorial courts looked and functioned like small-scale replicas of the royal palace. Sidon, for example, lay in the Persian satrapy of Beyond-the-River, whose capital was at Damascus. Architectural fragments excavated there indicate a provincial palace at Sidon whose elements imitated the palace of Darius at Susa.[38] Data from excavations at Ammon, Ramat Raḥel, and Lachish also suggest palaces in the Persian style at these provincial capitals. The use of Persian architectural and decorative motifs and gardens at these provincial capitals, as well as the processions, the daily banquets, and the presentations of gifts that are revealed on the reliefs, all served to convey the authority of Achaemenid royal culture throughout the empire.

The present discussion confirms and instantiates the results of archaeologists and anthropologists on the role of feasts in antiquity. Most important for the local economy was the redistribution of wealth that these banquets offered. In addition, these feasts established and reified relationships of social superiority and inferiority, creating a relationship of obligation.[39] Eating with the right company conferred honor, but being invited to the feast was not enough, since the banquets of the Persian courts also included distinctions in the seating arrangement of those attending.[40] The closer one was seated to the host, the higher one's social standing. The instability of rank and the capriciousness of royal or satrapal favor served to increase attendance, rivalry among the guests, and fawning on the host. The acceptance of a continually unequal pattern of hospitality at these feasts formally expressed the unequal relations of status and power, creating a firm patron–client relationship. While the official reason for the banquet may have been sharing wealth, generosity, and conviviality, underneath lay the legitimization of the unequal power relation between the noble and his host.

---

[38] M. C. Miller, *Athens and Persia*, 121–22.

[39] Michael Dietler, "Feasts and Commensal Politics in the Political Economy: Food, Power, and Status in Prehistoric Europe," in *Food and the Status Quest: An Interdisciplinary Perspective*, ed. Polly Wiessner and Wulf Schiefenhövel, Anthropology of Food and Nutrition 1 (Providence, RI: Berghahn, 1996), 87–125; Paul Freedman, "Medieval and Modern Banquets: Commensality and Social Categorization," in *Commensality: From Everyday Food to Feast*, ed. Susanne Kerner, Cynthia Chou, and Morten Warmind (London: Bloomsbury Academic, 2015), 99–108; Jacob L. Wright, "Commensal Politics in Ancient Western Asia: The Background to Nehemiah's Feasting," ZAW 122 (2010): 212–33, 333–52.

[40] Paul Freedman, *Food: The History of Taste* (London: Thames & Hudson, 2007); Freedman, "Medieval and Modern Banquets," 99–108.

SBL PRESS

New and Recent Titles

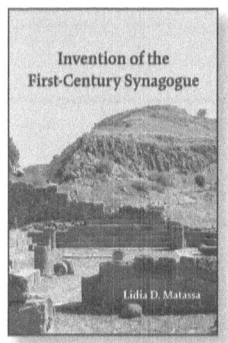

INVENTION OF THE FIRST-CENTURY SYNAGOGUE
Lidia D. Matassa
Jason M. Silverman and J. Murray Watson, editors
Electronic open access 978-0-88414-320-8
http://www.sbl-site.org/publications/Books_ANEmonographs.aspx
Paperback $39.95, 978-1-62837-218-2 288 pages, 2018 Code: 062826
Hardcover $54.95, 978-0-88414-319-2 Ancient Near East Monographs 22

ARCHAEOLOGY AND HISTORY OF EIGHTH-CENTURY JUDAH
Zev I. Farber and Jacob L. Wright, editors
Electronic open access 978-0-88414-348-2
http://www.sbl-site.org/publications/Books_ANEmonographs.aspx
Paperback $79.95, 978-1-62837-233-5 610 pages, 2018 Code: 062821
Hardcover $99.95, 978-0-88414-347-5 Ancient Near East Monographs 23

THE ANCIENT EGYPTIAN NETHERWORLD BOOKS
John Coleman Darnell and Colleen Manassa Darnell
Paperback $99.95, 978-1-62837-127-7 724 pages, 2018 Code: 061547
Hardcover $119.95, 978-0-88414-276-8 E-book $99.95, 978-0-88414-045-0
Writings from the Ancient World 39

HITTITE LOCAL CULTS
Michele Cammarosano
Paperback $69.95, 978-1-62837-215-1 538 pages, 2018 Code: 061557
Hardcover $89.95, 978-0-88414-313-0 E-book $69.95, 978-0-88414-314-7
Writings from the Ancient World 40

EVALUATING THE LEGACY OF ROBERT W. FUNK
Reforming the Scholarly Model
Andrew D. Scrimgeour, editor
Paperback $49.95, 978-1-62837-232-8 420 pages, 2018 Code: 061128
Hardcover $64.95, 978-0-88414-345-1 E-book $49.95, 978-0-88414-346-8
Biblical Scholarship in North America 28

STRENGTH TO STRENGTH
Essays in Honor of Shaye J. D. Cohen
Michael L. Satlow, editor
Paperback $79.95, 978-1-946527-11-0 730 pages, 2018 Code: 140363
Hardcover $99.95, 978-1-946527-12-7 E-book $79.95, 978-1-946527-13-4
Brown Judaic Studies 363

SBL Press • P.O. Box 2243 • Williston, VT 05495-2243
Phone: 877-725-3334 (toll-free) or 802-864-6185 • Fax: 802-864-7626
Order online at www.sbl-site.org/publications

JBL 137, no. 4 (2018): 833–851
doi: http://dx.doi.org/10.15699/jbl.1374.2018.452196

The Gods-Complaint:
Psalm 82 as a Psalm of Complaint

DANIEL MCCLELLAN
dan.mcclellan@gmail.com
University of Exeter, Exeter EX4 4RJ, UK

Psalm 82 has long resisted a consensus regarding its genre. While some scholars have noted that the psalm's language overlaps with that of the complaint genre, several features of the psalm appear to complicate that reading. As a result, the framework of the divine council is frequently given interpretive priority, which has resulted in a variety of solutions to the psalm's several interpretive difficulties and has also contributed to a general reluctance to consider the psalm within the literary context of the psalms of Asaph. I argue that the psalm's interpretive difficulties are best resolved by understanding the psalm as a complaint, specifically a complaint put into the mouth of YHWH and addressed to the gods of the nations—a "gods-complaint." This reading provides a new interpretive framework that may help resolve important questions related to the psalm's compositional background, rhetorical function, and theological influence.

The unique mythological themes of Ps 82 have long compelled scholars to consider it apart from the other psalms of the Asaph collection.[1] For many, the

[1] The literature on Ps 82 is phenomenally broad, but some notable contributions include Julian Morgenstern, "The Mythological Background of Psalm 82," *HUCA* 14 (1939): 29–126; James S. Ackerman, "An Exegetical Study of Psalm 82: A Thesis" (ThD diss., Harvard University, 1966); Gerald Cooke, "The Sons of (the) God(s)," *ZAW* 35 (1964): 29–34; Matitiahu Tsevat, "God and the Gods in Assembly: An Interpretation of Psalm 82," *HUCA* 40 (1969): 123–37; Hans-Winfried Jüngling, *Der Tod der Götter: Eine Untersuchung zum Psalm 82*, SBS 38 (Stuttgart: Katholisches Bibelwerk, 1969); Herbert Niehr, "Götter oder Menschen—eine falsche Alternative: Bemerkungen zu Ps 82," *ZAW* 99 (1987): 94–98; Simon B. Parker, "The Beginning of the Reign of God: Psalm 82 as Myth and Liturgy," *RB* 102 (1995): 532–59; Mark S. Smith, *God in Translation: Deities in Cross-Cultural Discourse in the Biblical World*, FAT 57 (Tübingen: Mohr Siebeck, 2008), 131–39; Peter Machinist, "How Gods Die, Biblically and Otherwise: A Problem of Cosmic Restructuring," in *Reconsidering the Concept of Revolutionary Monotheism*, ed. Beate Pongratz-Leisten (Winona Lake, IN: Eisenbrauns, 2011), 189–240; James M. Trotter, "Death of the אלהים in Psalm 82," *JBL* 131 (2012): 221–39, https://doi.org/10.2307/23488222; Brent A. Strawn, "The Poetics of Psalm 82: Three Critical Notes along with a Plea for the Poetic," *RB* 121 (2014): 21–46.

interaction with other divine beings, the possible distinction between YHWH and El, and possible links with the northern tradition have suggested a very early date of composition.[2] This would set the psalm apart from Pss 74 and 79, which appear to mention the destruction of the temple in Jerusalem and are often dated to the exilic or postexilic periods.[3] Indeed, Ps 82 is frequently interrogated in isolation from the rest of the psalms and by scholars interested primarily in what the psalm may reveal regarding much earlier Israelite conceptualizations of the divine council and of YHWH and El.[4] These scholars largely consider the divine council type-scene to be the most salient literary framework, with the psalm's likely liturgical setting providing a functional backdrop.[5]

In order to avoid awkward circumlocutions and confusion with the frequent references to plural deities, and in light of the unilateral use of masculine verbs and pronouns in the discussed texts, I use masculine pronouns in reference to YHWH throughout this article. Translations are my own unless otherwise noted.

[2] The Tetragrammaton nowhere appears in Ps 82, but, with the vast majority of readers, I understand the appellative אלהים to refer to YHWH, as it explicitly does in the surrounding psalms. The marked preference for אלהים over יהוה in Pss 42–83 has long been taken as an indication of the redactional obscuring of יהוה (which still appears forty-nine times), but the explanations for the inconsistency vary, and there is no textual support for that conclusion. I consider the question an open one. See Matthias Millard, "Zum Problem des elohistischen Psalters: Überlegungen zum Gebrauch von יהוה und אלהים im Psalter," in *Der Psalter in Judentum und Christentum*, ed. Erich Zenger and Norbert Lohfink, HBS 18 (Freiburg im Breisgau: Herder, 1998), 75–110; Laura Joffe, "The Elohistic Psalter: What, How and Why?," *SJOT* 15 (2001): 142–69; Frank-Lothar Hossfeld and Erich Zenger, "The So-Called Elohistic Psalter: A New Solution for an Old Problem," in *A God So Near: Essays on Old Testament Theology in Honor of Patrick D. Miller*, ed. Brent A. Strawn and Nancy R. Bowen (Winona Lake, IN: Eisenbrauns, 2003), 35–51; Joel S. Burnett, "Forty-Two Songs for Elohim: An Ancient Near Eastern Organizing Principle in the Shaping of the Elohistic Psalter," *JSOT* 31 (2006): 81–101.

[3] Some scholars identify the "sanctuary" (קדש) and meeting places mentioned in Ps 74:3 with cultic sites in the northern kingdom, which would facilitate a preexilic date for the psalm. See Michael D. Goulder, *The Psalms of Asaph and the Pentateuch: Studies in the Psalter, III*, JSOTSup 233 (Sheffield: Sheffield Academic, 1996), 36; Beat Weber, "Zur Datierun der Asaph-Psalmen 74 und 79," *Bib* 81 (2000): 521–32.

[4] The view that YHWH and El are distinguished in the psalm is promoted by Karl Budde, "Ps. 82:6f," *JBL* 40 (1921): 41–42, https://doi.org/10.2307/3259401; Otto Eissfeldt, "El and Yahweh," *JSS* 1 (1956): 29–30; Parker, "Beginning of the Reign of God"; Mark S. Smith, *The Origins of Biblical Monotheism: Israel's Polytheistic Background and the Ugaritic Texts* (Oxford: Oxford University Press, 2001), 48–49; David Frankel, "El as the Speaking Voice in Psalm 82:6–8," *JHebS* 10 (2010), art. 16, pp. 1–24, https://doi.org/10.5508/jhs.2010.v10.a16; and Ellen White, *Yahweh's Council: Its Structure and Membership*, FAT 2/65 (Tübingen: Mohr Siebeck, 2014), 24–33. Against these, see Tzevat, "God and the Gods in Assembly," 127–29; Michael S. Heiser, "The Divine Council in Late Canonical and Non-Canonical Second Temple Jewish Literature" (PhD diss., University of Wisconsin–Madison, 2004), 79–82.

[5] On the divine council type-scene, see E. Theodore Mullen, *The Assembly of the Gods: The Divine Council in Canaanite and Early Hebrew Literature*, HSM 24 (Chico, CA: Scholars Press, 1980); David M. Fleming, "The Divine Council as Type Scene in the Hebrew Bible" (PhD diss.,

On the other hand, Ps 82 aligns well with the themes of the Asaphite collection, and the terminology in the psalm overlaps significantly with that of the other Asaphite psalms. Form-critical analyses have largely been confined to commentaries and monographs focused on individual collections of psalms, but even there scholars have posited a wide variety of genres, including "prophetic liturgy," "prophetic oracle," "report of trial," and even "a peculiar mixing of psalm and oracle, where the oracle is the chief thing but is organically fitted into a short prayer."[6] A review of the notoriously broad scholarship reveals that the psalm has long resisted a consensus regarding genre as well as interpretation.

In this article, I argue that the interpretive difficulties of Ps 82 can be resolved by understanding the psalm as a complaint, and more specifically a "gods-complaint" put into the mouth of YHWH and directed at the gods of the nations. Following a discussion of the traditional approaches to Ps 82 and its interpretive difficulties and the complaint genre (using Ps 74 as a case study), I will interrogate Ps 82 using the complaint framework as an interpretive lens. I will argue that this particular framework facilitates the most parsimonious reading of the text, as well as a resolution to a number of the psalm's long-standing interpretive challenges. Finally, I will make some observations regarding what the framework may reveal about the psalm's composition and rhetorical function.

I. Conventional Approaches to Psalm 82

The most common interpretations of Ps 82 frame the psalm as a visionary account of a scene in the divine council. In verse 1, the God of Israel stands among the gods of the nations to accuse and condemn them. Most interpretations tend toward understanding the interrogatives of verse 2 to be accusatory questions, which are then followed in verses 3–4 by declarations of divine responsibilities for upholding justice.[7] The fifth verse is usually understood to be some manner of

---

Southern Baptist Theological Seminary, 1989); Min Suc Kee, "The Heavenly Council and Its Type-Scene," *JSOT* 31 (2007): 259–73; Robert P. Gordon, "Standing in the Council: When Prophets Encounter God," in *The God of Israel*, ed. Robert P. Gordon, UCOP 64 (Cambridge: Cambridge University Press, 2007), 190–204.

[6] For prophetic liturgy, see Mitchell Dahood, *Psalms*, 3 vols., AB 16–17A (Garden City, NY: Doubleday, 1968), 268. For prophetic oracle, see Craig C. Broyles, *Psalms*, NIBCOT 11 (Peabody, MA: Hendrickson, 1999), 335. For report of trial, see Erhard S. Gerstenberger, *Psalms: Part 2 and Lamentations*, FOTL 15 (Grand Rapids: Eerdmans, 2001), 113. Gerstenberger gives a second designation, "Praise and Petition," which is related to Broyles's broad division of the psalms into "praise and lament, or praise and petition" (*The Conflict of Faith and Experience in the Psalms: A Form-Critical and Theological Study*, JSOTSup 52 [Sheffield: JSOT Press, 1989], 35–36). For a "peculiar mixing of psalm and oracle," see Sigmund Mowinckel, *The Psalms in Israel's Worship*, trans. D. R. Ap-Thomas, 2 vols. (Oxford: Blackwell, 1962), 2:64.

[7] The question in verse 2 is labeled a "reproachful question" by Erich Zenger (in Frank-Lothar

verdict, with the prosecutor abruptly shifting address to the court or to the worshipers and announcing the gods' waywardness and incapacity to meet their duties. This is followed by the sentence in verses 6–7 consigning the gods to mortality. The petition of verse 8 calls upon YHWH to restore justice, as is his prerogative as judge over all the earth. The speaker here may be YHWH, El, the psalmist, or the community of worshipers.

While this outline roughly corresponds to the majority of readings of the psalm, there are a handful of interpretive difficulties that continue to be debated. One of the longest-standing questions has been the identity of the plural אלהים. Until about the mid-twentieth century, most scholars accepted that the אלהים were either disobedient angels or human judges referred to honorifically or metonymically as "gods" in the psalm.[8] These readings were primarily motivated by theological sensitivity, but the "judges" reading was supported by the ostensibly analogous use of אלהים in reference to humans in Exod 21:6 and 22:7, as well as by the claim that the neglected responsibilities mentioned in verses 2–4 were the primary purview of human kings and judges.[9] The latter has been recently adduced by James M. Trotter in support of his argument that the אלהים are best understood as the kings of the nations, who were considered divine by their constituents.[10]

Perhaps the most compelling question for contemporary scholars of early Israelite theology is the psalm's possible distinction of YHWH from El. Scholars have argued for some time now that in the earliest recoverable literary strata,

---

Hossfeld and Erich Zenger, *Psalms 2: A Commentary on Psalms 51–100*, trans. Linda M. Maloney, Hermeneia [Minneapolis: Fortress, 2005], 333) and an "indictment in the form of a question" by Marvin Tate (*Psalms 51–100*, WBC 20 [Dallas: Word, 1990], 335).

[8] Most precritical exegetes understood the gods of the narrative to be human judges, but on the weakness of that traditional reading, see Cooke, "Sons of (the) God(s)," 29–34; Tsevat, "God and the Gods in Assembly," 123–37. For a representative nineteenth-century voice, see Franz Julius Delitzsch, *Biblischer Commentar über die Psalmen*, BKAT (Leipzig: Dörffling & Franke, 1894), 546–49.

[9] On the problems with reading אלהים as a reference to humans in the Exodus verses, see Cyrus Gordon, "אלהים in Its Reputed Meaning of Rulers, Judges," *JBL* 54 (1935): 139–44, https://doi.org/10.2307/3259316; Anne E. Draffkorn, "Ilâni/Elohim," *JBL* 76 (1957): 216–24, https://doi.org/10.2307/3261571; David P. Wright, *Inventing God's Law: How the Covenant Code of the Bible Used and Revised the Laws of Hammurabi* (Oxford: Oxford University Press, 2009), 133–37 (and n. 57), 245–48, 252–58. For a somewhat recent attempt to defend the traditional view, see J. Robert Vannoy, "The Use of the Word hāʾĕlōhîm in Exodus 21:6 and 22:7, 8," in *The Law and the Prophets: Old Testament Studies Prepared in Honor of Oswald Thompson Allis*, ed. John H. Skilton, Milton C. Fisher, and Leslie W. Sloat (Philadelphia: Presbyterian and Reformed Publishing, 1974), 225–41.

[10] Trotter, "Death of the אלהים in Psalm 82," 221–39. The similar notion that the psalm can be thought of as referring to divine rule administered by human rulers is promoted in Niehr, "Götter oder Menschen," 94–98; Tate, *Psalms 51–100*, 341; Gerstenberger, *Psalms*, 114. Another minority view is that the psalm conflates two chronologically distinct perspectives, which is argued by Morgenstern, "Mythological Background," 114–26; A. Gonzalez, "Le Psaume LXXXII," *VT* 13 (1963): 293–309; and, to some degree, Tsevat, "God and the Gods in Assembly," 134.

YHWH was understood to be a second-tier deity subordinate to the high god El. The clearest attestation of this hierarchy is found in the version of Deut 32:8–9 preserved in 4QDeut^j (4Q37) and reflected in most ancient Greek translations of the passage.[11] According to the reconstruction of the text supported by those versions, the nations of the earth were divided up by Elyon "according to the number of the children of God," with the nation of Israel/Jacob going to YHWH, one of those children. Psalm 82 is considered an additional witness to this divine hierarchy. Among other considerations, verse 6 uniquely calls the deities "children of Elyon," which may obliquely allude to the distinction of the two deities in Deut 32:8. Additionally, the אלהים of verse 1 is/are taking a stand among the gods, while the אלהים of verse 8 is/are called upon to rise from an ostensible sitting position. According to the conventions of the type-scene, we are told, the presiding deity would have remained seated during the council, with a subordinate deity standing to act as prosecutor.[12] Others point out, however, that the evidence is mixed regarding the postures of judgment.[13] Recent analyses have suggested that the distinction between the two deities in the psalm may not be so clear.[14]

The identities of the speakers in verses 5 and 8 are also open questions. The former verse is widely understood as some manner of verdict being passed on the

---

[11] The end of verse 8 reads ἀγγέλων θεοῦ in most Greek witnesses, but this is a well-known substitution for the Hebrew בני אלהים. 4QDeut^j confirms this reconstruction, and the earliest known Greek witness reads "children of God" (John William Wevers, *Notes on the Greek Text of Deuteronomy*, SCS 39 [Atlanta: Scholars Press, 1995], 513). The beginning of verse 9 has καὶ ἐγενήθη in the Greek, which suggests ויהי in the source text. On this passage, see Patrick W. Skehan, "A Fragment of the 'Song of Moses' (Deut. 32) from Qumran," *BASOR* 136 (1954): 12–15; Paul Sanders, *The Provenance of Deuteronomy 32*, OtSt 37 (Leiden: Brill, 1996), 155–59; Michael S. Heiser, "Deuteronomy 32 and the Sons of God," *BSac* 158 (2001): 52–74; Innocent Himbaza, "Dt 32,8, une correction tardive des scribes: Essai d'interprétation et de datation," *Bib* 83 (2002): 527–48; Jan Joosten, "A Note on the Text of Deuteronomy xxxii 8," *VT* 57 (2007): 548–55; Smith, *God in Translation*, 139–43, 195–212.

[12] Kee "Heavenly Council," 263–68; Smith, *God in Translation*, 133 n. 4. Cf. Heiser, "Divine Council," 79–82.

[13] See, e.g., Machinist, "How Gods Die," 199–200.

[14] Smith, *God in Translation*, 135–36; Machinist, "How Gods Die," 195–203, esp. 203 and n. 41. Both highlight the possibility that the scene is an archaizing borrowing of older motifs. Some understand בעדת־אל in verse 1 (literally, "in the council of El") to indicate that El presides over the council in which YHWH pleads his cause, but this case is not strong. The designation El is used in reference to YHWH repeatedly throughout the Hebrew Bible, and it may just as well be a fixed or frozen formula. El's functional invisibility as a separate deity also argues against the distinction (also noted by both Smith and Machinist). Additionally, the LXX's συναγωγῇ θεῶν suggests an original עדת־אלים (Gonzalez, "Le Psaume LXXXII," 299; Tate, *Psalms 51–100*, 329 n. 1.d; cf., with some reservation, Oswald Loretz, *Psalmstudien: Kolometrie, Strophik und Theologie ausgewählter Psalmen*, BZAW 309 [Berlin: de Gruyter, 2002], 259). Finally, the psalms of Asaph already conflate YHWH/Elohim and El/Elyon (Pss 74:7–8, 18; 77:8–10; 78:35, 56; 83:2, 19). If the provenance of the psalm and its rhetorical function within the psalms of Asaph for which I argue below is correct, a distinction between the two deities can hardly be asserted.

gods (although some understand the group referred to as "they" to be the wicked, whom the gods favor).[15] Is the prosecuting deity addressing the rest of the council and referring to the gods in the third person? Is it the psalmist addressing the worshipers? Is it the presiding deity rendering a decision? There has not been wide agreement. The eighth verse is understood to call upon YHWH to establish justice over the earth, but within the divine council framework it is not entirely clear who is speaking. The question is not so widely debated in this verse, but David Frankel raises the possibility that the speaking voice in the psalm shifts from YHWH in verses 1–5 to El in verses 6–8. According to this reading, verse 5 is the concluding judgment of YHWH, and El takes over speaking with verse 6, rendering the judgment and calling upon YHWH to take over control of the nations.[16]

A final concern relates to the exact function of the language of verses 6–7. Here the gods are sentenced to mortality, but the structure is peculiar for the passing of a sentence:

6	a	אני־אמרתי אלהים אתם	I say, "You are gods,
	b	ובני עליון כלכם	children of the Most High, all of you";
7	a	אכן כאדם תמותון	nevertheless, you shall die like mortals,
	b	וכאחד השרים תפלו	and fall like any prince. (NRSV)

Elsewhere in the Hebrew Bible, אמרתי and אכן appear together where a misunderstanding finds correction or ignorance finds enlightenment (e.g., Zeph 3:7, Ps 31:22). Since Karl Budde's article in 1921, the psalm has been frequently interpreted to mean that the divine judge was—perhaps sarcastically—mistaken in thinking them deities.[17] This reading has not been widely accepted, but the most likely meaning—that the immortality of the gods is being revoked—represents a rather uncharacteristic use of the construction.[18]

II. The Complaint Genre

Jonathan Culler has asserted, "A work can only be read in connection with or against other texts, which provide a grid through which it is read and structured by establishing expectations which enable one to pick out salient features and give

---

[15] See, e.g., Goulder, *Psalms of Asaph*, 164: "The *They* of v. 5 are the רשעים, the *wicked* of v. 4." For a more "standard" perspective, see Tsevat, "God and the Gods in Assembly," 128–29.

[16] Frankel, "El as the Speaking Voice," 1–24. A similar conclusion is reached in White, *Yahweh's Council*, 33.

[17] Budde, "Ps. 82:6f," 39–42. Cf. Yair Zakovitch, "Psalm 82 and Biblical Exegesis," in *Sefer Moshe: The Moshe Weinfeld Jubilee Volume; Studies in the Bible and the Ancient Near East, Qumran, and Post-Biblical Judaism*, ed. Chaim Cohen, Avi Hurvitz, and Shalom M. Paul (Winona Lake, IN: Eisenbrauns, 2004), 213–28, here 222–24.

[18] See, e.g., Tsevat, "God and the Gods in Assembly," 129–30; Tate, *Psalms 51–100*, 330 n. 6a.

them a structure."[19] Similarly, Harry P. Nasuti writes in his study on genre in the Psalms that "it is only through association with other texts that one knows how to approach any particular text."[20] Both of these quotations get at the fact that hearers and readers construct meaning for texts by imposing certain expectations and conceptual structures based on the presence of conventionalized literary forms. As a basic example, if a modern text begins with "Once upon a time," an informed English-speaking reader will immediately assume a number of things about the text's intended form and function and will adopt a set of interpretive lenses related to those assumptions. While there are a number of different ways to conceptualize genre and its form, function, and study, it can be used to refer generally to a culturally salient grouping of those conventionalized forms, and this is how I use the term here.

I am concerned specifically with the literary forms understood to reify the genre of the complaint, specifically as found in the Psalms.[21] This is a modern framework that scholars apply to ancient texts, and therefore firm and clear boundaries should not be assumed.[22] There have been a handful of studies that have produced models for the psalm of complaint, and they overlap significantly in their identification of prototypical features. The model I adopt is a broadly representative one promoted by Craig C. Broyles.[23] For Broyles, the complaint is a subgenre within the broader genre of the lament, which is generally understood as a literary vehicle for the expression of grief or sorrow accompanied by a request for divine intervention. The complaint is related to the lament, but, rather than focus on the larger situation, the complaint concentrates on the responsible party, often striking a

---

[19] Jonathan D. Culler, *Structuralist Poetics: Structuralism, Linguistics and the Study of Literature* (Ithaca, NY: Cornell University Press, 1975; new ed., London: Routledge, 2002), 163.

[20] Harry P. Nasuti, *Defining the Sacred Songs: Genre, Tradition and the Post-Critical Interpretation of the Psalms*, JSOTSup 218 (Sheffield: Sheffield Academic, 1999), 52–53.

[21] I roughly espouse a prototype approach to genre, which is related to Wittgenstein's "family resemblances" approach. For two helpful discussions related to these approaches, see Carol A. Newsom, "Pairing Research Questions and Theories of Genre: A Case Study of the Hodayot," *DSD* 17 (2010): 241–59; Robert Williamson Jr., "Pesher: A Cognitive Model of the Genre," *DSD* 17 (2010): 307–31. For prototype theory in general, see Eleanor Rosch and Barbara B. Lloyd, eds., *Cognition and Categorization* (Hillsdale, NJ: Erlbaum, 1978); John R. Taylor, *Linguistic Categorization: Prototypes in Linguistic Theory*, 2nd ed. (Oxford: Clarendon, 1995).

[22] In fact, one of my primary concerns with the conventional approaches to genre vis-à-vis Ps 82 has been the assertion of necessary and sufficient features in the drawing of strict boundaries. As an example, Frankel insists that Ps 82 cannot be a complaint because "there is no atmosphere of distress or anguish in it" ("El as the Speaking Voice," 9; see also n. 39 below).

[23] Broyles, *Conflict of Faith*. For a discussion of the Psalter's laments and their relationship to the broader literary genre, see Carleen Mandolfo, "Language of Lament in the Psalms," in *The Oxford Handbook of the Psalms*, ed. William P. Brown (Oxford: Oxford University Press, 2014), 114–30. Susan Niditch includes an insightful discussion of the autobiographical dimensions of the lament in *The Responsive Self: Personal Religion in Biblical Literature of the Neo-Babylonian and Persian Periods*, AYBRL (New Haven: Yale University Press, 2015), 55–63.

rebuking tone.[24] Broyles identifies six features of the complaint: (1) the God-lament, (2) the confession of trust, (3) the reference to God's earlier saving deeds, (4) narrative and hymnic praise, (5) the petition, and (6) the assurance of being heard.

The individual features of the complaint are expressed in conventionalized ways, as well. The focal point of the complaint, the "God-lament," addresses YHWH's role in the distress, whether concessive or causative, usually through accusations, rhetorical questions, or both.[25] The two most common rhetorical questions employ the interrogative particles למה ("why?") and עד־מתי ("how long?"). The former rhetorically highlights the inexplicable nature of YHWH's actions or lack thereof, with the latter imposing a sense of urgency upon the complaint. The "confession of trust" is a rarer element of the complaint, and it offers praise regarding the deity's nature or regarding the deity's actions relevant to the distress under consideration. Very closely related is the assurance of being heard, which, according to Broyles, depicts YHWH's response to the complaint (שמע יהוה ["YHWH has heard"] in three of the four occurrences), and therefore is not a constituent element of the complaint proper. More common is the "reference to God's earlier saving deeds," which recounts YHWH's deliverance of his people in the past. That deliverance is usually related to the current suffering, and rhetorically "draw[s] out the contrast between the glorious past and the woeful present."[26] This juxtaposition serves rhetorically to express confidence that YHWH is capable of tackling the current situation while also reminding YHWH that he has yet to do so. The petition is another critical feature of the complaint, and in it the psalmist uses imperatives and negative jussives to appeal to YHWH for relief, whether through direct intervention or through the cessation of whatever neglectful or harmful treatment on the part of YHWH the psalmist sees as facilitating the people's suffering.[27]

Psalm 74 is a fairly standard example of a psalm of complaint. Its twenty-three verses are traditionally divided into three segments comprising verses 1–11, 12–17, and 18–23. The first section contains the bulk of the "complaint," addressing the destruction of the Jerusalem temple and the concomitant tragedies. The descriptions of the horrors visited upon YHWH's people by the unnamed enemy in verses 3b–9 are framed with the genre's stock rhetorical questions, למה ("why?"; vv. 1, 11) and עד־מתי ("how long?"; v. 10), as well as with the petitions taking the standard imperative form: זכר ("Remember!"; v. 2), הרימה פעמיך ("Lift up your steps!"; v. 3),

---

[24] Broyles, *Conflict of Faith*, 40: "Laments can be addressed to anyone; complaint must be addressed to the one responsible. A lament focuses on a situation; a complaint focuses on the one responsible. A lament simply bemoans the state of things; a complaint contains a note of blame and rebuke."

[25] Ibid., 55–82.

[26] Ibid., 42.

[27] Ibid., 46–48.

and כלה ("Destroy!"; v. 11).²⁸ The complaint is constituted by the rhetorical questions and the imperatives and jussives, as well as by the description of the enemy's actions with the resulting lamentable state of affairs. It has been noted by scholars that the complaint within Ps 74 reflects a heightened sense of urgency, omitting the initial invocation and fronting the rhetorical questions. In an effort to draw out a favorable response, the psalmist appeals to YHWH's concern for his own people and to the relationship established with them.

The second section, verses 12–17, abruptly shifts attention to proclaiming YHWH's mythopoetic creative acts, which are introduced as his "working salvation in the midst of the earth" (פעל ישועות בקרב הארץ; v. 12). The *vav* at the beginning of verse 12 is understood as an adversative-emphatic "Nevertheless!," which changes the tone in an effort to reassure YHWH that the complainant recognizes his power and mercy and knows he can remedy the situation. Within the complaint framework, this section functions as the "reference to God's earlier saving deeds," which may account for the framing of creation as salvific.²⁹ The introductory מקדם ("of old") and the acts described in the section hark back to Israel's mythological past, invoking Leviathan and the serpents of the primordial waters of chaos (cf. Isa 27:1; *KTU* 1.5 i.1–3, 27–30).³⁰ The allusion to YHWH's power over primordial monsters, combined with the organizational acts described in verses 15–17, suggests that the psalmist is recalling YHWH's power to render life and order out of chaos and disorder, which power is directly relevant to the chaos that has devastated the land of Israel.³¹

The final and shortest section of the psalm, comprising verses 18–23, resumes the petitions for YHWH's mercy and intervention, this time appealing to YHWH's sense of pride, covenant, and justice, alternating between imperatives and negative jussives in calling upon the deity to meet his obligations to his people. Here the additional motif of the ריב is included with the emphatic petition, "Rise up, O God! Plead your case!" (קומה אלהים ריבה ריבך).³² Erich Zenger states that this clause,

---

²⁸ Occurrences of נחלה ("inheritance"; v. 2), משכן־שמך ("dwelling place of your name"; v. 7), and the verb קנה ("acquire"; v. 2) in reference to Israel reflect the Deuteronomistic foundation of the author's conceptualization of YHWH's relationship with Israel. See Rainer Albertz, *Israel in Exile: The History and Literature of the Sixth Century B.C.E.*, trans. David Green, SBLStBL 3 (Atlanta: Society of Biblical Literature, 2003), 142–43; Hossfeld and Zenger, *Psalms 2*, 245; Marko Marttila, "The Deuteronomistic Heritage in the Psalms," *JSOT* 37 (2012): 78–79.

²⁹ On the "reference to God's earlier saving deeds," see Broyles, *Conflict of Faith*, 42–43.

³⁰ Nathaniel E. Greene has recently argued that this section is an interpolation that draws upon much earlier ideology ("Creation, Destruction, and a Psalmist's Plea: Rethinking the Poetic Structure of Psalm 74," *JBL* 136 [2017]: 85–101, https://doi.org/10.15699/jbl.1361.2017.156672).

³¹ Walter Brueggemann and William H. Bellinger Jr., *Psalms*, NCBiC (Cambridge: Cambridge University Press, 2014), 323.

³² The imperative קומה is found in over a dozen other laments, including eight other psalms where YHWH is the subject (Pss 3:8, 7:7, 9:20, 10:12, 17:13, 35:2, 44:27, 132:8). See J. Gamberoni, "קום," *TDOT* 12:605–6.

"challenges Yhwh, as saving judge, now at last to exercise his twofold office, namely effecting justice in the cosmos and in his people, *against* the oppressors and *for* the oppressed—out of mercy for the victims of injustice to judge or effect rescue."[33]

As has been noted by many scholars, this psalm is "in best accordance with the general scheme of Communal Complaint."[34] I have already noted the omission of the invocation, but two other elements of the complaint that we do not find in Ps 74 are the confession of trust and the assurance of being heard (cf. Pss 79:13, 80:19). The withholding of praise rhetorically challenges YHWH to do what has been done in the past, which punctuates the psalmist's desperation and the severity of the situation. This adds a rhetorical dynamic that we may find unexpected and even jarring, but in many ways the complaint functions precisely to question the integrity and justice of the moral framework over which YHWH has sovereignty. If Job's antagonists accurately reflect the then-contemporary conventional wisdom regarding the cosmic reciprocity of righteousness up to the exilic period, then those who diligently strive to serve YHWH have an honest case when they demand to know why he has not delivered. YHWH is either withholding what is owed, willfully ignoring the suffering of the righteous, setting his hand against them, or has forgotten his covenant and his people. The petitions and accusatory questions of the psalms of complaint raise all these possibilities and demand that YHWH make his people whole. Walter Brueggemann refers to these psalms as "Psalms of Disorientation" and describes them as responding to the failure of the system by seeking to reorient or restructure it.[35] Nasuti states that "those psalms that contend that the problem with the relationship is on God's part raise the unsettling possibility that the system itself has broken down."[36] To whom can the righteous turn if even the Most High either cannot or will not uphold justice and deliver the oppressed?

III. Psalm 82 as a Psalm of Complaint

One main reason Ps 82 has resisted classification as a complaint is that this classification makes it difficult to prioritize the divine council framework. The fact that segments of Ps 82 are closely linked with, or are to be identified as, elements of the complaint genre is acknowledged by a number of scholars, even as they insist that the conceptual space of the divine courtroom is to be foregrounded. Marvin Tate comments, for instance, "'How long?' (עד־מתי) is an expression found in some laments.... Here, however, the question has the character of a charge against the

---

[33] Zenger, *Psalms 2*, 250.
[34] Gerstenberger, *Psalms*, 79.
[35] Walter Brueggemann, *The Message of the Psalms: A Theological Commentary*, Augsburg Old Testament Studies (Minneapolis: Augsburg, 1984), 51–121.
[36] Nasuti, *Defining the Sacred Songs*, 70.

gods."³⁷ Psalms of lament are themselves frequently described as charges against God, however, so this is a distinction without a difference.³⁸ The notion of a psalm of complaint set in the mouth of God has rarely been considered.³⁹

While Ps 82 is only eight short verses, its structure and terminology are strikingly similar to those of Ps 74. As in Ps 74, the very first word addressed to the object of the complaint is the interrogative particle of a two-part accusatory rhetorical question: "How long [עד־מתי] will you render unjust judgment and show partiality to the wicked?" In Ps 74, the rhetorical questions of verse 1 are followed by imperatives intended to bring to God's attention his responsibility for the wellbeing of his people, which has been compromised. The remaining verses of the first section describe the lamentable state of affairs. Similarly, Ps 82:3–4 contains a series of imperatives intended to bring to the attention of the gods of the nations the proper administration of justice, which has likewise been compromised.

Psalm 82:5 has long been understood as a verdict, but, through the interpretive lens of the complaint, it makes more sense to view the verse as the consequence of the gods' neglect. Elsewhere in the Psalms, the foundations of the earth are set in place by YHWH and preserved by his administration of the cosmic order (Pss 93:1, 96:10, 104:5). Psalm 82 views that responsibility as shared by the gods, and the author indicts *them* rather than YHWH. As Patrick D. Miller has stated, "the maintenance of justice and righteousness is the foundation of the universe, the responsibility of the divine council, and the issue upon which hang both the stability of the universe and the stability and effective reality of the divine world."⁴⁰ For

---

³⁷ Tate, *Psalms 51–100*, 329. Tate also identifies קומה with the complaint genre, although "it seems to be more acclamation than supplication in this context" (339). Hermann Gunkel and Joachim Begrich list the petition of Ps 82:8 with the elements of the communal complaint (*Introduction to Psalms: The Genres of the Religious Lyric of Israel*, trans. James D. Nogalski, Mercer Library of Biblical Studies [Macon, GA: Mercer University Press, 1998], 90; German original, 1933).

³⁸ See, e.g., Zenger, *Psalms 2*, 393–94 (also quoting Bernd Janowski, "Die Toten loben JHWH nicht: Psalm 88 und das alttestamentliche Todesverständnis," in *Auferstehung / Resurrection: The Fourth Durham-Tübingen Research Symposium; Resurrection, Transfiguration and Exaltation in Old Testament, Ancient Judaism and Early Christianity*, ed. Friedrich Avemarie and Hermann Lichtenberger, WUNT 135 [Tübingen: Mohr Siebeck, 2001], 3–45); Brueggemann and Bellinger, *Psalms*, 210.

³⁹ Frankel suggests that קומה "accords with" the usage in the psalm of complaint but insists that "Psalm 82 is hardly a Song of Complaint," primarily on the grounds that the complainant shows no signs of distress and it would be uncharacteristic to petition to "save the downtrodden and unfortunate of the other nations" ("El as the Speaking Voice," 9–10). One exception is a note written by Patrick D. Miller in the *HarperCollins Study Bible*, which states that the complaint element "how long?" is "taken up by God on behalf of the victims of oppression" (Miller, "Psalms," *The HarperCollins Study Bible*, rev. and updated ed., ed. Harold W. Attridge et al. [San Francisco: HarperCollins, 2006], 800). I thank the *JBL* editors for bringing this exception to my attention.

⁴⁰ Patrick D. Miller, "Cosmology and World Order in the Old Testament: The Divine Council as Cosmic-Political Symbol," *HBT* 9 (1987): 53–78, here 68.

him, Ps 82:5b describes the consequence of the failure of the gods to uphold justice.[41] The first part of the verse should be interpreted in the same way: because the gods in Ps 82 have been derelict in their duties, the people of the nations lack knowledge and wander in darkness. The "they" of verse 5 are the denizens of the nations of the earth, not the gods. This is also the interpretation for which Brent A. Strawn argues, although without reference to the complaint genre.[42] Psalm 82:5 makes little sense as a verdict if the psalm functions as a psalm of complaint, but it fits the framework quite well as a description of the consequences of the deities' unjust judgment, favoritism, and neglect.

We must skip to verse 8 for the next complaint element, which is the petition "Rise up, O God!" (קומה אלהים). As mentioned above, the imperative קומה appears in several psalms, but there are only two occurrences in all of the Hebrew Bible with אלהים: Ps 74:22 and Ps 82:8. Here, the call to action is for YHWH to judge the earth (שפטה הארץ). The second half of the verse, אתה תנחל בכל־הגוים, could be read "You will inherit all nations," or as a jussive that carries on the imperative sense of קומה and שפטה: "*You* inherit all the nations."[43] As in Ps 74, the petition seeks a resolution to the oppression and suffering of the poor and the needy. In both instances, only YHWH can bring about the social justice so sorely needed among the people of Israel and the nations of the earth. It is important to note that the poor, the needy, and the orphan are not the discrete and literal victims of the negligence of the gods; they are stock metonymic figures who represent idealized victims associated with conventional conceptions of social justice and cosmic order.[44] The maintenance of that order was absolutely the purview of each nation's patron deity, so the argument that the victims of Ps 82 indicate that the אלהים are human rulers or ostensibly

---

[41] Ibid., 69: "The consequence of this is stated to be a shaking of the foundations of the world. The failure to maintain order, which in this instance is clearly seen to be the maintenance of righteousness in the moral sphere, that is, the resistance to a disorder that does in the poor and gives the rich and the wicked control, is seen to be manifest in a kind of cosmic disorder. The cosmos comes apart when righteousness is not maintained."

[42] Strawn, "Poetics of Psalm 82," 21–46. To summarize his argument: (1) the links with Isa 44:9, 18 (often appealed to in support of reading v. 5 as a judgment on the gods) are artificial, as the author there is addressing the inability of inanimate objects to perceive anything at all, not the ignorance and waywardness of sentient deities; (2) waywardness and a lack of knowledge and understanding generally refer to the oblivious wanderings of humans without the light of divine direction (Job 14:21, 29:3, Ps 92:7, Isa 1:3, 40:21, 50:10); (3) while the closest grammatical antecedents are the gods, the objects of the imperative הצילו, "Deliver!" are elided, and they are the semantic foci of verses 3–4.

[43] Cf. Dahood, *Psalms*, 2:271; Tate, *Psalms 51–100*, 332.

[44] See Morris Silver, "Prophets and Markets Revisited," in *Social Justice in the Ancient World*, ed. K. D. Irani and Morris Silver, Contributions in Political Science 354 (Westport, CT: Greenwood, 1995), 182–83: "The Ancient Near East designated victims by terms more or less conventionally translated as 'orphan,' 'widow,' 'poor person,' and 'peasant.' The referents are much less real-world social groupings than intellectual constructs. That is, the terms refer to the *ideal victim*" (emphasis original).

divine kings does not hold. The אלהים are the patron deities of the traditional seventy nations of the earth.[45]

Similar to Ps 74, Ps 82 lacks the complaint template's invocation, confession of trust, and assurance of being heard. Unlike Ps 74, however, Ps 82 also lacks the reference to earlier saving deeds. Psalm 82 is not directing the complaint at YHWH, however, and the gods have no righteous deeds in their background to champion. Indeed, they are the antagonists of the entire scene. This brings us to the psalm's other literary framework. The verses I have skipped over (vv. 1 and 6–7) constitute elements not of the complaint genre but of the divine-council narrative framework that establishes the setting of the complaint within the divine assembly. Whereas in other complaints the psalmist directs his complaint to YHWH for YHWH's failure to uphold the cosmic order vis-à-vis his people, here the complaint is being put into the mouth of the prosecuting attorney in the divine council. It is directed at the gods of the nations, who have failed to uphold the cosmic order vis-à-vis *their* people, disrupting the integrity of the cosmic order as a whole. This is a brilliant innovation on the complaint genre that weaves the conventionalized elements of the psalm of complaint into the case presented by the God of Israel against the gods of the nations. They are the ones ultimately responsible for the failure of social justice lamented in the third section of Ps 74, and this highlights a critical observation: Ps 82 employs the divine-council setting and the complaint framework to narrate the very ריב that YHWH is called upon to prosecute in Ps 74:22.

The first verse of Ps 82 sets the council scene, describing the divine judge standing (or rising) to take his place among the gods and immediately presenting the complaint in verses 2–5. Because the condemnation of the gods is a foregone conclusion, there can be no expectation of a favorable response. The gods are therefore condemned to mortality in short order in verses 6–7. The constraints imposed by the juxtaposition of the divine-council setting and the complaint motif account for the peculiar fact that the gods are called upon to repair the damage they have done but are given no opportunity to comply. The imperative petitions are necessary to satisfy the requirements of the complaint template, but the rhetorical goal is not to compel the gods to righteous judgment—it is, rather, to reorient the cosmos by deposing them.

The somewhat enigmatic use of אמרתי and אכן in verses 6–7 represents the first pivot in the two-part reorientation. The deity acknowledges the divinity of the gods but immediately revokes it by divine fiat to make way for YHWH's takeover. Strawn argues that אמרתי and אכן represent declarative acts that had previously rendered the deities divine but now revoke that divinity. Regardless of whether

---

[45] On this number and the relationship of the nations to patron deities, see Daniel I. Block, *The Gods of the Nations: Studies in Ancient Near Eastern National Theology*, 2nd ed., ETSS (Grand Rapids: Baker, 2000), 28–33; Darrell D. Hannah, "Guardian Angels and Angelic National Patrons in Second Temple Judaism and Early Christianity," *DCLY* 2007 (2007): 413–35.

אמרתי is understood to have divinized the gods of the nations, it is clear that verse 7 consigns them to mortality. The proximate cause of the convulsions of the cosmos has been removed. Conventional forms here provided the literary vehicles for concepts that had not yet been articulated in the literature but still needed the salience of traditional linguistic constructions—there were no literary templates for the de-deification of the divine council.[46]

With the work of the divine courtroom completed, the complaint elements can come back into focus. Normally, the issuer of the complaint concludes with petitions. The gods are gone in Ps 82, however, so YHWH has no one to whom he could issue the final petition. It falls back on the psalmist himself to call upon YHWH to rise up and fill the heavenly power vacuum left by the removal of the gods. Here is the rhetorical payoff of the psalm: YHWH alone will rule over the nations of the earth. This combination of divine-council scene and gods-complaint takes a new approach to the suffering of the poor and the orphan, shifting the blame to the gods of the nations for the breakdown in the stabilizing structures of cosmic justice and deposing them, finally achieving the reorientation sought by so many laments. This reading obviates the need to posit a distinction between YHWH and El—there is no room or reason for such a distinction. Not only is El functionally invisible throughout the psalm, but קומה is not indicative of the deity's seated position throughout the narrative.[47] Rather, it is a conventionalized complaint element that functions not as a reference to the physical posture of the subject of the imperative verb but as a call to action.[48] While YHWH had exercised rule over the gods of the divine council up to this point within the Israelite worldview, the ousting of the gods allows YHWH to take over direct rule of the nations and restore the cosmic structures of justice. This restructuring of divine sovereignty facilitates the worship of YHWH by those residing outside the land of Judah and ultimately becomes the concluding declaration of the psalms of Asaph (Ps 83:19): "Let them know that it is you—whose name is YHWH—who alone are Most High over all the earth."

---

[46] See Judith M. Hadley, "The De-Deification of Deities in Deuteronomy," in Gordon, *God of Israel*, 157–74. As many scholars have noted, Ps 82 has thematic parallels in other ancient West Asian literature where deities are demoted or killed. Among the best discussions is Parker, "Beginning of the Reign of God."

[47] On El's muted role, see Parker, "Beginning of the Reign of God," 538; Smith, *God in Translation*, 136; Machinist, "How Gods Die," 202–3.

[48] Machinist notes that the use of קומה elsewhere in the Psalms reflects a "call for action from the deity" (Machinist, "How Gods Die," 198 and n. 25).

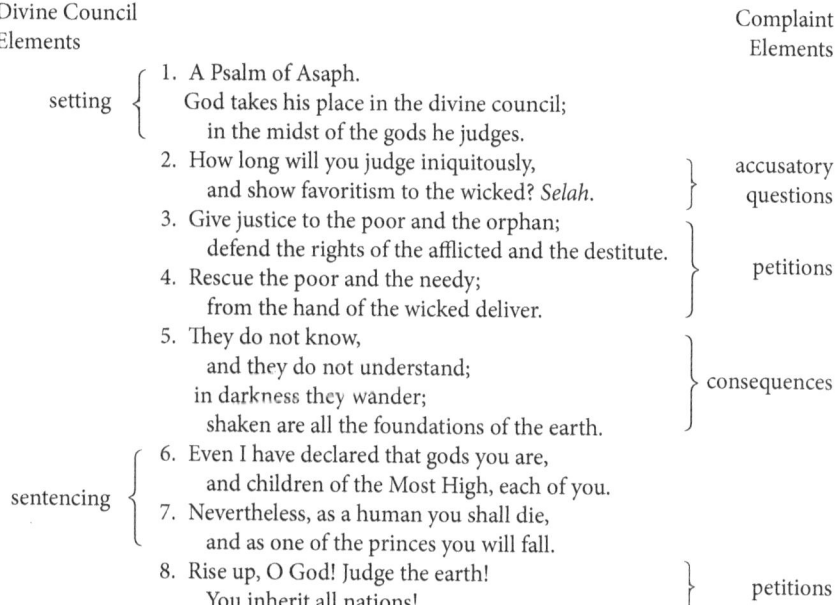

IV. Situating Psalm 82

Frank-Lothar Hossfeld and Erich Zenger have argued convincingly for viewing two main compositional arcs within the psalms of Asaph, running from Ps 74 to Ps 76 and from Ps 79 to Ps 82.[49] Both arcs begin with the communal complaints of Pss 74 and 79. In the second arc, Ps 80 is combined with Ps 79 as a continuation of that complaint. Psalms 75 and 81 are divine oracles, which provide the responses to the laments. In Ps 75:2–3, YHWH states, "I will appoint a time, and I, with uprightness, will judge. When the earth wavers, and all its inhabitants, it is I who steadies its pillars." Judgment is coming; YHWH alone may restore the order and steady the pillars of the earth. Psalm 81 admonishes Israel even as it responds to the lament: "My people did not listen to my voice. Israel did not satisfy me, so I turned them over to the stubbornness of their hearts, to follow after their own counsels. O, that my people would listen to me, that Israel would walk in my ways!

---

[49] Hossfeld and Zenger, *Psalms 2*, 250, 257–58, 271, 305, 307, 317, 325–26, 336. See also Erich Zenger, "Psalm 82 im Kontext der Asaf-sammlung: religionsgeschichtliche Implikationen," in *Religionsgeschichte Israels: Formale und materiale Aspekte*, ed. Bernd Janowski and Matthias Köckert, VWGTh 15 (Gütersloh: Mohn, 1999), 272–92.

I would soon humble their enemies, and turn my hand against their adversaries" (Ps 81:12–14).

Psalms 76 and 82 conclude the arcs with the intervention of YHWH. In the latter, YHWH indicts the gods of the nations and is called upon to take over in their place and restore the cosmic order. The final resolution is still off in the future; Ps 82 merely sets the table. In Ps 76, YHWH's abode has been established and the enemies have been vanquished. From the perspective of this psalm, the laments of the other psalms have been resolved (it was likely one of the later composed). It looks back on the fulfillment of the petition in Ps 82:8 when it declares in 76:9–10, "From the heavens you caused judgment to be heard; the earth feared and was silent when God rose up to judgment [בקום־למשפט אלהים], to save all the humble of the earth."

While this editorial theory fits Ps 82 comfortably into the thematic progression of the collection's compositional arcs, one might argue that the psalm was appropriated from an earlier context rather than composed to meet the rhetorical needs of the collection. Some linguistic and thematic features of the psalm make this unlikely, however. Most important to my discussion are Pss 74 and 79. Zenger described their relationship to each other as follows:

> At the very beginning Psalm 79, with its reference to Yhwh's "inheritance" and its "defilement" looks back to Psalm 74. This is true also of the conclusion in 79:13, whose reference to the people as "the sheep of your pasture" looks back to 74:1. Both psalms develop their laments with the questions "why?" (74:1, 11; 79:10) and "how long?" (74:10; 79:5), circling around the topoi of divine wrath, the deriding of God, and blasphemy of the divine name. Both psalms urge Yhwh to intervene, with an explicit appeal to his office as judge (74:22; 79:10–12).[50]

The differences between the two psalms, however, are also important. While Ps 74 is focused on offenses against YHWH committed by his generic enemies, Ps 79 emphasizes the suffering of the people at the hands of the nations, as well as the role of Israel's sin in that suffering. A primary appeal in Ps 79 is not just restoration but vengeance in the sight of all the nations. Here the gaze seems to be broadening beyond Israel and its immediate environs. For Zenger, Ps 79 is a theological interpretation of Ps 74 by a later author. Building on this, I suggest that Ps 82 is also looking back on Ps 79, but more directly on the first psalm of these compositional arcs, Ps 74. Psalm 82:8 seems to be a direct response to and fulfillment of the petition of Ps 74:22. The linguistic relationships and the resolution of the thematic tension within Ps 74 render it unlikely that Ps 82 was simply pulled off the shelf of complaints, dusted off, and conveniently inserted into the climax of this narrative arc.

Ideologically, Ps 82 fits best in an exilic setting, as well. As Peter Machinist argues, the petition in Ps 82:8 attempts to catalyze a transition in worldviews. It

---

[50] Zenger, *Psalms 2*, 305.

moves YHWH from a position of rule over the divine council to one of exclusive sovereignty over the nations. Machinist does not feel that a chronological relationship with the other psalms can be posited, but I disagree.[51] Psalms 74 and 79 attest to a view of YHWH as largely confined to Israel. Both psalms appeal to the vernacular of the Song of Moses (Deut 32:1-43) in connection with the destruction of the temple, referring to Israel as YHWH's "inheritance" without reference to any other nations under YHWH's immediate control. In these two psalms the nations do not call on the name of YHWH. In Ps 74 they revile that name. In Ps 79 they taunt YHWH and do not know him. The latter psalm pleads with YHWH to make his vengeance known among the nations. These texts push against the confines of a preexilic and early exilic worldview wherein YHWH is the God of Israel and the other gods are the patron deities of their own nations. This is the perspective when David laments in 1 Sam 26:19 that, in being kicked out of Israel—YHWH's "inheritance" (נחלה)—he is being forced to serve other gods. Similarly, in 2 Kgs 5:15-17, Naaman asks for cartloads of Israelite soil to facilitate YHWH's worship back in Syria, stating that there is no God in all the earth except in Israel. YHWH's political purview is the nation of Israel. I find no exceptions to this view in preexilic literature. YHWH is certainly presented as the god of gods who rules over the earth from the heavens, but the nations always take their directives from their own patron deities. The closest YHWH comes to governing another nation is through military-type incursions, which more closely fit a limited purview.[52]

For the exiled Judahites in Babylon, the cosmic order has been rocked; only bringing down the political barriers that separate them from their deity back in Israel can steady it. Psalm 82 provides for that restructuring of the cosmos and envisions a world unknown to the author of Ps 74. After the stewardships of the

---

[51] Machinist and White cite and reject Zenger's case for an Asaphite context for the composition of Ps 82, insisting that he attempts to make the case that the Asaphite psalms were all composed at or around the same time (Machinist, "How Gods Die," 236-37 n. 108; White, *Yahweh's Council*, 26). This, however, significantly misrepresents the case articulated by Zenger. His dating of the compositional histories of the psalms of Asaph spans from the eighth century BCE to the postexilic period (for instance, see Hossfeld and Zenger, *Psalms 2*, 226, 243-44, 263-64, 276, 311, 322, 340-41).

[52] The clearest example is 2 Kgs 3:27, where a military coalition that includes Israel has been promised victory over Moab by YHWH's prophet, but a last-minute sacrifice on the part of the Moabite king of his son and heir catalyzes a "great wrath" (קצף־גדול) that compels the Israelites to retreat. The text suggests that the offering of the king's son successfully catalyzed a response from the Moabite patron deity that drove off the invading forces. On this pericope, see Mordechai Cogan and Hayim Tadmor, *II Kings: A New Translation with Introduction and Commentary*, AB 11 (Garden City, NY: Doubleday, 1988), 40-52; John Barclay Burns, "Why Did the Besieging Army Withdraw? (II Reg 3,27)," *ZAW* 102 (1990): 187-94; Jon D. Levenson, *The Death and Resurrection of the Beloved Son: The Transformation of Child Sacrifice in Judaism and Christianity* (New Haven: Yale University Press, 1993), 14-17; Francesca Stavrakopoulou, *King Manasseh and Child Sacrifice: Biblical Distortions of Historical Realities*, BZAW 338 (Berlin: de Gruyter, 2004), 176-77; Smith, *God in Translation*, 116-18.

gods over the nations are vacated, the psalmist calls upon YHWH to take them over and extend his inheritance over all the earth. In this sense, Ps 82 represents the climax of the psalms of Asaph. The two narrative arcs running from Ps 74 to Ps 76 and from Ps 79 to Ps 82 reach a head in Ps 82 with the universalization of YHWH and his exaltation over the nations of the earth. There is little evidence for significant redaction after the initial composition, and the psalm should therefore be understood as composed precisely to serve the collection's rhetorical exigencies.[53] Thus, in agreement with Zenger, a date of composition in the late exilic or early postexilic period is most likely.[54] Even if one insists on an unrecoverable pre-Asaphite version, however, the parallels shared by the psalms would have been salient to any hearer or reader confronted with both psalms in their current positions within the Asaphite collection. The rhetorical function of Ps 82, therefore, as a response to Ps 74 and the climax of the psalms of Asaph would have been the dominant reading upon its inclusion in the corpus.

V. Conclusion

Psalm 82 was not written in a vacuum but in a literary context that facilitated its interpretation by its earliest hearers and readers. It shares a number of linguistic and thematic relationships with that context that have long been overlooked by scholars more interested in what the psalm reveals about early Israelite conceptualizations of deity than in how the text was intended to function. The psalm's interpretive challenges have endured for a few reasons. For instance, the psalm is difficult to interpret precisely because it makes use of conventional literary forms in *unconventional* ways, exactly as one would expect from a revolutionary reframing of the

---

[53] Apart from the plausible reconstruction of עדת־אלים in verse 1 based on the LXX's συναγωγῇ θεῶν.

[54] Objections to this dating on the grounds that the mythological and polytheistic parallels with earlier West Asian literature are too strong (Goulder, *Psalms of Asaph*, 160; Trotter, "Death of the אלהים," 233) privilege the assumption of an early and strict concept of monotheism that would have precluded the preservation of older themes. Of course, older themes are frequently preserved (Ps 74, for instance, makes use of the early *Chaoskampf* tradition [see n. 30 above]). I would refer the reader to Peter Hayman, "Monotheism—A Misused Word in Jewish Studies?" *JJS* 42 (1991): 1–15, here 8: "In some cases, we can see the old Canaanite gods still there in rabbinic Judaism, even retaining their old titles. Prince Yam, for example, lives on in the Babylonian Talmud and in some of the midrashim, and his opposition to Israel is located precisely where we should expect it: at the Sea of Reeds.... The mythological overtones of the crossing of the ים סוף are thus preserved in rabbinic Judaism as are numerous other remnants of older Canaanite beliefs.... There are rich, as yet unexplored, pickings in rabbinic midrash for scholars interested in the Canaanite background to Israelite religion." See also Jonathan Ben-Dov, "The Resurrection of the Divine Assembly in the Divine Title El in the Dead Sea Scrolls," in *The Comparative Perspective*, vol. 3 of *Submerged Literature in Ancient Greek Culture*, ed. Andrea Ercolani and Manuela Giordano (Berlin: de Gruyter, 2016), 9–31.

cosmological structures of divinity. In order for Ps 82 to gain purchase in the contemporaneous literary milieu, the author had to draw stabilizing connections with genres and motifs already in circulation but had to do so in a way that broke new conceptual ground and helped facilitate the overturning of long-held theological frameworks. Externally, scholars have struggled with the psalm because the divine-council framework has generally overshadowed other genre considerations, because an Asaphite compositional context demands a later date than many scholars would like, and because the placement of the complaint in the mouth of YHWH represents a significant innovation on the genre. This has resulted in less-than-satisfactory interpretive models that have been forced to draw literary contexts from second-millennium texts from Ugarit and elsewhere.

As this examination has shown, the use of עד־מתי in accusatory questions (followed by serial imperative petitions, including קומה) and the conventionalized call to action appeal directly to the elements of the complaint genre that are featured so heavily in the psalms leading up to Ps 82. If we remove the divine-council framework (vv. 1 and 6–7) and direct the remaining verses at YHWH rather than at the gods, the psalm would undoubtedly be classified as a psalm of complaint. As it stands, it was most likely composed in response to those other Asaphite complaints that blame YHWH for the destruction of Jerusalem and the exile of his people. The cosmological pillars of justice were rocked by these events, but the traditional complaint format could not provide the desired resolution. A new approach was formulated.

Rather than blame YHWH, Ps 82 expands the responsibility for the breakdown in justice to the other members of the divine council, who were equally responsible for regulating justice within their respective purviews and maintaining the cosmic order. The enemies in Pss 74 and 79 came from outside of Israel and thus outside of YHWH's purview, making their atrocities the responsibility of their respective patron deities. The complaint was placed in the mouth of YHWH and directed at the gods. Within the framework of the divine council, YHWH could pass judgment and effect the cosmic reorientation that Israel's liturgical pleas could not. By divine fiat, the gods' immortality was revoked, which allowed YHWH to expand his inheritance over all the nations of the earth and directly administer justice to his people scattered abroad. Psalm 82 is more than a divine-council scene, a prophetic liturgy, or a peculiar mixing of psalm and oracle; it is a gods-complaint that facilitated the most important turning point in the history of the conceptualization of the God of Israel.

New and Recent Titles

GROWING UP IN ANCIENT ISRAEL
Children in Material Culture and Biblical Texts
Kristine Henriksen Garroway
Paperback $45.95, 978-1-62837-211-3 356 pages, 2018 Code: 061729
Hardcover $60.95, 978-0-88414-295-9 E-book $45.95, 978-0-88414-296-6
Archaeology and Biblical Studies 23

INFANCIA Y LEGALIDAD EN
EL PRÓXIMO ORIENTE ANTIGUO DURANTE
EL BRONCE RECIENTE (CA. 1500–1100 A. C.)
Daniel Justel
Digital open-access, 978-0-88414-279-9
https://www.sbl-site.org/publications/Books_ANEmonographs.aspx
Paperback $55.95, 978-1-62837-203-8 420 pages, 2018 Code: 062825
Hardcover $75.95, 978-0-88414-280-5 Ancient Near East Monographs 20

EMPIRE AND GENDER IN LXX ESTHER
Meredith J. Stone
Paperback $49.95, 978-1-62837-231-1 354 pages, 2018 Code: 063552
Hardcover $64.95, 978-0-88414-343-7 E-book $49.95, 978-0-88414-344-4
Early Judaism and Its Literature 48

ADOPTING THE STRANGER AS KINDRED
IN DEUTERONOMY
Mark R. Glanville
Paperback $39.95, 978-0-88414-310-9 332 pages, 2018 Code: 062638
Hardcover $54.95, 978-0-88414-311-6 E-book $39.95, 978-0-88414-312-3
Ancient Israel and Its Literature 33

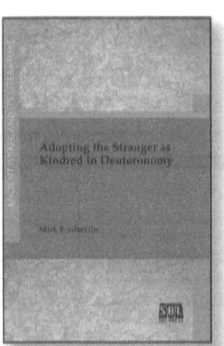

THE STUDIA PHILONICA ANNUAL XXX, 2018
Studies in Hellenistic Judaism
David T. Runia and Gregory E. Sterling, editors
Hardcover $58.95, 978-1-62837-230-4 244 pages, 2018 Code: 062230
E-book $58.95, 978-0-88414-342-0 Studia Philonica Annual 30

SBL Press • P.O. Box 2243 • Williston, VT 05495-2243
Phone: 877-725-3334 (toll-free) or 802-864-6185 • Fax: 802-864-7626
Order online at www.sbl-site.org/publications

Fluid Dynamics: The Interplay of Water and Gender in Nahum

WILLIAM BRIGGS
will_briggs@baylor.edu
Baylor University, Waco TX 76798

In light of the growing scholarly interest in gender in the Hebrew Bible, this article builds on the work of Cynthia Chapman and Julia O'Brien by demonstrating that the use of water imagery in Nahum contributes to the book's portrait of masculine conflict between YHWH and the king of Assyria. I argue two central theses: that water imagery constitutes a recurring motif in Nahum, as is evident in 1:4, 8; 2:7, 9; 3:8, 14; and that water imagery contributes to the gender dynamics present in the book. The water images in their present arrangement build on one another and, in doing so, contribute to the portrait of YHWH's masculine military might in Nah 1, presenting YHWH's victory over his enemies as assured. Subsequently, in Nah 2–3, water imagery contributes to the depiction of the shameful defeat of the king of Assyria and the violation of feminine Nineveh; it is the king's task to protect the feminine Nineveh in keeping with expectations for male behavior in the ancient Near East.

The small book of Nahum, which portrays the downfall of the Assyrian capital of Nineveh, packs a powerful punch of poetic artistry and provocative language and imagery. Scholars frequently remark on Nahum's rich literary features and "poetic excellence," even as they simultaneously struggle with difficult aspects of the book such as its depictions of violence and sexual humiliation.[1] What follows is an attempt to take both the book's artistry and its challenging depiction of gender relations into account, particularly with respect to the use of water imagery throughout Nahum.[2] While several scholars have noted the use of water imagery

---

[1] Scholars who make these two observations on the very same page include Walter Dietrich, *Nahum, Habakkuk, Zephaniah*, IECOT (Stuttgart: Kohlhammer, 2016), 25; Julia M. O'Brien, *Nahum*, Readings (London: Sheffield Academic, 2002), 13; Steven Tuell, *Reading Nahum–Malachi: A Literary and Theological Commentary*, Reading the Old Testament (Macon, GA: Smyth & Helwys, 2015), 11; William Wessels, "Nahum, an Uneasy Expression of Yahweh's Power!," *OTE* 11 (1998): 615–28, here 615.

[2] All verse numbers are from the MT.

in Nahum, its role as a recurring motif in the book remains underexplored, especially its role in the depiction of gendered conflict.[3] A detailed study of Nahum reveals that water imagery, which is found in 1:4, 8; 2:7, 9; 3:8, 14, constitutes a significant motif within the book as a whole. Furthermore, the water images in these verses build upon one another and highlight, reinforce, and occasionally unsettle ancient expectations for gender performance, mainly in relation to the masculine contest between YHWH and the king of Assyria.[4]

The first part of this study surveys the relevant scholarship. The second part demonstrates that water imagery is a prominent motif in the book of Nahum that contributes to the depiction of gendered conflict. In doing so, it will examine the six instances of water imagery in their immediate literary context, in relation to one another, and in the context of the book as a whole. Finally, the third section then relates the progression of aquatic imagery with respect to gender to proposed models for the development of the book of Nahum.

I. A History of Relevant Scholarship

History and Water in Nahum Research

As Michael Weigl observes, recent years have seen a growing gap between synchronic and diachronic approaches to the study of the book.[5] Many scholars have attempted to determine the book's compositional history through the use of redactional methods.[6] Others have approached Nahum from the synchronic perspective, arguing for its unity through a variety of structural and thematic claims.[7]

---

[3] See O'Brien, *Nahum*, 73–94.

[4] All uses of the name "Nahum" in this study are in reference to the literary work. Any reference to the person of the seventh-century prophet will be indicated accordingly.

[5] Michael Weigl, "Current Research on the Book of Nahum: Exegetical Methodologies in Turmoil?," *CBR* 9 (2001): 81–130.

[6] Among many other possible examples, see Dietrich, *Nahum, Habakkuk, Zephaniah*, 29–33; James Nogalski, *The Book of the Twelve: Micah–Malachi*, SHBC 18B (Macon, GA: Smyth & Helwys, 2011), 602–7; Bernard Renaud, "La composition du livre de Nahum: Une proposition," *ZAW* 99 (1987): 198–219; Heinz-Josef Fabry, *Nahum*, HThKAT (Freiburg im Breisgau: Herder, 2006), 87–94.

[7] Paul House, "Dramatic Coherence in Nahum, Habakkuk, and Zephaniah," in *Forming Prophetic Literature: Essays on Isaiah and the Twelve in Honor of John D. W. Watts*, ed. James W. Watts and Paul R. House, JSOTSup 235 (Sheffield: Sheffield Academic, 1996), 195–208, here 200–203; Marvin A. Sweeney, "Concerning the Structure and Generic Character of the Book of Nahum," *ZAW* 104 (1992): 364–77; Bob Becking, "Passion, Power, Protection: Interpreting the God of Nahum," in *On Reading Prophetic Texts: Gender-Specific and Related Studies in Memory of Fokkelien van Dijk-Hemmes*, ed. Bob Becking and Meindert Dijkstra, BibInt 18 (Leiden: Brill, 1996), 4–15; Duane L. Christensen, *Nahum: A New Translation with Introduction and Commentary*, AYB 24F (New Haven: Yale University Press, 2009), 42–48.

While the question of the text's historical development is certainly an important one, it will not be the primary focus of this study. The conclusions of this examination regarding water and gender in Nahum do not necessarily hinge on a developmental model for the book but rather work in conjunction with both diachronic and synchronic approaches. Nevertheless, the present study assumes the redactional model that is in large part common to the studies of Heinz-Josef Fabry, Walter Dietrich, and James Nogalski. For these scholars, most of Nah 2:2–3:19 was part of the earliest layer of Nahum, the psalm of 1:2–8 was added later, and the material in Nah 1:9–2:3 forms a bridge between these two larger sections of text.[8] The use of water imagery in Nahum, however, may offer some insight into these redactional processes behind the book's composition.

With regard to historical matters, which are closer to the subject of this study, a number of scholars have mentioned the prominence of aquatic features in the ancient city of Nineveh, whose downfall Nahum celebrates.[9] Scholars are divided on Nahum's knowledge and familiarity with the geography and architecture of Nineveh. Dietrich argues that Nahum's topographical descriptions reflect only a "rudimentary" knowledge of Nineveh, and Angelika Berlejung argues more generally against Nahum's being familiar with specific Assyrian sources. John Huddlestun and Aron Pinker, on the other hand, argue for Nahum's more intimate knowledge of the Assyrian capital and its fortifications.[10] In any case, Nineveh's fame as a river city that sits at the fork of the Tigris and the Khosr Rivers and that once boasted a tremendous system of waterworks makes the text's use of water imagery appropriate to its topographic context.[11] Indeed, the use of aquatic imagery in 2:7, 9 is

---

[8] James Nogalski offers a helpful overview of the many commonalities between the redactional models of these three scholars: "Preexilic Portions of the Book of the Twelve: Early Collections and Composition Models," in *Conference Proceedings to the Colloquium Biblicum Lovaniense LXV*, BETL (Leuven: Peeters, forthcoming).

[9] Tuell, *Reading Nahum–Malachi*, 36–37; J. J. M. Roberts, *Nahum, Habakkuk, and Zephaniah: A Commentary*, OTL (Louisville: Westminster John Knox, 1991), 65–66; Klaas Spronk, *Nahum*, HCOT (Kampen: Kok Pharos, 1997), 99–100; Ralph L. Smith, *Micah–Malachi*, WBC 32 (Waco, TX: Word, 1984), 83; Christensen, *Nahum*, 284–85, 293; John R Huddlestun, "Nahum, Nineveh, and the Nile: The Description of Thebes in Nahum 3:8–9," *JNES* 62 (2003): 97–110, here 106–8; Dietrich, *Nahum, Habakkuk, Zephaniah*, 70.

[10] Dietrich, *Nahum, Habakkuk, Zephaniah*, 25, 70; Angelika Berlejung, "Erinnerungen an Assyrien in Nahum 2,4–3,19," in *Die unwiderstehliche Wahrheit: Studien zur alttestamentlichen Prophetie; Festschrift für Arndt Meinhold*, ed. Rüdiger Lux and Ernst-Joachim Waschke, ABIG 23 (Leipzig: Evangelische Verlagsanstalt, 2006), 323–56; Huddlestun, "Nahum, Nineveh, and the Nile," 107; Aron Pinker, "Nineveh's Defensive Strategy and Nahum 2–3," *ZAW* 118 (2006): 618–25, here 620.

[11] Dietrich, *Nahum, Habakkuk, Zephaniah*, 64; Nogalski, *Micah–Malachi*, 624; Tuell, *Reading Nahum–Malachi*, 36–37; Roberts, *Nahum, Habakkuk, and Zephaniah*, 65; Spronk, *Nahum*, 29; Smith, *Micah–Malachi*, 83; Christensen, *Nahum*, 284–6.

particularly apt in this respect, as 2:7 mentions "river gates" (שערי הנהרות), while 2:9 likens Nineveh to a "pool of water" (ברכת־מים).[12]

Nevertheless, few scholars have drawn connections between the water images in 1:4, 8; 2:7, 9; 3:8, 14. Pinker links Nah 1:4 and 1:8 on the thematic level, noting that these verses and the psalm as a whole indicate YHWH's "supremacy over the forces of nature."[13] This observation is especially apt given the location of both of these verses within the partial acrostic psalm of 1:2–8,[14] which Elizabeth Achtemeier claims is the "theological key" to Nahum.[15] Klaas Spronk and Duane Christensen connect the opening of the river gates in 2:7 with the images of God's mastery over water in 1:4, 8. Spronk states that the root מוג ("melt") in 2:7 also occurs in 1:5, thereby connecting the opening psalm with the depiction of the downfall of Nineveh in chapter 2.[16]

Peter Machinist compares the fall of Nineveh in Nahum with other sources, arguing for the prominence of water as a destructive agent in Nahum. He observes that Nah 2:7, 9 describe Assyria as flooded and turned into a "watery pool," once again in conjunction with the Assyrian capital's situation along the Tigris and Khosr Rivers.[17] Huddlestun, however, appears to be the only scholar to connect the water imagery in all three chapters of Nahum, suggesting that 1:8; 2:7, 9; 3:8 are related through the book's "play on the ambivalent role of water, both as a means of protection and as the agent of destruction." Such a play, he contends, "may be an intentional literary strategy."[18]

Huddlestun's observation is consistent with the use of water imagery elsewhere in the Hebrew Bible, where water has both negative and positive attributes.[19] On the one hand, water is chaotic, threatening, or destructive in a number of texts, including Gen 1; 6–7; Exod 14–15; Deut 11:4; Judg 5:4, 21; Pss 32:6; 74:13–14; 77:16–20; 93:3–4; 104:5–9; Isa 51:9–10; and Jonah 2. On the other hand, water is

---

[12] Dietrich, *Nahum, Habakkuk, Zephaniah*, 65.

[13] Aron Pinker, "Nahum's Theological Perspectives," *JBQ* 32 (2004): 148–57, here 152.

[14] For a discussion of Nah 1:2–8 as an acrostic poem, see Julia M. O'Brien, *Nahum, Habakkuk, Zephaniah, Haggai, Zechariah, Malachi*, AOTC (Nashville: Abingdon, 2004), 35; Dietrich, *Nahum, Habakkuk, Zephaniah*, 49; Nogalski, *Micah–Malachi*, 609–11; Tuell, *Reading Nahum–Malachi*, 19–21; Roberts, *Nahum, Habakkuk, and Zephaniah*, 48; Becking, "Passion, Power, Protection," 4.

[15] Elizabeth Achtemeier, *Nahum–Malachi*, IBC (Atlanta: John Knox, 1986), 6.

[16] Spronk, *Nahum*, 95; Christensen, *Nahum*, 286.

[17] Peter Machinist, "The Fall of Assyria in Comparative Ancient Perspective," in *Assyria 1995: Proceedings of the 10th Anniversary Symposium of the Neo-Assyrian Text Corpus Project, Helsinki, September 7–11, 1995*, ed. S. Parpola and R. M. Whiting (Helsinki: Neo-Assyrian Text Corpus Project, 1997), 191.

[18] Huddlestun, "Nahum, Nineveh, and the Nile," 107.

[19] As pointed out especially by Erhard Gerstenberger ("Water in the Old Testament," in *Water Marks Our Life*, ed. Solange Lefebvre and Marie-Theres Wacker [London: SCM, 2012], 35–45); see also Robert Luyster, "Wind and Water: Cosmogonic Symbolism in the Old Testament," *ZAW* 93 (1981): 1–10.

life-giving, necessary for both the harvest (Deut 11:14; Jer 5:24; 14:1–9; Hos 2:5, 10–11) and the general flourishing of life (Gen 2:8–17; Exod 17:3; Num 24:6–7; Judg 4:19; 15:18–19; 1 Kgs 17:7; 18:1–6; Isa 41:17–19; Jer 14:1–9; Ezek 47:1–12).[20] Huddlestun does not expand much on his tantalizing observation, nor does he account for the occurrence of water imagery in Nah 3:14. Thus, there remains the possibility for further and more detailed examination of the role of water in the book of Nahum.

Gender in Nahum Scholarship

Scholars have sought to analyze the book of Nahum through the lens of contemporary concerns such as violence and human trafficking.[21] Yet many recent studies of the book focus on Nahum's depiction of gender relations.[22] These examinations have noted the importance of gendered language imagery in the book's exultation over the downfall of Assyria.[23]

Most striking in this regard are the masculine deity YHWH's actions against the personified feminine city of Nineveh and the masculine figure of the king of Assyria.[24] Cynthia Chapman avers that gendered language appears throughout Neo-Assyrian textual and iconographic materials from the ninth to seventh

---

[20] Water is also used figuratively in a number of instances: to convey the idea of being welcome or refreshing (Prov 25:25) or as powerful and oncoming (Hos 5:10; Amos 5:24) or as life-giving (Isa 58:11–12). See further Gerstenberger, "Water in the Old Testament," 41–44.

[21] See David G. Garber, "Facing Traumatizing Texts: Reading Nahum's Nationalistic Rage," *RevExp* 105 (2008): 285–94; Gregory D. Cook, "Human Trafficking in Nahum," *HBT* 37 (2015): 142–57; Daniel Timmer, "Boundaries without Judah, Boundaries within Judah: Hybridity and Identity in Nahum," *HBT* 34 (2012): 173–89; Wessels, "Nahum, an Uneasy Expression of Yahweh's Power!," 615–28.

[22] Leonard Mare and Johan Serfontein, "The Violent, Rhetorical-Ideological God of Nahum," *OTE* 22 (2009): 175–85; O'Brien, *Nahum*, 87–104; O'Brien, *Challenging Prophetic Metaphor: Theology and Ideology in the Prophets* (Louisville: Westminster John Knox, 2008), 101–24; Gerlinde Baumann, "Gott als vergewaltigender Soldat im Alten Testament? Ein Vergleich von Jes 47,2 und Nah 3,4–7," in *Machtbeziehungen, Geschlechterdifferenz und Religion*, ed. Bernhard Heininger, Stephanie Böhm, and Ulrich Sals (Münster: LIT, 2004), 55–60, 65–67; Cynthia R. Chapman, *The Gendered Language of Warfare in the Israelite–Assyrian Encounter*, HSM 62 (Winona Lake, IN: Eisenbrauns, 2004), 103–10, 150–53.

[23] Chapman, *Gendered Language of Warfare*, 20, 103–10; O'Brien, *Nahum*, 13, 98–100.

[24] The study of masculinity in the Hebrew Bible as a whole is a new and growing field of research. See David J. A. Clines, "David the Man: The Construction of Masculinity in the Hebrew Bible," in *Interested Parties: The Ideology of Writers and Readers of the Hebrew Bible*, JSOTSup 205 (Sheffield: Sheffield Academic, 1995), 212–41; Ovidiu Creangă, ed., *Men and Masculinity in the Hebrew Bible and Beyond*, Bible in the Modern World 33 (Sheffield: Sheffield Phoenix, 2010); Ovidiu Creangă and Peter-Ben Smit, eds., *Biblical Masculinities Foregrounded*, HBM 62 (Sheffield: Sheffield Phoenix, 2014); Stephan M. Wilson, *Making Men: The Male Coming-of-Age Theme in the Hebrew Bible* (New York: Oxford University Press, 2015).

centuries BCE and serves as an ideological and propagandistic tool in support of the Assyrian king and his efforts at expansion and control in the ancient Near East. These materials portray the king of Assyria as an unrivaled "ideal male" whose foes are defeated in battle. These foes are depicted as vanquished and feminized, having lost in a contest of masculinities on the battlefield. In several reliefs, the surrendering king cleans the feet of the mighty Assyrian king with his beard; in others, the women of a conquered city are led away single file while the bodies of their husbands and their king are strewn about on the battlefield. Images such as these, as well as textual materials calling the king a "shepherd" (similar to Nah 3:18) suggest not only the Assyrian conception of battle as a contest of masculinity but also the role of the male king who, like a husband, protects and provides for his people.[25]

Despite these rich comparative materials, Chapman is hesitant to frame the book of Nahum as a contest of masculinities, noting that the only explicit mention of the king of Assyria occurs in 3:18–19, when it is clear that "it is a contest that Yahweh has already won."[26] Instead, she rightly remarks that YHWH frequently directs his wrath against Nineveh, as in the dual declarations "I am against you" (הנני אליך) in 2:14 and 3:5.[27] At the same time, however, Chapman, followed by Dietrich, stresses the masculine failure of the Assyrian men; in her view, Nah 3:13 depicts the Assyrian troops as "women" (נשים) and YHWH as wreaking vengeance on Nineveh while "the king of Assyria sits totally incapacitated."[28]

Julia O'Brien, however, picks up on several aspects of the text of Nahum that Chapman forgoes in her analysis, convincingly framing the book as a struggle between two males, YHWH and the king of Assyria, that is "fought on the bodies of their women."[29] She points to the veiled threats and taunts against an anonymous male character at the end of both chapters 1 and 2. In 1:14, YHWH tells the still-anonymous Assyrian king, "I will prepare your grave, for you are worthless" (אשים קברך כי קלות), while 2:12–13 taunts the male lion for its inability to provide for its lioness and cubs.[30] O'Brien further mentions the gendered language of 1:13, which portrays YHWH as breaking "his rod" (מטהו), in reference to an anonymous masculine figure in 1:14, that is used to oppress Judah, as well as threatening that the male figure's name will no longer "be sown" (יזרע, niphal). Indeed, Nogalski argues that the logic of 1:9–2:3 requires that readers identify this anonymous masculine figure as the king of Assyria, who goes forth from Nineveh, conspires against YHWH (1:11), and relies on numerical strength to defeat his foes (1:12).[31] Nahum 1:12b–13 announces that the judgment against Nineveh is "good news for Judah

---

[25] Chapman, *Gendered Language of Warfare*, 1–10, 20–21, 39, 47.
[26] Ibid., 104. She also notes an anonymous appearance of the Assyrian king in 1:14.
[27] Ibid., 106.
[28] Ibid., 107, 110; Dietrich, *Nahum, Habakkuk, Zephaniah*, 83.
[29] O'Brien, *Nahum*, 73.
[30] Ibid., 64, 72.
[31] Nogalski, "Preexilic Portions of the Book of the Twelve."

and Jerusalem."³² To these observations one can add the appearance of the anonymous male character of 2:6, who "remembers his officers" (יזכר אדיריו) during the attack on Nineveh, even though it is too late to save the city.³³ These points support O'Brien's argument that the unnamed, threatened male figure throughout the book is the king of Assyria—information that is not revealed until the final two verses.³⁴ The portrait of an unnamed, threatened male figure throughout Nahum thus enables an analysis of the way in which this figure is portrayed in relation to expectations of masculinity.

For both Chapman and O'Brien, the absence and failure of the Assyrian king leads to the divine assault against the personified female character of Nineveh.³⁵ YHWH's sexual humiliation of Nineveh is most prominent in 3:4–7, in which YHWH lifts up Nineveh's skirts and throws filth at her exposed body. Yet the gender-charged portrait of YHWH's attack on Nineveh is not confined to this shocking section. The phrase "the gates of your land are wide open" (פתוח נפתחו שערי ארצך) in 3:13 has a sexual connotation (cf. Isa 3:16–26, Song 5:4–6).³⁶ The play between the term פת ("innermost parts") in Isa 3:17 and פתח ("gate") in Isa 3:26 in reference to the divine threat against Jerusalem equates the city with the female body and the gates with the "vaginal opening of the female body."³⁷ Elsewhere in Nahum, the leading away of "her maidservants" (אמהתיה) after the breaching of the city, the notion that the city is "exiled/uncovered" (גלתה, the same root used in 3:6 for the lifting up of Nineveh's skirts) in 2:8, and the general attack of a masculine figure against a feminine entity contribute to a deeply gendered portrait of violence.³⁸

Thus, the king of Assyria, through the assault on Nineveh, is shamed as a man through the violation and shaming of the female figure he is supposed to protect.³⁹ The failure of the Assyrian king to protect Nineveh stands in contrast to YHWH's

---

³² Ibid.

³³ Dietrich, *Nahum, Habakkuk, Zephaniah*, 69.

³⁴ O'Brien, *Nahum*, 72.

³⁵ Ibid., 66–68, 72; Chapman, *Gendered Language of Warfare*, 107, 110.

³⁶ Chapman, *Gendered Language of Warfare*, 109; O'Brien, *Nahum*, 70; Nogalski, *Micah–Malachi*, 632.

³⁷ F. Rachel Magdalene, "Ancient Near Eastern Treaty-Curses and the Ultimate Texts of Terror: A Study of the Language of Divine Sexual Abuse in the Prophetic Corpus," in *A Feminist Companion to the Latter Prophets*, ed. Athalya Brenner, FCB 8 (Sheffield: Sheffield Academic, 1995), 326–52, here 333.

³⁸ O'Brien, *Nahum*, 70; Spronk, *Nahum*, 76.

³⁹ This motif occurs elsewhere in the Hebrew Bible and in Neo-Assyrian texts, including in Esarhaddon's Succession Treaty and a treaty between Aššur-nerari V and Mati-ilu of Arpad, along with Isa 3:24–26; Jer 6:11–12, 24; and Mic 4:8–10. O'Brien, *Nahum*, 73, 93; Chapman, *Gendered Language of Warfare*, 42, 106–8; Susan Haddox, "Favoured Sons and Subordinate Masculinities," in Creangă, *Men and Masculinity*, 2–19, here 5–6; Ken Stone, "Gender Criticism: The Unmanning of Abimelech," in *Judges and Method: New Approaches in Biblical Studies*, ed. Gale A. Yee, 2nd ed. (Minneapolis: Fortress, 2007), 183–201, here 193.

protective role as a "stronghold on the day of distress" (מעוז ביום צרה) for "those who take refuge in him" (חסי בו) in 1:7. Nahum portrays YHWH as fulfilling the masculine role of protector that the king of Assyria is expected to fulfill.

Studies on masculinity in the Hebrew Bible, however, emphasize that feminization and identification or association with the feminine also bring shame upon a man.[40] This coheres with Chapman's and Dietrich's argument that Nah 3:13 contains a taunt against the fearsome Assyrian army.[41] That the downfall of Assyria is portrayed through the parallel depictions of the defeat of the king of Assyria (ch. 2) and the attack on feminine-personified Nineveh (ch. 3) suggests that Nahum associates the male king with the female city in order to shame the former figure. Nevertheless, the parallel fates of these two figures, coupled with their similarities, undermine the ancient assumptions regarding gender that Nahum employs with regard to the earthly entities in the book. It is clear, however, that gender plays an important role in Nahum's portrait of the downfall of Nineveh, primarily through the importance of expectations for masculine behavior in the text.

Water and Gender

Despite the prominence of water imagery in the text, scholars have not studied gender in Nahum through the lens of aquatic imagery. The studies of Richard Whitekettle and Julie Galambush regarding the association between water imagery and "the feminine" elsewhere in the Hebrew Bible, however, indicate the potential fruitfulness of such an endeavor.[42] Whitekettle observes that Leviticus conceptualizes the womb as a "wellspring" (מקר) that renders a woman impure whenever it overflows its boundaries, reflecting a homology in Levitical thought between womb and wellspring that was common in the ancient Near East.[43] From this point, Whitekettle argues that the treatment of the female reproductive system in the purity laws regarding puerperal and menstrual discharges in Lev 12:2–4 and 15:19–24 shares several features with that of the primeval world in Gen 1 and 6–9. He contends that the womb in Leviticus serves as a microcosm of the primeval macrocosm in Gen 1, 6–9 in that both Lev 12:2–4, 15:19–24 and Gen 1, 6–9 reckon with fluid boundaries. In each of these texts, when water—literal or figurative—remains within its "proper" boundaries, life is able to flourish, whereas when water

---

[40] Stone, "Gender Criticism," 188; Stone, *Sex, Honor, and Power in the Deuteronomistic History*, JSOTSup 234 (Sheffield: Sheffield Academic, 1996), 76.

[41] Chapman, *Gendered Language of Warfare*, 107, 110; Dietrich, *Nahum, Habakkuk, Zephaniah*, 83.

[42] Richard Whitekettle, "Levitical Thought and the Female Reproductive Cycle: Wombs, Wellsprings, and the Primeval World," *VT* 46 (1996): 376–91; Julie Galambush, *Jerusalem in the Book of Ezekiel: The City as Yahweh's Wife*, SBLDS 130 (Atlanta: Scholars Press, 1992).

[43] See Lev 12:6–7; 20:18; Whitekettle, "Levitical Thought and the Female Reproductive Cycle," 382–85.

goes beyond its bounds, the environment, whether the primeval topography or its uterine microcosm, is unable to be productive.[44]

Galambush likewise sees a connection between water and "the feminine," pointing to the portrait of Jerusalem in Ezek 40–48.[45] She argues that, in Ezekiel's closing vision, Jerusalem (the city) is similar to the personified female figure in Ezek 1–39 in that the city is a physically enclosed space like a mother that "shelters" its inhabitants and that the male deity YHWH jealously protects the city's innermost sanctum, with YHWH's honor dependent on preserving the inviolate nature of the city. Galambush further contends that the feminine city Jerusalem issues forth a clean stream of water from the entrance to the temple in Ezek 47:1–12, providing and sustaining life and connoting female sexuality, with the water serving as a "sort of amniotic fluid."[46]

The studies of Whitekettle and Galambush demonstrate the connection between water and gender in the Hebrew Bible. Nahum, however, presents a different picture. The Pentateuch and Ezek 40–48 portray water primarily in terms of its association with fertility. Nahum, on the other hand, uses aquatic imagery in relation to military combat and divine power. Nahum 1:4, 8 depict YHWH's struggle against river and sea and triumph over adversaries amid a flood, while 2:7, 9 offer historically cast uses of aquatic imagery, depicting the downfall of Nineveh through the opening of river gates to flood the city and the flight of its soldiers (though water's life-sustaining aspect is also present in 2:9). Likewise, Nah 3:8, 14 offer historically conditioned references to the downfall of Thebes and the siege preparations. For these reasons, the interpretive models of Whitekettle and Galambush are not readily applied to Nahum. I now turn to the text of Nahum, analyzing each occurrence of water imagery in both its immediate and its broader contexts.

II. Water and Gender in Nahum

The Mighty Male Divine Warrior in Nahum 1:4, 8

Though Nah 1:4, 8 do not speak of YHWH's conflict with Assyria, these two verses portray the deity's dealings with the aquatic realm and establish YHWH as a preeminent masculine warrior. In doing so, they set the stage for the depiction of gendered conflict with Assyria in the rest of the book. In 1:4a, YHWH is a deity who "rebukes the sea and dries it up" (גוער בים ויבשהו) and "lays waste to all the rivers" (כל הנהרות החריב). In 1:8, YHWH "makes a full end in/by a sweeping flood" (בשטף עבר כלה יעשה). Both 1:4 and 1:8 fall within a partial acrostic psalm, which

---

[44] Ibid., 386–89.
[45] Galambush, *Jerusalem in the Book of Ezekiel*, 151–57.
[46] Ibid., 153–55.

may have been a later addition to the prophetic book.[47] This psalm immediately follows the superscription of 1:1 and thereby provides a theological orientation to the book of Nahum, portraying God as a mighty and powerful warrior.[48] Indeed, compared to the remainder of the book, 1:2–8 contains a great deal more explicitly theological language and description of YHWH than is found in the rest of the book.

The psalm's presentation of YHWH as a mighty warrior arises not only from the unique description of the deity as an "avenger" (נקם) who "keeps wrath" (נוטר) against his enemies in 1:2 but also from the image of divine combat against the forces of nature and chaos throughout the rest of the psalm. As a number of scholars observe, the psalm draws heavily on and adapts ancient Near Eastern mythological motifs concerning the victory of the deity over the forces of chaos, including Baal's defeat of Prince Sea and Judge River, forces that are de-deified and turned into the natural features of the sea (ים) and the river (נהר) in Nah 1:4.[49] Even these powerful entities YHWH "rebukes," "dries up," and "lays waste." This description underscores the power and might of the avenging Divine Warrior, a powerful male figure who "exacts vengeance against his adversaries" (נקם ... לצריו, 1:2) and "by no means leaves [his enemies] unpunished" (נקה לא ינקה, 1:3).[50] In 1:2 YHWH is a "master of wrath" (בעל חמה, 1:2). This phrase implies power and control and echoes the gendered use of the term to mean "husband" (e.g., Exod 21:22; Deut 21:13; 24:4; Joel 1:8; Prov 31:11, 23, 28), a meaning that is played upon in Hos 2:18.

Thus, the image of YHWH's combat with sea in 1:4 supports the psalm's view of YHWH as a strong masculine figure who has power over his enemies. In 1:8, YHWH exercises his military might in or through a great flood; the preposition -ב at the beginning of the phrase בשטף, can imply both location and instrumentality.[51] YHWH is therefore capable of achieving victory "in the midst of a flood" or "by means of a flood." The former meaning coheres with the mythological language of

---

[47] Dietrich, *Nahum, Habakkuk, Zephaniah*, 9; Nogalski, *Micah–Malachi*, 602; Fabry, *Nahum*, 91–92; Renaud, "La composition du livre de Nahum," 208–9; Thomas Hieke, "Der Anfang des Buches Nahum I: Die Frage des Textverlaufs in der jetzigen Gestalt; Ein antithetisches Prinzip," *BN* 68 (1993): 13–17.

[48] Nogalski, *Micah–Malachi*, 602; Dietrich, *Nahum, Habakkuk, Zephaniah*, 29; Achtemeier, *Nahum–Malachi*, 5; Spronk, *Nahum*, 20; Joseph L. Mihelic, "The Concept of God in the Book of Nahum," *Int* 2 (1948): 199–207, here 202; Wessels, "Nahum, an Uneasy Expression of Yahweh's Power!," 618.

[49] Kevin Cathcart, "The Divine Warrior and the War of Yahweh in Nahum," in *Biblical Studies in Contemporary Thought: The 10th Anniversary Commemorative Volume of the Trinity College Biblical Institute 1966–1975*, ed. Miriam Ward (Burlington, VT: Trinity College Biblical Institute, 1975), 68–76, here 69–71; O'Brien, *Nahum*, 49; Tuell, *Reading Nahum–Malachi*, 23; Roberts, *Nahum, Habakkuk, and Zephaniah*, 50; Spronk, *Nahum*, 39.

[50] O'Brien interprets a number of Divine Warrior texts throughout the prophetic corpus through the lens of YHWH's masculinity (*Challenging Prophetic Metaphor*, 101–24).

[51] *IBHS*, 196–97.

the psalm and the latter with subsequent occurrences in the book (see below).[52] The use of water imagery in verses 4 and 8 thus emphasizes the invincible nature of YHWH, the mighty masculine warrior, and sets the stage for the assault on Nineveh in chapters 2–3.

Water In, Water Out: Nahum 2:7, 9

Nahum 2:7, 9 use water imagery in order to paint a picture of the assault on Nineveh. These verses are part of the first of two parallel poetic depictions of the downfall of Nineveh in chapters 2–3; the second is in 3:1–19 as the text shifts its focus to personified Nineveh.[53] Nahum 2:7 describes the state of the city during the attackers' successful assault: "the gates of the rivers are opened" (שערי הנהרות נפתחו). Meanwhile, 2:9 depicts the defeated city as "like a pool of water from whom waters flee" (כברכת מים מימי היא והמה נסים), and the departure of whose waters will not be stopped because "there is no one to turn [them around]" (אין מפנה). Though Nah 2:7, 9 almost certainly play on Nineveh's well-known aquatic topography as discussed above, these verses also connect to the motif of water in 1:4, 8 and contribute to the book's depiction of gendered conflict.

In this respect, Spronk's observation that the use of the root מוג in Nah 2:7 connects the first depiction of the fall of Nineveh in 2:2–14 with the opening psalm of 1:2–8 is instructive.[54] YHWH's appearance in Nah 1:5 causes the hills to melt (הגבעות התמגגו), while "the palace melts" (ההיכל נמוג) in 2:7. These descriptions, together with YHWH's declarations in 1:13, "I will break his yoke from upon you" (אשבר מטהו מעליך), and in 1:14, "I will prepare your grave" (אשים קברך), suggest divine causation for the fall of Nineveh in chapter 2. YHWH's threats, which appear to be addressed to Assyria's unnamed ruler, point to YHWH's inevitable triumph over his enemy in the masculine arena of battle.[55] The fall of the king's palace, a symbol of the king's power, offers tangible proof of the Assyrian ruler's shameful defeat.[56]

Reinforcing this portrait of the victory of YHWH in the contest of masculinities is the image in Nah 2:7 of the river gates opening, which would lead to the flooding of the Assyrian capital. This image recalls that of 1:8, in which YHWH "makes a full end" in and through a sweeping flood. YHWH's mastery over water thus provides yet another clue to the divine sanction that lies behind the assault of Nineveh. Through his destructive control over water, YHWH triumphs over the Assyrian king, who is portrayed as almost helplessly "remember[ing] his officers"

---

[52] Tuell, *Reading Nahum–Malachi*, 25.
[53] Nogalski, *Micah–Malachi*, 602; O'Brien, *Nahum*, 66.
[54] Spronk, *Nahum*, 95.
[55] Tuell, *Reading Nahum–Malachi*, 32; O'Brien, *Nahum*, 56.
[56] Chapman, *Gendered Language of Warfare*, 28.

(יזכור אדיריו) in 2:6 while the battle for Nineveh rages and his divinely backed assailants are on the verge of routing him and his forces.[57]

The description of Nineveh as a "pool of water" in 2:9 marks a shift in the usage of water imagery in Nahum. Each of the final three water images is related to a female entity. In the case of 2:9, the relationship of water to the female character of Nineveh is evident from the difficult phrase "from whom waters flee" (מימי היא והמה נסים).[58] But although female Nineveh is compared to a pool, her waters are portrayed as masculine entities through the use of the *qal* active participle נסים in the masculine plural form. This dual-gendered portrait of water in 2:9 serves two purposes. One is to demonstrate the "panicked flight" of anyone still capable of defending Nineveh.[59] Those fleeing the city are told emphatically to halt, evident in the double command "stay, stay!" (עמדו עמדו). Yet this command is to no avail, as a portrait of masculine failure to protect the city and to shepherd the people once again arises: "but there is no one to turn them around" (ואין מפנה), the *hiphil* masculine singular participle hinting that the failure lies at least in part with the anonymous Assyrian king. As Dietrich notes, the failure of the men—the water fleeing the pool—to defend the city leads to their "severe humiliation."[60]

The second is to build on YHWH's "rebuk[ing] the sea and dry[ing] it up" and "lay[ing] waste" to "all the rivers" (1:4). The portrait of Nineveh as a pool offers a stark contrast to YHWH's previous aquatic victory. In terms of scale, Nineveh pales in comparison to the mighty waters that YHWH has defeated. YHWH's victory over the city Nineveh is inevitable, just as was his victory over the king of Assyria. Furthermore, the image of Nineveh as a pool lacks the mythological connotations of Nah 1:4, which depicts YHWH's victory over the sea and the river. Indeed, if YHWH can triumph over the river and the sea, the text implies, what chance does a mere pool have against the mighty Divine Warrior?

These images also juxtapose notions of water as a source of chaos and peril with ideas of water as the source of life. While the mythological overtones of the river, sea, and flood signal a threat to life that YHWH defeats in the opening psalm, the pool of water in 2:9 offers an image of tranquillity that may sustain human, animal, and plant life.[61] Nevertheless, the "flight" of water from the pool in 2:9 also signals the downfall of Nineveh by implying that the city will no longer be able to support life as it once had. This image underscores the totality of YHWH's military victory over Assyria and contrasts with the depiction in Ezek 47:1–12, which

---

[57] Dietrich, *Nahum, Habakkuk, Zephaniah*, 64.
[58] Fabry, *Nahum*, 158, 162–63.
[59] Tuell, *Reading Nahum–Malachi*, 37.
[60] Dietrich, *Nahum, Habakkuk, Zephaniah*, 65.
[61] Passages in the Hebrew Bible that depict a "pool" (ברכת) of water as supporting life include 2 Kgs 20:20, Isa 22:9, and Eccl 2:6. See Gerstenberger, "Water in the Old Testament," 36–41.

portrays the new temple as issuing forth a life-giving stream that is able to support abundant plant, animal, and human life.[62]

Though the shift from masculine to feminine characters as YHWH's opponents from Nah 2:7 to 2:9 reinforces the portrait of YHWH as a powerful warrior, it also destabilizes (intentionally or unintentionally) typical gender assumptions in Nahum regarding the earthly entities. YHWH's triumph over river and sea in the opening psalm and subsequent defeat of the Assyrian king leave little doubt about the final defeat of Nineveh and the ultimate fate of the as-yet-unidentified male figure responsible for the city's defense. At the same time, however, both the still-anonymous king of Assyria and personified Nineveh, whose depiction as a woman is fleshed out in the subsequent chapter, portend the imminent downfall of the city itself and, by extension, the Assyrian Empire. Thus, Nahum folds male and female characters into its overall outlook on the historical Assyrian Empire, laying the literary groundwork for unsettling ancient gender binaries.

It may seem counterintuitive to claim that Nahum's parallel between the male king in chapter 2 and the female city in chapter 3—both figures serving as illustrations of Assyrian downfall—complicates and destabilizes ancient assumptions regarding gender and resists the drawing of a neat binary between male and female in Nahum. It is true that identification with a female figure brings shame upon the male figure,[63] and the parallel depictions of the fall of Assyria shame the masculine figure of the king by placing him in parallel with the female figure of Nineveh. Indeed, this implicit shaming of the king through his identification with a female figure complements his more explicit shaming through his defeat on the battlefield, itself a "feminizing" event in the ancient Near East.[64] Nevertheless, this melding of Nineveh and the king, together with the portrait of Nineveh in chapter 3, unsettles the gender assumptions in the book regarding the "human" entities, a topic that will be explored below in conjunction with water imagery.

Water and Women: Nahum 3:8, 14

The final two occurrences of water imagery pertain to the female figure of Nineveh and therefore play a key role in Nahum's portrait of the humiliation of the Assyrian king. In 3:8, the prophet asks Nineveh, "Are you better than Thebes, who sits upon the Nile, water all around her, whose might is the sea, her walls from the sea" (התיטבי מנא אמון הישבה ביארים מים סביב לה אשר חיל ים מים חומתה). In 3:14, the prophet commands her, "Draw for yourself water for the siege" (מי מצור שאבי לך). Each of these verses uses aquatic imagery to taunt Nineveh, conveying the

---

[62] See discussion of Galambush above; see her *Jerusalem in the Book of Ezekiel*, 154–55.
[63] Stone, *Sex, Honor, and Power*, 76; Stone, "Gender Criticism," 188.
[64] Wilson, *Making Men*, 33; Chapman, *Gendered Language of Warfare*, 20–58; Stone, "Gender Criticism," 193; Ela Lazarewicz-Wyrzykowska, "Samson: Masculinity Lost (and Regained?)," in Creangă, *Men and Masculinity*, 171–88, here 172–73.

message that water will offer her no security, whether in the form of physical defense or siege preparations. The lengthy question to Nineveh in 3:8 draws a comparison between two famous and powerful cities: Thebes in Upper Egypt and Nineveh, both of which are portrayed as feminine and the former of which was conquered by Assyria in 663 BCE.[65] Despite the military might of Thebes (Nah 3:9) and its advantageous position at a crook in the Nile, "even she became exiled" (גם היא לגלה, Nah 3:10).[66] Through this comparison, the prophet asserts that, just as aquatic topography did not prevent Thebes from falling, neither will it prevent Nineveh from falling.

This comparison between the two female cities supports the claim in Nah 3:4–7 that Nineveh will fall and, in doing so, be sexually humiliated by YHWH. Indeed, the root גלה in 3:10 recalls 3:5, where YHWH tells the personified city that he will "raise" her skirts over her face and show the world her "shame" (פלון). Such a horrific image of the city's downfall fits the biblical and ancient Near Eastern motif of the fall of a city as a sexual assault carried out by the attacking troops, or even by the deity.[67] This portrait of Nineveh's sexualized downfall imputes shame and dishonor not only to the fallen city but also to the male figure—in this case, the king of Assyria—who is supposed to protect her but instead has lost control over her body and her sexuality.[68] In keeping with O'Brien's conception of Nahum as a

---

[65] O'Brien, *Nahum*, 69; Dietrich, *Nahum, Habakkuk, Zephaniah*, 75; Nogalski, *Micah–Malachi*, 629; Tuell, *Reading Nahum–Malachi*, 46; Roberts, *Nahum, Habakkuk, and Zephaniah*, 74; Spronk, *Nahum*, 128; Huddlestun, "Nahum, Nineveh, and the Nile," 98; Dávid Benka, "Power of the Powerless and the Powerless Power: A Reading of Nahum," *BN* 161 (2014): 3–18, here 6, 14.

[66] While Thomas Schneider claims that the depiction of Thebes as surrounded by water arises from a mercenary soldier's knowledge of Thebes's topography and of the Nile's annual flooding that would have created an expansive aquatic defense for the city ("Nahum und Theben: Zum topographisch-historischen Hintergrund von Nah 3:8f," *BN* 44 [1988]: 63–73), Huddlestun, finding Schneider's claim unlikely, argues that Nahum models Thebes on Nineveh, given the prominence of Nineveh's massive waterworks and position along two rivers ("Nahum, Nineveh, and the Nile," 102–8). Regardless of the exact origin of this description of Thebes in Nahum, Thebes's proximity to water is likely to have prompted comparison between the two cities. See also Nogalski, *Micah–Malachi*, 69.

[67] See Pamela Gordon and Harold C. Washington, "Rape as a Military Metaphor in the Hebrew Bible," in Brenner, *Feminist Companion to the Latter Prophets*, 308–25; Magdalene, "Ancient Near Eastern Treaty-Curses," 339–48.

[68] O'Brien, *Nahum*, 73, 92, 102; Dietrich, *Nahum, Habakkuk, Zephaniah*, 79; Nogalski, *Micah–Malachi*, 629; Daniel Smith-Christopher, "Ezekiel in Abu Ghraib: Rereading Ezekiel 16:37–39 in the Context of Imperial Conquest," in *Ezekiel's Hierarchical World: Wrestling with a Tiered Reality*, ed. Stephen L. Cook and Corrine L. Patton, SymS 31 (Atlanta: Society of Biblical Literature, 2004), 141–57, here 152–53; Hilary Lipka, "Masculinities in Proverbs: An Alternative to the Hegemonic Ideal," in Creangă and Smit, *Biblical Masculinities Foregrounded*, 86–103, here 89; J. Cheryl Exum, "Feminist Criticism: Whose Interests Are Being Served?," in Yee, *Judges and Method*, 65–90, here 83.

contest of masculinities, the Assyrian king becomes emasculated; he is powerless and is not even mentioned in the text during the violation of feminized Nineveh.[69] That Nineveh experiences the same fate as Thebes, in spite of her impressive aquatic defenses, enhances all the more YHWH's status as an unrivaled masculine military figure who is able to defeat the very same foe that triumphed gloriously over Thebes.

The absence of the Assyrian king during the fall and sexual violation of Nineveh in Nah 3:4–7 continues in 3:14 as the prophet commands Nineveh to "draw water for the siege" (מי מצור שאבי). That this command is issued to the feminine figure of Nineveh is emphasized textually through the use of a second-person feminine singular imperative followed by the preposition ל- with a feminine singular pronominal suffix. The command to draw water (מי, masc. pl.) creates a subtle poetic parallel with Nah 2:9, in which Nineveh's waters (מי, masc. pl.) flee from her. Nineveh is thus urged to gain access to water and to find what defensive troops she can. Furthermore, the address to Nineveh to prepare for her own siege is remarkable and demonstrates a shift from 2:2, which contains a number of imperatives addressed to the still-unnamed masculine singular figure of the king of Assyria, challenging him to prepare for the assault on his city. Indeed, his disappearance from the defense of the city following 2:6 is emphasized through the lack of a male figure to turn the fleeing water back around in 2:9, the taunting line of questioning regarding the location of the male lion in 2:12–13, and YHWH's declarations "I am against you [fem. sg.]" and "the sword will consume your [fem. sg.] young lions" in 2:14.[70]

On another level, the command to Nineveh to prepare for her own defense by drawing her own water somewhat paradoxically elevates her to a status similar to that of the king of Assyria. Indeed, with respect to Nahum's use of imperatives, both the king and Nineveh are commanded to "gird/strengthen," with the prophet issuing a second-person masculine singular *piel* imperative to the former in 2:2 (חזק) and a second-person feminine singular *piel* imperative to the latter in 3:14 (חזקי). Rather than simply shaming the king through his identification with a female figure, this lexical parallel between the two figures elevates the stature of the female antagonist as an entity in her own right against which YHWH must fight. Even as Nah 3:4 derides Nineveh for her "prostitutions" (זנוני), it labels her a "mistress of sorceries" (בעלת כשפים), an unflinchingly negative depiction of her corrupting nature that also acknowledges her high status and power. The term בעלת occurs elsewhere in the Hebrew Bible only in 1 Sam 28:7 and 1 Kgs 17:17, to refer to a woman who has a degree of independence from masculine figures. The assertion

---

[69] O'Brien, *Nahum*, 73.

[70] While scholars rightly state that chapters 2 and 3 offer parallel accounts of Nineveh's downfall, the focus here is on the rhetorical movement of the text rather than on a claim of a straightforward "plot progression" between these two parallel scenes. See O'Brien, *Nahum*, 66; Nogalski, *Micah–Malachi*, 602.

that YHWH is a "lord of wrath" (בעל חמה) in Nah 1:2 furthers the portrait of Nineveh as a powerful but doomed woman.

Elevating the status of personified Nineveh further unsettles a binary, essentialized, patriarchal view of gender with respect to the "human" characters in Nahum. By acknowledging the power of personified Nineveh, the text portrays the city as a character whose power is at least equal to that of the king of Assyria, her supposed male protector. Nineveh's stature is "one who sells the nations" (המכרת גוים) in 3:4 and possesses fortresses and land (3:12–14), along with merchants and guards (3:16–17). These holdings match the Assyrian king's control of officers in 2:6 and nobles in 3:18. Furthermore, both the king and Nineveh are said to possess "people" (עמך in 3:13 [with a second-person fem. sg. pronominal suffix] and 3:18 [with a second-person masc. sg. pronominal suffix]). These textual clues indicate that Nineveh has power and stature beyond and independent of those of her supposed male protector. Indeed, O'Brien contends that the term זונה in 3:4 signifies a woman who has escaped a degree of male control and attained a level of agency beyond strict dependence on a male figure for protection.[71] The divine command to Nineveh to prepare for her own defense by drawing water not only signals the failure of the Assyrian king to protect his city but also depicts Nineveh in an active role in combat.[72]

Nahum's active portrait of Nineveh destabilizes the ancient binary expectations for the performance of gender roles with respect to the book's two Assyrian "characters" even as it reinforces YHWH's military might in defeating both male and female foes. Just as the Assyrian king suffers the shame of military defeat, so too will Nineveh, despite her siege preparations and watery defenses. The elevated stature of Nineveh in chapter 3, together with the implicit identification of the male king with female Nineveh created by the parallel depictions of Assyria's downfall, blurs the gender binary of earthly entities in Nahum. Both the male king and the

---

[71] O'Brien, *Challenging Prophetic Metaphor*, 102.

[72] The command to Nineveh to prepare for her own defense creates another problem for modern interpreters. It implies that Nineveh, a female figure, is responsible for her own defense against violation and that, if and when she fails to defend herself from assault, her sexual humiliation is her fault. An application of this principle to contemporary life and the continuing problem of sexual assault and violence is, at very least, extremely problematic and should be avoided. Accordingly, interpreters must be careful not to present descriptive analyses as prescriptive or normative mores in cases like Nahum's gendered project and the above discussion in no way is meant to portray YHWH's actions toward Nineveh as a paradigm for today with regard to either human action or conception of God. In light of these issues, William Wessels rightly recognizes that Nahum is an example of "resistance poetry" written by and for people under the thumb of the oppressive and violent Assyrian empire, as well as in recalling Assyrian oppression ("Nahum, an Uneasy Expression of Yahweh's Power!," 625). At the same time, it is important to acknowledge and work to counteract what O'Brien calls the "dark side of resistance movements," which may bring their own oppressive ideologies or actions to bear in struggling against oppression (*Nahum, Habakkuk, Zephaniah, Haggai, Zechariah, Malachi*, 48).

female city appear helpless in the face of YHWH's imminent victory; they meet the same fate and share the responsibility for the downfall of Assyria. Despite the assumed military prowess of the masculine figure, the king fails in the face of YHWH's army.

Drawing Together the "Flow" of Water Imagery in Nahum

As demonstrated above, Nahum employs water imagery in its portrait of gendered conflict. Its aquatic images build on one another, progressing rhetorically from a portrait of the imminently victorious masculine deity YHWH to the defeat of the king of Assyria, and finally to the abandoned female Nineveh. This sequence also moves from the depiction of YHWH's triumph in battle over the chaotic forces to the concrete account of YHWH's actions against Assyria's king and its capital. The psalm of Nah 1:2–8, which contains two occurrences of water imagery (vv. 4, 8), presents YHWH as a mighty masculine warrior of mythic proportions. The subsequent water images in 2:7, 9; 3:8, 14 personalize and concretize the grand portrait of YHWH's male military might that was introduced in the opening psalm.

Though these water images occur in different redactional units in Nahum, they provide a sense of forward movement within the text regarding YHWH's victory in the realm of masculine struggle, as well as a sense of unity across the book as a whole. Indeed, this forward movement toward YHWH's victory in masculine conflict is evident not only in the water images but also in the movement between direct addresses to the king of Assyria in Nah 1:14 and 3:19. While YHWH declares to the king of Assyria, "I will make your grave" (אשים קברך) in 1:14, the prophet taunts the king in 3:19 by declaring to him, "there is no alleviation for your fracture, your wound is lethal" (אין כהה לשברך נחלה מכתך), signaling a progression from preparation to imminent fulfillment of the divine threat. That such a progression, seen through the use of water imagery, takes place across different textual blocks within Nahum provides the book with a sense of structure and cohesiveness and allows the reader to view the individual units of varying style (e.g., poetry vs. prose) and form (hymn vs. prophetic taunt) as part of a coherent whole celebrating the downfall of a hated foe and oppressor.

I have assumed the compositional model of Nahum proposed by Fabry, Dietrich, and Nogalski, who view 1:2–8 as a later addition to the book, building on the largely preexisting corpus of 2:2–3:19. According to this model, the biblical writer responsible for the inclusion of 1:2–8 and its two instances of water imagery created an aquatic triptych of sorts that portrays YHWH as the powerful entity behind the fall of Assyria and Nineveh in particular. The opening psalm provides a theological lens through which the rest of the book may be read, establishing that YHWH is punishing Nineveh for its misdeeds. At the same time, however, the preexisting corpus of Nah 2:2–3:19 may have provided the writer behind the inclusion of 1:2–8 with literary grounds for adding the poem with its significant aquatic motif. This later inclusion of 1:2–8 would have cohered with book's already established emphasis on aquatic imagery. The appropriateness of the psalm for its literary context goes beyond the shared motif of water; the addition of 1:2–8 establishes a relationship between divine justice, military defeat, and aquatic imagery that continues through the rest of the book.

III. Conclusion

Water imagery constitutes a significant motif in the book of Nahum. The images in 1:4, 8; 2:7, 9; 3:8, 14 build on one another over the course of the book's three chapters. The aquatic imagery in Nahum also plays a role in what O'Brien calls the book's "gender project," which seeks to portray the conflict between YHWH and Assyria as a contest of masculinities between the Israelite deity and the king of Assyria that results in the shaming of the king of Assyria through military defeat and the violation of the feminine Nineveh.[73] At the same time, however, water imagery plays a role in the unsettling of essentialized, patriarchal, binary notions of gender with regard to human entities in the text. This study contributes to growing and important areas of study of Nahum and of the Hebrew Bible as a whole—the depiction of nature and of gender—while at the same time demonstrating a way for these two topics to be studied together.

[73] O'Brien, *Nahum*, 91.

Image in Text: Interpreting the Ephah Vision of Zechariah 5:5–11

JUSTIN J. WHITE
justin.white@yale.edu
Yale University, New Haven CT 06511

Considerable disagreement exists over the meaning of the ephah vision of Zech 5:5–11. I propose to read the ephah vision as a verbal replication of a common motif known in ancient Near Eastern tradition, represented in both text and image, of deities accompanied by winged hybrid creatures, or *Mischwesen*, who function as attendant creatures of the deity. In the resulting interpretation, I argue that the theme of the vision in Zechariah is a deportation of an Israelite goddess to Babylon, where a temple is established for her, all of which is accomplished by her attendant creatures. The ephah vision thus reflects the removal of the goddess and the totality of her cult from the Jerusalem temple. I conclude by offering a few thoughts on the rhetorical implications of the image–text dynamic in play in this reading of the vision.

Several features of the ephah vision of Zechariah have proven to be exceptionally difficult for scholars to interpret. The cultic language of the latter portion of the vision has been noted by many commentators, yet considerable disagreement exists over the meaning of the images in the vision.[1] I propose to interpret the ephah

I would like to offer my thanks to John J. Collins, Eibert J. C. Tigchelaar, Joel S. Baden, and James Nati, who read through previous iterations of this article and offered invaluable feedback. I would also like to thank the anonymous reviewers, whose exceptionally careful readings improved the argument herein.

[1] Elie Assis, "Zechariah's Vision of the Ephah (Zech. 5:5–11)," *VT* 60 (2010): 15–32; Mark J. Boda, *Haggai, Zechariah*, NIV Application Commentary (Grand Rapids: Zondervan, 2004), 303–16; Diana Edelman, "Proving Yahweh Killed His Wife (Zechariah 5:5–11)," *BibInt* 11 (2003): 335–44; Michael H. Floyd, "The Evil in the Ephah: Reading Zechariah 5.5–11 in Its Literary Context," *CBQ* 58 (1996): 51–68; Christian Jeremias, *Die Nachtgesichte des Sacharja: Untersuchungen zu ihrer Stellung im Zusammenhang der Visionsberichte im Alten Testament und zu ihrem Bildmaterial*, FRLANT 117 (Göttingen: Vandenhoeck & Ruprecht, 1977), 195–200; Mark C. Love, *The Evasive Text: Zechariah 1–8 and the Frustrated Reader*, JSOTSup 296 (Sheffield: Sheffield Academic, 1999), 205–14; Carol L. Meyers and Eric M. Meyers, *Haggai, Zechariah 1–8: A New*

vision by reading the vision as a verbal replication of a common motif known elsewhere in ancient Near Eastern visual and verbal culture. The use of iconographic approaches to the study of biblical texts has proliferated in the last ten years with promising results.[2] I seek to build on these results by considering how the visual cultures of the ancient Near East can help interpret the more enigmatic features of the text by providing a visual context for interpreting the visual phenomena described verbally in the vision.

I will begin by exploring the complicated issues involved in interpreting the various visual elements described in the vision, including the ephah, the "one woman," and the two winged women. Next I describe the ways in which similar elements manifest in both textual and visual instantiations of a common ancient Near Eastern motif of a deity flanked by its hybrid attendant creatures. I then offer an interpretation of the ephah vision in light of this motif, paying particular attention to the ways in which the disparate elements are linked together into a coherent replication of the motif. In conclusion, I offer a few thoughts on the rhetorical implications of the image–text dynamic in this vision.

I. The Vision in Zechariah 5:5–11

The vision opens when the interpreting angel exits the temple and draws the attention of the prophet to an object also exiting the temple.[3] The interpreting angel identifies the object as "the departing ephah" (האיפה היוצאת). Inside the ephah is a solitary item described by the interpreting angel as "this one woman" (זאת אשה אחת), who is small enough to fit within the ephah container, even with a round

---

Translation with Introduction and Commentary, AB 25B (Garden City, NY: Doubleday, 1987), 293–316; Susan Niditch, *The Symbolic Vision in Biblical Tradition*, HSM 30 (Chico, CA: Scholars Press, 1980), 160–67; David L. Petersen, *Haggai and Zechariah 1–8: A Commentary*, OTL (Philadelphia: Westminster, 1984), 254–62; Johannes Schnocks, "An Ephah between Earth and Heaven: Reading Zechariah 5:5–11," in *Tradition in Transition: Haggai and Zechariah 1–8 in the Trajectory of Hebrew Theology*, ed. Mark J. Boda and Michael H. Floyd, LHBOTS 475 (New York: T&T Clark, 2008), 252–70; Marvin A. Sweeney, *The Twelve Prophets*, Berit Olam, 2 vols. (Collegeville, MN: Liturgical Press, 2000), 2:618–23; Christoph Uehlinger, "Die Frau im Efa (Sach 5:5–11): Eine Programmvision von der Abschiebung der Göttin," *BK* 49 (1994): 93–103.

[2] For a helpful evaluation of the iconographic approach, see Ryan P. Bonfiglio, *Reading Images, Seeing Texts: Towards a Visual Hermeneutics for Biblical Studies*, OBO 280 (Fribourg: Academic Press; Göttingen: Vandenhoeck & Ruprecht, 2016), 1–16.

[3] The vision of the lampstand (Zech 4:1–14) depicts the restored presence of YHWH in the temple sanctuary (Floyd, "Evil in the Ephah," 53; Jeremias, *Die Nachtgesichte des Sacharja*, 180–81; Meyers and Meyers, *Haggai, Zechariah 1–8*, 272–77; Niditch, *Symbolic Vision*, 104–7; Petersen, *Haggai, Zechariah 1–8*, 227–28; Sweeney, *Twelve Prophets*, 612–13). In contrast with the sanctuary location of the lampstand vision, the ephah vision opens when the interpreting angel "goes out" (ויצא), thus exiting the temple (cf. Edelman, "Proving Yahweh Killed His Wife," 337; Sweeney, *Twelve Prophets*, 619).

lead cover sealing the opening.[4] The "woman" is soon accompanied by two winged anthropomorphic female creatures, who flank the one "woman" on either side as they use their wings to lift her into the sky. The vision concludes with the "woman" resting on her base in her newly established temple, presumably still accompanied by the winged women.

Scholars have grappled with the enigmatic presence of the ephah in the vision. The lexeme איפה occurs forty times in the Hebrew Bible and refers either to a predefined volumetric measure or a container that has a maximum capacity of the same measure. According to comparative evidence, the postexilic ephah was thirty-six liters.[5] As most commentators have noticed, the presence of the ephah in the context of the vision is problematic because an ephah is not large enough to contain a woman.[6] This disparity between the size of a woman and the limited size of an ephah has resulted in a number of interpretations.[7] Many have suggested that the ephah in the vision was larger than the size of a traditional ephah.[8] If the storage

---

[4] The verbal image of a cover is prompted by the round lead disk (כבר עפרת) that is lifted (נשאת) to reveal the woman inside the ephah. Though the issue is debated, most scholars suggest that the lead round is functioning as a lid in the vision, even if this was an atypical function for the weight (Boda, *Haggai, Zechariah*, 306; Edelman, "Proving Yahweh Killed His Wife," 337; Floyd, "Evil in the Ephah," 51; Meyers and Meyers, *Haggai, Zechariah 1–8*, 304; Niditch, *Symbolic Vision*, 167; Petersen, *Haggai, Zechariah 1–8*, 256; Sweeney, *Twelve Prophets*, 620; Uehlinger, "Die Frau im Efa," 97). Richly decorated round lids were known in Syria-Palestine and elsewhere in the ancient Near East (see esp. David Ben-Shlomo and Trude Dothan, "Ivories from Philistia: Filling the Iron Age I Gap," *IEJ* 56 [2006]: 1–38; M. Dothan, "A Decorated Ivory Lid from Tel Miqne-Ekron," *ErIsr* 27 [2003]: 83–90; Harry A. Hoffner Jr., "Hittite *Tarpiš* and Hebrew *Terāphîm*," *JNES* 27 [1968]: 61–68).

[5] According to Powell, the exact volume of the ephah varies between preexilic metrology and postexilic metrology. The preexilic ephah was used solely for dry measures and was probably between ten and twenty liters. Yet, based on the information from Ezek 45, the postexilic ephah was identified with the bath, which was typically used for liquid measures. Therefore, Powell suggests that in the early postexilic period an attempt was made to flatten the capacity measuring system between dry and liquid measures, probably under Babylonian influence (Marvin A. Powell, "Weights and Measures," *ABD* 6:897–908).

[6] Shlomo Marenof, "Note Concerning the Meaning of the Word 'Ephah,' Zechariah 5:5–11," *AJSL* (1931–1932): 264–67; Meyers and Meyers, *Haggai, Zechariah 1–8*, 296; Petersen, *Haggai, Zechariah 1–8*, 256; Uehlinger, "Die Frau im Efa," 96.

[7] A number of scholars have proposed a relationship between the frequent image of a "just" ephah elsewhere in the Hebrew Bible and the ephah in the present vision (e.g., Niditch, *Symbolic Vision*, 166–67; Petersen, *Haggai, Zechariah 1–8*, 256). This interpretation is supported by the images of the "lead round" (כבר עפרת) and the "stone of the lead" (אבן העפרת), both of which are related to the system of weights and balances. This interpretation, however, fails to explain the images of the latter half of the vision: the woman in the ephah, the winged creatures, the transportation of the ephah to Shinar, and the building of a temple.

[8] The Meyerses, Assis, and Love have tried to interpret the ephah in the context of the extraordinary elements of the other visions of First Zechariah. They have therefore all suggested that it may be the case that the ephah in the vision is extraordinarily large, such that it can fit an

device was considerably larger than an ephah, however, it seems strange that the vision would employ the term איפה at all, as it represents a very specific (and relatively small) measurement. Why not use the well-known and much larger חמר? In the preceding vision (Zech 5:1–4), the uncommonly large size of the scroll is detailed explicitly, and yet there is no such indication of an extraordinarily large ephah expressed in the ephah vision. The ephah depicted in the vision is thus most likely a typical ephah.[9] The question persists, however, as to why the ephah in the vision is such a small transportation device for a "woman," a topic to be discussed further below.

A number of scholars have sought to interpret the ephah in connection with cultic practice.[10] Scholars who attribute a cultic context to the ephah are influenced by the interpreting angel's identification of the ephah as "their guilt/eyes [עונם/עינם]" in all the land" (Zech 5:6). There is a text-critical problem at the heart of this statement, which makes for a difficult interpretation. The MT preserves עינם, while עונם is attested in the LXX and Syriac versions. Though many scholars have proposed maintaining the rendering of the MT,[11] it is probably best to understand the

---

adult woman (Assis, "Zechariah's Vision," 16 n. 30; Meyers and Meyers, *Haggai, Zechariah 1–8*, 297; Love, *Evasive Text*, 209).

[9] On this point see also Floyd, "Evil in the Ephah," 54–59; Sweeney, *Twelve Prophets*, 619; Eibert J. C. Tigchelaar, *Prophets of Old and the Day of the End: Zechariah, the Book of Watchers and Apocalyptic*, OtSt 35 (Leiden: Brill, 1996), 59–62; Uehlinger, "Die Frau im Efa," 94.

[10] On the basis primarily of his proposed relationship between the Hebrew term איפה and the Sumerian name E-pa, Shlomo Marenof proposed that the ephah designates the small, enclosed cella, often found at the top of a ziggurat ("Note Concerning 'Ephah,'" 265). Yet the translation of איפה as a term for a cult room atop a temple edifice is hardly warranted where it is used outside of Zechariah. It is therefore unlikely that the term refers to such a room in Zechariah. Others have identified the ephah as an object related to cultic observance by noting that elsewhere in the Hebrew Bible the ephah was used to carry grain offerings into the sanctuary (Boda, *Haggai, Zechariah*, 305; Meyers and Meyers, *Haggai, Zechariah 1–8*, 296). The only connection between the vision and grain offerings, however, is that provided by the presence of the ephah itself, which is not sufficient evidence to suggest a cultic identification. Noting a different sort of cultic association, Diana Edelman identifies the ephah as a coffin ("Proving Yahweh Killed His Wife," 338). Edelman does not provide an explanation of her proposition, noting only an article by Jeffrey Zorn ("Mesopotamian-Style Ceramic 'Bathtub' Coffins from Tell en-Nasbeh," *TA* 20 [1993]: 216–24), who describes several bathtub coffins of considerably differing sizes, ranging from 60 cm to 1.5 m in length with an average bathtub being approximately 95 cm long, 50 cm wide, and 50 cm high (218). The 200 liters of the average bathtub was more than five times the 36 liters of the postexilic ephah, which was itself more than a doubling of the preexilic ephah (Powell, "Weights and Measures," *ABD* 6:903). Even if the smallest bathtub Zorn discusses was supposedly representative of an ephah, it would have been 54 liters, which is still considerably larger than the postexilic ephah.

[11] Assis, "Zechariah's Vision," 25; Floyd, "Evil in the Ephah," 54–58; Meyers and Meyers, *Haggai, Zechariah 1–8*, 297–98; Sweeney, *Twelve Prophets*, 620–21. Of these, Assis is the only one who makes the proposition based on linguistic grounds. He suggests that the MT should be

statement of the interpreting angel in verse 6 in light of the angel's further comment in verse 8, identifying the "woman" in the ephah as "wickedness" (הרשעה). Several scholars have noted the association of רשעה with the veneration of deities other than YHWH.[12] Thus, the emendation to עונם after the LXX and Syriac versions is preferable, as it provides a close link between the ephah and its cargo.[13] Since the identification of the ephah as עונם is quite possibly contingent upon the identification of the "woman" inside it as הרשעה, the key issue for the passage is the identification of the "woman."

Unfortunately, the vision itself does not provide a clear identification of the "woman." The constellation of images surrounding her in the vision, however, might help clarify her identity. After the ephah with the "woman" inside departs from the temple, two winged women depart (יוצאת) from the temple to join the "woman." Their wings are described by the prophet as particularly storklike.[14] The two winged women immediately lift the ephah into the air and fly away with it. When asked by the prophet where the winged women are taking the "woman," the interpreting angel answers that they are tasked with transporting the woman and establishing her temple in Babylon. Scholars have offered a number of interpretations of the winged women, none of which has received widespread acceptance.[15]

---

preferred "because of the mismatch in this reading between the masculine noun עון and the feminine deictic זאת" (Assis, "Zechariah's Vision," 25). Floyd suggests that the lampstand in Zech 4:1–14 symbolically represents the *aniconic* presence of YHWH in the Jerusalem temple, which is positively envisioned as YHWH's royal rule, whereas the ephah serves as a "manifestation of divinity in human form," representing an alternative view of the divine "eye" based on an "'idolatrous' representation of divine royal rule" (Floyd, "Evil in the Ephah," 58–59). Yet non-anthropomorphic representation does not equate to aniconic representation. The lampstand thus iconically represents YHWH's divine presence in Zech 4:1–14. It is unlikely that Zech 4 would use an image as representative of YHWH's divine presence in order to convey a distaste for divine images.

[12] Christian Jeremias specifically identified the wickedness as "von der Verehrung anderer Gottheiten neben oder anstelle von Jahwe" (*Die Nachtgesichte des Sacharja*, 196). The Meyerses indicate that there are "several biblical passages in which 'wickedness' is associated with idolatry" (*Haggai, Zechariah 1–8*, 302). However, they preserve the reading of the MT in Zech 5:6. Sweeney proposes that the woman's identification as wickedness is appropriate "insofar as she represents a goddess figure" (*Twelve Prophets*, 621).

[13] The change from עונם to עינם is easily explained by confusion of *vav* and *yod*, a common scribal error preserved in the MT. For examples of *vav/yod* interchanges in the MT and Dead Sea Scrolls, see P. Kyle McCarter, *Textual Criticism: Recovering the Text of the Hebrew Bible* (Philadelphia: Fortress, 1986), 47; Emanuel Tov, *Textual Criticism of the Hebrew Bible*, 2nd ed. (Minneapolis: Fortress, 2001), 246–47; Tov, *Scribal Practices and Approaches Reflected in the Texts Found in the Judean Desert*, STDJ 54 (Leiden: Brill, 2004), 17.

[14] This feature has received considerable attention among commentators: Boda, *Haggai, Zechariah*, 307; Floyd, "Evil in the Ephah," 65–66; Love, *Evasive Text*, 205–14; Meyers and Meyers, *Haggai, Zechariah 1–8*, 206–7; Uehlinger, "Die Frau im Efa," 98.

[15] Assis proposes that, given his identification of the woman in the ephah as Samaria, the

Given the function of these winged women described by the interpreting angel, as well as the other visual aspects of the vision examined here, these women may be best understood as verbal instantiations of the visual phenomena of winged hybrid creatures, or *Mischwesen*, which are ubiquitous in ancient Near Eastern visual traditions. In these visual traditions such winged creatures—often partially anthropomorphic and partially theriomorphic in form—accompany deities as their divine attendant creatures, which both mark the presence of the deity and serve as tutelary figures. These visual traditions manifest in numerous artistic exemplars and are also known from ekphrastic[16] texts in the Hebrew Bible.

II. Winged Attendant Creatures in Text and Image

The motif of a deity with accompanying winged creatures was widely applied in biblical imagery, both ekphrastic and otherwise. Numerous ekphrastic texts in the Hebrew Bible portray the presence of YHWH as flanked by hybrid winged

---

two women represent "Israel and Judah" according to his principle "that all the female figures in the vision have something in common" ("Zechariah's Vision," 27–28). Edelman identifies them only as "heavenly minions," presumably tasked to do YHWH's bidding ("Proving Yahweh Killed His Wife," 335). The Meyerses identify the women as attendants of YHWH on the grounds that attendants of a goddess could not have "the power to carry her off" (*Haggai, Zechariah 1–8*, 306–7). Sweeney also identifies the women as attendants of YHWH (*Twelve Prophets*, 622). Floyd interprets the depiction of the women in light of his ironic reading of the vision and thus sees them as part of an unimpressive theophany of the "woman" in the ephah on analogy with YHWH's use of cherubim in theophanic texts ("Evil in the Ephah," 65–66). Uehlinger uses the distinctively storklike wings to identify the winged women. He proposes a parallel motif in Hittite, Neo-Assyrian, and biblical (Lev 14:49–53) purification rituals where birds are used to carry away impurities ("Die Frau im Efa," 98; cf. also David P. Wright, *The Disposal of Impurity: Elimination Rites in the Bible and in Hittite and Mesopotamian Literature*, SBLDS 101 [Atlanta: Scholars Press, 1987], 273 n. 150). The ritual described in Lev 14:49–53, however, is not related to temple impurity or to any sort of impurity prompted by unauthorized cultic practice. Moreover, Uehlinger's suggestion fails to explain the hybrid nature of the winged women, whose only avian characteristics are their wings.

[16] Ekphrasis is classically defined as a verbal representation of a visual representation. It is a rhetorical feature through which a visual object—or, more often, a work of visual art—is described verbally. See the definitions offered by Jaś Elsner, "Introduction: The Genres of Ekphrasis," *Ramus* 31 (2002): 1–18; Elsner and Shadi Bartsch, "Introduction: Eight Ways of Looking at an Ekphrasis," *CP* 102 (2007): i–vi; W. J. T. Mitchell, *Picture Theory: Essays on Verbal and Visual Representation* (Chicago: University of Chicago Press, 1994), 151–81; Ruth Webb, "Ekphrasis Ancient and Modern: The Invention of a Genre," *Word and Image* 15 (1999): 7–18.

creatures—the well-known כרבים.[17] In the ekphrastic texts describing the priestly tabernacle (Exod 25–31), two cherubim face each other, flanking the כפרת, with wings spread over it. That the presence of the deity is presupposed between the כרבים is made clear in Exod 25:22, which states that the deity delivers commands for the Israelites מעל הכפרת מבין שני הכרבים, "from over the mercy seat, from between the two cherubim" (cf. Num 7:89). Similarly, cherubim span the width of the inner sanctuary with wings outstretched in the art of the Solomonic temple (1 Kgs 6:23–28). The exact location of the divine presence relative to the cherubim is debated.[18] Several scholars have long contended that the presence of the deity was presupposed between the cherubim upon the inner wings of the cherubim, which served as the throne of YHWH.[19] The ark of the covenant, meanwhile, was situated under the inner wings of the two cherubim (1 Kgs 8:6–7; 2 Chr 5:7–8) and possibly served as the footstool of YHWH (1 Chr 28:2, Ps 132:7). This interpretation is likely influenced by the iconography of royal winged-sphinx thrones, known primarily through ancient visual depictions of such thrones. An example of one such image occurs on the well-known Late Bronze Age ivory plaque from Megiddo (fig. 1).[20] A similar scene is found on the sarcophagus of Ahiram, king of Byblos (fig. 2)

---

[17] For recent work on the biblical cherubim, see Raanan Eichler, "The Meaning of יֹשֵׁב הַכְּרֻבִים," ZAW 126 (2014): 358–71; and Alice Wood, Of Wings and Wheels: A Synthetic Study of the Biblical Cherubim, BZAW 385 (Berlin: de Gruyter, 2008).

[18] For a summary of the debate, see Eichler, "Meaning of יֹשֵׁב הַכְּרֻבִים," 358–65.

[19] Ronald S. Hendel, "The Social Origins of the Aniconic Tradition in Early Israel," CBQ 50 (1988): 365–82; Bernd Janowski, "Keruben und Zion: Thesen zur Entstehung der Zionstradition," in Ernten, was man sät: Festschrift für Klaus Koch zu seinem 65. Geburtstag, ed. Dwight R. Daniels, Uwe Glessmer, and Martin Rösel (Neukirchen-Vluyn: Neukirchener Verlag, 1991), 231–64; Othmar Keel, Jahwe-Visionen und Siegelkunst: Eine neue Deutung der Majestätsschilderungen in Jes 6, Ez 1 und 10 und Sach 4, SBS 84/85 (Stuttgart: Katholisches Bibelwerk, 1977), 15–45; Keel and Christoph Uehlinger, Gods, Goddesses, and Images of God in Ancient Israel, trans. Thomas H. Trapp (Minneapolis: Fortress, 1998), 167–73; Joel M. LeMon, Yahweh's Winged Form in the Psalms: Exploring Congruent Iconography and Texts, OBO 241 (Fribourg: Academic Press; Göttingen: Vandenhoeck & Ruprecht, 2010), 85–87; Tryggve N. D. Mettinger, No Graven Image? Israelite Aniconism in Its Ancient Near Eastern Context, ConBOT 42 (Stockholm: Almqvist & Wiksell, 1995), 19–20; Mettinger, "YHWH SABAOTH—The Heavenly King on the Cherubim Throne," in Studies in the Period of David and Solomon and Other Essays: Papers Read at the International Symposium for Biblical Studies, Tokyo, 5–7 December, 1979, ed. Tomoo Ishida (Winona Lake, IN: Eisenbrauns, 1982), 109–38.

[20] Keel and Uehlinger, Gods, Goddesses, and Images of God, 62, fig. 65, 168–69; LeMon, Yahweh's Winged Form, 6–7; Gordon Loud, The Megiddo Ivories, OIP 52 (Chicago: University of Chicago Press, 1939), pl. 4, 2a, and 2b. Given the relationship between thrones and royal imagery, it is understandable why ancient Levantine visual culture depicts cherub thrones as occupied almost exclusively by deities or kings (see Keel and Uehlinger, Gods, Goddesses, and Images of God, 168).

Figure 1. Ivory plaque, Megiddo, Late Bronze Age. Israel Museum, Jerusalem. © Erich Lessing / Art Resource, NY.

Figure 2. Sarcophagus of Ahiram, Byblos, thirteenth century BCE. National Archaeological Museum, Beirut. © Erich Lessing / Art Resource, NY.

These descriptions are corroborated by a plethora of texts describing visions of the deity with his winged attendant creatures. In the visions of Ezekiel, the hybrid anthropomorphic and theriomorphic features of the cherubim are described explicitly (Ezek 1:5–11; 10:8, 14, 21). These attendant creatures accompany the deity, whose divine radiance appears at least partially in anthropomorphic form (Ezek 1:26). The deity is seated on the throne (כסא), which is over the dome (רקיע) above the heads (על־ראשי) of the cherubim (Ezek 1; 10–11).[21] The imagery of these

[21] See the discussions of Eichler, "The Meaning of יֹשֵׁב הַכְּרֻבִים," 359–61; and Wood, *Of Wings and Wheels*, 50, 61–84, 95–139.

visions evokes the iconography of the royal winged-sphinx thrones even more than the ekphrastic descriptions of the cherubim "throne" from 1 Kings. In such a context, the divine presence remains simultaneously above (על) and between (בין) the cherubim. Similarly, YHWH rides upon the cherubim in the Song of David (2 Sam 22; Ps 18),[22] and the winged hybrid seraphim (שרפים) attend the enthroned representation of YHWH in Isa 6.[23]

In these examples, the texts provide clues to the identification of the hybrid creatures as the attendant creatures of the deity. In the visions of Ezekiel, the cherubim carry the glory (כבוד) of YHWH as it prepares to depart from the temple (Ezek 9–11). Wherever YHWH moves he is accompanied by his attendant cherubim, who use their wings to bear the deity through the air (Ezek 1:12, 24; 10:5, 16, 19; 11:22). The cherubim also offer fire to the man clothed in linen in obedience to YHWH's command (Ezek 10:7). Similarly, the cherubim use their wings to bear YHWH through the sky in the Song of David (2 Sam 22:11, Ps 18:10). The seraphim stand in attendance (עמדים) "above him" (ממעל לו), chant affirmation of the holiness of YHWH, and interact with Isaiah prior to YHWH's addressing Isaiah directly (Isa 6:2–3, 6–7). Likewise, these texts emphasize the foreboding presence of the creatures as fitting attendant creatures of YHWH. In the visions of Ezekiel, the cherubim move as fast as lightning (1:14) and the tumultuous (המלה) sound of their wings is equated with the sound of mighty water, the voice of the Almighty (שדי), and the sound of an army (1:24, 10:5). Similarly, in the vision of Isaiah the voices of the seraphim shake the door pivots of the stone sill (אמות הספים) in the temple (Isa 6:4). These textual features thus create a notion of these hybrid creatures as foreboding beasts who accompany YHWH to attend him, including serving as a primary mode of transportation.

Alongside these textual representations from the Hebrew Bible are numerous visual images of deities accompanied by winged hybrid creatures from the visual cultures of the ancient Near East. Such objects are attested throughout the Levant, extending also to Anatolia and Mesopotamia. While its interpretation has been

---

[22] There are slight variations in each account of the Song of David. Though the MT preserves the reading of a single cherub in both accounts, other versions, including the LXX and targumim, preserve the plural. As noted above, the verbal image of YHWH accompanied by attendant cherubim (plural) is far more common in the Hebrew Bible. For further discussion, see Stephen A. Geller, *Parallelism in Early Biblical Poetry*, HSM 20 (Missoula, MT: Scholars Press, 1979), 172; Frank Moore Cross and David Noel Freedman, "A Royal Song of Thanksgiving: II Samuel 22 = Psalm 18," *JBL* 72 (1953): 15–34, https://doi.org/10.2307/3261627; Douglas K. Stuart, *Studies in Early Hebrew Meter*, HSM 13 (Missoula, MT: Scholars Press, 1976), 184; Wood, *Of Wings and Wheels*, 88.

[23] Though the exact image of the שרפים in Isa 6 has remained a topic of debate, it is clear that the attendant creatures are winged hybrid creatures. For a variety of identifications, see John Day, "Echoes of Baal's Seven Thunders and Lightnings in Psalm XXIX and Habakkuk III 9 and the Identity of the Seraphim in Isaiah VI," *VT* 29 (1979): 143–51; Karen R. Joines, "Winged Serpents in Isaiah's Inaugural Vision," *JBL* 86 (1967): 410–15, https://doi.org/10.2307/3262795; Keel and Uehlinger, *Gods, Goddesses, and Images of God*, 272–74.

debated, one such object is the well-known tenth-century BCE terra-cotta stand from Taanach (fig. 3). The stand contains winged hybrid animals in its second and fourth registers—the former bear anthropomorphic heads whereas the latter appear to be wholly theriomorphic. These winged quadrupeds, identified by many as cherubim, flank what are arguably nonanthropomorphic representations of a deity, possibly YHWH.[24]

The visual motif is exceptionally well preserved in luxury ivory plaques, alluded to in the Hebrew Bible (see 1 Kgs 10:8, 22:39, Amos 6:4, Ezek 27:6).[25] These ivories come predominantly from workshops representing the distinct styles of Phoenicia, South Syria, and North Syria.[26] Indicative of the style known from North Syria, which has a tendency toward crowded, ill-proportioned images, is an ivory from Megiddo (fig. 4). The ivory depicts a winged hybrid creature flanking a sacred tree. The plaque preserves only half of the complete image—only one winged

---

[24] The representations in the second and fourth registers are possibly representations of YHWH—one in the form of a sun disc, the other in the form of a void (David Noel Freedman, review of *The Rise of Yahwism: The Roots of Israelite Monotheism*, by J. C. deMoor, and *The Early History of God: Yahweh and the Other Deities in Ancient Israel*, by Mark S. Smith, *JBL* 110 [1991]: 693–98, here 698, https://doi.org/10.2307/3267667; Judith M. Hadley, *The Cult of Asherah in Ancient Israel and Judah: Evidence for a Hebrew Goddess*, UCOP 57 [Cambridge: Cambridge University Press, 2000], 172–76; Tryggve N. D. Mettinger, "The Veto on Images and the Aniconic God in Ancient Israel," *SIDA* 10 [1979]: 15–29, here 27; Glen Taylor, *Yahweh and the Sun: Biblical and Archaeological Evidence for Sun Worship in Ancient Israel*, JSOTSup 111 [Sheffield: JSOT Press, 1993], 24–37). On the other, less-well-known tenth-century BCE terra-cotta stand from Taanach, similar winged quadrupeds also flank a central image of a stylized tree flanked by ibexes (Susan Ackerman, "At Home with the Goddess," in *Symbiosis, Symbolism, and the Power of the Past: Canaan, Ancient Israel and Their Neighbors from the Late Bronze Age through Roman Palaestina*, ed. William G. Dever and Seymour Gitin [Winona Lake, IN: Eisenbrauns, 2003], 455–68, here 456; Hadley, *Cult of Asherah*, 153, 165–69, 172; Othmar Keel, *Goddesses and Trees, New Moon and Yahweh*, JSOTSup 261 [Sheffield: Sheffield Academic, 1998], 41; Keel and Uehlinger, *Gods, Goddesses, and Images of God*, 154–55).

[25] The motif also occurs on numerous other types of visual objects from throughout ancient Near East, including wall reliefs, seals of all kinds, plaques, and cult stands. For examples and a brief discussion of such an array of objects, see LeMon, *Yahweh's Winged Form*, 27–58.

[26] Richard D. Barnett, *Catalogue of the Nimrud Ivories in the British Museum: With Other Examples of Ancient Near Eastern Ivories in the British Museum* (London: Trustees of the British Museum, 1957), 43; Barnett, "Phoenician and Syrian Ivory Carving," *PEQ* (1939): 4–19; Keel and Uehlinger, *Gods, Goddesses, and Images of God*, 234; Irene J. Winter, "Establishing Group Boundaries: Toward Methodological Refinement in the Determination of Sets as a Prior Condition to the Analysis of Cultural Contact and/or Innovation in the First Millennium BCE Ivory Carving," in *Crafts and Images in Contact: Studies on Eastern Mediterranean Art of the First Millennium BCE*, ed. Claudia E. Suter and Christoph Uehlinger, OBO 210 (Fribourg: Academic Press; Göttingen: Vandenhoeck & Ruprecht, 2005), 23–42; Winter, "Phoenician and North Syrian Ivory Carving in Historical Context: Questions of Style and Distribution," *Iraq* 38 (1976): 1–22; Wood, *Of Wings and Wheels*, 181.

Figure 3. Terra-cotta stand, Taanach, tenth century BCE. Israel Museum, Jerusalem. © Zev Radovan, Jerusalem.

Figure 4. Ivory plaque, Megiddo, ninth or eighth century BCE. Israel Museum, Jerusalem. © Erich Lessing / Art Resource, NY.

FIGURE 5. Ivory plaque, Nimrud, eighth or seventh century BCE. The Metropolitan Museum of Art, New York. Photograph courtesy of the Metropolitan Museum of Art, New York, Rogers Fund, 1964.

creature and half of the sacred tree on each ivory.[27] An ivory from Nimrud, depicting another human-headed winged sphinx, is indicative of the Phoenician style, which is typically better balanced and more sophisticated than its North Syrian counterpart (fig. 5).[28] This ivory bears iconography similar to that attested in fig. 4 inasmuch as the sphinx faces the sacred tree. In the Nimrud ivory, however, the sphinx tramples a nude human who reaches out for the sacred tree. It is likely that this iconographic element suggests that the attendant creature was effective in protecting the tree. Stylistically, this protective feat barely affects the attendant creature, whose body remains in the standard striding position and whose anthropomorphic face remains impassive. Thus, while the North Syrian style emphasizes the massive size and disproportionately imposing presence of the sphinx, the Phoenician style focuses attention on the majesty and elegance of the creature.[29] Each style attempts to portray the attendant creature differently, yet in a way that

---

[27] Irene J. Winter, "Is There a South Syrian Style of Ivory Carving in the Early First Millennium B.C.?," *Iraq* 43 (1981): 101–30.

[28] The more sophisticated style of the Phoenician works has been noted primarily by identifying Egyptian elements in their artistry (Barnett, *Catalogue of the Nimrud Ivories*, 62, 155–61; Barnett, "The Nimrud Ivories and the Art of the Phoenicians," *Iraq* 2 [1935]: 185–99; Keel and Uehlinger, *Gods, Goddesses, and Images of God*, 234; Winter, "Phoenician and North Syrian Ivory Carving," 1–11; Wood, *Of Wings and Wheels*, 181).

[29] Winter, "Phoenician and North Syrian Ivory Carving," 7–8.

communicates that the sphinx is a fitting creature to guard the deity, represented in each depiction as the sacred tree.

Two ivories from Arslan Tash highlight variations in anthropomorphic and nonanthropomorphic representations of deities and their attendant creatures (fig. 6 and fig. 7). In fig. 6 the two hybrid theriomorphic creatures, typically identified

FIGURE 6. Ivory plaque, Arslan Tash, ninth century BCE. National Museum, Aleppo. © Erich Lessing / Art Resource, NY.

FIGURE 7. Ivory plaque, Arslan Tash, eighth century BCE. Musée du Louvre, Paris. © Musée du Louvre, Dist. RMN-Palais / Raphael Chipault / Art Resource, NY.

as ram-headed griffins, are completely without anthropomorphic characteristics. Likewise, the deity is here represented as the sacred tree (i.e., nonanthropomorphic). In contrast to the figures considered thus far, which contained nonanthropomorphic representations of the deity and limited anthropomorphic characteristics of the attendant creatures, fig. 7 depicts two winged anthropomorphic creatures flanking an anthropomorphic image of an infant Horus on a raised lotus flower.[30] This ivory is indicative of a style known as South Syrian or Intermediate, which is described as being between the well-balanced Phoenician style and the ill-proportioned North Syrian style.[31] The two winged creatures are facing each other with their wings outstretched over the central image of the male deity. The iconography of the ivory portrays the wings of the creatures forming an enclosed circle around the deity, which likely suggests a tutelary function of these creatures.[32] The two winged creatures are represented as anthropomorphic with the exception of their wings, while the deity is represented completely in anthropomorphic form.

In summary, the motif of a deity with winged hybrid attendant creatures is well known in the visual cultures of the ancient Near East as well as in the biblical textual tradition. Differences in both the biblical textual tradition and the ancient Near Eastern visual tradition include variations in the anthropomorphic and theriomorphic characteristics of the attendant creatures and depictions of deities in anthropomorphic and nonanthropomorphic forms. The textual tradition preserves literary features that hint at the particular attendant roles the creatures fulfilled and that describe the foreboding presence of the divine attendant creatures. Likewise in the visual tradition, a range of visual features such as styles, compositions, and iconographies contributed to a notion of the attendant creatures as tutelary figures, fit to protect both the deity and the deity's realm.

III. Image in Text: Interpreting the Ephah Vision

Many of the enigmatic features of the ephah vision seem to accord well with the tradition in both its textual and its visual manifestations. Given these continuities,

---

[30] This ivory is part of a related series of ivories discovered at Arslan Tash, which were originally interpreted by François Thureau-Dangin to represent the birth of Horus (François Thureau-Dangin et al., eds., *Arslan-Tash*, Bibliothèque archéologique et historique 16 [Paris: Paul Geuthner, 1931], 92–97). The series also contains five plaque fragments depicting a sacred tree flanked by winged women (Winter, "Is There a South Syrian Style of Ivory Carving," 104).

[31] Georgina Herrmann, *Commentary and Catalogue*, vol. 1 of *Ivories from Room 37 Fort Shalmaneser*, Ivories from Nimrud (1949–1963) 4 (London: British School of Archaeology in Iraq, 1986), 6; Winter, "Is There a South Syrian Style of Ivory Carving," 6–17.

[32] In offering a typology of wing iconography in Syro-Palestinian art, LeMon has argued that wings, whether on birds or on numinous hybrid creatures, commonly function as a sign of protection (*Yahweh's Winged Form*, 27–58).

it seems appropriate to interpret these as textual manifestations of this broader ancient Near Eastern motif. The winged women are thus likely the winged hybrid attendant creatures of the "woman." This identification seems to be confirmed not only by their description as winged hybrid creatures but also by the tasks they perform for the "woman."[33] Just as the cherubim do with YHWH in the biblical textual tradition, these hybrid anthropomorphic creatures bear the "woman" through the sky. The winged women are also given the other attendant duty of the construction of a temple (בית) dedicated to the "woman" in Shinar (i.e., Babylon). Once the temple is completed the "woman" will rest (הניחה) upon her base (על־מכנתה) in her temple, undoubtedly with her attendant creatures alongside, reminiscent of YHWH resting on his throne in his temple with his attendant creatures in the visions of Ezekiel and Isaiah.

Returning to the question of the identity of the "woman" in view of these continuities with the tradition and the portrayal of such hybrid creatures as the attendant creatures of deities, I suggest that the "woman" between the winged hybrid attendant creatures is almost certainly a deity. According to the terminology of the vision (i.e., אשה), the "woman" was likely represented as anthropomorphic in form. The relatively small size of a traditional postexilic ephah precludes the possibility that the "woman" in the ephah is the size of an adult woman. Since the representation of the goddess is anthropomorphic in form and since it is unlikely that the ephah in the vision is larger than a traditional postexilic ephah, the "woman" in the vision is probably either a miniature human woman or a cult image in the form of a woman. It seems unlikely that the "woman" in the vision is a miniature human, given that her size is intimated only by the relatively small size of the ephah and is not expressed in more explicit language, such as is found elsewhere in the visions of Zechariah to describe the unusual size of objects (Zech 5:1–4).[34] It is more likely that the "woman" is an anthropomorphic cult image. This conclusion is supported by other evidence from within the vision. The "woman" in the vision never performs any action but is only acted upon: the "woman" is transported by her winged attendant creatures in a transportation device (v. 9) and is lifted and thrown by the interpreting angel (v. 8).[35] Moreover, the final image of the vision is

---

[33] Jeremias rightly identifies the *Mischwesen* as "in den Darstellungen altorientalischer Kunst," which he substantiates by listing a considerable number of Mesopotamian and Syro-Palestinian images testifying to the iconographic tradition of winged creatures (*Die Nachtgesichte des Sacharja*, 199 n. 19). He does not, however, recognize the creatures as the attendant creatures of the "woman" in the vision, a problem shared by Boda (*Haggai, Zechariah*, 307).

[34] Uehlinger has likewise suggested that the visions present a consistent, imaginable realism and that, therefore, a miniature living woman would be outside this scope of realism ("Die Frau im Efa," 96).

[35] Zechariah 5:7 indicates that the "woman" was sitting in the ephah, but this is almost immediately followed by the interpreting angel throwing her back into the ephah (v. 8). The vision thus implies that the interpreting angel removed the "woman" from the ephah before throwing her back in.

the "woman" resting upon her base in her Babylonian temple, a position reserved for cult images.

The identification of the ephah vision as representing the deportation of an anthropomorphic cult image raises another question about how the ephah vision fits into the literary context of First Zechariah. Michael H. Floyd has noted the importance of comparing the motifs of the ephah vision with common motifs in the vision of the lampstand (Zech 4:1–14).[36] In the lampstand vision, the prophet sees a bowl with seven lamps atop a gold lampstand flanked by two olive trees, which pour oil through golden pipes into the bowl atop the lampstand. The interpreting angel identifies the seven lamps as the seven eyes of YHWH (v. 10) and the two olive trees as "two anointed ones" (שני בני־היצהר) who stand by the "Lord of the whole earth" (אדון כל־הארץ, v. 14). Though the identification of the two olive trees is debated, most scholars agree that the lampstand represents the reestablished presence of YHWH in the temple, thus locating the vision of the lampstand in the temple sanctuary.[37] This nonanthropomorphic representation of YHWH is part of a recurrent theme throughout First Zechariah depicting the return of the presence of YHWH to Jerusalem.[38]

In the context of the ephah vision, the prior location of the ephah—and, more importantly, the anthropomorphic cult image it contains—in the Jerusalem temple indicates that the cult dedicated to the "woman" in the ephah had been previously established in the temple.[39] The interpreting angel's identification of her transportation device as עונם suggests the removal of the totality of "their" veneration of the unnamed goddess in the temple.[40] The immediate context provides no clear ante-

---

[36] Floyd, "Evil in the Ephah," 52–53. Sweeney (*Twelve Prophets*, 619–20) reiterates the points made by Floyd.

[37] Floyd, "Evil in the Ephah," 53; Jeremias, *Der Nachtgesichte des Sacharja*, 180–81; Meyers and Meyers, *Haggai, Zechariah 1–8*, 272–77; Niditch, *Symbolic Vision*, 104–7; Petersen, *Haggai, Zechariah 1–8*, 227–28; Sweeney, *Twelve Prophets*, 612–13.

[38] Zech 1:16–17; 2:4–5, 10–13; 3:9; 4:14; 6:12–13, 15; 8:3, 8, 9, 15, 21–23.

[39] Floyd agrees, though he hesitates to say anything except that the cult image was used in the temple ("Evil in the Ephah," 67–68). Sweeney proposes that the "woman" was the "Queen of Heaven" from Jer 44 and Ezek 8, whom he identifies as Ishtar (*Twelve Prophets*, 620). In his identification Sweeney follows Margaret Barker, "The Evil in Zechariah," *HeyJ* 19 (1978): 12–27; and Mathias Delcor, "La vision de la femme dans l'Epa de Zach, 5:5–11 à la lumière de la littérature hittite," *RHR* 187 (1975): 137–45. Tigchelaar agrees that the "woman" is a goddess but suggests the possibility that she represents "goddesses as such" and thus resists any particular identification of the "woman" (*Prophets of Old*, 61).

[40] Petersen comments, "If *rišʿāh* can be used to describe the improper act, then *ʿāwôn* refers to the sin guilt incurred by such action" (*Haggai, Zechariah 1–8*, 257). Though Petersen's nuanced understanding of עון is too narrow, his interpretation of the terms as a reference to the specific sin and the collective implication of the sin is helpful. Gary Anderson proposes that, when the term עון is used in collocation with the verb נשא, it has a primary and a secondary meaning—"sin" and "punishment," respectively (*Sin: A History* [New Haven: Yale University Press, 2009], 16–26). Anderson suggests that the conditions determining whether עון will take its primary or secondary

cedent for the third-person masculine plural suffix on עון in Zech 5:6, which has led to disparate identifications of the cultic violators.[41] It is most likely that the third-person masculine plural suffix refers to those who performed the past cultic violation associated with the goddess in the ephah. Thus, the totality of their cultic betrayal could refer to the veneration of the goddess in the temple dedicated to YHWH prior to its destruction.

The return of the presence of YHWH to the Jerusalem temple presumably precipitates the deportation of the divine presence of the goddess to Babylon. Several scholars interpret this deportation of the "woman" as the removal of idolatry in preparation for YHWH's return to the temple.[42] Undoubtedly this interpretation is a reaction to the identification of the "woman" in the ephah as הרשעה by the

---

meaning are always contextual but contingent on the contextual meaning of the term נשא, which can mean either to "bear/carry" or to "forgive." Central to his explanation of the term עון is that it indicates a *burden* that must be borne, thus the result of previous action. Anderson's work builds on the earlier work of Baruch Schwartz ("Term or Metaphor: Biblical *nōśē ʿăwōn/pešaʿ/ḥeṭ*" [Hebrew], *Tarbiz* 63 [1994]: 149–71; and Schwartz, "The Bearing of Sin in Priestly Literature," in *Pomegranates and Golden Bells: Studies in Biblical, Jewish, and Near Eastern Ritual, Law, and Literature in Honor of Jacob Milgrom*, ed. David P. Wright, David Noel Freedman, and Avi Hurvitz [Winona Lake, IN: Eisenbrauns, 1995], 3–21).

[41] The Meyerses propose that the third-person masculine plural suffix refers to the "two females," which they explain by suggesting that the suffix is a survival of the dual form, which does not distinguish masculine from feminine (*Haggai, Zechariah 1–8*, 298). It should be noted that the Meyerses maintain the MT עינם, which they suggest refers to the visibility of the ephah. Yet it is difficult to understand why the interpreting angel would specify that the ephah is visible to creatures who have not yet appeared in the vision. Sweeney suggests that, "although the referent for 'their' is not specified, it would have to refer to the Persian authorities who ruled Judah from Babylon, to which the woman in the ephah is about to be sent" (*Twelve Prophets*, 620). Sweeney's unique suggestion is based on his preservation of "their eye" in Zech 5:6, which he juxtaposes with the "eyes of YHWH" in 6:10. The new worshipers of the goddess in Babylon, however, are not referred to anywhere in the context of the vision, let alone being identified as Persian authorities. In addition, it is unclear why the ephah, as the eyes of Persian officials, would be held in contrast with YHWH's eyes if the woman—not the ephah—is representative of the goddess.

[42] Boda, *Haggai, Zechariah*, 308; Jeremias, *Die Nachtgesichte des Sacharja*, 195–96; Meyers and Meyers, *Haggai, Zechariah 1–8*, 313–16. The use of the lid to cover the ephah has been a main contributing factor for many scholars who have proposed that the "woman" represents collective idolatry. In Hittite mythological and incantation texts, bronze cauldrons with lead lids were used in connection with the capturing of spirits or demons in the depths of the sea and the netherworld (see Wright, *Disposal of Impurity*, 263–64). Hoffner suggests that in the incantation texts "whatever is put into those cauldrons and covered with the lead lids cannot under any circumstances ever come up out again" ("Hittite *Tarpiš* and Hebrew *Terāphîm*," 66). The Hittite texts do not help clarify the contents of the ephah in the vision, as the contents of the cauldrons in the Hittite texts vary considerably. One mythological text contains a list of things that are put into the cauldron, which includes an evil spirit/demon, bloodshed, sorrow, tears, grief, and disease (Delcor, "La vision de la femme dans l'épha," 141–43; Hoffner, "Hittite *Tarpiš* and Hebrew *Terāphîm*," 65). Though the Hittite texts do not help identify the woman, they do clarify the function of the lead round as a lid.

interpreting angel. Nonetheless the interpretation of the "woman" as collective idolatry leaves three important questions unanswered: (1) Why is the deity in the temple at the time of YHWH's return depicted as a "woman"? (2) Why does the vision employ familiar ancient Near Eastern imagery representing a single deity?[43] And (3) if the goddess represents condemnable idolatry, why is her cult deported and reestablished elsewhere instead of being destroyed in Jerusalem?[44]

The simplest answer to the first two questions is likely that the "woman" is a venerated goddess from Judah's past. The established place of the goddess in the temple in Jerusalem at the time of her deportation may provide a clue to her identity. In the record of Manasseh's cultic misdeeds, he established פסל האשרה in the Jerusalem temple along with the other altars he had set up in it (2 Kgs 21:7).[45] Though אשרה in the Hebrew Bible typically refers to the wooden cult object, it appears that this Asherah was a cult image, given the common function of פסל,[46] and likely anthropomorphic in form.[47] The move from the representation of Asherah by the nonanthropomorphic wooden cult object to an anthropomorphic representation is consistent with a general proliferation of anthropomorphic representations of deities in the eighth and seventh centuries.[48] Though the image of the goddess Asherah was recorded as being established in the temple during the reign of Manasseh, her cult apparently persisted in Judah at least until the cult reforms of Josiah and likely until the destruction of the temple.[49] While it is far

---

[43] The only images of divine presence in all of the visions of First Zechariah are the visions of YHWH's divine presence and the vision of the "woman" in 5:5–11.

[44] This question prompted the entire work of Assis, which resulted in his identification of the "woman" in the ephah as Samaritans ("Zechariah's Vision," 17).

[45] Many have suggested that this occurrence is the earliest record of an anthropomorphic representation of a deity being placed in the temple in Jerusalem (Mordechai Cogan and Hayim Tadmor, *II Kings: A New Translation with Introduction and Commentary*, AB 11 [Garden City, NY: Doubleday, 1988], 268; Menahem Haran, *Temples and Temple-Service in Ancient Israel: An Inquiry into the Character of Cult Phenomena and the Historical Setting of the Priestly School* [Oxford: Clarendon, 1977; repr., Winona Lake, IN: Eisenbrauns, 1985], 278–79).

[46] Christoph Dohmen, "פסל," *TDOT* 12:30–38; Frederick E. Greenspahn, "Syncretism and Idolatry in the Bible," *VT* 54 (2004): 480–94.

[47] Keel and Uehlinger note that the "linen clothing" woven by the female temple personnel for the cult image in 2 Kgs 23:7 accords well with iconographic evidence from Iron Age IIC that nearly exclusively depicts the female form of goddesses as clothed (*Gods, Goddesses, and Images of God*, 336). See also Hadley, *Cult of Asherah*, 72–74; for a survey of additional perspectives on 2 Kgs 21:7, see 68–71.

[48] Keel and Uehlinger note the isolated anthropomorphic representations of a goddess in the eighth century BCE, with a proliferation in the seventh century BCE (*Gods, Goddesses, and Images of God*, 198–204).

[49] Though Josiah's destruction of the cult objects related to the worship of Asherah (2 Kgs 23:4, 6–7) may have resulted in a break in Asherah veneration in the temple in Jerusalem, the historian indicates that all the kings of Judah after Josiah leading up to the destruction of the temple performed "evil in the eyes of YHWH" according to the practice of their ancestors (2 Kgs

from certain that the "woman" is Asherah, there is one additional detail in the vision that further suggests it as a possible identification. The interpreting angel identifies the woman as הרשעה. The interpreting angel's use of this term to identify the "woman" is possibly a play on words. הרשעה and אשרה are separated phonetically only by metathesis of the ר and ש.[50] Identifying the "woman" as הרשעה can thus be seen simultaneously as an indictment of her cult and nearly a statement of her name. Asherah could therefore fit the location of the "woman" in the temple, the depiction of the "woman" as female, and the reason that the "woman" is depicted in a manner commonly used to represent a single deity.[51]

Yet the final question still remains. Why was her cult deported and set up in Babylon? The deportation of divine images is mentioned elsewhere in the Hebrew Bible. According to 2 Chr 25:14-16, after defeating the Edomites, Amaziah brought

---

23:32, 37; 24:9, 19). This seems to presume a resumption of Manasseh's policies with regard to the cult (see Hadley, *Cult of Asherah*, 59; Ziony Zevit, *The Religions of Ancient Israel: A Synthesis of Parallactic Approaches* [New York: Continuum, 2001], 476). Though the historian does not say so explicitly, it is likely the case that one of these kings reestablished the cult of Asherah in the temple in Jerusalem.

[50] This point is noted also by the Meyerses (*Haggai, Zechariah 1-8*, 303) and Edelman ("Proving Yahweh Killed His Wife," 336).

[51] There remains considerable disagreement over the identification of Asherah as an Israelite goddess. Many scholars interpret the cumulative biblical, archaeological, inscriptional, and iconographic data as sufficient to suggest that there was a goddess Asherah in monarchic Israel (see Susan Ackerman, *Under Every Green Tree: Popular Religion in Sixth-Century Judah*, HSM 46 [Atlanta: Scholars Press, 1992]; John J. Collins, *The Bible after Babel: Historical Criticism in a Postmodern Age* [Grand Rapids: Eerdmans, 2005], 99-129; John Day, *Yahweh and the Gods and Goddesses of Canaan*, JSOTSup 265 [Sheffield: Sheffield Academic, 2000], 42-67; William G. Dever, *Did God Have a Wife? Archaeology and Folk Religion in Ancient Israel* [Grand Rapids: Eerdmans, 2005]; Hadley, *Cult of Asherah*; Keel and Uehlinger, *Gods, Goddesses, and Images of God*; Saul M. Olyan, *Asherah and the Cult of Yahweh in Israel*, SBLMS 34 [Atlanta: Scholars Press, 1988]; Zevit, *Religions of Ancient Israel*; among many others). Other scholars, however, interpret these data as dissociated from the earlier West Semitic goddess by the biblical period (see J. A. Emerton, "'Yahweh and His Asherah': The Goddess or Her Symbol?" *VT* 49 [1999]: 315-37; Christian Frevel, *Aschera und der Ausschliesslichkeitsanspruch YHWHs: Beiträge zu literarischen, religionsgeschichtlichen und ikonographischen Aspekten der Ascheradiskussion*, 2 vols., BBB 94, [Weinheim: Beltz Athenäum, 1995]; P. Kyle McCarter Jr., "Aspects of the Religion of the Israelite Monarchy: Biblical and Epigraphic Data," in *Ancient Israelite Religion: Essays in Honor of Frank Moore Cross*, ed. Patrick D. Miller, Paul D. Hanson, and S. Dean McBride [Philadelphia: Fortress, 1987], 137-55; Mark S. Smith, *The Early History of God: Yahweh and the Other Deities in Ancient Israel*, 2nd ed. [Grand Rapids: Eerdmans, 2002]; among others). There is, of course, a distinction to be made between actual cultic practice in monarchic Judah and postexilic retrospective rumination on the possible reasons for cultic violations by prior, preexilic generations. It seems entirely reasonable that the author of First Zechariah could associate the cultic misdeeds of the generation that saw the exile with "this one woman," whose presence in the temple is attested in multiple places in the biblical tradition, regardless of the historical metaphysics of אשרה in monarchic Judah.

the gods of the people of Seir back to Judah, where he instituted their cult. In this text, much as with the goddess of the ephah vision, not only were the statues themselves brought to a different place, but they were also set up in that new place for resumed veneration. Similarly, in Jer 48:7 the prophet portends that Chemosh will go forth into exile with his priests and his attendants, thus indicating the deportation of the totality of his cult. Likewise, the goddess in the ephah vision is accompanied by her attendant creatures in her deportation to Babylon indicating the removal of the entirety of her cult and, more importantly, the locus of her presence.[52] In this regard, the removal of the divine presence of the goddess is quite similar to Ezekiel's vision of the presence of YHWH leaving the Jerusalem temple, accompanied by his attendant cherubim (Ezek 8–11).

IV. Conclusion: Texts and Images

I have argued that the ephah vision of Zechariah draws on a common ancient Near Eastern motif of deities accompanied by their hybrid attendant creatures, attested in both text and image. Up to this point I have reserved the question of *how* the vision takes up the visual motif into its verbal rhetoric. As alluded to above, the vision, while expansively descriptive, allows some elements of the visual motif to remain implicit. The description of the winged women takes up an entire verse (v. 9), with emphasis on their anthropomorphic form, their storklike wings, and their bearing of the ephah into the sky by means of their wings capturing the wind. Moreover, the interpreting angel offers further description of their role vis-à-vis the "woman" in response to Zechariah's question (vv. 10–11). This notable visual description is juxtaposed with the complete lack of visual description of the "woman," who is described only as "sitting" (יושבת). And yet the presence of hybrid creatures attending to an individual in the context of the vision as a whole is remarkably reminiscent of the motif of deities and their attendant creatures explored above.

---

[52] The deportation of divine images and entire cults is also notably mentioned in two Akkadian *ex eventu* prophetic texts—the Marduk prophecy and the Uruk prophecy. The Marduk prophecy is a prophetic reflection of the removal of the cult of Marduk from Babylon three times after each of three conquests of Babylon in the mid- to late second millennium BCE. The Uruk prophecy tells of the deportation of the *lamassu* (i.e., the protective goddess) of Uruk and her cult to Babylon by an unjust king. The cult of the *lamassu* remains instituted in Babylon until a just king arises who returns the *lamassu* and her cult to Uruk. It is likely that the just king who returned the *lamassu* was Nebuchadnezzar II, which probably locates the production of this text in the late Neo-Babylonian period (Hermann Hunger and Steven A. Kaufman, "A New Akkadian Prophecy Text," *JAOS* 95 [1975]: 371–75; and Matthew Neujahr, *Predicting the Past in the Ancient Near East: Mantic Historiography in Ancient Mesopotamia, Judah, and the Mediterranean World*, BJS 354 [Providence, RI: Brown Judaic Studies, 2012], 27–41, 50–58).

The vision seems to rely on features well attested in both visual and textual manifestations of this motif, to which it alludes through inclusion of these visual phenomena in its textualized vision. In this way the vision might be characterized as ekphrasis, which in antiquity included not only verbal descriptions of visual works of art but also people or visual experiences. A complete discussion of the poetics of ekphrasis in the vision is, unfortunately, outside the scope of this article. Yet at this point it is necessary to acknowledge that the verbal articulation of the prophet's visual experience includes a dynamic interaction between the visual and the verbal (i.e., image and text). Thus, while knowledge of the motif can help interpret some of the enigmatic features of the vision as images in text as explored here, further consideration of the poetics of ekphrasis in visionary contexts remains an important desideratum of future research.

JOHN THE BAPTIST IN HISTORY AND THEOLOGY
Joel Marcus

"No one can understand the historical Jesus without first coming to grips with John the Baptist. In a study that is massively researched, brimming with insights, and engagingly written, Joel Marcus has provided a compelling account that should be the definitive statement of our generation."—Bart D. Ehrman, University of North Carolina at Chapel Hill

296 pp., hc and ebook, $59.99

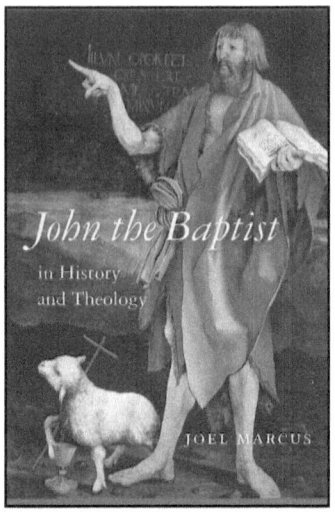

BATHSHEBA SURVIVES
Sara M. Koenig

"Although Bathsheba appears in a mere seventy-six verses in the Hebrew Bible, her character survives in ways that are at once fascinating and surprising, and Sara Koenig is an astute and delightful guide to the material. Deftly moving between the Bible, art, music, theology, politics, film, fiction, and television, Koenig brings Bathsheba to life over and over again by sensitively elucidating the ways a wide range of interpreters have brought their particular concerns, questions, and creative energies to the text."—Amy Erickson, Iliff School of Theology

192 pp., 20 b&w illus., hc and ebook, $49.99

To Order: 800-537-5487
www.uscpress.com

Manuscript, Voice, and the Construction of Pseudepigraphal Identities: Composing a Mutable David in Some Qumran Psalms Scrolls

GREGORY PETER FEWSTER
greg.fewster@mail.utoronto.ca
University of Toronto, Toronto, ON M5R 2M8, Canada

Through an analysis of varying configurations of the persona of David in some Qumran scrolls, I argue for an approach to the study of ancient pseudepigraphy that prioritizes manuscripts over reconstructed and idealized literary works. Three data sets ground the study: three fragments from Cave 4 that contain Pss 33 and 69; 4Q522, a paraphrase of Joshua that incorporates Ps 122; and finally two groupings of 11QPs[a], the Ascents collection and the material following "David's Last Words." I observe how the "I" voice of a given psalm or group of psalms joins third-person description to constitute David's authorial persona in ways distinctive to the text inscribed on a given manuscript. Accordingly, this article aligns with studies that see the enlargement and mutability of authorial figures in the expanding archive of early Jewish literature and with more recent calls to view texts as material objects that reflect their context of production.

Many manuscripts found among the Qumran scrolls contain psalms, and some of these are explicitly associated with authorial figures, including David. The objective of this article is to inquire into the mutability of the image of David through different compositional strategies and editorial arrangements of psalmic material. I engage with a number of recent developments in the study of pseudepigraphy in early Judaism, many of which observe the development and enlargement of ideal figures through ascribed qualities and roles. These largely literary assessments of the development of pseudepigraphal identities could benefit from a more materialist approach to early Jewish pseudepigraphy, and the pseudepigraphal construction of David among Qumran psalms scrolls offers an opportunity to explore this dynamic.

I argue that the production of pseudepigraphal authorial identities in the psalms emerges dynamically from a synthesis between third-person description and the authorial "I" voice of the psalms themselves. Third-person description that ascribes a psalm to David or engages in more detailed narration produces expectations for the reading of the following psalm(s) and thus rebounds back onto the Davidic persona itself. In order to illustrate this dynamic and diverse relationship, I will explore three sets of data: three psalm fragments from Cave 4, the inclusion of Ps 122 in a paraphrase of Joshua (4Q522), and two larger groupings in 11QPs^a. While it is true that over time pseudepigraphal identities, such as that of David, accumulate and develop shape and detail, different aspects of this persona are selected and enhanced in a variety of manuscripts.

I. Pseudepigraphy and Authorship in Early Judaism

An important development in the study of Jewish literature is the recognition that attribution itself is a rather late development, preceded by the production of anonymous texts.[1] Such a shift in compositional practice raises questions about the motivations and strategies associated with attribution—pseudepigraphal attribution in particular—though challenges to those questions persist.[2] One way of approaching this question, attested in the recent work of Bart Ehrman, understands false attribution of ancient texts to be forgery or a species of literary deceit.[3] Years

---

[1] See Annette Yoshiko Reed, "Pseudepigraphy, Authorship and the Reception of 'the Bible' in Late Antiquity," in *The Reception and Interpretation of the Bible in Late Antiquity: Proceedings of the Montréal Colloquium in Honour of Charles Kannengiesser, 11–13 October 2006*, ed. Lorenzo DiTommaso and Lucian Turcescu, Bible in Ancient Christianity 6 (Leiden: Brill, 2008), 467–90, here 476; Karel van der Toorn, *Scribal Culture and the Making of the Hebrew Bible* (Cambridge: Harvard University Press, 2009), 28, 31–33. This view replaces an earlier one, in which false or misattribution as a compositional strategy deviated from earlier practices of authentic attribution.

[2] Scholars identify various challenges facing the study of Jewish pseudepigraphy, many of which derive from Christian and modern Western ideas about Scripture and authorship. Eibert J. C. Tigchelaar ("Forms of Pseudepigraphy in the Dead Sea Scrolls," in *Pseudepigraphie und Verfasserfiktion in frühchristlichen Briefen / Pseudepigraphy and Author Fiction in Early Christian Letters*, ed. Jörg Frey et al., WUNT 246 [Tübingen: Mohr Siebeck, 2009], 85–101, here 85–89) suggests that the category of apocryphal/pseudepigraphal texts derives from Christian views of a chronologically prior and closed canon, while Michael E. Stone ("The Dead Sea Scrolls and the Pseudepigrapha," *DSD* 3 [1996]: 270–95, here 270) points to the Protestant roots of the category. Hindy Najman states that such a view of pseudepigraphy stems from modern notions of authorship and textual ownership (*Seconding Sinai: The Development of Mosaic Discourse in Second Temple Judaism*, JSJSup 77 [Leiden: Brill, 2003], 1–7). Alternatively Devorah Dimant suggests that part of the reason that the categories have remained in use is because many of the previously unknown texts from Cave 4 have remained unpublished for so long ("Apocrypha and Pseudepigrapha at Qumran," in *History, Ideology and Bible Interpretation in the Dead Sea Scrolls: Collected Studies*, FAT 90 [Tübingen: Mohr Siebeck, 2014], 153–70, here 153–54).

[3] See Bart D. Ehrman, *Forgery and Counterforgery: The Use of Literary Deceit in Early Christian Polemics* (Oxford: Oxford University Press, 2013); and a specific discussion of his

earlier, Morton Smith suggested that blanket uses of the language of forgery can detract from serious historical study of pseudepigraphal texts.[4] However, he continued to use the term, articulating a distinction between false attribution (forgery) and misattribution.[5] Smith's distinction is a productive one, although the interest in pseudepigraphy as forgery addresses a certain set of questions that focus on issues of authorial and editorial intention. But these are not the questions prompting this article, which asks: what is the significance of associating texts with authorial figures and how are such identities constructed and leveraged? In order to address these questions, I draw upon two phenomena treated in recent scholarship: ancestral/founders discourse and textual agglomeration.

In *Seconding Sinai*, Hindy Najman treats examples of "Mosaic discourse" found in several texts, including Deuteronomy, Jubilees, and the Temple Scroll (11QT). She argues that creative rewriting of Sinaitic revelation (i.e., the giving and interpretation of the Torah) is the operation of a "founders discourse."[6] Rather than take credit for their interpretation of the law, the composers of those texts situated their interpretive exercises in the activity and experience of Moses, the founder of nomic discourse.[7] Similar attributive strategies appear in texts such as 4 Ezra and in material associated with David, as Najman and Eva Mroczek argue.[8] In these instances, new texts draw on qualities and activities ascribed to these and other characters from earlier literature in ways that are relevant to contemporary challenges facing Judean communities. Accordingly, 4 Ezra is able to construct a figure that encapsulates the various roles (scribe, teacher, prophet, and lawgiver) that are required to help members of the Jewish community recover an idealized past of Torah observance.[9] In David's Compositions (4QPs^a XXVI–XXVII), David

---

typology of forgery in "Apocryphal Forgeries: The Logic of Literary Deceit," in *Fakes, Forgeries, and Fictions: Writing Ancient and Modern Christian Apocrypha*, ed. Tony Burke (Eugene, OR: Cascade, 2017), 33–49.

[4] Morton Smith, "Pseudepigraphy in the Israelite Literary Tradition," in *Pseudepigrapha I: Pseudopythagorica: Lettres de Platon, Litterature pseudépigraphique juive*, vol. 1 of *Pseudepigrapha*, ed. Kurt von Fritz, Entretiens sur l'Antiquité classique 18 (Geneva: Vandoeuvres, 1971), 191–215, here 192–93. For Smith, psalms serve as a primary example of misattribution (195–96).

[5] Ibid., 194–95.

[6] Najman here appeals to Michel Foucault's treatment of authorship and the author function. In particular, Foucault discusses the activity of the authorial claim, whereby a writer claims to represent what a particular figure associated with that kind of discourse would have said. See Najman, *Seconding Sinai*, 9–13; Michel Foucault, "What Is an Author?," in *Textual Strategies: Perspectives in Post-Structuralist Criticism*, trans. Josué V. Harari (Ithaca, NY: Cornell University Press, 1979), 141–60.

[7] See Najman, *Seconding Sinai*, 16–17, where she notes four features of Mosaic discourse.

[8] See esp. Eva Mroczek, *The Literary Imagination in Jewish Antiquity* (Oxford: Oxford University Press, 2016).

[9] Hindy Najman with Itamar Manoff and Eva Mroczek, "How to Make Sense of Pseudonymous Attribution: The Case of 4 Ezra and 2 Baruch," in *A Companion to Biblical Interpretation in Early Judaism*, ed. Matthias Henze (Grand Rapids: Eerdmans, 2012), 308–36, here 312–15;

operates as the ideal scribe of liturgy who inaugurates psalmic activity, whereby the scribes who emulate him are legitimized in their production of new and revised texts.[10]

For both Najman and Mroczek, pseudepigraphy functions through scribal attempts to emulate ideal figures of antiquity, often in an effort to validate sets of responses to contemporary events. When rewritten in newly composed texts, these figures often accumulate idealized qualities that had not previously been associated with them. If the invocation of an ideal figure such as Moses facilitates a certain connection with the past, it is the particular construction of that pseudepigraphal identity in that text that enables the connection. These studies demonstrate instances where new texts conflate virtues and qualities into a single figure. This article will explore the inverse.

Loren Stuckenbruck has made a similar intervention with respect to Enochic literature; his attention to the compositional histories of texts enhances our ability to conceive of the development of pseudepigraphic identities. He notes that some of the earliest invocations of the Enoch character use him as a means of opening up a long-past, though ostensibly significant, period of time. Anonymous scribes grounded their insights about the present in the antediluvian period, enabling readers to reconceptualize the present through an imagined past.[11] Enochic literature is an interesting place to explore these dynamics since it is a tradition subject to a lengthy and complex textual history. As Stuckenbruck notes, the earliest stratum (1 En. 6–11) of the Book of the Watchers (1 En. 1–36) contains no mention of Enoch. As the Enochic "I" began to be imposed upon this third-person narrative, that "I" took on a sort of pseudepigraphal momentum.[12] The result was an assemblage of generic blending that produced a complex and contoured set of Enochic images, including that of the scribe (e.g., 1 En. 12:4–5; 13:6; 15:1; 91–108). The Enochic corpus thus poignantly illustrates the way in which the agglomeration and collection of literary materials produces complex pseudepigraphal identities.[13]

Najman, *Past Renewals: Interpretive Authority, Renewed Revelation and the Quest for Perfection in Jewish Antiquity*, JSJSup 53 (Leiden: Brill, 2010), 236–42.

[10] See esp. Eva Mroczek, "Moses, David and Scribal Revelation: Preservation and Renewal in Second Temple Jewish Textual Traditions," in *The Significance of Sinai: Traditions about Sinai and Divine Revelation in Judaism and Christianity*, ed. George J. Brooke, Hindy Najman, and Loren T. Stuckenbruck, TBN 12 (Leiden: Brill, 2008), 100–108; Mroczek, "Psalms Unbound: Ancient Concepts of Textual Tradition in 11QPsalms^A and Related Texts" (PhD diss., University of Toronto, 2011), 137–84. Jed Wyrick also understands David's Compositions to emphasize the scribal activity of David in consonance with his status as a composer of psalms (*The Ascension of Authorship: Attribution and Canon Formation in Jewish, Hellenistic, and Christian Traditions*, HSCL 49 [Cambridge: Harvard University Press, 2004], 90–92).

[11] Loren T. Stuckenbruck, "The Epistle of Enoch: Genre and Authorial Presentation," *DSD* 17 (2010): 387–417, here 395–96.

[12] Ibid., 397–99.

[13] See also the discussion by Michael Knibb, concerning the pluriformity of "books of

The pseudepigraphal connection to ancestral discourse contributes to an exercise of imagination that encourages further and continued use of pseudepigraphal identities. While Najman and Mroczek have emphasized pseudepigraphy as the appeal to and construction of idealized figures associated with certain types of activities, Stuckenbruck has demonstrated how textual agglomeration and the blending of literary forms contributes to a complex and contoured imagining of the pseudepigraphal figure. Pseudepigraphal attribution was not necessarily a feature of the texts' initial composition. Rather, pseudepigraphal identities were constructed and accentuated over time. While pseudepigraphy as a literary strategy may be evocative of authorship, set in the context of textual composition and transmission, it may be conceived of as an emergent feature of editorial activity.[14] Put another way, as editors redact texts through agglomeration and collection, the production of a pseudepigraphal identity appears alongside and as a result of that editorial activity.

Stuckenbruck's insight emerges from reconstructing redactional activity and thus imagining the historical movement of a fluctuating text. In contrast, I take a materialist turn, whereby manuscripts themselves become the primary data from which I discuss the construal of pseudepigraphal identities. Liv Ingeborg Lied distinguishes between three terms: work, text, and manuscript. Whereas "text" simply refers to words on a page, "manuscripts" are material artifacts that contain texts, and "works" are complete and idealized textual entities.[15] The distinction between "work" as an idealized text and "manuscript" as a material artifact is crucial, as it directs attention to the configuration of texts in material objects and the demands those particular configurations make on their being read. Further, the emphasis on manuscripts recognizes the human labor required to produce manuscripts without relying on appeals to editorial intention as definitive of pseudepigraphal identity.

II. Pseudepigraphy in the Psalms and Psalm Manuscripts from Qumran

Since composing and redacting literary works contributed to the development of an authorial persona, as seen in works including Deuteronomy, Jubilees, 1 Enoch,

---

Enoch" reflected in the existing manuscript witnesses and various versions ("The *Book of Enoch* or *Books of Enoch*: The Textual Evidence for *1 Enoch*," in *Essays on the Book of Enoch and Other Early Jewish Texts and Traditions*, SVTP 22 [Leiden: Brill, 2009], 36–55).

[14] This contrasts with Karel van der Toorn's statement that "Pseudepigraphy is the doing of the author; attributed authorship is the work of the editor" (*Scribal Culture*, 36).

[15] See Liv Ingeborg Lied, "Text–Work–Manuscript: What Is an 'Old Testament Pseudepigraphon,'" *JSP* 25 (2015): 150–65, here 152–53. As we will see concerning the book of Psalms, its existence and status as a "work" are highly contested. This distinction is useful here, even when scholars allow for a considerable degree of fluctuation and variation in their conception of the book of the Psalms as a "work."

and 4 Ezra, the same can be said of psalm materials. The character of such redaction, however, should not be overdetermined by a conception of an ideal or authoritative "book of Psalms." Accordingly, I consider here psalms as smaller textual units that underwent extensive compilation and redaction, apparent in manuscripts of the psalms.[16] Many of the psalm manuscripts also include introductory material that can be read as a type of authorial incipit. Although these incipits do not claim authorship in a historical sense, they produce an association with particular figures that, in the period from which these fragment derive, can be called "authorial."[17] While it is difficult to say what effect psalm collections might have on the construction of authorial personas, the fragmentary state of these psalms manuscripts provides an opportunity to think about the effect of authorial incipits upon a given psalm's pseudepigraphal character.[18] As in the MT Psalter, the

---

[16] Here I follow Mika Pajunen's recent argument that the Qumran psalms collective attestation to a "book of Psalms" is a "statistical illusion" ("Perspectives on the Existence of a Particular Authoritative Book of Psalms in the Late Second Temple Period," *JSOT* 392 [2014]: 139–63). See similar arguments in Mroczek, *Literary Imagination*, 38–44. Rather, the scrolls merely attest to the existence of individual psalms and groupings of psalms as parts of larger collections. Cave 4, Cave 1, and Cave 11 especially contained numerous fragments of previously known and unknown psalms dating from a range of periods. Unfortunately, little remains of the Cave 4 fragments, yet Patrick W. Skehan, Eugene Ulrich, and Peter W. Flint note that, upon early examination, Hartmut Stegemann considered some of the fragments (e.g., 4QPs^a, 4QPs^c) to be the remains of full Psalters. It is not clear what is meant here by a "full Psalter." See Skehan, Ulrich, and Flint, "Psalms," in *Qumran Cave 4.XI: Psalms to Chronicles*, by Eugene Ulrich et al., DJD XVI (Oxford: Clarendon, 2000), 7–170, here 7–8, 49.

[17] Brevard S. Childs notes that "whatever the expression לדוד may once have meant, the claim of authorship now seems most probable" ("Psalm Titles and Midrashic Exegesis," *JSS* 16 [1971]: 137–50, here 138). It is unlikely that the preposition ל attached to names like דוד was originally authorial attribution. The meaning of the preposition is broad enough to indicate dedication or attribution, and calling a psalm "of David" does not necessarily signal authorship. This is evident in psalms like Ps 51, which uses the ל in potentially two senses (i.e., to the director and of David). Childs, however, alludes to subsequent interpretations of these incipits that take them as authorial attribution. He notes also incipits that locate the psalm in David's life. Additionally, the tradition of attributing to David authorship of psalms emerges in works like David's Compositions, rabbinic tradition, and some Greek translations of the psalms that used the genitive rather than the dative. See Albert Pietersma, "David in the Greek Psalms," *VT* 30 (1980): 213–26, here 213–18, on this latter point. See also Sigmund Mowinckel, *The Psalms in Israel's Worship* (Grand Rapids: Eerdmans, 1962), 76–78; and Mroczek, *Literary Imagination*, 58–61, who especially troubles the idea that the preposition ל should be considered "authorial" but points to expanded psalm headings and additional literatures that place the given composition "in David's mouth."

[18] As Childs notes, while the psalm incipits have been largely ignored by historical critics for providing information about the composition of the psalms because of their secondary character, they still can provide insight pertaining to their reception and the exegetical activity directed toward them ("Psalm Titles and Midrashic Exegesis," 137).

Qumran psalms have a considerable range of authorial attribution. Familiar incipits mention David, the sons of Asaph, the sons of Korah, and so on. There are also a number of other psalms, unknown before the discovery of the scrolls, that bear unfamiliar or less-familiar authorial incipits such as תהלה לעבדיה (a psalm of Obadiah, 4Q380).[19]

Moshe Bernstein suggests that psalms are often instances of what he calls "decorative pseudepigraphy" in contrast to "authoritative" or "convenient" pseudepigraphy, all of which refer to the extent to which a text makes use of authorial attribution.[20] This set of designations recognizes that pseudepigraphy is not a monolithic category with singular intentions and strategies. Rather, it emphasizes that the relationship between authorial attribution, the authorial voice, and the content of the text varies in strength. By calling individual psalms instances of decorative pseudepigraphy, Bernstein indicates that the attribution "is not organic to the text and often the supposed author is linked to the text only by the title."[21] He does not give this label to all psalms, however. He notes that Ps 151A is an example of strong pseudepigraphy, whereby the Davidic attribution is maintained by the contents of the psalm. In order to analyze a given psalm's pseudepigraphical character, Bernstein's model draws a sharp distinction between the expectations established by a prose incipit and the extent to which the following psalm confirms or draws from that expectation.

Bernstein is correct to draw attention to this relationship. In doing so, however, he construes the addition of an authorial incipit as an authority-conferring function, dependent on an already robust and established persona that could simply be attached to an existing text or be generative of a new text. But, as shown by Najman, Mroczek, and Stuckenbruck, authorial personas, even of an ancient figure, are both dependent on existing traditions about that figure and produced by

---

[19] The most well known are probably the psalms found in 4Q380 and 4Q381, first edited by Eileen Schuller. Four of them bear authorial incipits: 4Q380 1 II, 8 תהלה לעבדיה, "a psalm of Obadiah"); 4Q381 24, 4 (ם[הי]תהלה לאיש האל, "a psalm of a man of God"); 31, 4 (תפלה ל...מ[לך], "a prayer of ... king"); 33 + 35, 8 (תפלה למנשה מלך יהודה, "a prayer of Manasseh, king of Judah"). See Eileen M. Schuller, *Non-Canonical Psalms from Qumran: A Pseudepigraphic Collection*, HSS 28 (Atlanta: Scholars Press, 1986).

[20] See Moshe Bernstein, "Pseudepigraphy in the Qumran Scrolls: Categories and Functions," in *Pseudepigraphic Perspectives: The Apocrypha and Pseudepigrapha in Light of the Dead Sea Scrolls; Proceedings of the International Symposium of the Orion Center for the Study of the Dead Sea Scrolls and Associated Literature, 12–14 January, 1997*, ed. Esther G. Chazon and Michael E. Stone, STDJ 31 (Leiden: Brill, 1999), 1–26, here 18. Authoritative pseudepigraphy appeals to the name of a famous character in antiquity to lend authority to a literary work, such as the halakic interpretation of the Torah. Convenient pseudepigraphy is slightly weaker than authoritative techniques, where an authorial ascription lends some weight to a strong authorial "I," such as in testamentary literature. Finally, decorative pseudepigraphy bears no ostensible relation to the contents of the text itself (3–7).

[21] Ibid.

the text that has received this attribution.²² The editorial production of pseudepigraphal texts constructs an authorial tradition as much as it responds to one. Thus, for psalms, there is a dialectic between the authorial attribution and the content of the psalm itself that propels an interpretation of the psalm in the context of the psalmist's life and developing image of that psalmist. This is precisely what we see in later compositions as David is perceived as the psalmist par excellence and psalms are composed (e.g., Ps 151) that reflect a more consonant relationship between incipit and content.²³

This statement can be supported by a more diverse and detailed analysis of psalms as pseudepigrapha. Bernstein's notion of decorative pseudepigraphy implicitly appeals to a disjunction of voice between authorial incipit and the psalm itself, suggesting that at least the ancient psalms were given their incipit at some point in the history of their transmission. This disjunction of voice pivots on a linguistic distinction between third-person discourse and first-person discourse. Without the third-person voice, the reader is forced to make meaning by reading into the expressions of the authorial "I" in the psalm. By contrast, the third-person description reflected in an authorial incipit draws the reader outside the psalm for a brief moment, functioning almost narratively for the reader. The "narrator" constructs readerly expectation through the third-person voice and through its superscriptive position. Thus, the ability for the reader to identify the voice of the psalm is now guided by the incipit.

The strength of a pseudepigraphon (i.e., its authorial construction) is not dependent on one of these voices at the expense of the other. Rather, as I will explore with the following two psalms from Cave 4 (Ps 69 and Ps 33), it is the relationship between the two that contributes to the construction of the authorial identity. Crucial for these readings is an appreciation of the status of each Qumran manuscript as an artifact. The material (including textual) particularities of each scroll and scroll fragment need not be understood as features that more or less accurately reflect an ideal composition. Rather, each of these manuscripts reflects editorial decisions and accidents of transmission that make demands on how it can be read.²⁴ These scrolls, in various ways, materially configure a Davidic persona.

---

²²Mroczek also observes that many scholars have tended to propose the attribution of authority as a rationale for pseudonymous attribution (*Literary Imagination*, 52–53). She notes, however, that attribution may simply celebrate or develop the image of a figure or, following Reed ("Pseudepigraphy, Authorship," 477), that attribution may position the figure as a tradent or guarantor of a tradition.

²³See Mroczek, *Literary Imagination*, 78–85, for a discussion of the expansion of the Jewish imaginary of David, which includes his role as composer of psalms.

²⁴See, e.g., the programmatic essay by Hugo Lundhaug and Liv Ingeborg Lied, "Studying Snapshots: On Manuscript Culture, Textual Fluidity, and New Philology," in *Snapshots of Evolving Traditions: Jewish and Christian Manuscript Culture, Textual Fluidity, and New Philology*, ed. Liv Ingeborg Lied and Hugo Lundhaug, TUGAL 175 (Berlin: de Gruyter, 2017), 1–19.

Psalm 69:1–19 is found in col. III of 4QPsᵃ, and its incipit includes the expected לדויד but also bears what is likely musical instruction, למנצח על שושנים ("To the director, according to Lilies").²⁵ In keeping with Bernstein's category "decorative pseudepigraphy," there is nothing in the psalm that connects with what we know about the life of David, except perhaps that the enigmatic phrase from Ps 69:9, כי קנא[ת ביתכה] אכלתני ("zeal for your house has consumed me," 4QPsᵃ III, 30) could be connected with David's temple preparation. It is not, however, a potential connection to the historical David that creates the Davidic quality of the psalm. Rather, the simple incipit softly associates the psalm with David—perhaps even as the source of the words. The effect of this association is the positioning of David as the type of person who is oppressed by his many enemies and can only call on YHWH for deliverance. In fact, this is a sentiment offered in many other Davidic psalms and, as we will see, is integral to the construction of Davidic personas in 11QPsᵃ.

Portions of Ps 33 are attested in 4QPsᵃ and 4QPsᵍ, following the final verses of Ps 31 without Ps 32 intervening.²⁶ These two fragments, however, can be distinguished by the inclusion of the Davidic incipt לדויד שיר מזמור ("Of David. A Song. A Psalm") in 4QPsᵍ, which does not appear in the 4QPsᵃ or in the MT. The question remains, What effect does the presence or absence of the incipit have on the reading of the psalm and its construction of a Davidic persona?

4QPsᵃ 4 I: Ps 31:23–25 → Ps 33:1²⁷

ואני אמרתי בחפזי נגרזתי מנגד עיניכ[ה	] 3
אהבו את יהוה כול חסידי[ו אמנם] נ[וצר	] 4
[יהוה ומשלם על יתר עשה גאוה חזקו ויאמץ לבבכם כול המיחלים ליהוה]	] 5
[³³רננו צדיקים ביהוה לישרים נאוה תהלה הודו ליהוה בכנור בנבל [עשור זמרו לו	] 6

    3 [And I said in my haste, "I am cut off from your sigh]t."
    4 [Love the Lord, all who are belove]d. [T]he faithful ones
    5 [the Lord preserves, and repays with abundance those who are proud. Be strong and have courage in your heart, all of you who wait on the Lord.]
    6 [Praise the Lord, righteous ones. To the upright, praise is fitting. Thank the Lord with the lyre, with the harp of] ten strings make melody to him.

---

²⁵ See the text in Skehan, Ulrich, and Flint, "Psalms," 20.
²⁶ Skehan, Ulrich, and Flint note that the provenance of 4QPsᵍ has been disputed. It was initially acquired from bedouin, and some scholars consider it to be from among the Naḥal Ḥever finds. Further investigation, however, has confirmed J. T. Milik's initial assessment that it came from Cave 4 (Skehan, Ulrich, and Flint, "Psalms," 145).
²⁷ Text is from Skehan, Ulrich, and Flint, "Psalms," 12; my translation.

4QPsq I: Ps 31:24–25 → Ps 33:1[28]

1 [33]נוצר יהוה ומשלם על יתר עו[שה גא[וה ח[ז[ק[ו ויאמץ ל[ב[בכם כול המיחלים ליהוה
2 [   ] [   ]   לדויד שיר מזמור
3 רננו צדיקים ביהוה לישרים נ[אוה תהלה[ ]הוד[ו לי]ה[ו]ה בכנור בנבל
עשור זמרו לו שירו

1 [the LORD preserves, and repays with abundance those who ar]e pro[ud.] B[e] stro[ng and have courage] in your [h]eart, all of you who wait on the LORD.]
2 [ ] [ ]Of David. A Song. A Psalm.
3 [Praise the LORD, righteous ones. To the upright, prais]e is fitting.[ ]Than[k th]e Lo[R]D with the lyre, with the harp of ten strings make melody to him, singing.

Gerald Wilson has argued that, throughout books 1–3 of the MT Psalter, psalms lacking an incipit function as an extension of the psalm that preceded it. He observes a number of thematic relations between Pss 32 and 33 that suggest that together they performed a liturgical function early on in their transmission history. Wilson suggests that the variation in the incipit in these two fragments from Qumran points to diverse attempts to negotiate the absence of a superscription for Ps 33.[29] This proposal, which would hold only if Ps 31 in 4QPsa had a Davidic incipit (as it does in the MT), suffers since thematic linkages between Pss 31 and 33 are not as strong as between Pss 32 and 33. On the other hand, at least one scribe considered Ps 33 worthy of its very own Davidic attribution.

Notably, Ps 33 does not maintain a strong "I" voice in the same way that we saw with Ps 69. Instead, it is overwhelmed with imperatives that call for praising YHWH for all the impressive things he has done. The beginning of this psalm makes several references to musical instruments, including a lyre (הודו ליהוה בכנור, "Thank the LORD with the lyre," v. 2), a ten-stringed harp (לו בנבל עשור זמרו, "with the harp of ten strings make melody to him," v. 2) and strings (היטיבו נגן, "play the stringed instrument well," v. 3). Without the Davidic incipit, these references fit comfortably within general liturgical practices of playing instruments to YHWH. With the inclusion of the Davidic incipit, however, these references correlate to the tradition of David the musician. Especially if we envision a liturgical context for Ps 33, in the version in 4QPsq, the skillful playing of music in praise of YHWH for his mighty acts was overlaid with David's own example of doing the same.

These examples illustrate in part the way in which an authorial incipit works together with the content of the psalm to construct an authorial identity. This is not a consistent synergy, however, since the strength and direction of the authorial voice vary from psalm to psalm. Further, the presence or absence of an authorial

---

[28] Text is from Skehan, Ulrich, and Flint, "Psalms," 147; my translation.
[29] Gerald H. Wilson, "The Use of 'Untitled' Psalms in the Hebrew Psalter," *ZAW* 97 (1985): 404–13, here 405–8.

incipit of the same psalm greatly alters the readers' reception of the authorial voice. This sort of shifting between the authorial "I" and third-person description is fairly simple in the context of a single psalm or a collection of psalms, but pseudepigraphal identities accumulate great contour and complexity in larger and more complete compositions.

III. David as the Fulfillment of Joshua in 4Q522

As Mroczek observes, manuscripts of the psalms reflect an interesting variety of genres and uses. While some manuscripts do not leave clear evidence of their initial compositional shape, there are at least four examples of psalm manuscripts that likely did not appear in a Psalter.[30] I am interested here in 4Q522, a fragment that many have argued belonged to a literary composition often given the title Apocryphon of Joshua.[31] Regardless of whether 4Q522 is part of a larger work, the twenty-six fragments of the document comprise a manuscript that tells the story of Joshua and the conquest of Canaan. But this manuscript also includes Ps 122.

4Q522 should not be called a Davidic pseudepigraphon in the sense of a whole work being attributed to David, since the Davidic attribution of the psalm in frag. 22 is an isolated instance of construing a Davidic voice.[32] Rather, it is Joshua's voice

---

[30] Eva Mroczek, "The Hegemony of the Biblical in the Study of Second Temple Literature," *JAJ* 6 (2015): 2–35, here 7–13.

[31] Two manuscripts, 4Q378 and 4Q379, are the most secure witnesses to this reconstructed work, accompanied by 4Q522. Carol A. Newsom proposed the title Apocryphon of Joshua in her edition of those two manuscripts ("'The Psalms of Joshua' from Qumran Cave 4," *JJS* 39 [1988]: 56–73; Newsom, "4Q378 and 4Q379: An Apocryphon of Joshua," in *Qumranstudien: Vorträge und Beiträge der Teilnehmer des Qumranseminars auf dem internationalen Treffen der Society of Biblical Literature, Münster, 25.–26. Juli 1993*, ed. Heinz-Josef Fabry, Armin Lange, and Hermann Lichtenberger, SIJD 4 [Göttingen: Vandenhoeck & Ruprecht, 1996], 35–85). Others have suggested additional texts for inclusion, and it was Tov who first validated the notion that there were six manuscripts (4Q123, 4Q378, 4Q379, 5Q9, 4Q522, and Mas 1039-211) that should be considered collectively to constitute the Apocryphon. Although he would prefer to give the work the name "paraphrase of Joshua," he continues with the term "apocryphon" since it is by now well established in the literature ("The Rewritten Book of Joshua Found at Qumran and Masada," in *Biblical Perspectives: Early Use and Interpretation of the Bible in Light of the Dead Sea Scrolls: Proceedings of the First International Symposium of the Orion Center for the Study of the Dead Sea Scrolls and Associated Literature, 12–14 May 1996*, ed. Michael E. Stone and Esther G. Chazon, STDJ 28 [Leiden: Brill, 1998], 233–56, here 233). Most recently, Ariel Feldman has argued that five of the manuscripts enumerated by Tov (not including the text from Masada) belonged to five separate compositions. For Feldman, the implication is that the book of Joshua was subject to rich exegetical activity (*The Rewritten Joshua Scrolls from Qumran: Texts, Translations, and Commentary*, BZAW 438 [Berlin: de Gruyter, 2014], 187–93).

[32] The first line is barely discernible, but the hook and lower portion of the final *dalet* in לדויד are quite evident in the top right-hand corner of the fragment. See Émile Puech, *Qumran Cave*

that emerges strongly in preceding fragments. Fragment 9 of 4Q522, however, provides the largest remaining portion of the text that includes both a speech of Joshua and a transition that introduces David as an important figure. This fragment retains portions of two columns; the first includes a list of place-names that had been conquered and remained to be conquered by Joshua. Emanuel Tov suggests that column II, beginning with the mention of Sinai, continues on from the previous column in describing towns that Joshua had not conquered.[33] The mention of Sinai facilitates the transition to a speech by Joshua that justifies the fact that he did not conquer Jerusalem or establish the tent of meeting, thereby anticipating David's future military success and the establishment of the temple by David and Solomon.[34]

Neither David nor Solomon is mentioned by name; the text uses circumlocutions.[35] But the text is not entirely favorable toward Joshua either. He admits fault for not consulting God through the Urim and Thummim, which allowed him to be deceived by the Canaanites (II, 9–12). Devorah Dimant suggests, therefore, that the "passage implies criticism of Joshua for infringement of the Torah, and praise for David and Solomon as the ideal rulers who carried out the divine purpose to the full."[36] The text positions David and his nation- and temple-building activity to overshadow Joshua's only partial nation-building activity, with the inclusion of Ps 122 at the end of 4Q522 contributing most significantly to David's prominence.[37] David's voice is immediately foregrounded by the incipit "A Song of Ascents, of

---

4.XVIII: Texts hébreux (5Q521–4Q528, 4Q576–4Q579), DJD XXV (Oxford: Clarendon, 1998), 68; Puech, "Un autre fragment du Psaume 122 en 4Q522 (4Q522 26)," *RevQ* 20 (2001): 129–32, here 130–32, for a reconstruction. The second article by Puech includes a fifth fragment of the psalm (the twenty-sixth of the entire manuscript) that had been previously thought to be part of 4Q538. An English edition is also included in Skehan, Ulrich, and Flint, "Psalms," 169–70; Feldman, *Rewritten Joshua Scrolls*, 151.

[33] See Tov, "Rewritten Book of Joshua," 242–44. These place-names, however, differ from what is found in Joshua (Feldman, *Rewritten Joshua Scrolls*, 153).

[34] Tov, "Rewritten Book of Joshua," 244–45. This basic reading is followed also in Devorah Dimant, "The *Apocryphon of Joshua*—4Q522 9 ii: A Reappraisal," in *History, Ideology and Bible Interpretation*, 348–51.

[35] David is referred to as the son of Jesse, the son of Perez, the son of Judah (כי הנה בן נולד ליש̇י בן פרץ בן יה[ודה], 9 II, 3), and Solomon is later referred to as his (i.e., David's) youngest son (ובנו הקטן, 9 II, 6). Instead, the text highlights the priestly figures who will serve at the temple, namely, Zadok and the sons of Phinehas (II, 6–7).

[36] Dimant, "*Apocryphon of Joshua*," 351.

[37] Feldman considers the inclusion of an entire psalm in a work of "rewritten Bible" unusual, and along with Tov remains incredulous as to why Ps 122 would be included in the composition. Why is Jerusalem being praised in a composition set in a period when Jerusalem is yet to be conquered? (*Rewritten Joshua Scrolls*, 165; see also Tov, "Rewritten Book of Joshua," 249). This incredulity is actually the main reason why Tov (235, 249–50) is cautious about linking frags. 22–25 to the rest of the fragments of 4Q522, even though they bear all the physical markings of belonging to the same composition.

David" ([שיר המעלות לדוי[ד], 22, 1). The content of the psalm, associated with David, fits well with what we can discern from the larger text represented in 4Q522.

1 [שיר המעלות לדוי]ד שמחתי ב[אומרים ל]י ב[ית יהוה נלך עמדות היו]
2 [רגלינו בשעריך]ירושלם ירו[של]ם הבנוי[ה כעיר שחוברה לה יחדיו ששם]
3 [עלו שבטים] שבטי יה עדות לישראל להוד[ות לשם יה]וה כי שם י[שבו]
4 [כסאות למ]שפט כסאות לבית דויד שאל[ו שלום י]רושלם ישליו
5 [אוהביך יהי שלום] בח[י]לך [ש]ל[ו]ם בארמו[נותיך למען]אחי ורעי אד[ברה]
6 [נא שלום בך למען בית יהו]ה [אלהינו אבקשה] שלום ל]ך
] [   ] 7

1 [A Song of Ascents. Of Davi]d. I rejoiced when[they said] to me, ["We are going to the]H[ouse of YHWH". Our feet stood]
2 [inside your gates,]O Jerusalem, Jeru[sale]m buil[t up, a city knit together, to which]
3 [tribes would make pilgrimage,] the tribes of YHWH,—as was enjoined upon Israel—to pra[ise to the name of YH]WH. There
4 [the thrones of jud]gement [stood], thrones of the house of David. Pra[y for the well-being of Je]rusalem;
5 [May those who love you be at peace. May there be peace] within your ram[pa]rts, and [p]e[a]ce in [your] cita[dels. For the sake] of my kin and friends I pr[ay]
6 [for your well-being; for the sake of the house of YHW]H [our God, I seek] yo[ur] peace.[38]

David expresses relief and gratitude at the prospect of going up to the house of the Lord (ב]ית יהוה), now established at Jerusalem with its protective walls and towers. Whereas Joshua's speech depicted a period when some places in Canaan remained to be conquered and the house of YHWH needed to be protected from the remaining residents, Ps 122 encapsulates a future period when Israelites feel peace in the land and David himself dwells in Jerusalem. This peace is maintained both by the power of God and by the strength of the Davidic dynasty. Curiously, the Davidic voice, signaled by the incipit, refers to the establishment of the Davidic dynasty as having already occurred. This appears as a strange anachronism—but evidently not strange enough to warrant a different authorial incipit.

The extant text of 4Q522 is largely a rewriting of the story of Joshua's conquest of Canaan. This story in 4Q522 includes Joshua's own admission of the failure of his conquest of Canaan and the future expectation of the establishment of the temple by individuals whose identities are only hinted at. The identity of one of these temple builders, David, is made explicit by the inclusion of Ps 122 near or at the end of this text. The psalm effectively confirms Joshua's expectations of the conquering of Jerusalem and the establishment of God's house there and places its fulfillment in the voice of David himself. While the authorial incipit of Ps 122 itself

---

[38] The text and translation are taken, with minor changes, from Feldman, *Rewritten Joshua Scrolls*, 151. See his n. 29 for other editions.

rather weakly evokes a Davidic persona, its inclusion in the larger narrative helps to construe David as the fulfillment of patriarchal anticipation and divine expectation of a subdued Canaan. As we will see, this is not the only function of Ps 122 among the Qumran scrolls, as it is included with other Psalms of Ascent in 11QPs[a], the text to which I now turn.

IV. Constructing David in 11QPs[a]

11QPs[a] is the largest psalm collection from Qumran and contributes greatly to a construction of a Davidic persona. Scholars are divided, however, with respect to the significance of 11QPs[a] as a witness to multiple editions of the Psalter or as a liturgical composition that consciously altered the MT arrangement of the Psalms while adding material not found in the MT Psalter.[39] This debate importantly comes to bear on the status of psalms collections as "works."[40] The status of 11QPs[a] as a "manuscript" whose shape has a bearing on ancient conceptions of David, is of primary concern here. Issues of textual history and editorial behavior are important only for providing contrast to better apprehend the shape of the text in 11QPs[a]. In what follows, I will explore the degree to which the shape of 11QPs[a] has significance for the construction of Davidic personas in 11QPs[a], with reference to the two

---

[39] In James A. Sanders's initial treatments of the scroll, he argued that 11QPs[a] represented a legitimate edition of the Psalter that preceded the fixity and closure of the Psalter reflected by later Masoretic Psalters. See, e.g., James A. Sanders, "Variorum in the Psalms Scroll (11QPs[a])," *HTR* 59 (1966): 83–94. This position has been more or less supported, especially in the work of Peter W. Flint (*The Dead Sea Psalms Scrolls and the Book of Psalms*, STDJ 17 [Leiden: Brill, 1997], 202–27) and to a lesser degree by Gerald Wilson ("The Qumran Psalms Manuscripts and the Consecutive Arrangement of Psalms in the Hebrew Psalter," *CBQ* 45 [1983]: 377–88). In contrast, several studies consider the shape of MT Psalter to have been fixed prior to the composition of 11QPs[a] (or its exemplars). Thus, according to a number of proposed rationales, including liturgical and eschatological, 11QPs[a] represents a reshaping of the MT Psalter. For the liturgical rationale, see Patrick W. Skehan, "Liturgical Complex in 11QPs[a]," *CBQ* 35 (1973): 195–205; and M. H. Goshen-Gottstein, "The Psalms Scroll (11QPs[a]): A Problem of Canon and Text," *Text* 5 (1966): 22–33. For the eschatological rationale, see Ben Zion Wacholder, "David's Eschatological Psalter 11Q Psalms[a]," *HUCA* 59 (1988): 23–72; and Ulrich Dahmen, *Psalmen- und Psalter-Rezeption im Frühjudentum: Rekonstruktion, Textbestand, Struktur und Pragmatik der Psalmenrolle 11QPs[a] aus Qumran*, STDJ 49 (Leiden: Brill, 2003). Marko Marttila affirms both emphases (*Collective Reinterpretation in the Psalms: A Study of the Redaction History of the Psalter*, FAT 13 [Tübingen: Mohr Siebeck, 2006], 234). Mroczek criticizes the distinction between a scriptural text proper and a liturgical function as somehow distinct from other presumed uses of a scriptural text ("Psalms Unbound," 48–51).

[40] As Mroczek has recently argued, the debate itself is predicated on a view of publication and textuality that does not accurately reflect ancient ideas about textual fixity (*Literary Imagination*, 19–50). Furthermore, William Yarchin has recently shown that the shape of the MT Psalter itself (which he prefers to call the Textus Receptus) continued to be fluid in shape and ordering (though not contents) until the early modern period ("Were the Psalms Collections at Qumran True Psalters?," *JBL* 134 [2015]: 775–89, https://doi.org/10.15699/jbl.1344.2015.2898).

subunits under examination: the micro-collection of Pss 120–32 in 11QPs[a], which makes up a major portion of the so-called Psalms of Ascent, and the final grouping of texts in 11QPs[a] from David's Last Words to Ps 151B.

David among the Psalms of Ascent

The Psalms of Ascent in the 11QPs[a] Psalter represent one of the larger and more familiar groupings found also in later Psalters.[41] 11QPs[a] showcases notable differences in order and placement of the Ascent psalms.[42] Notably, Pss 133 and 134 have been located elsewhere in the scroll and not with the other Psalms of Ascent. Psalm 133 appears in col. XXIII between Ps 141 and Ps 144, and Ps 134 is located in the final col. XXVIII right before Ps 151.[43] As Flint argues, this relocation helps to make the micro-collection more Davidic. In addition to the repetition of שיר המעלות, which gathers the psalms together into a distinctive group, the authorial incipits that accompany many of the superscriptions contribute to a sense of Davidic authorship. If the consensus view that Ps 120 was originally present in the scroll is correct, then the Psalms of Ascent in 11QPs[a] begin with a Davidic attribution and end with Ps 132, in which David is the subject of the psalm.[44] The psalms

---

[41] Many scholars agree that the collection of Ascent psalms was compiled not long after the exile, though there is disagreement whether the psalms were composed as a group or underwent layers of composition. For example, on the basis of a number of factors including word repetition, shared syntax, and thematic unity, Hendrik Viviers considers this collection to have been composed by a single author ("The Coherence of the Maʿalôt Psalms [Pss 120–134]," ZAW 106 [1994]: 275–89, here 286–87). On the other hand, Loren D. Crow has suggested that a number of repeated formulas throughout the psalms reflect the hand of a later redactor. He, in fact, proposes that Pss 121, 122, 132, 133, and 134 were composed by the later scribe (*The Songs of Ascents [Psalms 120–134]: Their Place in Israelite History and Religion*, SBLDS 148 [Atlanta: Scholars Press, 1996], 129–58).

[42] Flint notes the possibility that 1QPs[b] may represent a psalms scroll that contained only the Ascent micro-collection. The extant fragments include portions of Pss 126, 127, and 128 (*Dead Sea Psalms Scrolls and the Book of Psalms*, 31). That its ordering is identical to the MT in the small portion that we have does not encourage distinct discussion here.

[43] Curiously, Pss 135 and 136 continue on, with Ps 119 occupying the place where Pss 133 and 134 might have otherwise been expected. Ryan M. Armstrong argues that Pss 133 and 134 fit nicely in the Ascents collection, which suggests that their location elsewhere is a purposeful editorial move ("Psalms Dwelling Together in Unity: The Placement of Psalms 133 and 134 in Two Different Psalms Collections," JBL 131 [2012]: 487–506, https://doi.org/10.2307/23488251). As we will see below, I do not agree with his precise explanations, but I do agree with his more general point that their relocation contributes to the notion that 11QPs[a] underwent purposeful shaping. It is also worth noting that the joining of Pss 141, 133, and 144, is duplicated in 11QPs[b], frag. 7a–e. See Florentino García Martínez, Eibert J. C. Tigchelaar, and A. S. van der Woude, *Qumran Cave 11.II: 11Q2–18, 11Q20–31*, DJD XXIII (Oxford: Clarendon, 1998), 45.

[44] Skehan writes that "there can be no serious doubt that lines 20–25 of the [column ii] contained Ps 120" ("Liturgical Complex in 11QPs[a]," 196 n. 8). This judgment has been generally followed or assumed by Wacholder ("David's Eschatological Psalter 11Q Psalms[a]," 46), Wilson

in between are punctuated with authorial incipits. While Ps 127 was likely attributed to Solomon (the portion that would have contained שיר המעלות has deteriorated), several others have Davidic incipits. Psalms 122 and 123 are attributed to David—the MT Ps 123 is not. The beginning of Pss 124 and 131 have been lost, but both are Davidic in the MT.[45]

A maximalist reconstruction of these psalms produces a distinct Davidic quality on the basis of the authorial incipits. In 11QPs[a], the Ascents collection concludes with Ps 132 rather than with Pss 133 and 134, as it does in the MT. What is striking about Ps 132 is that, while it does not bear a Davidic incipit, David has become the subject of the psalm. Thus, the Davidic quality of this micro-collection is not exclusively an authorial one. Over the course of these שיר המעלות, David composes psalms about going up to Jerusalem, requesting mercy, the salvation of God in the face of violent enemies, and humility toward God. These psalms are followed by an anonymous psalm that confirms the sentiments of the Davidic "I" in the previous psalms and locates the actions described in the previous psalms in the Davidic dynasty.[46] Further, as Ryan Armstrong has noted, in what was likely the earlier Ascents collection, Ps 132 is the final royal psalm and the following two psalms emphasize unity (invoking the image of Aaron's beard) and mutual blessings between the congregation and YHWH.[47] By locating Pss 133 and 134 elsewhere in the scroll, the Ascents micro-collection produces a thoroughgoing Davidic quality that closes with a strong emphasis on the integrity of the Davidic dynasty and the weakness of their enemies.[48]

Comparing 11QPs[a] and 4Q522 provides an additional opportunity to observe the mutability of Davidic personas on the basis of variation in manuscript shape.[49] In 11QPs[a], the David of Ps 122 is constructed on the basis of the flow of the Ascents collection. In this case, repeated authorial incipits provide a consistent sense of the Davidic "I" that is subsequently confirmed by the anonymous third-person voice

---

("The Qumran Psalms Scroll [11QPs[a]] and the Canonical Psalter: Comparison of Editorial Shaping," *CBQ* 59 [1997]: 448–64, here 450, 459), Michael Chyutin ("The Redaction of the Qumranic and the Traditional Book of Psalms as a Calendar," *RevQ* 16 [1994]: 367–95, here 374), and Flint (*Dead Sea Psalms Scrolls and the Book of Psalms*, 187, 191).

[45] For an edition of the text of these materials, see James A. Sanders, *The Psalms Scroll of Qumran Cave 11 (11QPs[a])*, DJD IV (Oxford: Clarendon, 1965), 24–27.

[46] This is especially striking since the sentiment of request for mercy in Ps 123—Davidic in this collection—leads off Ps 132.

[47] See Armstrong, "Psalms Dwelling Together in Unity," 497.

[48] Marttila suggests that Ps 132 is a climax of the Ascents psalms on the basis of its Davidic interest, which corresponds to the Davidic emphasis of the entire scroll (*Collective Reinterpretation*, 224).

[49] In addition to the shifts in the construction of a Davidic persona, there is some textual variation between the two manuscripts. 11QPs[a] writes the divine name in paleo-Hebrew script, whereas 4Q522 uses square script. Further, in line 6, 11QPs[a] reads "I will seek your good [טובה]" with the MT, while 4Q522 reads "I will seek your peace [שלום]."

in Ps 132. This greatly contrasts 4Q522, in which Ps 122 is isolated from the Ascents collection and incorporated into a paraphrase of Joshua. Whereas the David of the 11QPs^a Ascents collection initiates activities including going up to Jerusalem or thanking God for protection from enemies that is picked up and retrospectively asserts their continuance in the Davidic dynasty, the David of 4Q522 is himself the fulfillment of the expectation of habitation in Jerusalem.

David in Transition and the Close of 11QPs^a

Interest in the final columns of 11QPs^a has been dominated by attention to the prose piece "David's Compositions." It is indeed strange to find a prose piece in a psalter, and this is enhanced by the fact that it follows the final verses of "David's Last Words," otherwise found in 2 Sam 23:1–7, and precedes three additional psalms that conclude with Ps 151.[50] However, David's Compositions has garnered attention for its potential to illuminate the editorial logic of 11QPs^a as a whole, precisely because of its emphasis on David's activity as a scribe, psalmist, and prophet.

More pressing, however, is the issue of compositional integrity. While significant emphasis on David is provided by David's Compositions and its position near the end of the scroll, many scholars consider it part of an epilogue or colophon.[51] Mroczek argues strongly against this position and notes that such labeling makes it seem as though David's Compositions was an afterthought or somewhat distinct from the Psalter proper.[52] This emphasis on David proves to be one of the most compelling reasons for most commentators to consider a high level of editorial intention, yet this approach requires that the editorial goals cohere with selected

---

[50] For an edition of the text of these materials, see Sanders, *Psalms Scroll of Qumran Cave 11*, 48–49.

[51] Skehan ("Liturgical Complex in 11QPs^a," 202–5) and Wacholder ("David's Eschatological Psalter 11Q Psalms^a," 55) see the Hymn to the Creator as the beginning of a set of supplementary materials to the Psalter proper. Yarchin also assumes that David's Compositions is "part of a colophon near the end of the scroll" ("Scripture as a Spiritual Phenomenon: The Evidence of the 11Q Psalms Scroll Colophon," *BBR* 22 [2012]: 363–81, here 366.

[52] Mroczek, *Literary Imagination*, 72–74, followed by David Willgren, *The Formation of the "Book" of Psalms: Reconsidering the Transmission and Canonization of Psalmody in Light of Material Culture and the Poetics of Anthologies*, FAT 2/88 (Tübingen: Mohr Siebeck, 2016), 124–26. The position that David's Compositions functions as an epilogue is further weakened by other proposals that view the functional ending of the scroll occurring at different points. Armstrong argues that the doxology at the end of Ps 134 concludes the Psalter, leaving 151 as an epilogue ("Psalms Dwelling Together in Unity," 495). Others suggest that the scroll logically ends after David's Compositions while the remaining materials were later additions (Dahmen, *Psalmen- und Psalter-Rezeption*, 307; Marttila, *Collective Reinterpretation*, 227). Wyrick appears to head in this direction. While he states that "this note was affixed to the end of an entire scroll of Psalms," he goes on to appeal to Ps 151 as he downplays David's status of prophet in the period when 11QPs^a was composed (Wyrick, *Ascension of Authorship*, 89–91, esp. 89).

beliefs of the Qumran community.[53] Editorial intention, however, including appeals to sectarian themes from external and corroborating evidence, is not a necessary datum in the analysis of how the materiality of the scroll itself makes demands on its reading. The latter part of the scroll, which includes much Davidic material, does not materially set itself apart from the rest of the text of the scroll, as Mroczek points out. She observes that the hand and layout of the materials of 11QPs^a remain consistent and does not visually differentiate prose from poetry or text from paratext.[54] This is not to say that there are not internal groupings that hold together on the basis of thematic logic or earlier and discrete collections; in fact, my analysis benefits from such groupings. But the material features of 11QPs^a encourage us to regard the work as a unity, which makes demands on a reading of the Davidic persona constructed therein.

While there may be no shift in the appearance of the text between prose and poetry, the final columns of 11QPs^a exhibit drastic shifting between the authorial "I" and third-person description. This shifting can be seen first in David's Last Words as well as in the transition from David's Compositions to the final three psalms of the scroll. Not much remains of David's Last Words except the final line, which begins column XXIII, and the fragmentary state of the text argues against drawing conclusions about its construction of David.[55]

Following David's Last Words is the piece called David's Compositions. This text consists of the lengthiest third-person description in the entire scroll and as such is able to depict David and his extensive compositional activity with an efficiency and directness that could not otherwise be achieved through the use of David's voice in a psalm. Accordingly, I accept Mroczek's argument that this piece does much to construct David as the quintessential psalmist who inspires additional compositions.[56] Yet the consistent emphasis in the secondary literature on this prose piece as constructive of a Davidic persona fails to appreciate the relationship between third-person description and the authorial "I" of psalms. In 11QPs^a, David's Compositions is followed by a series of psalms, many of which possess brief

---

[53] For example, Chyutin proposes that the Psalter was arranged on the basis of the calendar ("Redaction of the Qumranic and the Traditional Book of Psalms," 367–95). Flint argues for a general Davidization of the Psalter paired with a structuring based upon the solar calendar (*Dead Sea Psalms Scrolls and the Book of Psalms*, 192–95), while Wacholder argues that the Davidic character anticipates an eschatological descendant of David ("David's Eschatological Psalter 11Q Psalms^a," 32–72).

[54] In this instance, she fails to see how scholars can distinguish the authorial voice of David in the earlier psalms from the authorial voice of David in David's Last Words as part of a postscript and legitimation of the arrangement of that Psalter ("Psalms Unbound," 107, 116–17).

[55] This portion of 2 Samuel is not extant among the Samuel scrolls of Qumran, so it is impossible to use such information to reconstruct column XXII.

[56] See the works cited in n. 10 above.

Davidic incipits that construe David as the voice of the authorial "I."[57] Given the strength with which David's Compositions emphasize David's activity as a psalmist, the subsequent Davidic incipits of Ps 140 and Ps 151A heighten the sense of the Davidic voice in the following psalms, compared to the psalms included earlier in the scroll.

The flow of the final psalms' content paints a very different picture of David than is typically emphasized in treatments of 11QPs[a]. Certainly David's image as the composer of psalms is confirmed by the incipits of Pss 140 and 151A. In the remaining psalms, however, the now-heightened authorial voice is concerned with the defeat of YHWH's enemies and David's own role in that defeat as the ruler of YHWH's people. The first psalm after David's Compositions is attributed to David (למנצח מזמור לדוד, "To the leader, a psalm, of David"; 11QPs[a] XXVII, 12) and expresses the general plea to YHWH to deliver him from enemies. This is followed by the likely unattributed Psalm of Ascent (Ps 134), which encourages the giving of blessing to YHWH from his house. Finally, the scroll moves to Ps 151A + B, which are also placed in the mouth of David.

Prior to the discovery of 11QPs[a], Ps 151 was known only from Greek versions and translations of the Greek. In contrast to the lengthy incipit of LXX Ps 151, which overemphasizes the Davidic attribution and sets the composition at David's defeat of Goliath, 11QPs[a] simply names it a Hallelujah of David the son of Jesse.[58] The psalm is divided into two portions here, since the Hebrew version is longer and the scribe began the so-called Ps 151B on a new line.[59] This longer version depicts the ascent of David, opening with a pastoral image of the young David, who plays the lyre in praise of God. It steadily builds as David narrates his transition from shepherd to king, stating that YHWH took him from behind the flock and anointed him as a leader.[60] Psalm 151B begins at this point, but unfortunately most of it has

---

[57] Flint labels this portion "Mainly Davidic Pieces" and suggests (as he does for other portions of the Psalter) that the unattributed Ps 134 is "Davidicized" by its being sandwiched between two David psalms (*Dead Sea Psalms Scrolls and the Book of Psalms*, 192–94). What I have not seen argued is that Ps 134—whose first verses have been lost—could have been given a Davidic ascription, which would not be entirely unprecedented given that we have already seen it happen in Ps 123.

[58] Sanders, *Psalms Scroll of Qumran Cave 11*, 49.

[59] Andrew C. Witt provides a helpful parallel of the Greek and Hebrew versions, effectively illustrating the expanded material of the Hebrew ("David, the 'Ruler of the Sons of His Covenant' [מושל בבני בריתו]: The Expansion of Psalm 151 in 11QPs[a]," *Journal for the Evangelical Study of the Old Testament* 3 [2014]: 77–97, here 84–85).

[60] Witt sees this transition as an effect of the division of Ps 151A from 151B ("David, the 'Ruler,'" 95). This transition at Ps 151B is considerably stronger when following the reading recently proposed by Dimant. Her reconstruction differs from Sanders's, who saw third-person endings in lines 5–6, whereas Dimant views them as first-person endings. The result is a complaint that neither the mountains nor trees witness to David's playing but YHWH notices anyway ("David's Youth in the Qumran Context [11QPs[a] 28:3–12]," in *Prayer and Poetry in the Dead Sea*

been lost. The portion that remains, however, elaborates on this moment of transition, where David was anointed and hints at his encounter with Goliath. The LXX version includes one verse that slightly parallels 11QPs[a] XXVIII, 11 and one additional verse:

⁶ ἐξῆλθον εἰς συνάντησιν τῷ ἀλλοφύλῳ,
καὶ ἐπικατηράσατό με ἐν τοῖς εἰδώλοις αὐτοῦ·
⁷ ἐγὼ δὲ σπασάμενος τὴν παρ' αὐτοῦ μάχαιραν
ἀπεκεφάλισα αὐτὸν καὶ ἦρα ὄνειδος ἐξ υἱῶν Ισραηλ.

I went to meet the foreigner
and he cursed me with his idols.
But after drawing his sword,
I beheaded him and removed the disgrace from the sons of Israel.[61]

Sanders states that the Greek and extant Hebrew differ so much already that the unparalleled Greek verses cannot provide a base for conjecturing the end of the psalm.[62] Yet the relation between these two versions of the entire psalm is one of rough correspondence, where the Hebrew consistently has expanded the content with respect to the Greek version. Notably, in Ps 151B, the first two lines of the Hebrew expand upon the single verse in the Greek.[63] It is plausible that whatever lines remained roughly corresponded with what we find in the LXX version, that is, David's slaying of Goliath.[64] This entire psalm, thus, represents David's own reflection on his transition from pastoral musician to warrior king, defined by removing the lyre from David's hands and placing in them the sword of Goliath.

Many recent readings of "David" in 11QPs[a], guided especially by the final texts of the scroll, tend to emphasize his status as musician or psalmist par excellence. The image of David produced in 11QPs[a], however, is slightly more contoured. I suggest that beginning with David's Compositions, the scroll moves in a precise

---

Scrolls and Related Literature: Essays in Honor of Eileen Schuller on the Occasion of Her 65th Birthday, ed. Jeremy Penner, Ken Penner, and Cecilia Wassen, STDJ 98 [Leiden: Brill, 2011], 97–114, here 101, 105–7). This transition produces a more pronounced image of David than Sanders's suggestion that the psalm emphasizes YHWH's choice of David on the basis of humility and beauty of soul (*Psalms Scroll of Qumran Cave 11*, 61).

[61] Text from Alfred Rahlfs, *Septuaginta: Id est Vetus Testamentum graece iuxta LXX interpretes*, rev. ed. (Stuttgart: Deutsche Bibelgesellschaft, 2006), 164; my translation.

[62] James A. Sanders, *The Dead Sea Psalms Scroll* (Ithaca, NY: Cornell University Press, 1967), 100.

[63] See Sanders's comparison (*Psalms Scroll of Qumran Cave 11*, 60). I am not suggesting that the shorter Greek version represents an earlier composition upon which the version in 11QPs[a] enlarged. Although Sanders thought that the Qumran version was earlier, recent proposals have positioned the Greek as temporally prior or have viewed both as stemming from an earlier tradition still. See Witt, "David, the 'Ruler,'" 86–87.

[64] In the DJD edition, Sanders does suggest that enough text remains to infer that the psalm relates the Goliath episode (*Psalms Scroll of Qumran Cave 11*, 61).

trajectory that is facilitated by the heightened authorial attribution and the Davidic "I" in Pss 140 and 151. This trajectory begins with the image of David as a musician and composer of psalms and ends with an autobiographical emphasis on David as warrior king, a transition that pivots on praise to YHWH and entreaty that he protect his people from enemies. While I am not ready to suggest that this trajectory defines the David of 11QPs[a], the pairing of elaborate third-person description in David's Compositions with the autobiographical account of David's ascension as ruler of YHWH's people and slayer of Goliath projects a powerful image of David as the ascendant king and warrior, which takes precedence over his capacity as a psalmist at the close of the psalm and the larger psalter of which it is a part.[65]

V. Conclusion

I set out to describe and analyze the construction of the pseudepigraphal identity of David among the psalms at Qumran and the mutability of that image in different arrangements. My proposal rested on the claim that pseudepigraphy emerges from editorial manipulation and alteration of texts and that attention to individual manuscripts is revealing of such pseudepigraphal identities, which can be compared between texts. Among psalms manuscripts, textual agglomeration through editorial activity enables a synergy between the authorial "I" of the psalm proper and the third-person description reflected in incipits and other adjacent material. In the case of 4Q522, David's image in Ps 122 contributes primarily to a narrative of the conquest of Canaan, whereby David and his son complete the task of Joshua. Small fragments of psalms give David's persona only limited shape. 4QPs[q] produces an image of David as a musician due to the Davidic incipit and musical references in the body of the psalm. But this image is muted, especially when compared to the production of a Davidic persona in 11QPs[a]. In that manuscript, image construction operates on a much larger scale, where attributed psalms and narratives of David's activities combine to produce an image of David as the ideal psalmist, though it concludes by reminding readers of David's status as warrior-king.

Considerable and interesting variation in the emergent Davidic persona is evident through examining several different (portions of) manuscripts, as manuscripts rather than as witnesses to works (to return to Lied's terminology). This methodological suggestion offers a counterpoint to recent assessments of pseudepigraphy in early Judaism that often emphasize more general and expansive authorial images that are reflected in selected idealized works. Early Judaism was literarily

---

[65] This argument, then, contrasts with Witt's suggestion that David's example as a musician of praise pairs with his image as warrior ("David, the 'Ruler,'" 95–96). It seems to me that his suggestion underplays the transition I have been describing.

productive, with much of its literature adding contour and color to the personas of characters who were becoming increasingly famous. A corollary of this productivity, however, includes editorial and scribal work in the production of new manuscripts, which are pluriformal and variant, as the scrolls show us. Attention to specific manuscripts, their editorial logic, and material constitution props up another—and I think complementary—point in the dialectical emergence of pseudepigraphic identities in early Jewish literature.

The Social Condition of Lepers in the Gospels

MYRICK C. SHINALL JR.
ricky.shinall@vanderbilt.edu
Vanderbilt University Medical Center, Nashville, TN 37232

It has become a common interpretive assumption that the people with leprosy whom Jesus encounters in the gospels would have been shunned by Second Temple Jewish society, which makes Jesus's interactions with them all the more remarkable. In this article, I examine the underpinnings of this assumption by attending carefully to what is said about leprosy in the Hebrew Bible as well as in Second Temple and rabbinic sources. I argue that the evidence for the exclusion of the leprous from first-century Jewish society is much less certain than is generally realized. Without this assumption, the gospel texts themselves do not convey the message that lepers were excluded. Indeed, there is evidence in the gospels that lepers had relatively unhindered social access. Interpretations that see the overcoming of social stigma in Jesus's healings of leprosy stem not so much from consideration of the textual evidence as from a latent tendency to construe Judaism negatively in order to make Jesus appear in a more positive light.

It is widely held that a man in possession of leprosy in the gospels must be in want of community. When interpreting Jesus's healing of lepers (Matt 8:2–4, Mark 1:40–45, Luke 5:12–15, 17:12–18), commentators and rigorous historical-critical scholars have either argued or assumed that ostracism of lepers and taboos against contact with them constitute the background for interpreting these pericopae.[1]

---

[1] Ezra P. Gould, *A Critical and Exegetical Commentary on the Gospel according to St. Mark*, ICC (New York: Scribner's Sons, 1896), 30–32; Alfred Plummer, *A Critical and Exegetical Commentary on the Gospel according to St. Luke*, ICC (New York: Scribner's Sons, 1900), 149, 403; Martin Dibelius, *From Tradition to Gospel*, trans. Bertram Lee Woolf (Cambridge: James Clarke, 1971), 74; Alan Hugh McNeile, *The Gospel according to St. Matthew: The Greek Text with Introduction, Notes, and Indices* (London: Macmillan, 1952), 102; Joseph A. Fitzmyer, *The Gospel according to Luke I–IX: Introduction, Translation, and Notes*, AB 28 (Garden City, NY: Doubleday, 1981), 572–74; Gerd Theissen *The Miracle Stories of the Early Christian Tradition*, trans. Francis McDonagh, SNTW (Edinburgh: T&T Clark, 1983), 146; Joachim Gnilka, *Das Matthäusevangelium*, 2 vols., HThKNT (Freiburg im Breisgau: Herder, 1986), 1:296; W. D. Davies and Dale C.

Although a few scholars have challenged these assumptions, a tacit consensus has developed that Jesus's interactions with the leprous occurred within a purity system that socially isolated lepers.[2] This consensus about the social condition of lepers in Second Temple society has gained traction outside the guild of biblical studies and has found its way into related academic fields and into the life of the church.[3] I challenge this consensus and argue that neither the gospel texts nor the available background information on Second Temple Judaism demands that we read the leprous characters of the gospels as outcasts.[4]

Allison, *A Critical and Exegetical Commentary on the Gospel according to St. Matthew*, 3 vols., ICC (London: T&T Clark, 1991), 2:11–12; Darrell L. Bock, *Luke*, 2 vols., BECNT 3 (Grand Rapids: Baker, 1994), 1:464–65; Joel Marcus, *Mark 1–8: A New Translation with Introduction and Commentary*, AB 27 (New York: Doubleday, 2000), 206–9; François Bovon, *Luke 1: A Commentary on the Gospel of Luke 1:1–9:50*, trans. Christine M. Thomas, Hermeneia (Minneapolis: Fortress, 2002), 174–76; Frederick Dale Bruner, *Matthew: A Commentary*, 2 vols., rev. and exp. ed. (Grand Rapids: Eerdmans, 2004), 1:373; R. T. France, *The Gospel of Matthew*, NICNT (Grand Rapids: Eerdmans, 2007), 305; John T. Carroll, *Luke: A Commentary*, OTL (Louisville: Westminster John Knox, 2012), 127. Ulrich Luz provides the rare interpretation of the story without any mention of exclusion (*Matthew: A Commentary*, 3 vols., Hermeneia [Minneapolis: Fortress, 2001–2007], 2:5–7). Adela Yarbro Collins does not explicitly state that the leper in Mark 1:40–45 was an outcast, but she strongly implies it by noting that the pronouncement of purification enabled his reintegration into society and by citing injunctions on the quarantine of lepers in the Dead Sea Scrolls as background for the pericope (*Mark: A Commentary*, Hermeneia [Minneapolis: Fortress, 2007], 178–80). John P. Meier questions the taboo against touching lepers but accepts that lepers were ostracized from social and religious life (*Law and Love*, vol. 4 of *A Marginal Jew: Rethinking the Historical Jesus*, AYBRL [New Haven: Yale University Press, 2009], 411–13).

[2] For the rare scholar who has questioned the exclusion of the leprous from Second Temple society, see John J. Pilch, "Understanding Biblical Healing: Selecting the Appropriate Model," *BTB* 18 (1988): 60–66. Yet more recent work by Pilch assumes exclusion of the leprous and those who touch them from Second Temple society; see his "Improving Bible Translations: The Example of Sickness and Healing," *BTB* 30 (2000): 129–34, here 131.

[3] See, e.g., Mary Ann McColl and Richard S. Ascough, "Jesus and People with Disabilities: Old Stories, New Approaches," *Journal of Pastoral Care and Counseling* 63 (2009): 1–11, here 3; Bruce T. Morrill, *Divine Worship and Human Healing: Liturgical Theology at the Margins of Life and Death* (Collegeville, MN: Liturgical Press, 2009), 84; Steven J. Sainsbury, "AIDS: The Twentieth-Century Leprosy," *Dialogue* 25 (1992): 68–77; Chris U. Manus and Bolaji O. Bateye, "The Plight of HIV and AIDS Persons in West Africa: A Contextual Re-reading of Mk 1:40–45 and Parallels," *AsJT* 20 (2006): 155–69; Bobby Ross, "Modern-Day Lepers: Churches Try to Balance Grace and Accountability Toward Sex Offenders," *Christianity Today* 53, no. 12 (2009): 16–17, here 16; Maggi Dawn, "The Untouchables," *The Christian Century* 124, no. 20 (2007): 18.

[4] In modern usage, the term *leprosy* refers to chronic infection with the mycobacterium *M. leprae*, which affects the skin and peripheral nerves, a condition also known as Hansen's disease. "Leprosy" also translates the Hebrew term צָרַעַת (which entered Greek as λέπρα), which refers to a skin ailment that does not neatly correspond to Hansen's disease or to any other single dermatologic condition. In this article, I use the term *leprosy* and its cognates to refer to the condition that the ancient authors called צָרַעַת or λέπρα without any presuppositions concerning how the condition would be classified among modern disease(s). See John J. Pilch, "Leprosy," *NIDB* 3:635–37.

Questioning the degree of isolation of lepers fits into the current debates about the social significance of impurity in Second Temple Judaism. Students of early Judaism debate whether purity was salient for Jews only when they approached the temple (and so irrelevant for most of the people most of the time) or if there existed a drive to maintain purity in daily life away from the temple.[5] Even positing a widespread and thoroughgoing concern with purity in Jewish daily life does not thereby establish the social condition of bearers of impurity. A spectrum of Jewish attitudes toward interacting with bearers of impurity would have been compatible with a serious concern for purity in day-to-day life. On one end of the spectrum would be complete avoidance of the impurity bearer, and on the other end would be completely unhindered interactions followed by purification if these interactions transmitted impurity. Being impure does not per se imply being a pariah.

The relevant question for this investigation of leprosy is not whether lepers were considered unclean but rather whether their uncleanness brought them social isolation. With reference to Jesus's interactions with lepers, the leading issues are twofold: In the Second Temple period, were lepers shunned in ways that involved exclusion from normal social intercourse? And was there was a specific taboo against touching lepers, the act that figures so prominently in Jesus's healing of the single leper (Matt 8:2–4 // Mark 1:40–45 // Luke 5:12–15)? I argue that exegetes need not, and indeed should not, read the stories of Jesus's healings of lepers in light of a general social exclusion of the leprous or a specific taboo against touching them. To demonstrate this larger thesis, I elaborate three subsidiary arguments:

1. Jewish sources outside the New Testament present inconsistent evidence for the exclusion of lepers and taboos against touching them. This evidence does not justify reading such exclusion or taboo into the stories of Jesus's encounters with the leprous.

2. The gospel texts themselves do not provide evidence that lepers suffered from such exclusion or taboos but in some cases offer counterevidence for such treatment of lepers.

3. Reading such exclusion into the gospel stories creates a number of problems, not the least of which is insidious anti-Judaism.

I. The Mosaic Legislation and Its Application

When citing evidence for the stigma attached to people with leprosy in Jesus's time, interpreters most commonly point to the laws in Lev 13–14. John Pilch's explanation is typical:

---

[5] John C. Poirier, "Purity beyond the Temple in the Second Temple Era," *JBL* 122 (2003): 247–65, https://doi.org/10.2307/3268445.

When Jesus or anyone touched a so-called "leper" in the Biblical stories, no "mark" transferred from the afflicted person to Jesus. Pollution, however, did transfer. Jesus was viewed as now being unclean as these petitioners were unclean. The consequence of such pollution was obligatory separation from the holy community (Lev 13:45–46).[6]

Leviticus serves as evidence for (1) the exclusion of people with leprosy from Jewish society and (2) the taboo against touching such people since they communicated uncleanness by contact. A close reading of Lev 13–14, however, fails to confirm these two supposed facts of Second Temple Jewish life.

The two chapters in Leviticus devoted to leprosy say little about the social condition of the person with leprosy. Leviticus extensively attends to the procedure for identifying leprosy and its resolution in people (13:1–44), the ritual for cleansing a formerly leprous person (14:1–21), and the identification and management of leprosy in cloth (13:47–59) and buildings (14:22–54). Although the stipulations about how the Israelites treated leprous houses and cloths may have some implications about how they treated leprous people, it is not immediately clear how the handling of these inanimate objects corresponded to behavior toward people. Only two verses speak directly to the lepers' social condition:

> The person who has the leprous disease shall wear torn clothes and let the hair of his head be disheveled; and he shall cover his upper lip and cry out, "Unclean, unclean." He shall remain unclean as long as he has the disease; he is unclean. He shall live alone; his dwelling shall be outside the camp. (Lev 13:45–46 NRSV)

This treatment of lepers is corroborated in Num 5:2: "Command the Israelites to put out of the camp everyone who is leprous, or has a discharge, and everyone who is unclean through contact with a corpse."

Both Numbers and Exodus stipulate that lepers should be excluded from *the camp* (המחנה). The statute presumes the exodus setting, when Israel lived in a camp but says nothing explicitly about what to do with lepers once the Israelites established permanent settlements. The stipulation that the leper "shall live alone" could be interpreted to apply even after the exodus, but how this should be carried out is not specified. Second Temple Jews had several plausible options for interpreting these statutes. A strict reading could take the statutes to have applied only when the Israelites lived in the camp. A more expansive reading might see in the analogy between the tabernacle and the temple a correspondence between the camp and Jerusalem, so that lepers should be excluded from Jerusalem. An even more expansive reading could see any Jewish settlement as the successor to the camp, so that every Jewish city, village, and town would exclude the leprous. The latter option would raise more interpretive questions: How many dwellings constituted a settlement that must exclude the leprous? What determined the boundary of such settlements? How far outside the boundary were the leprous to live? Moreover, were the

---

[6] Pilch, "Improving Bible Translations," 131.

restrictions only on where lepers could reside, or were lepers excluded from even entering these restricted zones? The text of Leviticus and Numbers cannot answer these questions, which concern the interpretation of the Torah in Jesus's day.

The statutes also remain silent about how and whether lepers transmit impurity to others. Although the sections of Leviticus on leprous cloths and buildings indicate transmissibility, the text never explicitly states whether and how leprous human beings transmit impurity either to other human beings or to inanimate objects. Statements such as "contact with lepers had to be avoided and lepers had to warn others not to come close to them (Lv 13:45)," imply that Leviticus lays out how the leprous are to interact with other people.[7] Leviticus 13:45, however, simply instructs the leper how to dress (in torn clothes), how to wear his hair (disheveled), and how to behave (to cover his upper lip and cry out, "Unclean! Unclean!"). The text does not mention anyone whom the leper warns to stay away. Lepers behave like mourners: they wear torn clothing, they have disheveled hair (Gen 37:29, 37:34, Lev 10:6, 21:10, Judg 11:35, 2 Sam 1:11, 1 Kgs 21:27, 2 Kgs 2:12, Job 1:20, Esth 4:1), and they cover the upper lip (Ezek 24:17, 24:22). In this posture of mourning, the cry of "Unclean! Unclean!" directed at no one in particular could just as easily be a lament as it could be a warning to some passerby.[8]

Levitical legislation clearly lays out the ways that humans could contract uncleanness through contact: from animal carcasses (11:27–28, 39–40), from men with an abnormal discharge (15:5–11), from semen (15:18), from menstruating women (15:21–24), and from women with an abnormal discharge (15:25). In all cases the text describes the contact that transmits impurity and how the person who contracts impurity becomes clean again. By contrast, the text is silent with respect to how lepers transmit impurity to other people and has no instructions for how to remove the impurity once contracted. Since priests closely examined people to identify the presence and resolution of leprosy, they logically should have been greatly interested in the process by which they could return to a state of purity if they accidentally touched a leper during their examinations. If Jews dreaded the touch of lepers as much as New Testament exegetes often claim, Leviticus's lack of instructions for managing this impurity is surprising.[9]

These two verses from Leviticus, along with Num 5:2, show those with leprosy adopting behaviors associated with mourning and exclusion from the camp. The

---

[7] Francois P. Viljoen, "Jesus Healing the Leper and the Purity Law in the Gospel of Matthew," *IDS* 48, no. 2 (2014): art. 1751, pp. 1–7, here 3, https://doi.org/10.4102/ids.v48i2.1751.

[8] Hyam Maccoby, *Ritual and Morality: The Ritual Purity System and Its Place in Judaism* (New York: Cambridge University Press, 1999), 125. Other interpreters recognize the similarities to mourning yet nevertheless posit that the behaviors constitute a warning. See Baruch A. Levine, *Leviticus* ויקרא: *The Traditional Hebrew Text with the New JPS Translation*, JPSTC (Philadelphia: Jewish Publication Society, 1989), 82; Jacob Milgrom, *Leviticus 1–16: A New Translation with Introduction and Commentary*, AB 3 (New York: Doubleday, 1991), 803–4.

[9] Meier, *Law and Love*, 411–12.

text remains silent about the interactions they are to have with other people: how they are to acquire food and clothing, how they are to migrate with the rest of the Israelites when it is time to move the camp, what happens to their children or other dependents. Nor are there instructions for how the nonleprous are to treat them, with the exception of the instructions to priests on examining them and performing their purification rites. Into these silences, interpreters have inserted unsubstantiated claims that Leviticus and Numbers describe the leprous as cut off from their fellow Israelites and socially equivalent to the dead.[10]

In his delineation of the purity system, Jacob Milgrom attempts to fill these lacunae in the purity codes. Milgrom explicates the underlying logic of the modes of transmission, the quarantines, and the purification rituals that the Priestly legislation promulgates for the various types of impurity.[11] Based on the extensiveness of the purification rituals assigned to lepers, Milgrom detects a hierarchy of impurities; leprosy, having the most extensive purification ritual, sits atop the hierarchy. The hierarchy of impurities correlates with how these impurities are communicated. Impurities that are lower on the hierarchy are transmitted by touch and by being in an enclosed space. It stands to reason that leprosy, as the highest impurity, would be transmitted in the same ways. Impurity becomes a problem when it contacts the holy (sacred offerings, priests, the sanctuary) because such contact is dangerous to the community. The law thus assigns levels of quarantine or isolation to bearers of impurity based on how their impurity is transmitted to prevent inadvertent contamination of someone or something else that then contacts the holy. The common denominator that Milgrom identifies behind the impurities is death (or at least the absence of life). In his analysis, the purity system reflects an impulse to keep the holy separate from the manifestations of death.[12]

Milgrom's system does not entail the categorical isolation of those with leprosy that other interpreters so often envision. According to Milgrom, only contact between the impure and the holy is dangerous; contact between the impure and the common is a problem only if the resulting contamination is not recognized and the appropriate purification rites are not performed.[13] Israelites could freely interact with leprous people as long as they purified themselves afterwards before contacting a holy thing or person. Although the necessity of subsequent purification makes close contact with lepers inconvenient, the system Milgrom posits does not imply

---

[10] Gnilka, *Das Matthäusevangelium*, 296; Marcus, *Mark 1–8*, 208; Bovon, *Luke 1*, 175; Johnson M. Himuhu, *Leviticus: The Priestly Laws and Prohibitions from the Perspective of Ancient Near East and Africa*, StBibLit 115 (New York: Lang, 2008), 343–44; Felix Chingota, "Leviticus," in *Africa Bible Commentary*, ed. Tohunboh Adeyemo (Grand Rapids: Zondervan, 2010), 150; Samuel E. Ballentine, *Leviticus*, IBD (Louisville: Westminster John Knox, 2002), 108.

[11] Milgrom's system is set out in detail in his *Leviticus 1–16*, 986–1000, and in a more abbreviated form in his later *Leviticus: A Book of Ritual and Ethics* (Minneapolis: Fortress, 2004), 141–50.

[12] Milgrom, *Leviticus 1–16*, 1000–1004.

[13] Milgrom, *Leviticus: A Book*, 144.

that such contact was forbidden or that the leprous were therefore cut off from all social intercourse.[14]

This system proposed by Milgrom fills the gaps that Leviticus and Numbers leave about regulating contact with leprous people.[15] Milgrom's work presumes that regulations about purity and impurity spring from an intelligible underlying way of thinking. His critical assumption is that an internally consistent system generated the Levitical regulations, an assumption that may or may not be true.[16] Without presupposing this consistency, one cannot use such a system to discover the unstated regulations about those with leprosy.

To discern the degree of social isolation that the leprous experienced in Jesus's day, one must examine evidence closer in time to the setting of the gospels. Like the Pentateuch, however, these later sources do not present a comprehensive picture concerning lepers' exclusion.

Josephus discusses the social situation of lepers in the first century, but his is but one voice in the often fractious ancient debates about what conformed to Jewish law.[17] Moreover, Josephus had an obvious concern to cast the Jews, their traditions, and their heroes in a positive light and to counter gentile calumnies about Jews, even if that meant stretching the evidence.[18] This latter caution is salient because much of Josephus's discussion of leprosy comes in the context of refuting pagan historians who claimed that Moses himself had leprosy and that the Israelites originated as lepers and other outcasts from Egyptian society.[19]

When retelling the promulgation of the Mosaic laws in *Jewish Antiquities*, Josephus says that Moses "expelled from the city those whose bodies were attacked by leprosy" (*Ant.* 3.261) and adds, "He banished the leprous completely from the city—associating with no one and in no way differing from a corpse" (*Ant.* 3.264).[20] Like Leviticus, Josephus sets the banishment in the context of the exodus, but instead of describing banishment from the camp, Josephus describes banishment from "the city," suggesting that he views Jerusalem as the successor of the camp.[21]

---

[14] Maccoby, *Ritual and Morality*, 125.

[15] Jonathan Klawans, "Ritual Purity, Moral Purity, and Sacrifice in Jacob Milgrom's *Leviticus*," *RelSRev* 29.1 (2003): 20.

[16] For the challenge to Milgrom's and others' recent attempts to systematize the purity constructions of the Hebrew Bible, see T. M. Lemos, "Where There Is Dirt, Is There System? Revisiting Biblical Purity Constructions," *JSOT* 37 (2013): 265–94, here 280–81.

[17] Daniel R. Schwartz, *Reading the First Century: On Reading Josephus and Studying Jewish History of the First Century*, WUNT 300 (Tübingen: Mohr Siebeck, 2013), 167–68; Jonathan Klawans, *Josephus and the Theologies of Ancient Judaism* (Oxford: Oxford University Press, 2012), 137–79.

[18] Louis H. Feldman, *Studies in Josephus' Rewritten Bible*, JSJSup 58 (Leiden: Brill, 1998), 546–51, 557–60.

[19] See Josephus, *Ant.* 3.265; *Ag. Ap.* 1.227–251; 1.288–303; 1.304–320; Tacitus, *Hist.* 5.3.1.

[20] Translation from Louis H. Feldman, *Flavius Josephus: Judean Antiquities 1–4; Translation and Commentary*, FJTC 3 (Leiden: Brill, 2000), 308.

[21] Ibid. For an argument that Josephus here intends all the cities of Israel, see Hannan

Corroborating this reading are Josephus's comments in *Jewish War* that lepers cannot live in Jerusalem or participate in the Passover sacrifice (*J.W.* 5.227, 6.426). Further confirmation comes from *Against Apion*, where Josephus tells of Moses promulgating the purification ritual for the person who recovered from leprosy as a precondition for such a person to "enter the holy city" (*Ag. Ap.* 1.282).[22]

In *Against Apion*, Josephus states that Moses prescribed a high degree of social isolation for the leprous. Having just summarized the gentile historian Manetho's assertion that Moses suffered from leprosy, Josephus writes:

> And it is clear from his [Moses's] own statements that he did not suffer any physical misfortune of this sort, for he prohibited the leprous from staying in a city or living in a village requiring that they travel about alone with their clothes torn; and he regards as unclean anyone who touches them or lives under the same roof. (*Ag. Ap.* 1.281)[23]

Josephus has expanded the strictures on social contact with the leprous from what he reports in *Jewish Antiquities* (and from what is in the Pentateuch) to emphasize the incongruity between Moses's supposed leprosy and the harsh laws about leprosy that he promulgated. Of any source examined so far, this passage from *Against Apion* corresponds most closely to the extensive ostracism of the leprous that so many interpreters take to be the background of the gospel stories. Several factors, however, militate against taking Josephus's description at face value: (1) the polemical agenda to maximize the inconsistency between Moses's legislation and his personal affliction with leprosy; (2) the more limited exclusion from "the city" described in *Jewish Antiquities*; (3) the description in *Against Apion* of the purification ritual as enabling the formerly leprous person to enter the holy city without reference to its necessity for reentering villages or otherwise reintegrating with society; and (4) the setting of this prohibition in the context of the exodus without an explicit claim that such prohibitions carried force in Josephus's day.[24] Josephus certainly points toward some level of marginalization of lepers in Second Temple society, but the extent of this marginalization remains uncertain.

The Dead Sea Scrolls also give little reliable evidence concerning the degree of exclusion of the leprous from Second Temple society. The Temple Scroll forbids those with leprosy from entering Jerusalem (11Q19 XLV, 17–18) and also stipulates that there should be a location to the east of Jerusalem where those with leprosy

---

Birenboim, "Expelling the Unclean from the Cities of Israel and the Uncleanness of Lepers and Men with a Discharge according to 4Q274 1 i," *DSD* 19 (2012), 28–54, here 37.

[22] Translation from John M. G. Barclay, *Flavius Josephus: Against Apion; Translation and Commentary*, FJTC 10 (Leiden: Brill, 2007), 151.

[23] Translation from ibid.

[24] Thomas Kazen argues that Josephus must be referring to contemporary practice since his description of the restrictions on leprosy differ from those of Moses (*Jesus and Purity Halakhah: Was Jesus Indifferent to Impurity?*, rev. ed., ConBNT 38 [Winona Lake, IN: Eisenbrauns, 2010], 113).

should be placed (XLVI, 17–18). The scroll goes on to instruct the readers to make places "in every city [בכול עיר]" (XLVIII, 14) for those with leprosy so that the leprous "do not enter your cities and defile them [לוא יבואו לעריכמה וטמאום]" (XLVIII, 15).[25] It is not clear whether the author envisions the leprous to be confined in one area of the city or in an area just outside the city. In another document, the author mandates that lepers should reside twelve cubits (about sixteen feet) from any other house and should maintain this distance when speaking with the nonleprous (4Q274 1 I, 1–2).[26] Here the leprous are separated from others, but the stipulated distance is not great and the author clearly envisions leprous people talking to the nonleprous.[27] Like Josephus, the Dead Sea Scrolls indicate exclusion of the leprous from Jerusalem and some degree of exclusion from other cities, but the extent to which the Dead Sea Scrolls represent actual Second Temple practice is debatable. Although the scrolls witness a tendency to marginalize lepers, they simultaneously envision social intercourse between the leprous and nonleprous.

Looking for evidence of social exclusion in other Second Temple sources adds little to the picture from Josephus and the Dead Sea Scrolls. Pseudo-Philo briefly mentions the sacrifices required for the cleansing of lepers but does not comment on lepers' social status (LAB 13:3). The mention of the law for cleansing lepers is the only gloss by Pseudo-Philo on the purity regulations of Leviticus; thus, leprosy serves as a paradigmatic impurity in the work. Philo himself mentions leprosy in a number of places, but he tends to use the condition as a symbol for impurity and vice rather than comment on how other people treated actual lepers.[28]

Another instance of leprosy's status as paradigmatic impurity and its suitableness for metaphors about sin comes in the Syriac version of the apocryphal Ps 155: "The sins of my childhood remove from me; / and my insolence do not remember against me. / O Lord, cleanse me from the evil leprosy / and do not let it again return to me" (5 Apoc. Syr. Ps. 3:12–13 [trans. Charlesworth and Sanders, *OTP* 2:624]).

---

[25] The scroll here also stipulates that those with a discharge, menstruating women, and parturients should be thus segregated even though the latter two are not excluded from the camp in the Torah. Hannan Birenboim argues that those with leprosy are excluded from the city while menstruants and parturients are quarantined within it, but the text does not differentiate ("'The Place Which the Lord Shall Choose,' the 'Temple City,' and the 'Camp' in '11QT^A,'" *RevQ* 23 [2008]: 357–69, here 368).

[26] The text is actually somewhat vague and other possible explanations for the referent exist, but the most plausible reading is that it refers to a person with leprosy. See Birenboim, "Expelling the Unclean," 40.

[27] Thomas Kazen argues that these stipulations refer to the leprous person in the process of purification rather than leprous people in general based on the assumption that 4Q274 and the Temple Scroll reflect a coherent purity system across the Dead Sea Scrolls ("4Q274 Fragment 1 Revisited—or Who Touched Whom? Further Evidence for Graded Impurity and Graded Purifications," *DSD* 17 [2010]: 68), much as Milgrom assumes for Leviticus.

[28] See Philo, *Alleg. Interp.* 1.49; *Worse* 16; *Posterity* 47; *Unchangeable* 123–131; *Planting* 111; *Sobriety* 49; *Dreams* 1.202; *QG* 2.29.

Here the curing of leprosy symbolizes the extirpation of sinfulness. The Hebrew version of this psalm contained in the Dead Sea Scrolls, however, has the speaker asking God to cure him of the evil "plague" (נגע), and not "leprosy" (צרעת, 11Q5 XXIV, 12). Apparently, the metaphor worked with either leprosy or a less-specific affliction. Philo and Syriac Psalm 155 attest to the power of leprosy as a symbol of impurity and sin but do not provide information about the social condition of the leprous.

The Pentateuch and the Second Temple literature refer to the exclusion of lepers, but they also imply some level of participation in Jewish society. A similar pattern emerges in the early rabbinic regulations for those with leprosy. The Mishnah explicitly lays out a graded system of impurity, much like the one Milgrom posits for Leviticus (m. Kelim 1:1–5). Lepers contaminate others by touch or by being in enclosed spaces together (m. Kelim 1:1, m. Neg. 13:7). However, the Mishnah does not stipulate that lepers be totally excluded from society. They are to be sent out from walled cities, which implies that they could remain in smaller settlements (m. Kelim 1:7). The Mishnah gives special instructions on how lepers might attend the synagogue—a small partition separates the leprous person from the rest of the congregation (m. Neg. 13:12). The Tosefta likewise makes allowance for the leprous person to attend synagogue (t. Neg. 7:11) and also to have sexual intercourse (t. Neg. 8:6).[29] The interpreter of the Tannaitic regulations on leprosy must question how much rabbinic pronouncements reflect practice, rather than the rabbis' fantasies of their own authority.[30] Regardless of whether these practices existed outside the rabbinic imagination, the system thus envisioned does allow some participation of the leprous in society.[31]

In summary, the available evidence provides an inconsistent picture of the degree of the leper's social stigma in Jesus's time. The actual evidence from the Second Temple era is fragmentary, consisting primarily of scattered references in Josephus and the Dead Sea Scrolls. Rabbinic literature gives a more detailed description of how leprosy fits into a system of purity and impurity, but the rabbis do not emphasize the exclusion of the leprous. Much like Leviticus itself, the rabbinic literature focuses mostly on how to diagnose leprosy rather than on how to exclude the afflicted from society. In any case, due to its later dating, rabbinic literature cannot reliably illustrate early first-century Jewish practice. Although the sources describe some level of ostracism for the leprous in some places, the weight

---

[29] Jacob Neusner, *The Tosefta: Translated from the Hebrew* (New York: Ktav, 1977), 166.

[30] Mira Balberg, "Rabbinic Authority, Medical Rhetoric, and Body Hermeneutics in Mishnah Negaʾim," *AJSR* 35 (2011): 323–46, here 336–37.

[31] Kazen argues that these rabbinic stipulations allowing some participation for the leprous represent a relaxing of restrictions that postdates the first century (*Jesus and Purity*, 111–12). These scruples about using Tannaitic data to investigate Second Temple practice do not prevent Kazen from using the Mishnah to provide evidence for the transmissibility of the leper's impurity in Jesus's time (*Jesus and Purity*, 112–13).

of the sources does not warrant the assumption that Second Temple Jews made a consistent effort to avoid social and physical contact with lepers.

II. Stories of the Leprous

If Jewish ostracism of the leprous underlies the gospel narratives, one would expect such ostracism to figure prominently in narratives about lepers in the Hebrew Bible as well. Yet social isolation figures only sporadically in these stories, further evidence that the segregation of leprous people varied over time and location.

Moses is the first character mentioned in the Hebrew Bible to experience leprosy. At the burning bush, when Moses asks God for signs to prove to the Israelites that God has sent him, God turns Moses's hand white with leprosy and then removes the leprosy (Exod 4:6–7). Moses never subsequently uses this sign. This brief mention of Moses's leprous hand may have been the source of (or a response to) the claim by historians such as Manetho that Moses himself had leprosy.[32] Whatever the provenance of this story of Moses's leprosy, the text makes no mention of any exclusion or isolation of Moses. The story demonstrates God's power to inflict and remove leprosy.[33]

Moses's sister Miriam is the next biblical character to experience leprosy (Num 12:1–16). She and Aaron grumble against Moses, and, as punishment, God afflicts her with leprosy. Aaron, horrified, asks Moses to pray for Miriam's healing. God responds, "If her father had but spit in her face, would she not bear her shame for seven days? Let her be shut out of the camp for seven days, and after that she may be brought in again" (Num 12:14 NRSV). Here the leprosy serves as divine punishment much as it served as evidence for divine action in Exod 4:6–7.[34]

Unlike Moses's brief affliction, however, Miriam's leprosy does involve exclusion—she must stay out of the camp for seven days. Yet the text relates this exclusion not to uncleanness but to shame. Miriam should be ashamed of her behavior and so should bear her shame for seven days outside the camp. Nor does Miriam's exclusion conform to the pattern laid down in Leviticus. Numbers never states that Miriam's leprosy resolved; the text reports only that Moses prayed for its resolution.

---

[32] Thomas Römer, "Tracking Some 'Censored' Moses Traditions Inside and Outside the Hebrew Bible," *HBAI* 1 (2012): 64–76, here 69. The LXX, Targum Onkelos, Philo (*Moses* 1.79), and Josephus (*Ant.* 2.273) omit any reference to leprosy in the story. For the argument that such an omission is a response to the charges of Manetho and his ilk, see C. Houtman, "A Note on the LXX Version of Exodus 4,6," *ZAW* 97 (1985): 253–54.

[33] William H. C. Propp, *Exodus 1–18: A New Translation with Introduction and Commentary*, AB 2 (New York: Doubleday, 1999), 209.

[34] Dirk Schinkel, "Mirjam als Aussätzige? Zwei Bemerkungen zu Num 12," *ZAW* 115 (2003): 94–101.

If one assumes that Moses's prayer was immediately effective, then according to Leviticus Miriam could have entered the camp immediately after sacrificing a bird, bathing, and shaving her head. In the camp she would have had to live outside her tent for seven days until she completed the last part of the cleansing ritual (Lev 14:1–9). Instead, Miriam lives outside the camp for seven days and performs no purification rituals. Although the story of Miriam does connect leprosy with exclusion, it does so not on the basis of the Levitical rules but on the basis of shame.[35] Thus, while Miriam's story provides evidence for leprosy leading to exclusion, its divergence from the Levitical stipulations shows the inconstancy of this exclusion throughout the biblical tradition.

Even more famous than Miriam's case of leprosy is that of Naaman (2 Kgs 5:1–8). There is no indication that Naaman suffers exclusion due to his leprosy. Naaman's leprosy does not prevent him from becoming an accomplished warrior, taking a wife, or accessing the royal courts of Aram and Israel. Commentators noting Naaman's social access have suggested that his disease must have differed from the "true" leprosy that entailed social isolation.[36] The text, however, provides no basis for differentiating Naaman's leprosy from that depicted in Leviticus. Rather than provide evidence for a different type of leprosy, the story of Naaman offers evidence for a nonuniform level of social stigma attaching to leprosy.

Prior to his cleansing, Naaman seemingly has access to whomever he chooses, except for Elisha himself who communicates via his servant (2 Kgs 5:10). Although Elisha meets Naaman face to face after his cleansing (5:15–19), the text does not mention that Elisha eschewed the first meeting to avoid contact with the leprous Naaman. Indeed, the prophet readily exposes his servant to contact with Naaman (5:10). Elisha's servant Gehazi attempts some double-dealing with Naaman after the latter's cure, for which the prophet inflicts leprosy on Gehazi and his descendants forever (5:20–27). Despite this curse, the next time Gehazi appears, he speaks with the king of Israel and enjoys the same ready access to court that Naaman did (2 Kgs 8:4–5).[37] In the story of Naaman, leprosy, through both its remedy and its infliction, manifests Elisha's connection to God. The story contains no evidence of social exclusion attached to the affliction.

The story of Naaman has special relevance for investigating the background of the gospel narratives on leprosy because Luke explicitly mentions it. In Jesus's encounter in the Nazareth synagogue, the story of Naaman becomes part of Jesus's polemic against his fellow Nazarenes that a prophet is not accepted in his hometown (Luke 4:23–29). Incidentally, Jesus's mention that there were "many lepers in

---

[35] Jacob Milgrom, *Numbers* במדבר: *The Traditional Hebrew Text with the New JPS Translation*, JPSTC (Philadelphia: Jewish Publication Society, 1990), 98.

[36] Mordechai Cogan and Hayim Tadmor, *II Kings: A New Translation*, AB 11 (New York: Doubleday, 1988), 63; John Gray, *I and II Kings: A Commentary*, OTL (Philadelphia: Westminster, 1970), 504.

[37] Nachman Levine, "Twice as Much of Your Spirit: Pattern, Parallel, and Paronomasia in the Miracles of Elijah and Elisha," *JSOT* 24 (1999): 25–46, here 31.

Israel" (4:27) in Elisha's time suggests his assumption that there was a place for lepers in society. Jesus brings up the healing of Naaman as an illustration of a prophet's work with gentiles rather than with Jews. For Luke's purposes, the example develops the theme of gentile inclusion in Jesus's work.[38] It also illustrates that an evangelist can use a Hebrew Bible story about a leprous person without any reference to social isolation or stigma.

Shortly after the story of Naaman, the Deuteronomistic Historian recounts the siege of Samaria by King Ben-hadad of Aram, an episode in which four lepers play a significant role. Unbeknownst to the people of Samaria, God terrifies the besieging army, causing them to flee in the night. The next morning four lepers sitting outside the gates of the city decide to go that day to surrender to the Arameans. Approaching the camp, they find it deserted and announce to the inhabitants of Samaria that the siege has been lifted (2 Kgs 7:3–10).

In this story, the exclusion of the leprous from the city of Samaria plays a key role. It is because the lepers spend the siege outside the city walls that they are the first to explore the deserted Aramean camp. The text implies, however, that the lepers had access to the city as well. As they formulate their plan to surrender to the Arameans, they say to one another, "Why should we sit here until we die? If we say, 'Let us enter the city,' the famine is in the city and we shall die there, but if we sit here, we shall also die" (2 Kgs 7:3–4 NRSV). These leprous men believe that they could gain admittance to the city, but that it would be fruitless to do so since they would starve there.[39] The biblical text presents exclusion from the city as the condition of leprous people, which implies social isolation, but it simultaneously implies that, at least under emergency conditions, the leprous men could enter the city.[40]

The last major character in the Hebrew Bible with leprosy is King Azariah of Judah, also called Uzziah. Second Kings gives only the briefest account of his leprosy and its consequences: "The Lord struck the king, so that he was leprous to the day of his death, and lived in a separate house [בבית החפשית]. Jotham the king's son was in charge of the palace, governing the people of the land" (2 Kgs 15:5). The NRSV translates the description of Azariah's dwelling place as "in a separate house," but the meaning of the phrase בית החפשית is far from clear. The word חפשית occurs only in this verse and in its parallel in 2 Chr 26:21 also describing the leprous king's dwelling. Its meaning apparently remained obscure to the translators of the LXX, who simply transliterated the word in both verses that tell how the king dwelt ἐν οἴκῳ αφφουσωθ.[41]

---

[38] Bovon, *Luke 1*, 156; John C. Poirier, "Jesus as an Elijianic Figure in Luke 4:16–30," *CBQ* 71 (2009): 349–63, here 361–62.

[39] Gray, *I and II Kings*, 524; Maccoby, *Ritual and Morality*, 124.

[40] The LXX and targumic versions of this story similarly present entry into the city as an option for the leprous men. In his retelling, Josephus explicitly states that there was a law that barred the leprous men from Samaria and that the leprous men spoke about the futility of entering the city even if they were hypothetically admitted (*Ant.* 9.74–75).

[41] For debate about the meaning of the phrase, see Gray, *I and II Kings*, 620; Cogan and

Whatever the nature of this בית החפשית, it seems to be separate from the palace so that Jotham must rule as prince regent in Azariah's place. It is not clear from the text of 2 Kings whether Azariah resides inside or outside Jerusalem. The parallel verse in 2 Chronicles states, "King Uzziah was leprous to the day of his death, and being leprous lived in a separate house [בבית החפשית], for he was excluded from the house of the LORD. His son Jotham was in charge of the palace of the king, governing the people of the land" (2 Chr 26:21). The Chronicler likewise fails to mention whether Uzziah lived outside Jerusalem, but the note that he was excluded from the house of the LORD seems overspecific if the king was indeed excluded from the whole of the city as well. The LXX of both 2 Kings and 2 Chronicles similarly fails to say whether Uzziah dwelled in the city or outside of it. However, in their retellings, both Targum Jonathan (2 Kgs 15:5, 2 Chr 26:21) and Josephus (*Ant.* 9.226–227) have Uzziah banished from Jerusalem.

While the Chronicler does not further specify the degree of Uzziah's exclusion, he does provide much more information about the cause of the leprosy. Uzziah attempted to usurp the priestly prerogative by offering sacrifice in the temple. For this sacrilege God smote the king with leprosy (2 Chr 26:16–20). Leprosy serves as divine punishment for Uzziah in 2 Chronicles just as it did for Miriam in Numbers and Gehazi in 2 Kings. Throughout these stories from the Hebrew Bible, leprosy recurs as a divine punishment, and its relief as a divine blessing offered by God or God's agents Moses and Elisha. These stories show that leprosy has a valence beyond social exclusion, a valence connecting leprosy with divine action. When Jesus heals leprosy, he performs an action associated in the Hebrew Bible with God and God's most illustrious prophets irrespective of any purity considerations.[42]

These stories of leprosy from the Hebrew Bible only intermittently illustrate social exclusion associated with the disease. Moses, Naaman, and Gehazi experience no exclusion, while Miriam, Uzziah, and the four Samarian men do. Even when the leprous characters do experience social isolation, no consistent pattern of ostracism appears. Miriam's exclusion from the camp does not fit the Levitical statutes and is motivated by concerns about shame rather than purity. The four men could enter Samaria if they wish. Uzziah lives outside the palace but not necessarily outside Jerusalem. These stories, taken together with the legal material reviewed in the last section, show a diversity of exclusionary practices across time and space rather than a uniform application of Levitical regulations throughout Israel's history.

Tadmor, *II Kings*, 166–67; Ralph W. Klein, *2 Chronicles: A Commentary*, Hermeneia (Minneapolis: Fortress, 2012), 380; Wilhelm Rudolph, "Ussias 'Haus der Freiheit,'" *ZAW* 89 (1977): 418; Pancratius C. Beentjes, "'They Saw That His Forehead Was Leprous' (2 Chr 26:20): The Chronicler's Narrative on Uzziah's Leprosy," in *Purity and Holiness: The Heritage of Leviticus*, ed. M. J. H. M. Poorthuis and J. Schwartz, JCPS 2 (Leiden: Brill, 2000), 61–72, here 68.

[42] Friedrich Avemarie, "Jesus and Purity," in *New Testament and Rabbinic Literature*, ed. Reimund Bieringer et al., JSJSup 136 (Leiden: Brill, 2010), 255–80, here 263.

My argument in this and the previous sections is not that lepers faced no exclusion or marginalization in Second Temple society. As we have seen in both the narrative and legal materials, some level of exclusion of lepers is apparent across sources and over the centuries. Nevertheless, these exclusionary practices varied over time and space and are counterbalanced by references to lepers' integration within society. This variation suggests that when examining a Second Temple text about a leper (such as a gospel story), one should refrain from assuming a priori that the leper is socially marginalized. One must rely on the texts themselves to speak about the degree of marginalization of their leprous characters.

III. Leprosy in the Gospels

The gospels do not indicate that lepers were outcasts and, indeed, they often provide evidence of their inclusion. This inconsistency in the texts has not stopped interpreters from assuming that all lepers experienced isolation. Such interpretations rely on what might be called "heads I win, tails you lose" exegesis—any hints at isolation are evidence of social constraints for lepers, while any social contact indicates boldness and compassion in disregarding these strictures.

The story of Jesus's healing the single leper (Matt 8:2–4 // Mark 1:40–45 // Luke 5:12–15) illustrates the interpretive acrobatics involved in reading the gospels against the background of presumed social isolation. Although the substance of the story is much the same in all three versions, each evangelist sets it differently. Matthew sets the story immediately after the Sermon on the Mount, when great crowds were following Jesus (8:1). Matthew makes no mention of the crowd reacting to the approach of the leper in 8:2. One might take the crowd's nonreaction as evidence that close contact with a leper did not trouble these Galilean Jews, but if one is determined to read ostracism into the story it can be done: one can assume that the crowd dissipated between verse 1 and verse 2 or that the crowd was stunned by the leper's boldness in approaching.[43] The presence of a crowd does not stand in the way of an interpreter determined to see social isolation.

Luke sets the same story in a city: "And it happened while he was in one of the cities, behold a man full of leprosy, and seeing Jesus and falling upon his face he begged him" (Luke 5:12). My rather wooden translation here reflects the fact that the text does not describe the entrance into the city of either Jesus or the leper—both are simply there, and the man sees Jesus, which precipitates the action. To interpret this story on the assumption of widespread isolation of the leprous, one must read the leper as an intruder in the city, his boldness motivating him to

---

[43] France, *Gospel of Matthew*, 307; Curtis Mitch and Edward Sri, *The Gospel of Matthew*, Catholic Commentary on Sacred Scripture (Grand Rapids: Baker Academic, 2010), 126.

violate social norms in search of Jesus.[44] Yet this element is absent. Although Mark does not explicitly provide a setting for the encounter between Jesus and the leper, he implies that it occurred in a populated area since Jesus was going through Galilee proclaiming his message in the synagogues (Mark 1:39). It is only after his fame from cleansing the leper spreads that Jesus can no longer enter a town but must stay in the countryside (1:45). All three evangelists set the story in ways that challenge the notion that the leprous were excluded from Galilean society.[45]

The crux of all three versions comes as Jesus touches the man and his leprosy leaves him (Matt 8:3 // Mark 1:41–42 // Luke 5:13). Jesus frequently heals by touch (Matt 8:15 // Mark 1:31; Matt 8:25 // Mark 5:41 // Luke 8:54; Matt 8:20 // Mark 5:29 // Luke 8:44; Mark 7:31–37; 8:22–26). Elijah and Elisha also heal through physical contact (1 Kgs 17:21, 2 Kgs 4:34), as do other healers in the Hellenistic world (Philostratus, *Vit. Apoll.* 4.45; Tacitus, *Hist.* 4.81; Suetonius, *Vesp.* 7.2).[46] This review has shown that no Levitical prohibition about touching a leper existed and that strictures against contact with lepers varied over time and location. It may have been that physical contact with the leprous was not prohibited in first-century Galilee.[47] The three evangelists present the leprous man as having ready access to Jesus and note no hesitation on Jesus's part in touching the man and no reaction of shock from any spectators. Nevertheless, many interpreters take Jesus's touching of the leper to be his flouting of Jewish purity concerns in the name of compassion and a demonstration of the ability of his holiness to overcome impurity.[48]

---

[44] Carroll, *Luke*, 126–27. Kazen provides an alternative by seeing the urban location as the result of Luke's ignorance of Jewish customs of excluding the leprous from cities (*Jesus and Purity*, 118). When Luke reports later that the ten lepers of 17:12–19 kept their distance, he provides evidence of Jewish practice (119). Details that counter the ostracism of lepers are secondary accretions, while details that confirm their ostracism constitute traces of the original tradition.

[45] Pilch, "Understanding Biblical Healing," 65.

[46] Kazen recognizes all these parallels but still sees in the mention of Jesus's touching a leper an emphasis intended to highlight Jesus's rejection of purity restrictions (*Jesus and Purity*, 106). See also Marcus, *Mark 1–8*, 206.

[47] Carl R. Kazmierski, "Evangelist and Leper: A Socio-Cultural Study of Mark 1.40–45," *NTS* 38 (1992): 37–50, here 43–44.

[48] David E. Garland, *Reading Matthew: A Literary and Theological Commentary on the First Gospel*, Reading the New Testament (New York: Crossroad, 1993; repr., Macon, GA: Smyth & Helwys, 2001), 107; Bruner, *Matthew*, 1:376; McNeile, *Gospel according to St. Matthew*, 102; Grant R. Osborne, *Matthew*, Zondervan Exegetical Commentary on the New Testament (Grand Rapids: Zondervan, 2010), 284–85; Charles H. Talbert, *Matthew*, Paideia (Grand Rapids: Baker Academic, 2010), 112; Mitch and Sri, *Matthew*, 126; Daniel J. Harrington, *The Gospel of Matthew*, SP 1 (Collegeville, MN: Liturgical Press, 2007), 113; Camille Focant, *The Gospel according to Mark: A Commentary*, trans. Leslie Robert Keylock (Eugene, OR: Pickwick, 2012), 80; Marcus, *Mark 1–8*, 206; Bovon, *Luke 1*, 175; Carroll, *Luke*, 127; Luke Timothy Johnson, *The Gospel of Luke*, SP 3 (Collegeville, MN: Liturgical Press, 1991), 95–96; Plummer, *Gospel according to St. Luke*, 149; Gould, *Gospel according to St. Mark*, 30, 32; M. Eugene Boring, "The Gospel of Matthew," *NIB* 8:89–505, here 225.

Luke adds a second encounter between Jesus and the leprous in the healing of the ten lepers (17:12–19). Although no physical contact occurs in this story, in contrast to the story of the single leper in 5:12–15, a determined exegete can find exclusion in both stories. With respect to the single leper, John T. Carroll comments, "The man's boldness in entering the city already suggests that he is willing to press beyond conventional social boundaries"; but about the ten lepers, he says, "Fittingly for persons in a perpetual state of ritual impurity by virtue of their skin lesions, they keep their distance."[49] Likewise, Darrell L. Bock observes that in the first instance Jesus "touches the leper, an act that makes him unclean, but that visualizes his desire to show compassion, even at a cost," while in the second encounter, "ten lepers intend to speak with him, but they cannot approach him because of their despised disease."[50] Contact with the leprous demonstrates a bold rejection of ritual laws, while distance demonstrates these laws' power to exclude. Heads I win, tails you lose.

Jesus's supposed flouting of the purity taboos by touching the leper fits awkwardly with his immediate instructions that the man should present himself to the priest and undergo the rites of purification prescribed in the Pentateuch (Matt 8:4 // Mark 1:44 // Luke 5:14). This is the only explicit reference in the gospels to the Mosaic legislation on leprosy. The incongruity of Jesus supposedly violating the law in one moment then immediately ordering conformity to the law can be explained as Jesus's concern for the social reintegration of the former leper.[51] The operative assumption is that the man can reintegrate into society only if he completes the Mosaic purification.[52] If Jesus's instruction is motivated by his desire to allow the man to reintegrate into society, then the man's behavior in Mark is strange. After healing the man, Jesus orders, "See that you say nothing to anyone, but go show yourself to the priest and offer for your cleansing that which Moses commanded as a testimony to them" (1:44 NRSV). The man does not comply with this command: "But [δέ] he went out and began to proclaim it freely and to spread the word" (1:45). The man successfully spreads the word of Jesus even though he fails to follow Jesus's command and apparently does not immediately go to the priests for his cleansing.[53] The man's effectiveness in spreading Jesus's fame would be odd if the ceremony he forgoes were a precondition for his acceptance in society.

The story of this man's healing has a parallel in the noncanonical Egerton Gospel. Whether this version represents a gloss on one or more of the Synoptics or an independent witness to this tradition, it nevertheless provides further evidence of how early followers of Jesus thought about the social condition of the leprous.[54]

---

[49] Carroll, *Luke*, 126, 343.
[50] Bock, *Luke*, 1:465, 2:1401.
[51] France, *Gospel of Matthew*, 308; Focant, *Gospel according to Mark*, 81; Carroll, *Luke*, 127.
[52] Kazen, *Jesus and Purity*, 101.
[53] Marcus, *Mark 1–8*, 210.
[54] For the relationship of the Egerton Gospel to the canonical gospels, see Tobias Nicklas,

In this version, the leper tells Jesus about how he acquired his leprosy: "Teacher Jesus, while traveling with lepers and eating with them in the inn I myself also became leprous" (2.12–15).[55] This version presumes that the leprous and non-leprous travel together and eat together in inns, hardly the outcast state so often taken to be the lot of lepers.[56]

Matthew and Mark narrate one further encounter of Jesus with a leprous character that calls into question the idea that leprosy necessarily entailed exclusion from society. In the last week of his life, Jesus stays in Bethany "at the house of Simon the leper" (Matt 26:6 // Mark 14:3). It is here that Jesus is anointed by the woman with the expensive ointment in the sight of his disciples. Apparently, none of these people has any problem being in a leper's house. Moreover, Simon the leper is allowed to live within the community of Bethany. To explain how Simon could be described as a leper yet live integrated into society, some scholars assume that he has previously been healed without citing any evidence that λεπρός was used to describe a person who was formerly leprous.[57] If one reads the story freed from the assumption that the leprous must have been excluded from Second Temple society, then Simon's living in a house and hosting a dinner does not require special explanation.

None of these gospel stories demands that we envision the leprous characters as being excluded from any aspect of society. In fact, many of the stories provide indirect evidence for the participation of lepers in the society of Jesus's time. Without bringing to the gospels the dubious assumption that leprosy in Jesus's time meant ostracism, interpreters would not find social isolation in the texts themselves.

IV. The Roots of the Problem

The gospel texts offer no compelling evidence for the social exclusion of the leprous. Other Jewish literature shows varying levels of exclusion across time and

---

"The 'Unknown Gospel' on *Papyrus Egerton 2*," in *Gospel Fragments*, ed. Thomas J. Kraus, Michael J. Kruger, and Tobias Nicklas, OECGT (Oxford: Oxford University Press, 2009), 96–100.

[55] Here taking the reconstruction proposed by H. Idris Bell and T. C. Skeat, *Fragments of an Unknown Gospel and Other Early Christian Papyri* (London: Trustees of the British Museum, 1935). This reconstruction has retained the most widespread acceptance; see Nicklas, "'Unknown Gospel,'" 42; Bart D. Ehrman and Zlatko Pleše, *The Apocryphal Gospels: Texts and Translations* (Oxford: Oxford University Press, 2011), 250.

[56] Bothered by the incongruity of this reconstruction with the shunning of lepers, Karl F. W. Schmidt proposed a reconstruction that would render the quoted fragment, "Teacher Jesus, you who visit lepers and eat with tax collectors at the inn, have mercy. I myself am also the same" ("Ein bisher unbekanntes Evangelienfragment: Einblicke in die Arbeitsweise eines alten Evangelisten," *TBl* 15, no. 2 [1936]: 34–45, here 35). This reconstruction has been widely rejected as being too long to fit the papyrus (Nicklas, "'Unknown Gospel,'" 50). Kazen, however, prefers this reading so that he can argue that Egerton does not provide evidence against the ostracism of the leprous (*Jesus and Purity*, 125–26).

[57] France, *Gospel of Matthew*, 974; Osborne, *Matthew*, 950; Harrington, *Matthew*, 362.

place. In light of this thin evidential basis, one might wonder how the exclusion of the leprous from Jewish society became such an interpretive commonplace.

One reason might be a scholarly bias toward systemization. The references to the social situation of lepers are few and scattered widely over centuries of Jewish literature. By assuming uniformity over time and space, scholars can allow these disparate materials to inform one another. Assuming a stable system allows extrapolation from one text to another to create a fuller picture than can be gained by looking at each individual text discretely. A system gives the scholar more material about which to talk and write.

Yet this bias toward systemization cannot explain why the social status of the leprous is construed so negatively. Milgrom's interpretation of Leviticus represents the pinnacle of systemization, but his work in no way implies a state of wretched isolation for the leprous. There must be more than a scholarly predilection for systems at work to explain why so many commentators take ostracism to be the implied state of the lepers whom Jesus heals.

The pedigree of this line of interpretation stretches back to John Chrysostom. In his exegesis of Matt 8:2–4, Chrysostom assumes that the law forbade touching lepers and that Jesus healed by touch to demonstrate that he was not subject to the law. He goes on to compare this episode to Elisha's healing of Naaman. Chrysostom ignores all the social contact that Naaman has in the story and seizes upon Elisha's refusal to speak to him face to face as evidence that the law forbade Elisha's contact with the leprous Naaman (*Hom. Matt.* 25.2). The Elisha story serves as the background for Jesus, but Jesus surpasses this background as he ignores the law that held Elisha so rigidly. This contrast between the law-bound Elisha and the law-free Jesus continues to find its way into modern commentaries.[58]

Chrysostom makes clear what is at stake in this line of interpretation as his exegesis continues. He must explain why Jesus, who so readily defies the law by touching the leper, commands the man to show himself to the priest:

> Here again, to fulfill the law, for he did not everywhere set it aside nor everywhere keep it, but sometimes did one and sometimes the other. He set it aside to prepare for the coming philosophy, but he kept it to hold back the impudent speech of the Jews for a while and to stoop to their weakness. (*Hom. Matt.* 25.3; my translation)

Chrysostom maintains Jesus's Jewish identity, but he also requires Jesus to transcend the Judaism that Chrysostom so negatively constructs.[59] For Chrysostom, as for so many other Christian interpreters, Judaism serves what Jonathan Z. Smith has identified as a double function: "On the one hand it has provided apologetic scholars with an insulation for early Christianity, guarding it against 'influence' from its 'environment.' On the other hand, it has been presented by the very same

---

[58] E.g., Focant, *Gospel according to Mark*, 80.
[59] Joshua Garroway, "The Law-Observant Lord: John Chrysostom's Engagement with the Jewishness of Christ," *JECS* 18 (2010): 591–615.

scholars as an object to be transcended by early Christianity."[60] By construing Second Temple society as totally isolating the leprous, exegetes can simultaneously locate Jesus firmly within a Jewish milieu and have him transcend his social location by touching and healing the leper.

Making Jesus look good by contrasting him with a negatively constructed Judaism is nothing new for Christian exegetes. For modern interpreters, however, this construction of Judaism has an added advantage. Reading Jesus's healing work against a supposed background of social isolation allows the modern exegete to move attention from Jesus as a miracle worker toward Jesus as an advocate for inclusivity. Such interpretations make Jesus relevant in a world that cares deeply about inclusion but that has little room for miracles. Whatever the attractions of such a relevant Jesus, he comes at the price of the interpreter abdicating historical-critical responsibility and defaming Jesus's Jewish contemporaries in the process.

V. Conclusion

Although the tone of this article has been largely critical, it is not meant as a personal criticism of any of the interpreters quoted or cited. Indeed, I imagine the suggestion that their interpretations were implicitly anti-Jewish would dismay all the authors cited, with the exception of Chrysostom. From Sunday school on, Christians are taught that leprosy brought shunning in Jesus's day, so it is not surprising that academic work in biblical studies reflects this common conception. I intend here to criticize a way of thinking that pervades the church and the academy, not just the specific authors whom I mention.

Nor do I mean to imply that there was no social exclusion of lepers in Second Temple society. Although the evidence is fragmentary and often contradictory, some level of exclusion of the leprous recurs throughout the sources. What I have shown is that the categorical isolation of the leprous does not appear in Jewish texts the way it is so often assumed and that we have very little information on what level of isolation, if any, lepers experienced in first-century Galilee. Moreover, the gospel texts themselves do not presuppose, and in some cases actually refute, the idea that lepers were banished from the society of Jesus's day. The lack of evidence for readings that presuppose the wholesale exclusion of lepers should be reason enough for exegetes of the gospels to drop this line of interpretation. That such readings involve slandering Judaism for the sake of a relevant Christianity make it all the more imperative that we find better ways to approach these texts.

---

[60] Jonathan Z. Smith, *Drudgery Divine: On the Comparison of Early Christianities and the Religions of Late Antiquity*, Jordan Lectures in Comparative Religion 14 (Chicago: University of Chicago Press, 1990), 83.

The Willoughby Papyrus: A New Fragment of John 1:49–2:1 (P134) and an Unidentified Christian Text

GEOFFREY SMITH
gssmith@utexas.edu
University of Texas at Austin, Austin, TX 78748

Formerly in the possession of Harold Willoughby, professor of early Christian origins at the University of Chicago, this unpublished fragment of the Gospel of John in Greek created a stir when it appeared briefly on a well-known auction site in January 2015. Having obtained permission from the owner to edit and publish the manuscript, I offer in this article the results of my analysis of the so-called Willoughby Papyrus, which I have assigned to the third or fourth century. On the basis of new images of the fragment, I provide a transcription of the text, discuss its apparent bookroll format, and assess its text-critical value. Finally, I present the secondary text on the verso and offer some tentative suggestions about its literary character. Though no more than six fragmentary lines survive on either side, the Willoughby Papyrus is of historical interest for three reasons: (1) it is a rare example of a New Testament fragment in which "God" is not abbreviated as a *nomen sacrum*, a "sacred name"; (2) it furnishes scholars with the first defensible example of a New Testament text written on the front side of an unused bookroll; and (3) it preserves six lines from an otherwise unknown Christian literary text. The Willoughby Papyrus has the potential to provide fresh insight into the emergence and standardization of *nomina sacra* conventions, the transition from the bookroll to the codex, and the circulation of canonical and noncanonical Christian writings.

The Willoughby Papyrus is a small fragment that consists of John 1:49–2:1, the final portion of the calling of Nathaniel and the beginning of the wedding at Cana on the recto (→) and an Unidentified Christian Text on the verso (↓).[1] The

I am grateful to Roger Bagnall, Larry Hurtado, Brice Jones, AnneMarie Luijendijk, Brent Nongbri, and Jennifer Knust for their comments on this article. Support for this research was received from the Institute for the Study of Antiquity and Christianity at The University of Texas at Austin.

[1] The polyvalence of the terms *recto* and *verso* can cause confusion. Michael Kruger

text of John on the recto has received the Gregory-Aland designation P134 from the Institut für Neutestamentliche Textforschung. On the basis of the style of the handwriting, both sides of the fragment were likely copied sometime in the third or fourth century CE. Formerly in the private collection of Harold Willoughby, professor of early Christian origins at the University of Chicago, this previously unknown Greek fragment created a stir when news of its existence spread in January 2015.[2] Having obtained permission from the owner to edit and publish the manuscript, I offer in the present article the results of my analysis of the so-called Willoughby Papyrus. I discuss what is known about the circumstances of discovery and rediscovery of the papyrus and, on account of increasing concerns about the legal circumstances under which artifacts have been acquired, demonstrate that it complies with the 1970 UNESCO convention on cultural property. On the basis of new images that I took of the fragment, I also provide a transcription of the text, discuss its peculiar format and *nomina sacra* conventions, and assess its text-critical value. Finally, I present the Unidentified Christian Text on the verso (↓) and offer some provisional thoughts on its literary character. Though no more than six fragmentary lines survive on either side, the Willoughby Papyrus is of historical interest for three reasons: (1) it is a rare example of a New Testament fragment in which "God" is not abbreviated as a *nomen sacrum*, a "sacred name"; (2) it furnishes scholars with the first defensible example of a New Testament text written on the front side (→) of an unused bookroll; and (3) it preserves six lines from an otherwise unknown Christian literary text.[3] For these reasons the Willoughby Papyrus

---

summarizes the problem well: "In a strict sense, the term 'recto' simply refers to the front of a folio and the 'verso' to the back. However, as these terms were applied to papyrus and parchment manuscripts, the recto became associated with the side of the manuscript with the better writing surface (which was normally used as the front of the page). Thus, 'recto' became associated with the side with horizontal fibers on papyrus manuscripts and with the flesh side of parchments manuscripts. Likewise, 'verso' was often (though not exclusively) used to refer to the side with vertical fibers on a papyrus manuscript and to the hair side of a parchment manuscript" (*The Gospel of the Savior: An Analysis of P.Oxy. 840 and Its Place in the Gospel Traditions of Early Christianity*, TENTS 1 [Leiden: Brill, 2005], 21). Confusion arises in those instances in which the front or "recto" of a manuscript page is not written with the fibers on papyrus or on the flesh side of a parchment. For this reason I follow the practice of many other editors in referencing a side by its fiber direction (i.e., → or ↓), rather than by the terms *recto* or *verso* alone.

[2] For a biographical sketch of Harold R. Willoughby and a comprehensive list of his special lectureships and publications, see *Early Christian Origins: Studies in Honor of Harold R. Willoughby*, ed. Allen Wikgren (Chicago: Quadrangle Books, 1961), 150–59. The papyrus received attention again in November 2016, when various media outlets reported on its discovery. See especially Jennifer Schuessler, "Greek New Testament Papyrus Is Discovered on eBay," *New York Times*, 20 November 2015, http://www.nytimes.com/2015/11/21/books/greek-new-testament-papyrus-is-discovered-on-ebay.html.

[3] As many are well aware, the notion of a New Testament canon in the early Christian period is somewhat artificial, and there is much to be gained by studying texts now in the New Testament alongside early Christian texts that did not make it into the New Testament. Indeed, the format,

has the potential to provide fresh insight into the emergence and standardization of *nomina sacra* conventions, the transition from the roll to the codex, and the circulation of canonical and noncanonical Christian writings.

I. Harold R. Willoughby

The fragment once belonged to Harold R. Willoughby, a scholar of ancient religion and noted bibliophile.[4] Throughout the 1920s, 1930s, and 1940s, Willoughby worked closely with colleague Edgar J. Goodspeed to amass a collection of manuscripts for the University of Chicago from dealers and private collectors in the United States and abroad.[5] Willoughby was instrumental in acquiring several illuminated manuscripts, including the Rockefeller McCormick New Testament (MS 965), a complete Byzantine New Testament with more than ninety illustrations, and the Silver Gospels (MS 951), an Armenian manuscript bound in silver.[6] He even purchased a Greek lectionary that was formerly used as an oath book for patrons of Colosimo's Cafe, a Chicago restaurant owned and operated by notorious mobster

---

scribal conventions, and literary content of the Willoughby Papyrus challenge long-standing assumptions about the material differences between New Testament and extracanonical manuscripts. Yet to illustrate the fragment's unique characteristics, I find it useful to compare it to existing New Testament fragments. This approach allows me to highlight its peculiarities as a New Testament manuscript and also has the practical advantage of allowing me to draw upon data gleaned from New Testament papyri (*nomina sacra* conventions, format, etc.) that are not yet readily available from extracanonical papyri. I have no doubt, however, that in subsequent studies the Willoughby fragment will contribute to ongoing efforts to blur the distinction between scriptural and nonscriptural scribal conventions in Christianity's early centuries. For efforts to move beyond the canonical/extracanonical divide, see Eldon Jay Epp, "The Oxyrhynchus New Testament Papyri: 'Not without Honor except in Their Hometown'?" *JBL* 123 (2004): 5–55, https://doi.org/10.2307/3268548; and AnneMarie Luijendijk, "Sacred Scriptures as Trash: Biblical Papyri from Oxyrhynchus," *VC* 64 (2010): 217–54. For a broader discussion of the issue, see David Brakke, "Scriptural Practices in Early Christianity: Toward a New History of the New Testament Canon," in *Invention, Rewriting, Usurpation: Discursive Fights over Religious Traditions in Antiquity*, ed. Jörg Ulrich, Anders-Christian Jacobsen, and David Brakke, Early Christianity in the Context of Antiquity 11 (Frankfurt am Main: Lang, 2012), 263–80.

[4] At the time of his death, Harold Willoughby owned approximately thirty-five hundred rare books, many of them Bibles. His private collection was purchased by North Park College and Theological Seminary in 1963. See "North Park Gets Professor's Rare Religion Library," *Chicago Sun Times*, 3 February 1963.

[5] See Edgar Goodspeed, "New Manuscript Acquisitions," *The University of Chicago Magazine*, January 1930, 137–42; Harold R. Willoughby, "Manuscript Hunting in Chicago," *The University of Chicago Magazine*, December 1930, 65–68; and Willoughby, "A Year of Manuscript Acquisitions," *The University Record*, July 1930, 139–46.

[6] "The Goodspeed Manuscript Collection," http://goodspeed.lib.uchicago.edu/collection.php.

Jim Colosimo. The experience, in Willoughby's own words, "brought gangland suddenly near."[7] Given that Willoughby interacted with a number of manuscript dealers over a period of three decades, it is not possible to determine where or when he acquired the papyrus.

That the manuscript belonged to Willoughby can be established on the basis of its appearance as "MS 4" in a list entitled "Manuscript Collection of H. R. Willoughby," written in his own hand (fig. 1; compare his signature in fig. 2), and the mention of "A papyrus Fragment Mounted on glass—John 1" in an inventory of his estate prepared after his death in 1962 (fig. 3). Although not absolutely certain, it would seem reasonable to conclude that, since Willoughby designated only MS 4 as a "papyrus," among the seven listed manuscripts "MS 4" was the only papyrus. The remaining six Greek and Latin manuscripts were likely parchments, and their whereabouts are at present unknown.

MS Collection of
H R Willoughby
ms1, Greek, Psalms 105–136, 36 fols
ms2, Greek, υποθεσις and κεφαλαια for Gospel of John, 1 fol
ms3, Greek, Mt 9:18–26, 9:1–5, 1 fol
ms4, Greek, Jn 1:50–51, Papyrus Fragments.
ms5, Latin, Sermones of Petrus Chrysologus, 2 fols
ms6, Latin, Book of Hours 1 fol
ms7, Greek, Mt 22:30–23:9, 1 fol

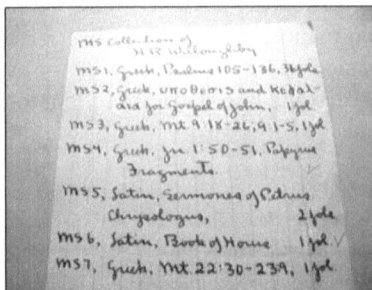

FIGURE 1. Inventory of Willoughby's personal manuscript collection written in his own hand. Photo by the anonymous owner of the fragment.

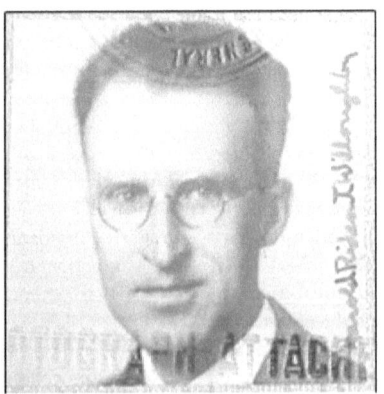

FIGURE 2. Willoughby's signed passport photo. Photo by the anonymous owner of the fragment.

A papyrus Fragment Mounted on glass -- John 1
A Leaf, illuminated, from the Book of Hours, Italy 1510
A miniature Greek Cursive Psalter - 11th Century -
has 36 leaves Book of Psalms 105-136.

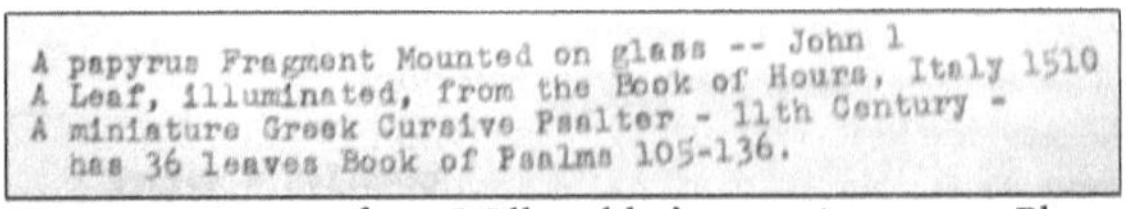

FIGURE 3. Excerpt from Willoughby's estate inventory. Photo by the anonymous owner of the fragment.

[7] Willoughby, "Manuscript Hunting in Chicago," 67.

Margaret Mitchell has recently come across additional documentation of this fragment among the papers of Harold Willoughby in the Special Collections Research Center at the Regenstein Library. In box 10 she found a folder labeled by Willoughby himself "Chicago, Willoughby Coll. Ms. Papyrus Frags. Jn. 1:50, 51 2 neg. 3 ½ x 5." The folder contains only two negatives of the recto and verso of the Willoughby papyrus apparently taken prior to its mounting (figs. 5 and 7). These early images also show a large detached fragment, which was later attached when the papyrus was mounted. Additionally, I have been able to determine on the basis of the images of the negatives provided to me by Mitchell that the negatives were taken at the latest not long after 1951 or 1952. Printed on the edge of the negatives are the words "Eastman – Nitrate – Kodak." On account of the combustibility of nitrate, which caused several fires in cinemas and film vaults in the late nineteenth and early twentieth centuries, Kodak began to phase out nitrate in the late 1940s, a process that was complete by 1951 or 1952. At this point Kodak switched to acetate film and replaced the word "Nitrate" with "Safety."[8] In other words, Harold Willoughby must have acquired the papyrus at a time when nitrate film was still available.

Even if we cannot determine precisely where or when he acquired the fragment, the handwritten inventory, estate paperwork, and negatives demonstrate that the papyrus was part of Harold Willoughby's personal collection prior to his death in 1962 and that he imaged the papyrus already in or before the early 1950s. Therefore, the fragment complies fully with the 1970 UNESCO convention on cultural property.[9]

Provenance, that is, documentation of a manuscript's circulation in the modern era, is but one of a cluster of interrelated issues that have in recent years risen to the forefront of scholarly conversations about the proper handling of ancient artifacts. As the recent contributions of William Johnson and Roberta Mazza make clear, even when a manuscript's provenance is secure, ethical questions linger, and scholars cannot ignore such issues.[10] The Willoughby Papyrus raises questions about private collections and scholarly access. Though images of the manuscript

---

[8] See https://www.kodak.com/motion/support/technical_information/storage/storage_and_handing_of_processed_nitrate_film/default.htm; see also www.kodak.com/motion/About/Chronology_Of_Film/1940-1959/default.htm.

[9] For the details of the resolution, see "Convention on the Means of Prohibiting and Preventing the Illicit Import, Export and Transfer of Ownership of Cultural Property 1970," http://portal.unesco.org/en/ev.php-URL_ID=13039&URL_DO=DO_TOPIC&URL_SECTION=201.html. On the significance and implementation, see, e.g., Patricia Gerstenblith, "Implementation of the 1970 UNESCO Convention by the United States and Other Market Nations," in *The Routledge Companion to Cultural Property*, ed. Jane Anderson and Haidy Geisman (New York: Routledge, 2017), 70–88; and Gerstenblith, "The Meaning of 1970 for the Acquisition of Archaeological Objects," *JFA* 38 (2013): 364–73.

[10] William Johnson, "The Oxyrhynchus Distributions in America: Papyri and Ethics," *BASP* 49 (2012): 209–22; and Roberta Mazza, "Papyri, Ethics, and Economics: A Biography of P.Oxy. 15.1780 ($\mathfrak{P}^{39}$)," *BASP* 52 (2015): 113–42.

are now available (figs. 6 and 8, http://ntvmr.uni-muenster.de/manuscript-workspace?docID=10134), whether scholars will be able to examine the fragment for themselves in the future remains, at present, uncertain. One can only hope that the fragment will one day find its way into an open collection.

The Willoughby Papyrus also exposes the unsettling relationship between scholarship and economics. The present article and subsequent scholarship on the fragment will likely increase the monetary value of the manuscript, should it change hands in the future. As troubling as this may be for scholars like myself who view manuscripts not as commodities but as cultural heritage, one should note that the Willoughby fragment is not unique in this respect. The efforts of scholars who worked on P28 (P.Oxy. 12.1538), which the Pacific School of Religion sold to private collector Gifford Combs for an undisclosed sum in 2015, or P39 (P.Oxy. 15.1780), which in 2003 the Colgate Rochester Divinity School sold through Sotheby's to a private collector for a record $400,000 (now part of the Green collection), likely increased the monetary value of these New Testament papyri as well. I doubt many scholars intend to inflate the price tags of the manuscripts they study, but the need to be aware of and reflect on the relationship between scholarship and the antiquities market will only increase as manuscripts continue to surface from private collections and more and more institutions contemplate selling off their textual treasures to private collectors in order to balance budgets. There are no easy solutions to the host of ethical questions raised by scholars such as Johnson and Mazza, but acknowledging the dilemmas we face is a step in the right direction.

Following Willoughby's death the papyrus was kept in a suitcase with a collection of his papers. In about 1990 the suitcase changed hands and was stashed away in an attic. The significance of its contents was largely forgotten until recently, when the new owner, a descendent of Willoughby who inherited some of his papers, opened the suitcase and happened upon the fragment. In the owner's words, "I recently took time to go through [the suitcase] and [the papyrus] fell out from a stack of letters/papers."[11] The fragment made a brief appearance on a popular auction site in early January 2015, and, with the help of Brice Jones, who called attention to the fragment on his blog and prepared a preliminary transcription and analysis of its text, both scholars and collectors became aware of the existence of this previously unknown fragment from the Fourth Gospel.[12] Once informed of its significance, the owner chose to end the auction before the fragment sold. I am grateful to the owner for recognizing the historical value of the papyrus and for allowing me to make available to the scholarly community images and an edition of this intriguing manuscript. I offer the present edition on the basis of a brief,

---

[11] Private correspondence with the owner on 5 January 2015. The owner has asked to remain anonymous.

[12] Brice Jones, "A Greek Papyrus of the Gospel of John for Sale on eBay," *Brice C. Jones: An Academic Website Devoted to Papyrology and More*, posted 4 January 2015, https://www.bricecjones.com/blog/a-greek-papyrus-of-the-gospel-of-john-for-sale-on-ebay.

in-person examination and images I took of the papyrus in March 2015. At present the manuscript has not been multispectrally imaged, nor has the papyrus been subjected to carbon 14 testing. Because many forged manuscripts have surfaced in recent years, most notably the Gospel of Jesus's Wife, one should exercise extra caution when working with manuscripts that lack a secure location of discovery.[13] Nothing about the Willoughby fragment or its history, however, strikes me as suspicious and would lead me to doubt the authenticity of the manuscript.

II. The Willoughby Papyrus

The Willoughby Papyrus consists of three fragments, the largest of which measures 7 cm wide by 4.5 cm tall. Fragments 2 and 3 each measure less than 1 cm square. Ink traces are visible on fragments 2 and 3 but are too small to suggest any letterforms. I have not yet successfully placed them alongside the larger fragment. All three fragments have been semiprofessionally mounted between two plates of glass and labeled "John I, 50–51," perhaps by Willoughby himself.[14]

A vertical crease flanked by symmetrical insect holes indicates that the papyrus was folded at least once in antiquity. The fold may have left the recto (→) exposed since the papyrus on the Gospel of John side is worn and even stained, whereas the papyrus on the Unidentified Christian Text side appears to have been protected from the elements. Evidence of a possible second fold runs vertically through the upstroke of τ in αναβαινοντας ("ascending") on → line 5.

Similarities in letterforms and the overall impression of the hands suggest that the same scribe may have copied both the Gospel of John and the Unidentified Christian Text. On the basis of the available evidence, it is not possible to know how long an interval—if any—separated the copying of the text of John on the recto from the copying of the text on the verso. There are, however, slight differences in the ink hue and stroke thickness between the writing on each side. In the Unidentified Christian Text, the strokes are generally thin and the ink is rich.[15] By comparison, the text of John appears to have been written with a blunter stylus and in

---

[13] In its short life, the Gospel of Jesus's Wife has generated an impressive bibliography. See especially *HTR* 107.2 (2014) and *NTS* 61.3 (2015), both of which include numerous articles on the Gospel of Jesus's Wife.

[14] Regrettably, the mounting tape used has started to yellow and curl in at least one place. I have recommended to its owner that the papyrus be professionally remounted at some point in the near future. This would allow one to attempt to place fragments 2 and 3, replace the translucent tape with transparent tape, and relabel the two sides of the fragment "John 1:49–2:1" and "Unidentified Christian Text." The papyrus would also benefit from multispectral imaging (MSI).

[15] The differences in ink hue are more pronounced in the amateur infrared images I took of the fragment. Proper MSIs will help determine the degree to which the inks differ.

an ink diluted with water or mixed with some other ingredient.[16] These differences suggest that, if a single scribe did indeed copy both texts, the scribe did so in two separate writing events. It is not possible to determine how long the scribe would have waited before writing out the second text, but we can be confident that the scribe copied John's Gospel first because it is written along the fibers.

The handwriting on the Willoughby fragment belongs to Pasquale Orsini and Willy Clarysse's group 2b, a group that had its origins in second- and third-century bureaucratic and chancery writing styles.[17] Orsini and Clarysse divide group 2b into two subgroups, the Alexandrian stylistic class and the Alexandrian chancery script of Subatianus Aquila; the handwriting on the Willoughby Papyrus shares features with both. Several New Testament manuscripts belong to this group, but the most striking parallels to the hand of the Willoughby Papyrus are found in P77, P90, and P103. While examples of this hand appear from the second through fourth centuries, the use of the apostrophe to separate doubled consonants in ↓ line 6 suggests a date after 200 CE.[18] Therefore, the Willoughby Papyrus was likely copied sometime in the third or fourth century CE.

Several scribal features appear throughout the text. An apostrophe separates doubled consonants in ευαγ'γελιζεϲθαι ("to proclaim the gospel") in ↓ line 6.[19] Interlinear marks appear on the recto (→) between [αυ]τω ("to him") and οτι ("namely") in line 2, above the first letter of οψεϲθε ("you will see") in line 4, and over the first letter of αναβαινοντας in line 5. The first and third resemble acute accent marks, and the second resembles what Eric Turner calls a "form 1" smooth breathing mark.[20] Traces of what could be additional acute markings are visible over the ε in [πιϲτε]υειϲ ("do you believe?") in → line 3. No interlinear marks appear in the Unidentified Christian Text. The three certain marks may serve as smooth breathing marks over initial vowels, and the two possible marks could function as additional lectional aids. While the lack of interlinear markings in the Unidentified Christian Text may not be significant, it could indicate that the Gospel of John and the Unidentified Christian Text were not intended to be read in the same way. For example, interlinear markings could suggest a public rather than a private reading context.[21] *Nomina sacra* appear on both sides of the papyrus and include [α̅ν̅]ο̅υ̅ for

---

[16] The apparent difference in ink hue may also be due to the fact that the fragment was possibly folded leaving the ink used to copy the Gospel of John exposed to the elements.

[17] Pasquale Orsini and Willy Clarysse, "Early New Testament Manuscripts and Their Dates: A Critique of Theological Palaeography," *ETL* 88 (2012): 443–74, here 458–59.

[18] Eric G. Turner, *Greek Manuscripts of the Ancient World*, 2nd ed. (London: University of London Institute of Classical Studies, 1987), 11 n. 50.

[19] Ibid., 11.

[20] Ibid.

[21] For recent discussions about the connection between lectional aids and public reading, see Scott D. Charlesworth, "Public and Private—Second- and Third-Century Gospel Manuscripts," in *Jewish and Christian Scripture as Artifact and Canon*, ed. Craig A. Evans and H. Daniel Zacharias, SSEJC 13 (London: T&T Clark, 2009), 148–75; Larry W. Hurtado, *The Earliest Christian*

ἀνθρώπου ("of man") in → line 6, π̅ρ̅α̅ for πατέρα ("Father") in ↓ line 2, and θ̅ν̅ for θεόν ("God") in ↓ line 3. Curiously, the scribe has not abbreviated "God" in → line 5 but has instead written θεοῦ out in full. Given the informal nature of the hand, it is not possible to determine on the basis of available space alone whether Ἰησοῦς ("Jesus") in → line 2 and υἱόν ("Son") in → line 6 were abbreviated. But since the scribe abbreviated ἀνθρώπου in → line 6, the immediately preceding υἱόν was probably also abbreviated.[22]

Inconsistent use of *nomina sacra* is unusual but not unparalleled in the New Testament papyri. Consider for example the uneven application of a *nomen sacrum* for πνεῦμα ("Spirit") in P46 (P. Beatty 2/P.Mich. Inv. 6238). In some instances the scribe writes πνεῦμα and related terms out in full and in others the scribe prefers a *nomen sacrum*. As Joel Estes has recently demonstrated, the distinction between *plene* ("full") and abbreviated spellings of πνεῦμα and related terms does not correspond to a distinction between lesser spirits and the Holy Spirit in P46.[23] The

---

Artifacts: Manuscripts and Christian Origins (Grand Rapids: Eerdmans, 2006), 155-89; and AnneMarie Luijendijk, "Reading the *Gospel of Thomas* in the Third Century: Three Oxyrhynchus Papyri and Origen's Homilies," in *Reading New Testament Papyri in Context / Lire des papyrus du Nouveau Testament dans leur contexte*, ed. Claire Clivaz and Jean Zumstein, BETL 242 (Leuven: Peeters, 2011), 241-67. As a New Testament text with lectional aids copied with the fibers of a roll, the Willoughby John calls into question the universality of Hurtado's claim that Christian rolls were likely meant for private, not public, reading (Hurtado, "The Greek Fragments of the Gospel of Thomas as Artefacts: Papyrological Observations on Papyrus Oxyrhynchus 1, Papyrus Oxyrhynchus 654 and Papyrus Oxyrhynchus 655," in *Das Thomasevangelium: Entstehung - Rezeption - Theologie*, ed. Jörg Frey, Edzard E. Popkes, and Jens Schröter, BZAW 157 [Berlin: de Gruyter, 2008], 19-32, esp. 30).

[22] I do not place too much weight on the likelihood of *nomina sacra* in the lacunae; whether the scribe abbreviated "Jesus" and "Son" is ultimately unknowable. The pitfalls of staking too much on reconstructed *nomina sacra* are apparent in the speculative debates over whether one should reconstruct the full or contracted form of Ἰησοῦς in the lacunae of P52 (P.Rylands Gk. 457). See C. H. Roberts's initial assessment in *An Unpublished Fragment of the Fourth Gospel in the John Rylands Library* (Manchester: Manchester University Press, 1935), and the subsequent exchange between Christopher Tuckett ("P52 and Nomina Sacra," *NTS* 47 [2001]: 544-48), Charles E. Hill ("Did the Scribe of P52 Use the Nomina Sacra? Another Look," *NTS* 48 [2002]: 587-92), and Hurtado ("P52 [P.Rylands Gr 457] and the Nomina Sacra: Method and Probability," *TynBul* 54 [2003]: 1-14). An important difference between P52 and the Willoughby Papyrus, however, is that, unlike P52, where no visible *nomina sacra* have survived, the Willoughby Papyrus does contain *nomina sacra* in the surviving text. On the basis of the scribe's conventions, we can make an educated guess about what may have been lost in the lacunae. On the pitfalls of scholarly reconstructions in general, see most recently Thomas Kraus, "Reconstructing Fragmentary Manuscripts—Chances and Limitations," in *Early Christian Manuscripts: Examples of Applied Method and Approach*, ed. Thomas Kraus and Tobias Nicklas, TENTS 5 (Leiden: Brill, 2010), 1-38.

[23] Joel Estes, "Reading for the Spirit of the Text: Nomina Sacra and πνεῦμα Language in P46," *NTS* 61 (2015): 566-94.

scribe was simply not consistent.[24] Thus, to find terms inconsistently abbreviated in the Willoughby Papyrus, while unusual, is not without precedent.

What is striking about the inconsistent application of *nomina sacra* in the Willoughby Papyrus is the particular word in question. Unlike πνεῦμα, θεός takes its place alongside κύριος ("Lord"), Ἰησοῦς ("Jesus"), and Χριστός ("Christ") as one of four words thought to appear regularly as *nomina sacra* in New Testament papyri.[25] Take P46 again: despite inconsistencies in the appearance of πνεῦμα, the terms θεός, κύριος, Ἰησοῦς, and Χριστός are always rendered as *nomina sacra* when applied to revered beings. On the basis of his detailed analysis of the *nomina sacra* in P46, Estes arrives at the following conclusion: "Thus, the four earliest *nomina sacra*—θεός, κύριος, Ἰησοῦς, and Χριστός—display considerable consistency in P46. With few exceptions, they are used in a 'sacred' sense, and are only written in full to distinguish between the true God or Lord and false gods or lords."[26] The habits of P46 are representative of a broader tendency among scribes of New Testament papyri to abbreviate θεός, κύριος, Ἰησοῦς, and Χριστός as *nomina sacra*. Accordingly, Larry Hurtado remarks that to find "an actual instance of a copy of [a New Testament] text in which unabbreviated forms of these key words were used would be a

---

[24] Estes argues that the inconsistent use of *nomina sacra* for πνεῦμα and related terms "may illustrate wider theological ambiguities among some early Christian communities concerning the status and role of the Holy Spirit" (ibid., 566).

[25] A. H. R. E. Paap lists only one instance of a *plene* spelling of "God" in the sacral sense in the Greek New Testament papyri through the fifth century CE: P.Mich. 130 (Paap no. 8), a third-century copy of the Shepherd of Hermas that in one instance reads θεω rather than the expected $\overline{\theta\omega}$, a reading that Roberts characterizes as "probably a scribal error" (*Manuscript, Society, and Belief in Early Christian Egypt*, Schweich Lectures 1977 [London: British Academy, 1979], 38 n. 4). Even though the Shepherd of Hermas is not considered by most today to be canonical, many early Christians considered it to be Scripture and copied it according to scriptural scribal customs; thus for our purposes the *nomina sacra* conventions in Michigan Hermas are relevant. See A. H. R. E. Paap, *Nomina Sacra in the Greek Papyri of the First Five Centuries A.D.: The Sources and Some Deductions*, PLB 8 (Leiden: Brill, 1959), 6. On account of Paap's observation that the vocative form of θεός was apparently not abbreviated (100), I am not including instances of θεέ among the exceptions. It is also important to keep in mind that his survey of *nomina sacra* is current only through New Testament papyri published prior to 1959. Additionally, here and below I recognize that maintaining a rigid distinction between canonical and noncanonical writings when analyzing Christian manuscripts from the second through fourth centuries—a period when the New Testament as we know it was still taking shape—not only is anachronistic but also has the potential to give rise to misleading conclusions about Christian scriptural scribal conventions. Rather than redraw the traditional boundary customarily at work in New Testament manuscript studies by advocating a capacious understanding of Christian Scripture, one that includes, inter alia, P.Oxy. 655 and P.Oxy. 2949 (the Gospel of Thomas and the alleged Gospel of Peter both copied on the recto [→] of book rolls), I prefer to place the Willoughby John—with its "peculiar" format and *nomina sacra* conventions—alongside manuscripts of the traditional New Testament canon in order to problematize from within the very notion of unique "canonical" or "scriptural" scribal practices.

[26] Estes, "Reading for the Spirit of the Text," 578.

notable exception."²⁷ If, as I argue below, the Willoughby Papyrus once belonged to a continuous copy of the Gospel of John, we now have such a "notable exception." If, on the other hand, the scribe excerpted this passage from the Gospel of John as part of an occasional or private text, then the Willoughby Papyrus joins a small group of nonliterary Christian papyri that abbreviate these four key terms inconsistently if at all.²⁸ Yet, given that the Willoughby Papyrus hails from at least a century after our earliest New Testament papyri and that the scribe abbreviates ανθρώπου to [αν]ου only a line later (not to mention the abbreviation of θν for θεόν in line 3 of the Unidentified Christian Text), the *plene* θεοῦ in → line 5 may not be a relic from an era when Christian *nomina sacra* conventions were still emerging but the product of an inconsistent or inattentive scribe.²⁹ Nonetheless, the full spelling of θεοῦ in → line 5 is noteworthy and should contribute to future research into the origin, development, and use of *nomina sacra* in the biblical papyri.³⁰

The hand of the Willoughby Papyrus is informal and occasionally inclines slightly to the right. The letters ε, θ, o, and c are narrow with the exception of the horizontal stroke of ε, which can extend well beyond the vertical plane established

---

²⁷ Hurtado, "P52 (P.Rylands Gr 457) and the *Nomina Sacra*," 5 n. 15.

²⁸ See, e.g., P.Lond. 413 (TM 10051), P.Oxy. 407, and P.Oxy. 1786. See also the subliterary and documentary texts with full spellings of these terms in Paap, *Nomina Sacra*, 6–75. See also Roberts, *Manuscript, Society, and Belief*, 37–38.

²⁹ Roberts distinguishes two kinds of deviations in *nomina sacra* conventions: "In any period there are very occasional eccentric forms, most of which occur once only and then usually in a badly written manuscript, the result of the misunderstanding or vagaries of a particular scribe." In other instances, however, unusual forms "represent an experimental phase in the history of the system when its limits were not clearly established." The challenge is to determine to which of the two classes the *plene* spelling of "God" in the Willoughby John belongs (Roberts, *Manuscript, Society, and Belief*, 39, quoted by AnneMarie Luijendijk, *Greetings in the Lord: Early Christians and the Oxyrhynchus Papyri*, HTS 60 [Cambridge: Harvard University Press, 2008], 66). See also Bruce Metzger, *Manuscripts of the Greek Bible: An Introduction to Greek Palaeography* (New York: Oxford University Press, 1981), 37.

³⁰ The Willoughby Papyrus could lend support to Don Barker's recent "tentative proposal" for locating the origin of the Christian *nomina sacra* in the Semitic custom of contracting personal names. As evidence for this hypothesis, Barker points to the use of *nomina sacra* in P.Lond.Lit. 207, a third-century fragment from a Psalms scroll in which κύριος and ἄνθρωπος are written as *nomina sacra*, but θεός is not ("P.Lond.Lit. 207 and the Origin of the *Nomina Sacra*: A Tentative Proposal," *Studia Humaniora Tartuensia* 8.A.2 [2007]: 1–14). Barker is building upon the prior work of A. Millard, "Ancient Abbreviations and the *Nomina Sacra*," in *The Unbroken Reed: Studies in the Culture and Heritage of Ancient Egypt in Honour of A. F. Shore*, ed. Christopher J. Eyre, M. Anthony Leahy, and Lisa Montagno Leahy, Occasional Publications of the Egypt Exploration Society 11 (London: Egypt Exploration Society, 1994), 221–26. In addition to comparable use of *nomina sacra*, similarities in hand, date, and format between the Willoughby Papyrus and P.Lond. Lit. 207 suggest that further comparison of the two would be fruitful. For other theories about the origin of the *nomina sacra*, see Larry W. Hurtado, "The Origin of the Nomina Sacra: A Proposal," *JBL* 117 (1998): 655–73, https://doi.org/10.2307/3266633; Hurtado, *Earliest Christian Artifacts*, 112–20; and Roberts, *Manuscript, Society, and Belief*, 26–48.

by the top and bottom arcs (see especially ↓ line 5). Distinctive letterforms include wedged-shaped α with occasional overhanging top stroke (see the first α on → line 5 and ↓ line 2); ε with elongated horizontal stroke; μ with a curved center stroke that rests on the bottom line; ν with second stroke that consistently connects above the midpoint of the second vertical; υ formed in one continuous stroke; and β, ζ, ι, κ, ξ, ρ, and ψ that extend below the bottom line. With the exception of the combination ει, in which the horizontal stroke of the ε consistently connects to the upstroke of the ι (see the occurrences of ει on → lines 3 and 4), and τω (→ line 2), where the top stroke of the τ drops to form the initial down stroke of the ω, letters are individually formed. Hooks appear in varying lengths at the stroke-ends of γ, η, ι, κ, ν, π, ρ, τ, υ, and ψ. These serifs are reminiscent of the stroke-ends on some of the letterforms seen in P52 (P. Ryl. Gk. 457),[31] but they more closely resemble the exaggerated hooks found in later hands influenced by bureaucratic scripts. The hand of the Willoughby Papyrus belongs to Orsini and Clarysse's "cursive and informal documentary" group, while also exhibiting features of chancery scripts.[32] Similar hands appear in the following dated papyri: P.Flor. 208 (256 CE); P.Flor. 268 (ca. 249–268 CE); and P.Panop. 27 (323 CE). Biblical papyri copied in similar hands that have been assigned dates on the basis of paleography alone include P.Oxy. 3.402 (= P9; 275–325 CE; all dates are according to Orsini and Clarysse); P.Oxy. 10.1228 (MS Gen 1026/13 = P22; 250–300 CE); and P. Mich. 137 (= P37; 250–300 CE). In light of these parallels, the Willoughby Papyrus likely dates to 250–350 CE. This proposed date is supported by the use of apostrophe to separate doubled consonants in ευαγ'γελιζεϲθαι in ↓ line 6, a scribal feature that appears more frequently after ca. 200 CE.[33]

The format of the Willoughby Papyrus is unusual. Even though there is writing on both sides of the papyrus, the fragment does not come from a codex. After the Gospel of John was copied, the papyrus was turned over and rotated 180° in order to copy the Unidentified Christian Text; in other words, if one flips the John fragment horizontally the Unidentified Christian Text is upside-down. That the biblical text appears on only one side of the papyrus raises two possibilities about its original format: either the fragment from John's Gospel was part of a noncontinuous text, such as an amulet, or it belonged to a bookroll.[34] Both the fold lines

---

[31] For discussion of P52's ornamental "flourishes" or "hooks," see Roberts, *Unpublished Fragment*, 13; Brent Nongbri, "The Use and Abuse of 𝔓52: Papyrological Pitfalls in the Dating of the Fourth Gospel," *HTR* 98 (2005), 23–48, here 28, 43; and Hurtado, "P52 (P.Rylands Gr 457) and the *Nomina Sacra*," 4.

[32] Orsini and Clarysse, "Early New Testament Manuscripts," 443–74.

[33] Turner, *Greek Manuscripts*, 19.

[34] Eldon Jay Epp defines continuous texts as "MSS containing (originally) at least one NT writing in continuous fashion from beginning to end" ("The Papyrus Manuscripts of the New Testament," in *The Text of the New Testament in Contemporary Research: Essays on the Status Quaestionis*, ed. Bart D. Ehrman and Michael W. Holmes, SD 46 [Grand Rapids: Eerdmans, 1995], 3–21, here 5). For a fresh analysis of many of the noncontinuous biblical papyri, see Brice Jones,

on the papyrus and the fact that it contains material from a gospel raise the possibility that the Willoughby Papyrus is an amulet. Amulets were often folded,[35] and excerpts from the gospels are common in biblical amulets. Among the 186 "certain," "probable," and "possible" Egyptian Christian amulets in Greek and Latin catalogued by Theodore de Bruyn and Jitse Dijkstra, twenty-five include excerpts from the canonical gospels.[36] Most of these amulets draw upon an established repertoire of biblical texts: gospel incipits; the Lord's Prayer; and passages about protection, healing, or other manifestations of divine power, for example, Matt 4:23: "Jesus went throughout Galilee, teaching in their synagogues and proclaiming the good news of the kingdom and *curing every disease and every sickness among the people*" (NRSV).[37]

Though not a common text in the biblical amulets, the wedding at Cana did belong to this repertoire. P.Vind. G 2312 (de Bruyn/Dijkstra no. 59) is an amulet that has been dated as early as the fourth century and as late as the seventh.[38] It quotes Ps 90:1–2, Rom 12:1–2, and John 2:1–2. The juxtaposition of these particular verses, culminating in the beginning of the wedding at Cana led the text's first editor to suggest that the amulet functioned as a wedding charm.[39] Recently Joseph Sanzo

---

New Testament Texts on Greek Amulets from Late Antiquity, LNTS 554 (London: Bloomsbury T&T Clark, 2016).

[35] Theodore de Bruyn and Jitse Dijkstra, "Greek Amulets and Formularies from Egypt Containing Christian Elements: A Checklist of Papyri, Parchments, Ostraka, and Tablets," *BASP* 48 (2011): 163–216, here 172. See also de Bruyn, "Papyri, Parchments, Ostraca, and Tablets Written with Biblical Texts in Greek and Used as Amulets: A Preliminary List," in Kraus and Nicklas, *Early Christian Manuscripts*, 145–89, here 149–50.

[36] De Bruyn and Dijkstra, "Greek Amulets and Formularies," 163–216. Not included in this statistic are P.Oxy. 16.1928, which alludes to the four Gospels, and P.Berl. 11710, a fragment from an otherwise unknown apocryphal gospel. Since the publication of de Bruyn and Dijkstra's list, two additional gospel amulets in Greek have been published: P.Oxy. 76.5073 and P.Ryl. Gk. Add. 1166.

[37] This verse appears in *BKT* (*Berliner Klassikertexte*) 6.7.1 (de Bruyn/Dijkstra no. 4) and *PGM* P4 (*P.Oxy.* 8.1077; de Bruyn/Dijkstra no. 19). See also Theodore de Bruyn, "Appeals to Jesus as the One 'Who Heals Every Illness and Every Infirmity' (Matt 4:23, 9:35) in Amulets in Late Antiquity," in *The Reception and Interpretation of the Bible in Late Antiquity: Proceedings of the Montréal Colloquium in Honour of Charles Kannengiesser, 11–13 October 2006*, ed. Lorenzo DiTommaso and Lucian Turcescu, Bible in Ancient Christianity 6 (Leiden: Brill, 2008), 65–81.

[38] C. F. G. Heinrici assigned the papyrus to the fourth century (*Die Leipziger Papyrusfragmente der Psalmen*, Beiträge zur Geschichte und Erklärung des Neuen Testaments 4 [Leipzig: Dürr, 1903], 31–32). Carl Wessely assigned it to the sixth or seventh century (*Le plus anciens monuments du Christianisme écrits sur papyrus (II)*, PO 18.3 [Paris: Firmin-Didot, 1924], 411). Most recently, Brice Jones has argued for a date of fifth or sixth century (*New Testament Texts on Greek Amulets*, 172).

[39] Carl Wessely, *Catalogus papyrorum Raineri: Series Graeca, Pars I: Textus graeci papyrorum qui in libro "Papyrus Erzherzog Rainer-Führer durch die Ausstellung Wien 1894" descripti sunt*, 2 vols., StPP 20 (Leipzig: E. Avenarius, 1920–1922), 1:294.

has proposed an alternative purpose for the amulet.[40] By copying the beginning of the wedding at Cana, Sanzo argues, the ritual specialist was invoking not Jesus's blessing upon a marriage but his ability to work miracles. When interpreted alongside Ps 90:1–2, a passage that appears often in healing amulets, and Rom 12:1–2, which reads "living soul" in place of "living sacrifice," Sanzo concludes that P.Vind. G 2312 "was not an amulet for newly-weds. It is more likely that we are dealing with a general healing or protective amulet."[41] Despite these differing interpretations, the appearance of John 2:1–2 in P.Vind. G 2312 demonstrates that the wedding at Cana belongs to the repertoire of known appropriations of the gospels in biblical amulets, either as a promise of God's blessing on a marriage or as a reassurance of divine power.

One could appeal to P.Vind. G 2312 to support an argument for identifying the Willoughby Papyrus as the fragmentary remains of a biblical amulet. Such an argument could be augmented by appeal to P.Berl. 11710, an amulet with cord still attached that preserves an apocryphal dialogue between Nathaniel and Jesus. As commentators have noted, the conversation between Nathaniel and Jesus in P.Berl. 11710 resembles Nathaniel's exchange with Jesus during his calling in John 1:47–51.[42] With both Jesus's exchange with Nathaniel and the wedding at Cana attested in the corpus of biblical amulets, it is tempting to conclude that the Willoughby Papyrus is a fragment from a biblical amulet. But even if the two episodes appear in the corpus of Christian amulets, the presence of *both* of these passages in sequential order in the Willoughby Papyrus leaves little doubt that what is being copied out is the biblical narrative, not isolated pericopes excerpted for their magical import. Aside from incipits, which are occasionally quoted at length, I know of no Greek gospel amulets in which a scribe copied out multiple pericopes in sequential order.[43]

---

[40] Joseph Sanzo, *Scriptural Incipits on Amulets from Late Antique Egypt: Text, Typology, and Theory*, STAC 84 (Tübingen: Mohr Siebeck, 2014), 166–68.

[41] Ibid., 167.

[42] For editions of and commentary on P.Berl. 11710, see Andrew Bernhard, *Other Early Christian Gospels: A Critical Edition of the Surviving Greek Manuscripts*, LNTS 315 (London: Clark, 2006), 102; Bart D. Ehrman and Zlatko Pleše, *The Apocryphal Gospels: Texts and Translations* (New York: Oxford University Press, 2011), 237–39; J. K. Elliott, *The Apocryphal New Testament: A Collection of Apocryphal Christian Literature in an English Translation* (Oxford: Clarendon, 1993), 42–43; Hans Leitzmann, "Ein apokryphes Evangelienfragment," *ZNW* 22 (1923): 153–54; and Aurelio de Santos Otero, *Los Evangelios apócrifos: Colección de textos griegos y latinos, versión crítica, estudios introductorios y comentarios*, rev. ed., BAC 148 (Madrid: Biblioteca de Autores Christianos, 2003), 80.

[43] One could point to P.Oxy. 64.4406 (de Bruyn/Dijkstra no. 122 = P105) as an example of a gospel amulet with multiple passages quoted. P.Oxy. 64.4406 is a fragment from a fifth- or sixth-century codex of Matthew's Gospel that preserves Matt 27:62–64 and 28:2–5. On the basis of a small thread still attached to the fragment, J. David Thomas concluded that P.Oxy. 4406 was once used as an amulet. Yet its format leaves no doubt that the fragment once belonged to a Matthew

Even if the Willoughby Papyrus was not likely copied as an amulet, it still may belong to another class of noncontinuous texts, such as a writing exercise, an aide-mémoire, or a *hermeneia* of the Gospel of John. In theory these other possibilities cannot be ruled out, but in the absence of any positive evidence such as remnants of a cord, an unexpected margin or *vacat* suggesting an interruption in the biblical narrative, or the appearance of the term ἑρμηνεία ("interpretation"), the possibility that the Willoughby Papyrus belonged to a noncontinuous biblical text remains remote. The fact that the manuscript has fold marks does not count as positive evidence that it was a noncontinuous text. While it is true that many noncontinuous biblical texts were folded (see, e.g., P.Oxy. 2.209 = P10), continuous biblical texts can have visible crease marks as well.[44] Consider the horizontal and vertical fold marks on P.Oxy. 10.1229 (= P23), a fragment from the letter of James written on a leaf from a codex. This fragment may have been removed from a codex and reused as an amulet or aide-mémoire, but that it may have been folded and repurposed as an amulet says nothing about whether it belonged to a continuous or noncontinuous text. Despite the fold marks, P.Oxy. 10.1229 originally belonged to a continuous biblical text copied out in codex format.[45] With P.Oxy. 10.1229 in mind, the fold marks on the Willoughby Papyrus leave open the possibility that it was reused as an amulet, an aide-mémoire, or some other kind of text that was kept on one's person. However, they do not necessarily speak to the original design of the fragment.

The available evidence instead suggests that our fragment from the Gospel of John was part of a continuous copy of the Fourth Gospel in roll format. The overwhelming majority of New Testament papyri were copied out in codices. On the rare occasion that New Testament texts were written on rolls, they are copied on the back of inscribed rolls. Examples include British Library Pap. 1532 (P.Oxy. 4.657 + PSI 12.1292 = P13), multiple numbered columns from the Epistle to the Hebrews written on the back of the Epitome of Livy (P.Oxy. 4.668), and P.IFAO inv. 2.31 (= P98), a copy of Revelation written on the back of a documentary text.[46] P.Oxy. 10.1228 (= P22), two columns of the Gospel of John written against the fibers, may also have been copied onto the back of a roll, but the fact that the extant portion of

---

codex and was only later repurposed as an amulet. In other words, Matt 27:62–64 and 28:2–5 were not chosen specifically for the amulet; they happened to be the portion of the biblical text that survived on the repurposed fragment.

[44] For a recent study of P.Oxy. 2.209 and its function, see AnneMarie Luijendijk, "A New Testament Papyrus and Its Documentary Context: An Early Christian Writing Exercise from the Archive of Leonides (P.Oxy. II 209/P¹⁰)," *JBL* 129 (2010): 575–96, https://doi.org/10.2307/25765953.

[45] Don Barker, "The Reuse of Christian Texts: *P.Macquarie inv.* 360 + *P.Mil.Vogl.inv* 1224 (𝔓⁹¹) and *P.Oxy.* X 1229 (𝔓²³)," in Kraus and Nicklas, *Early Christian Manuscripts*, 129–43, here 137–38.

[46] For a recent study of the often neglected phenomenon of the Christian roll, see Luijendijk, "Reading the *Gospel of Thomas*," 247–54.

the other side is uninscribed leaves open the possibility, however remote, that P.Oxy. 10.1228 comes from a one-sided roll copied against the fibers.[47] P.Oxy. 8.1079 (= P18), a leaf with Exodus on the recto (→) and Revelation on the verso (↓) was once regarded as another instance of a New Testament reused roll, but recently Brent Nongbri has made a strong case in favor of seeing both texts as belonging to a single, albeit eclectic, codex.[48] New Testament texts copied onto the backs of rolls are reused manuscripts and thus are rolls of convenience not by design. For this reason they are not necessarily artifacts from an earlier era in which Christians preferred the roll to the codex.[49]

A strong argument that the Gospel of John side of the Willoughby Papyrus was copied onto an unused bookroll can be made on the basis of an often-overlooked feature of reused rolls to which Nongbri has recently called attention. In nearly every example of a Christian literary text written on the reverse of a reused roll, the scribe rotated the roll 180° before copying the new text. For example, the text of Hebrews in British Library Pap. 1532 (P.Oxy. 4.657 + PSI 12.1292 = P13) is copied upside down in relation to the Epitome of Livy (P.Oxy. 4.668). Other examples of this practice include two copies of the Psalms, PSI 8.921 and P.Lips. 1.97; P.IFAO inv. 2.31 (= P98); and P.Mich. inv. 44 and P.Oxy. 69.4705, the two copies of the Shepherd of Hermas on reused rolls. According to Nongbri, "the only Christian literary text on the reverse of a reused roll not known to me to be written right-side up relative to the 'recto' is P.Oxy. 4 654, a fragment of the Gospel of Thomas copied on the reverse of a land register."[50] While a comprehensive review of the available evidence is in order, Nongbri's preliminary findings indicate that, when Christians reused rolls, they preferred to rotate them 180° prior to copying the new text.

The reason for the seemingly peculiar practice becomes apparent when a scenario offered by William Johnson is imagined:

> A roll that has been rolled back up after reading will have the beginning of the recto (→) text as the outermost part of the roll. To begin writing on the verso, the roll must be rotated 180° so that writing can proceed from left to right,

---

[47] C. H. Roberts and T. C. Skeat consider P22 to be aberrant and do not incorporate it into their analysis of Christian rolls (*The Birth of the Codex* [London: British Academy, 1983], 39–40). Kurt Aland suggests that the scribe may have added leaves at the end of the used roll (*Studien zur Überlieferung des Neuen Testaments und seines Textes*, ANTF 2 [Berlin: de Gruyter, 1967], 114). See also Luijendijk, "Reading the *Gospel of Thomas*," 251.

[48] Brent Nongbri, "Losing a Curious Christian Scroll but Gaining a Curious Christian Codex: An Oxyrhynchus Papyrus of Exodus and Revelation," *NovT* 55 (2013): 77–88.

[49] PSI inv. 108 (= P93), a fragment of John 13 written along the fibers, is likely a noncontinuous text on a sheet rather than a continuous copy of John on a roll.

[50] Nongbri adds an important caveat to this statement: "P.Oxy. 10.1228, a copy of parts of two columns of the Gospel of John written against the fibers (↓) is blank on the 'recto' (→); so we cannot tell the orientation of the two sides" ("Losing a Curious Christian Scroll," 87 n. 26).

resulting in the beginning of the verso (↓) text and the beginning of the recto (→) text being at the same end of the papyrus but upside-down relative to one another.[51]

On the other hand, one could appeal to P.Oxy. 4.654 and imagine a scenario in which an unrolled roll is flipped and reused, in which case the verso (↓) text would not appear upside-down relative to the recto (→) text. But the manuscript record suggests that more often than not Christians rotated rolls for reuse while they were still rolled up. Rotating a rolled-up roll was likely more manageable than rotating an unrolled roll, which could extend for several feet.

Rotating a roll 180° prior to reuse can account for the otherwise perplexing format of the Willoughby Papyrus, wherein two distinct literary texts are written on either side of the papyrus, upside-down in relation to each other. Thus, the most likely explanation is that the Gospel of John was copied onto the recto (→) of a roll, and then at some later time when the same scribe decided to copy another Christian literary text on the verso (↓), he or she rotated the rolled-up papyrus 180° before copying out the Unidentified Christian Text (fig. 4).[52] If this assessment is correct,

---

[51] Nongbri, "Losing a Curious Christian Scroll," 87, on the basis of personal correspondence with William Johnson on 7 September 2011.

[52] If the same scribe did copy both the Gospel of John and the Unidentified Christian Text, then the Willoughby Papyrus would be an example of an opisthograph, a roll inscribed on both sides by a single scribe. For other examples of opisthographs, see, e.g., the P.CtYBR inv. 2082(A) + P.CtYBR inv. 2082(B), two separate works of Isocrates copied by the same scribe. In his edition of the text, Alan Samuel offers some interesting thoughts on the advantage of single-scribe opisthographs and their possible place in the history of ancient bookmaking: "The copying of texts back to back is rare, but not unparalleled. The procedure achieves not only a conservation of papyrus, but probably more important, a saving of storage space. There is also the advantage that, if the sides are read in sequence, the roll upon completion is in fact re-rolled. This papyrus gives us some insight into the attempts to overcome the disadvantages of the roll, attempts which were never really successful. The roll, inherently awkward, with inevitable difficulty of reference, with its cumbersomeness for reading and inconvenience for storage, had to be replaced. It may have been opisthograph rolls like this one, solving some but not all of the problems of the roll, which led to opisthograph writing on sheets to be bound together, forming the codex, the great innovation which totally changed the nature of books" ("An Early Papyrus Text of Isocrates: P. Yale Inventory 2082," in *Homage to a Bookman: Essays on Manuscripts, Books and Printing Written for Hans P. Kraus on His 60th Birthday, Oct. 12, 1967*, ed. Hellmut Lehmann-Haupt [Berlin: Mann, 1967], 17–23, here 20). While in my opinion Samuel exaggerates the clumsiness of the roll, he is right to point out that opisthographs and codices both have the advantage of "saving storage space." It is entirely possible that a similar interest in saving space compelled the scribe of the Willoughby Papyrus to copy two literary texts on a single roll, even as most of the scribe's Christian contemporaries opted to save space by making use of the codex format. See also Susan A. Stephens, *Yale Papyri in the Beinecke Rare Book and Manuscript Library II*, ASP 24 (Chico, CA: Scholars Press, 1985), 42–49 and pls. 1 and 2. One finds mention of opisthographs in Pliny the Younger (*Ep.* 3.5.17; discussed in Harry Gamble, *Books and Readers in the Early Church: A History of Early Christian Texts* [New Haven: Yale University Press, 1995], 267 n. 21), who reports that his uncle left him 160 notebooks inscribed on both sides.

then the Willoughby Papyrus furnishes us with the first known instance of a New Testament text copied onto the recto (→) of a papyrus roll.[53] As one scholar has recently remarked, "throughout antiquity the book roll was the primary vehicle for literature. Its use for a Christian text, however, contravenes strong Christian preference for the codex as book format. In the material world of early Christian manuscripts, book rolls stand out."[54] As a New Testament text written on an unused roll, the Willoughby John not only stands out; it is peerless.

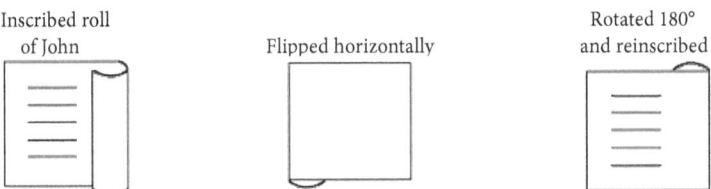

FIGURE 4. Explanation of the Format of the Willoughby Papyrus

Despite the lack of physical evidence for New Testament texts copied on the recto (→) of bookrolls, there is reason to believe that early Christians did occasionally write their texts out in roll format. Given that the earliest Jesus followers belonged to a renewal movement *within* Judaism, they likely adopted the Jewish practice of copying their own sacred writings onto rolls. Glimpses of this practice survive in the Acts of Peter, a late second-century apocryphal work in which Peter "rolls up" a gospel scroll.[55] Likewise, in the second-century Acts of the Scillitan Martyrs, a group of Christians claims to possess "books and letters of Paul" in a *capsa*, a cylindrical container designed to hold multiple bookrolls (12). Literary reports such as these affirm that, despite the dearth of physical evidence for first-order Christian bookrolls, copies of New Testament texts such as the Gospels and the Pauline Epistles did circulate in roll format. If the Willoughby Papyrus in indeed a fragment from a bookroll, it helps to close the gap between the literary and papyrological records.

Since margins do not survive on either side of the Willoughby Papyrus, the precise alignment of the extant text cannot be known. On the basis of the reconstructed text of John, we can determine that the recto (→) would have contained approximately 40 to 45 letters per line and columns would have measured approximately 17 cm wide. Such broad columns are exceptional when compared to

---

[53] Independent confirmation that the Willoughby John belonged to a roll comes from its estimated original format, which is nearly identical to British Library Pap. 1532 (P.Oxy. 4.657 + PSI 12.1292 = P13), the Hebrews reused roll. See discussion below.

[54] Luijendijk, "Reading the *Gospel of Thomas*," 247–48.

[55] "When Peter came into the dining-room he saw that the gospel was being read. And *rolling it up* he said …" (Acts Pet. 20). Translation from J. K. Elliott, *Apocryphal New Testament: A Collection of Apocryphal Christian Literature in an English Translation* (Oxford: Clarendon, 2009), 413 (emphasis added). See also Gamble, *Books and Readers*, 80–81.

non-Christian prose rolls, which usually measure between 4 and 8 cm wide.[56] Column widths in P.Vind. G2316, a fourth-century roll of Isocrates's *Ad Nicolem*, are remarkably wide, though they still extend only 15.9 cm.[57] Greek poetry rolls can sometimes extend to more than 20 cm wide, but such great length is the result of dividing the Greek text up into metrical units.[58] For this reason, Greek verse manuscripts are not suitable *comparanda* for the Willoughby John. There is evidence to suggest, however, that Christian rolls could have exceptionally broad columns. The format of British Library Pap. 1532 (P.Oxy. 4.657 + PSI 12.1292 = P13) is strikingly similar to the Willoughby John. Lines contain an average of 40 letters, and columns would have measured approximately 17 cm wide.[59] Even if the columns of the Willoughby John appear exceptionally wide when compared to non-Christian prose rolls, they are quite in keeping with the broad columns of P13. With averages of 40+ letters per line and column widths of approximately 17 cm, the Willoughby John and P13 exhibit line lengths that are more common in literary codices than rolls.[60]

Written on the back of the John roll and likely in the same hand is an Unidentified Christian Text. Unfortunately, very little text survives, and its precise literary character cannot be determined. Nonetheless, the content of the surviving text raises the possibility that the fragment belongs to a Christian apologetic work with narrative elements, such as an apocryphal acts, martyrdom text, or apology. The progression of the text is as follows:

1. theological statement: τον π(ατε)ρα και ̣ ̣ ̣ [...] τον θ(εο)ν
2. assurance that a particular house(hold) is of one mind: [πα]ς οικος ην ομοτονω[c]
3. claim about the abstract principles of government: [τα ηγ]εμονικα τελε[ι]ν
4. preaching of the gospel to a person or group: ευαγ'γελιϲεϲθαι α[υτω/ α[υτοιc

All that survives of the theological statement is a string of divine names in the accusative that is too generic to comment upon. Following the theological statement is a new clause beginning with the adverb μεταξυ followed by postpositive δε, an expression that often signals a shift in time in a narrative. Representative of this

---

[56] William Johnson, *Bookrolls and Scribes in Oxyrhynchus*, Studies in Book and Print Culture (Toronto: University of Toronto Press, 2004), 101–2.

[57] Ibid., 174.

[58] See ibid., 175–84, table 3.2.

[59] I have arrived at these statistics on the basis of my own calculations of letters per line and line lengths in PSI 12.1292.

[60] What this observation means for the historical development of book technology, however, remains to be determined.

usage is Dio Chrysostom's *Or.* 1 (*1 Regn.* 52), where he describes getting lost while wandering in exile: "As I walked along the Alpheus on my way from Heraea to Pisa, I succeeded in finding the road for some distance. But all at once [μεταξὺ δέ] I got into some woodland and rough country, where a number of trails led to sundry herds and flocks, without meeting anybody or being able to inquire my way."[61] The expression could signal a similarly abrupt shift in narrative in the Willoughby Papyrus as well.

Next comes a claim that a household stands in agreement. The expression "[the entire] household was uniformly" ([πα]ς οικος ην ομοτονω[ς]) is reminiscent of the unity statements in the Acts of the Apostles (e.g., 2:46–47), where members of the fledgling church are "in one accord" (ὁμοθυμαδόν), have favor with "all the people" (ὅλον τὸν λαόν), and share meals "from house to house" (κατ' οἶκον).

From an assurance of unanimity the text moves to what appears to be a claim about perfecting the abstract principles of government. Even though the reading of this line is tentative, the expression has echoes of Philo's *Embassy to Gaius*. Philo places on the lips of an unruly Gaius the following criticism of ignorant authorities: "But some persons in their shameless audacity dare to put themselves forward as interpreters and perfecters of the principles of government [ἱεροφαντεῖν καὶ τελεῖν τὰ ἡγεμονικά], when in reality they scarcely ought to be enrolled among those who have any understanding whatever of the matter" (*Legat.* 56.5–6).[62] Implicit in the expression [τα ηγ]εμονικα τελε[ι]ν in the Willoughby Papyrus might be a similar critique of authority; the expression could have been placed paradoxically on the lips of an ignorant politician, or perhaps the unified household in the previous line is claiming that Christians are able to perfect the imperfect principles of government at work in the world.

In the last line of the fragment we encounter the preaching of the gospel. The voice of the infinitive ευαγ'γελιζεςθαι can be taken as middle ("to preach the gospel") or passive ("to be preached the gospel"). Since the middle voice is more common, it is more likely that the following α introduces the person (α[υτω]) or group (α[υτοις]) to whom the gospel is preached. Less likely, but still possible, is that ἀπό follows the infinitive and introduces the person or group that preaches the gospel. A similar expression appears in 1 Clem. 42.1: "The apostles were given the gospel for us *by the Lord Jesus Christ*" (οἱ ἀπόστολοι ἡμῖν εὐηγγελίσθησαν ἀπὸ τοῦ κυρίου Ἰησοῦ Χριστοῦ) (trans. Ehrman, LCL).

The themes of theology, unity, critique of government, and proclamation are admittedly generically Christian, but they coalesce in apocryphal acts, martyrdom texts, and other types of apologetic works such as apologies, sermons, and

---

[61] Trans. J. W. Cohoon (LCL) with slight modification. See also, e.g., Dio Chrysostom, *Borysth.* 24 (*Or.* 36); and Eusebius, *Praep. ev.* 10.9.

[62] Trans. Charles Duke Yonge, *The Works of Philo Judaeus, the Contemporary of Josephus*, 4 vols. (London: H. G. Bohn, 1854–1890).

theological treatises. Unfortunately the text is too fragmentary to identify further the Willoughby Unidentified Christian Text.

III. Edition, Notes, and Images

In the notes below I offer a collation of the biblical text against the 28th edition of Nestle-Aland, *Novum Testamentum Graece* (NA[28]); sigla and manuscript abbreviations are detailed in the introduction to that edition. For fuller apparatuses of this passage in the Gospel of John, see Reuben J. Swanson, *New Testament Greek Manuscripts: Variant Readings Arranged in Horizontal Lines against Codex Vaticanus* (Pasadena, CA: William Carey International University Press, 1995); and the CNTTS [Center for New Testament Textual Studies] New Testament Critical Apparatus. In the final variation unit I have reported the reading of P.Vind. G 2312, a Greek amulet that preserves John 2:1–2.[63] In each of the three variation units where the reading is certain, the text of the Willoughby Papyrus agrees with P66 P75 ℵ A L W^s and *l*2211. Additionally, the fragment contains no singular readings and agrees with the text of John as established by the editors of NA[28] in each of the three variation units where the reading is certain.

→ John 1:49–2:1 (P134)

```
       ] . . ςιλ .[.]. [1-2] . . . .[ραηλ                              John 1.49
   απεκριθη ιης και ειπεν αυ]τω οτι ειπον coι οτι [ειδον                50
   cε υποκατω της cυκης πιcτε]υεις μειζω τ . . . [ων οψη
   και λεγει αυτω αμην αμην λεγω] υμειν οψεσθε τον ο[υ]ρα[νον            51
 5 ανεωγοτα και τους αγγελους το]υ θεου αναβαινοντας κ[αι
   καταβαινοντας επι τον υν του αν]ου και [τη] ημερ[α] τη [τρ-          2.1
```
→

1 Visible ink traces are too faint to determine whether the text reads βαcιλευc ει (so P75 A B L W^s Ψ f^1 33. 579. *l*2211) or ει ο βαcιλευc (so P66 ℵ K Γ Δ Θ f^{13} 565. 700. 892. 1241. 1424 𝔐 sy^h; Ir^{lat} Epiph).

2 ιης: It is not possible to determine on the basis of available space whether the scribe wrote ιηcουc or ιης (or perhaps ιc) here.

[63] I recognize that noncontinuous biblical texts are not traditionally reported in collations, but I share Brice Jones's desire to see these manuscripts taken seriously both as witnesses to the text of the New Testament and as instances of scriptural reception in late antiquity. "Our hope in producing this work," Jones writes with reference to his recent study of biblical amulets, "is that others will be able to benefit from a collection of these neglected ancient witnesses and to use them, where appropriate, within text-critical research. We also hope that the analyses of individual amulets and their contexts will enrich a larger area of inquiry concerning what these artifacts reveal about the lives and religious perspectives of the late antique Egyptian Christians who used them" (*New Testament Texts on Greek Amulets*, 27).

ὅτι: P66 P75 ℵ A B L Wˢ Ψ f¹³ l2211 a b r¹ ¦ om. K Γ Δ Θ f¹ 33. 565. 579. 700. 892. 1241. 1424 𝔐 lat.

3 [υποκατω της cυκης]: υπο την cυκην (so P66) is not likely here given the available space.

μειζω: μειζων (so P75 Δ 579. 1424. l2211) is possible, but less likely. μειζονα (so P66 ℵ; Epiph) can be ruled out given the available space between ζ and the following τ.

4 υμειν: leg. υμιν. For ει/ι interchange, see Francis T. Gignac, *Phonology*, vol. 1 of *A Grammar of the Greek Papyri of the Roman and Byzantine Periods*, TDSA 55 (Milan: Cisalpino-La Goliardica, 1976), 1:189–91.

οψεcθε: so P66 P75 ℵ B L Wˢ 579. l2211 lat; Epiph ¦ απ αρτι οψεcθε A K Γ Δ Θ Ψ f¹·¹³ 33. 565. 700. 892. 1241. 1424 𝔐 e q r¹ sy

6 τον υ̅ν̅: It is not possible to determine on the basis of available space alone whether the scribe wrote υιον or υ̅ν̅, but given that ανθρωπου is abbreviated, υἱόν was likely also abbreviated.

ημερ[α] τη [τρ(ιτη)]: τριτη ημερα B Θ f¹³ (P.Vind. G 2312)

↓ Unidentified Christian Text
Diplomatic Transcription
     ]. [....]. . .[
   ].τονπ̅ρ̅ακαι. . .[
   ]τονθ̅ν̅μεταξυδε[
   ]ϲοικοϲηνομοτ. . .[
5].μο.ικατελ.[.]ν.[
   ]ευαγ'γελιζεϲθα . α[
     ]. . .[

Reconstruction
↓]. [....]. . .[...
   ]. τον π(ατε)ρα και . . .   ...] the Father and [...
   ] τον θ(εο)ν. μεταξυ δε [...] God. Meanwhile [...
   ... πα]ϲ οικοϲ ην ομοτονω[ϲ   ...the entire] household was uniformly [...
5 ...τα ηγ]εμονικα τελε[ι]ν .[...] to perfect the principles of government [...
   ] ευαγ'γελιζεϲθαι α[υτοιϲ   ...] to proclaim the gospel [to them ...
   ]. . .[...
↓

2 There is a *vacat* between και and τον. See the similar space between θ(εο)ν and μεταξυ in line 3.

4 [πα]ϲ οικοϲ: also possible is [ο ολο]ϲ οικοϲ.

ομοτονω[ϲ]: After examining a digital image of the manuscript, Luijendijk and Roger Bagnall noted that the papyrus may be misaligned in line 4, and they suspected that, once realigned, the ink traces may suggest λ rather than μ. Luijendijk offers ὁλοτελής as a possibility. Though I think the fragments are properly aligned and still prefer μ, I offer the reconstruction ομοτονω[ϲ] tentatively, pending an in-person reexamination of the papyrus.

5 [τα ηγ]εμονικα: [ο ηγ]εμονικος is also possible, but the available space seems too small for ος.

6 ᾳ[υτοις]: I take the voice of ευαγ'γελιζεςθαι to be middle, so ᾳ[υτω] is also possible. One could also interpret the infinitive as passive, in which case ἀπό plus an agent in the genitive would be expected. See, e.g., 1 Clem. 42.1.

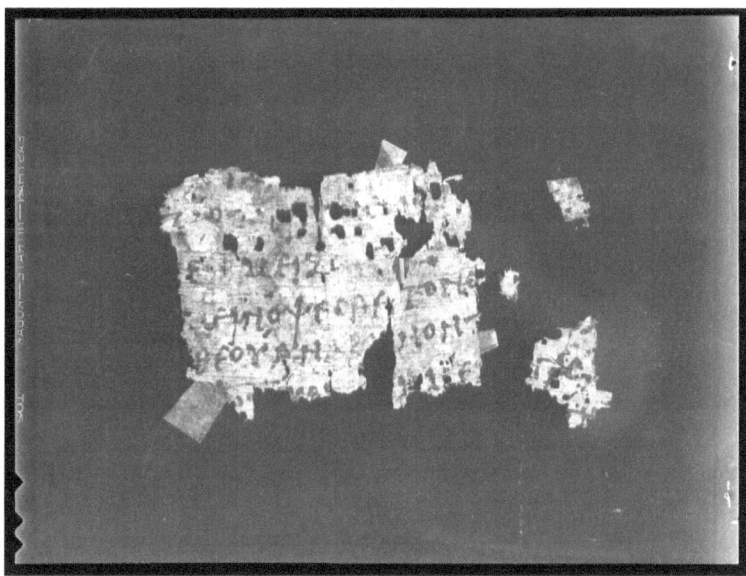

FIGURE 5. Negative of the Willoughby Papyrus (→) prior to mounting. Courtesy of the Special Collections Research Center, The University of Chicago

FIGURE 6. Willoughby Papyrus (→) John 1:49–2:1

958   *Journal of Biblical Literature* 137, no. 4 (2018)

Figure 7. Negative of the Willoughby Papyrus (↓) prior to mounting.
Courtesy of the Special Collections Research Center, The University of Chicago

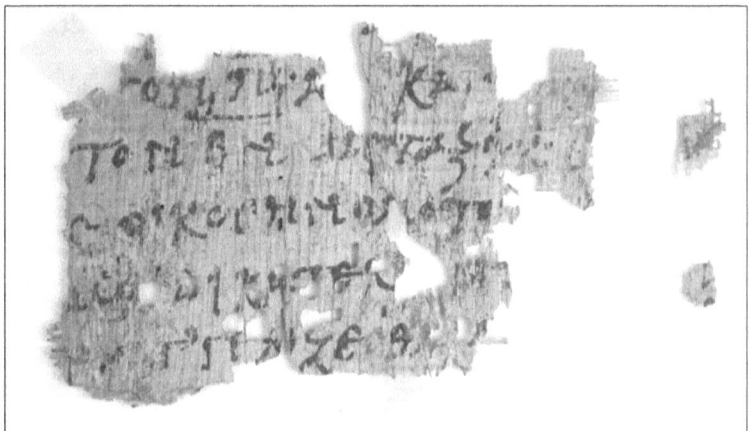

Figure 8. Willoughby Papyrus (↓) Unidentified Christian Text

Ekklēsia outside the Septuagint and the *Dēmos*: The Titles of Greco-Roman Associations and Christ-Followers' Groups

RICHARD LAST
richardlast@trentu.ca
Trent University, Peterborough, ON K9L 0G2, Canada

This article proposes a methodological shift away from setting Paul's usage of the group designator ἐκκλησία against the backdrop of the LXX corpus and the Greek δῆμος assemblies and toward understanding Christ-followers' adoption of the title in light of naming conventions in Greco-Roman associations. Assessing naming patterns in associations and exploring possible connections between titles and behaviors leads to the new possibility that association titles, including Paul's, generally connote little more than the ideal of cohesiveness among members and corporate identity. Previous arguments that ἐκκλησία represented for Paul political subversion, continuity with Judean ethnicity, or conscious modeling on civic ἐκκλησίαι are deemed especially unlikely. Paul did not explicitly attribute such connotations to the title nor did association titles generally reflect political orientation or ethnic identity. The possibility of Pauline innovation necessarily remains, but it should not be assumed a priori.

Paul need not have put much thought into what he called the groups he formed. In fact, the basic connotation inherent in the title on which he settled, ἐκκλησία, is a call for togetherness—the idea stressed by almost every other known ancient association's title. Nonetheless, interpreters tend to propose complex explanations for Paul's selection of this title. These explanations emerge from dualisms or binary frameworks for thinking about Christ-followers' ethnic identity and posture toward the polis. For example, some interpreters have framed Paul's usage of

I am grateful to Richard Ascough for providing feedback on an earlier draft of this article. Translations are my own. Greek epigraphic and papyrological abbreviations follow G. H. R. Horsley and John A. L. Lee, "A Preliminary Checklist of Abbreviations of Greek Epigraphic Volumes," *Epigraphica* 56 (1994): 129–69; and John F. Oates, Roger S. Bagnall, and William H. Willis, *Checklist of Editions of Greek Papyri and Ostraca*, 5th ed., BASPSup 9 (Oakville, CT: American Society of Papyrologists, 2001).

ἐκκλησία as either mimicry of Greco-Roman civic discourse or continuity with the ἐκκλησίαι of the LXX. Others have instead emphasized Paul's usage of ἐκκλησία as either counterimperial or ideologically normative.[1]

While I share an interest in the significance of the group designator ἐκκλησία for Paul and the members of his groups, it seems appropriate to shift the methodology by which this topic is approached. Traditionally, the approach has been to study different groups that were called ἐκκλησίαι, including the Israelite people in the LXX and the voting citizens in a polis. This endeavor typically leads to the conclusion that Paul's groups identified somehow as fictive versions of either the Israelite people or the male voting citizens of a polis. In the search for the group identity of Christ-followers in light of the title ἐκκλησία, several scholars have proposed that the title asserted that Paul's groups were distinct from associations, the known examples of which apparently never adopted ἐκκλησία as a title.[2] I find it difficult

---

[1] See section I below for a review. While these studies emphasize one side of a binary over the other, many commentators allow space for both sides of the Greek-Roman civic/LXX binary—that is, the idea that ἐκκλησία for Paul carried allusions to both the people of Israel and also the male voting citizens of a Greek (and later, Greco-Roman) polis. Paul Trebilco explicitly recognized that this double meaning would be inherent in ἐκκλησία, given its currency in both traditions ("Why Did the Early Christians Call Themselves ἡ ἐκκλησία?," NTS 57 [2011]: 440–60, here 456 n. 84).

[2] For the argument that Christ-followers' groups chose ἐκκλησία to mark themselves as distinct from associations, see Wayne A. Meeks, *The First Urban Christians: The Social World of the Apostle Paul*, 2nd ed. (New Haven: Yale University Press, 1983), 79; Hans-Josef Klauck, *The Religious Context of Early Christianity: A Guide to Graeco-Roman Religions*, SNTW (Edinburgh: T&T Clark, 2000), 54; and Young-Ho Park, *Paul's Ekklesia as a Civic Assembly: Understanding the People of God in Their Politico-Social World*, WUNT 2/393 (Tübingen: Mohr Siebeck, 2015), 214–15. Already by 1880, Edwin Hatch had observed that Christ groups and associations "had the same names for their meetings" (*The Organization of the Early Christian Churches: Eight Lectures Delivered before the University of Oxford, in the Year 1880*, Bampton Lectures [London: Rivingtons, 1881], 30 n. 11). Hatch identified IGLAM 1381–1382 = LBW 1381–1382 (Aspendus, Pamphylia, Asia Minor); IDelos 1519 = CIG 2271 = AGRW 223 (Delos, Aegean; 153/152 BCE). Since that time, researchers have scrutinized, subtracted from, and added to Hatch's examples of this phenomenon. The result is that we now know of three inscriptions attesting to associations that referred to their meetings as ἐκκλησίαι: IDelos 1519 = CIG 2271 = AGRW 223 (Delos, Aegean; 153/152 BCE); IG 12.6.1 133 (Samos, Aegean; second century BCE); and Louis Robert, *Le sanctuaire de Sinuri près de Mylasa*, Mémoires de l'Institut français d'archéologie de Stamboul 7, Bibliothèque archéologique et historique de l'Institut français d'archéologie d'Istanbul 8 (Paris: É. de Boccard, 1945) no. 73 = Louis Robert, "Decret d'une syngeneia Carienne au sanctuaire de Sinuri," *Hellenica* 7 (1949): 59–68. For a persuasive rejection of Hatch's IGLAM 1381–1382 as examples of this phenomenon (and also of OGIS 488), see Ralph John Korner, "Before 'Church': Political, Ethno-Religious, and Theological Implications of the Collective Designation of Pauline Christ-Followers as Ekklēsiai" (PhD diss., McMaster University, 2014), 57–87, esp. 59–67. See now the published version of Korner's dissertation: *The Origin and Meaning of* Ekklēsia *in the Early Jesus Movement*, Ancient Judaism and Early Christianity 98 (Leiden: Brill, 2017). See also John S. Kloppenborg, "Edwin Hatch, Churches, and Collegia," in *Origins and Method: Towards a New Understanding of Judaism and Christianity; Essays in Honour of John C. Hurd*, ed. Bradley H.

to accept the assumption behind this argument—namely, that Paul was aware that no association ever called itself an ἐκκλησία (assuming from our incomplete data that truly no association ever used the title). Yet the evidence shows that some associations did use ἐκκλησία for their meetings, and therefore this term would not have marked Christ-followers' groups as distinct.[3]

Greater clarity cannot be achieved on the questions that recent studies have asked of Paul's title, ἐκκλησία, because Paul did not articulate why he chose ἐκκλησία, did not state what it meant to him, and neglected to identify what it was supposed to connote to members.[4] It is difficult, therefore, to determine the extent to which his use of ἐκκλησία conveyed these groups' connection to the people of Israel, or their symbolic status as the male voting citizens of a polis. It is also difficult to judge whether the title expressed a conscious effort to model these groups after the voting assemblies of the δῆμος in Greek cities.

One can nevertheless contribute to the current discussion of Paul's selected title, ἐκκλησία, by exploring naming conventions in the very types of groups that Paul called ἐκκλησίαι. These include neighborhood collectives, occupational guilds, cultural minority networks, domestic associations, and broadly what we might construe as Greco-Roman associations.[5] In the present article, I explore emphases

---

Maclean, JSNTSup 86 (Sheffield: JSOT Press, 1993), 212–38, esp. 231; Richard Ascough, "Matthew and Community Formation," in *The Gospel of Matthew in Current Study: Studies in Memory of William G. Thompson, S.J.*, ed. David E. Aune (Grand Rapids: Eerdmans, 2001), 97–126, esp. 113; Philip A. Harland, *Associations, Synagogues, and Congregations: Claiming a Place in Ancient Mediterranean Society* (Minneapolis: Fortress, 2003), 106, 182; Harland, *Dynamics of Identity in the World of Early Christians: Associations, Judeans, and Cultural Minorities* (New York: T&T Clark, 2009), 44; and Park, *Paul's Ekklesia*, 56–61. For abbreviations used herein in connection with papyri and inscriptions, see Richard A. Ascough, Philip A. Harland, and John S. Kloppenborg, Associations in the Greco-Roman World, http://www.philipharland.com/greco-roman-associations/.

[3] For an overview of language common to Pauline letters and association documents, see Richard S. Ascough, "Voluntary Associations and the Formation of Pauline Churches: Addressing the Objections," in *Vereine, Synagogen und Gemeinden im kaiserzeitlichen Kleinasien*, ed. Andreas Gutsfeld and Dietrich-Alex Koch, STAC 25 (Tübingen: Mohr Siebeck, 2006), 149–83.

[4] Trebilco concedes that Paul nowhere links the title of his associations (ἡ ἐκκλησία τοῦ θεοῦ) with the ἐκκλησία of Israel in the LXX (*Self-Designations and Group Identity in the New Testament* [Cambridge: Cambridge University Press, 2012], 174). Likewise, Gregory K. Beale has observed that Paul neither directly connects ἐκκλησία with any other political language nor contrasts the Christ-followers' ἐκκλησίαι with civic ἐκκλησίαι ("The Background of ἐκκλησία Revisited," *JSNT* 38 [2015]: 151–68, here 166; Trebilco, "Early Christians," 445). See also the recent comments to this effect in Erich S. Gruen, "Synagogues and Voluntary Associations as Institutional Models: A Response to Richard Ascough and Ralph Korner," *Journal of the Jesus Movement in Its Jewish Setting* 3 (2016): 125–31, here 130–31.

[5] For my own inclusive description of the analytic category Greco-Roman association, see Richard Last, *The Pauline Church and the Corinthian Ekklēsia: Greco-Roman Associations in Comparative Context*, SNTSMS 164 (Cambridge: Cambridge University Press, 2016), 23–43; and Last, "The Other Synagogues," *JSJ* 47 (2016): 330–63. Vaia Touna's recent dissertation ("Acts of Identification and the Politics of the 'Greek Past': Religion, Tradition, Self" [Ph.D. diss., University

that ἐκκλησία shared with other association titles and what might have differentiated this title from other association titles.[6]

As a way to organize the massive database of association names, I offer a typology of association titles in section II.[7] The usage of civic titles (such as ἐκκλησία) fits well within the typology, but the phenomenon of appropriating civic titles requires special attention because of its direct relevance to understanding the supposed connection between Paul's usage of a civic title and the apparently negative posture of his groups to civic ideology. This will be discussed in section III.

Several unexplored nuances in the title ἐκκλησία become recognizable through comparison with the titles of associations. For example, little has been made of the fact that Paul named his groups after the act of invitation, emphasizing openness and hospitality, whereas some other associations turned restrictive features of their membership into titles (e.g., πλατεῖα ["street"], γειτνίασις ["neighborhood"], ἐργασία ["business"]). Still other titles naturalized the companionship of members (e.g., φράτρα). These designators need not indicate, however, that those groups enforced restrictive recruitment policies, limiting membership to residents on the given street or to practitioners of a certain occupation. Rather, titles such as πλατεῖα, ἐργασία, and φράτρα essentialized the groups' identities according to their members' place of residence, occupation, cult preference, and so on.[8] It is also

---

of Alberta, 2015]) has provided renewed cause to avoid the descriptors "voluntary [associations]," "private [associations]," and "religious [associations]" when referring to the types of groups that typically fall into the association category. Touna, however, goes too far in my estimation when suggesting that the category itself "would not be possible without fundamentally distinguishing between private vs. public, voluntary vs. non-voluntary, religious vs. profane, all in an effort to create identities by drawing boundaries and creating limits" (117). The researchers with whom Touna engages often apply the term *association* to groups that (fully known to the researchers themselves) cannot be understood as private as opposed to public (e.g., the πολιτεύματα of Hellenistic Egypt; the *vici* in Augustan Rome) or as voluntary as opposed to compulsory (e.g., many domestic and occupational associations). The religious/secular binary, while present in older scholarship that employed function-based typologies of associations—characterizing some associations as religious, others as social (e.g., funerary associations)—is less prominent now.

[6] This new approach will also help to determine whether the term ἐκκλησία was irreplaceably special to Paul and Christ-followers for its ethnic or political connotations (why else study the connotations of Paul's usage of the word exclusively in light only of other entities called ἐκκλησίαι?). Jorunn Økland's observation that "ἐκκλησία is in itself a fairly empty term" is an exception (*Women in Their Place: Paul and the Corinthian Discourse of Gender and Sanctuary Space*, JSNTSup 269 [London: T&T Clark, 2004], 135).

[7] The idea of typologizing association names goes back to Franz Poland, *Geschichte des griechischen Vereinswesens* (Leipzig: Teubner, 1909), 5–172. Poland merged the discussion of association titles with his overview of types of associations, but many titles cannot be mapped onto specific types of associations.

[8] Recently, John Kloppenborg and Richard Ascough suggested a correlation between association membership and locational convenience. Using a guild of leather workers from Saittai (Lydia) as an illustration, they proposed that it "no doubt consisted mainly of leather workers, but it might have had a few non-leather worker members who happened to live on or near that street"

fascinating to compare Paul's title, ἐκκλησία, with the many other association titles that were developed from a range of words that, like ἐκκλησία, come from language typically used to describe the act of coming together. Especially interesting in this respect is that such titles tend to come from the names of institutions that were part of the organizational structure of a polis or confederacy. If the civic titles that associations selected as their own designators tended to convey the basic idea of a call to come together—and little else is recoverable—one wonders why so much more (ethnic identity, fictive civic status, political subversion, etc.) should be attributed to Paul's title. These attributions cannot be defended by rejecting the relevance of association material; Paul himself gives no affirmation that the title was supposed to characterize the ethnic or political identities of members.[9]

I. A Surplus of Meaning

A. *A Primarily Judean Context*

The appearance of ἐκκλησία in Judean literature has offered one framework for assessing nuances beyond "assembly" that Christ-followers might have heard in the designator.[10] The Hebrew Bible's two terms for "assembly" are עדה and קהל. The LXX uses ἐκκλησία only for קהל, which typically denotes ad hoc meetings of the whole people of Israel or, occasionally, the people themselves.[11] This background has set the course for understanding Judean connotations in Paul's usage of the title. Recently, Gregory K. Beale further established the LXX background by highlighting that even Paul's phrase ἡ ἐκκλησία (τοῦ) θεοῦ (בקהל האלהים), occasionally considered a "semantic neologism" or at least insignificant for understanding Paul's language,[12] finds an important LXX predecessor in Neh 13:1 (2 Esd 23:1) and appears in various passages in Philo.[13] For Beale, Paul's usage of ἐκκλησία conveys that "the early Christian 'assembly' ... is the continuation of the true Israelite 'assembly of God' in the new covenant age, which implicitly stands in

---

in John S. Kloppenborg and Richard S. Ascough, *Attica, Central Greece, Macedonia, Thrace*, vol. 1 of *Greco-Roman Associations: Texts, Translations, and Commentary*, BZAW 181 (Berlin: de Gruyter, 2011), 2; cf. John S. Kloppenborg, "Membership Practices in Pauline Christ Groups," *Early Christianity* 2 (2013): 183–215, here 192.

[9] See n. 4 above.

[10] "Judean literature" (as I use the phrase) is the body of texts pertaining to the laws, myths, and customs associated with Jerusalem and the surrounding territory.

[11] Korner, "Before 'Church,'" 103–7; Park, *Paul's Ekklesia*, 64–67; I. Howard Marshall, "New Wine in Old Wine-Skins: V. The Biblical Use of the Word 'Ekklēsia,'" *ExpTim* 84 (1972–1973): 359–64, here 359; cf. Trebilco, "Early Christians," 446–48.

[12] Udo Schnelle, *Apostle Paul: His Life and Theology*, trans. M. Eugene Boring (Grand Rapids: Baker Academic, 2005), 560.

[13] Philo, *Drunkenness* 213, *Confusion* 144; *Alleg. Interp.* 3.81. Schnelle is aware of analogous phrases in Philo and LXX Neh 13:1 (*Apostle Paul*, 560 n. 4).

contrast, or as an alternative, to the civic 'assemblies of the world.'"[14] It is difficult to demonstrate that ἐκκλησία meant anything this specific to Paul, so this conclusion is surprisingly precise. Beale represents well a common outcome in studies that situate Paul's usage of ἐκκλησία in analogies from Judean literature: namely, the idea that the title reflected Pauline groups' identity as "Judean" rather than "Greek"—an unnecessary binary when studying the membership profile of Paul's culturally diverse groups. In Beale's version of the model, the title also positions Paul's groups as subversive rather than supportive of civic ideology in their poleis.

Yet, if Paul selected a title that was meant to attribute Judean ethnic identity to Christ-followers, why choose ἐκκλησία over, say, συναγωγή? Paul Trebilco, on whose work Beale relied heavily, replies to this question with the suggestion that Christ-followers (specifically, the Greek-speaking Judeans in Jerusalem whom Trebilco argues first introduced the title into the Jesus movement) selected ἐκκλησία because the term συναγωγή was already employed by "'non-Christian' Jews" from whom Christ-followers sought differentiation.[15]

The practice of selecting the second-best title when the most-desired one was already in use has been suggested also for foreign military associations on Cyprus. Dorothy Thompson theorized that cultural minority military associations in Ptolemaic Cyprus chose the designator κοινόν over the more natural choice, πολίτευμα, in order to avoid confusion with other groups called πολίτευμα on the island. Thompson describes these other πολιτεύματα as ones "of the more traditional type."[16] Unfortunately, Thompson did not elaborate any further about what these "traditional πολιτεύματα" might be. Thomas Kruse recently wondered if Thompson had in mind poleis on Cyprus that had been there prior to Ptolemaic rule.[17] In any case, the reason Thompson suspected that the Cyprian associations would have preferred the title πολίτευμα, had it been "available," is that this was the title employed by similar foreign military groups with the same legal rights as the

---

[14] Beale, "Background of ἐκκλησία," 166. Trebilco, from whom Beale builds his model, stresses that his interpretive paradigm does not imply that other Judeans are excluded from the Judean God's covenant in the minds of the Christ-believers under investigation ("Early Christians," 458 and passim). Trebilco proposes that, with the term ἐκκλησία, *"members of the ἐκκλησία could express their continuity with the OT people of God, the OT 'assembly', without claiming that they alone were the heirs of that people"* (449–60; emphasis added).

[15] Trebilco, "Early Christians," 456 (cf. 453–59).

[16] See Dorothy J. Thompson, "The Idumaeans of Memphis and the Ptolemaic politeumata," in *Atti del XVII Congresso Internazionale di Papirologia (Napoli, 19–26 maggio 1983)*, 3 vols. (Naples: Centro Internazionale per lo Studio dei Papiri Ercolanesi, 1984), 1069–75, here 1073–74.

[17] Thomas Kruse, "Ethnic *Koina* and *Politeumata* in Ptolemaic Egypt," in *Private Associations and the Public Sphere: Proceedings of a Symposium held at the Royal Danish Academy of Sciences and Letters, 9–11 September 2010*, ed. Vincent Gabrielsen and Christian A. Thomsen, Scientia Danica: Series H, Humanistica, 8 vol. 9 (Copenhagen: Det Kongelige Danske Videnskabernes Selskab, 2015), 270–300, here 294.

Cyprian associations but residing elsewhere under Ptolemaic rule (namely, in Egypt). On Thompson's model, this led the cultural minority military associations to choose κοινόν.

Kruse, though, questioned how much confusion a title might actually cause if the groups bearing the title were very different: on the one hand, local political institutions (perhaps even cities) and, on the other hand, "newly founded *politeumata* consisting of foreign mercenary soldiers from outside Cyprus."[18] To be sure, the difference between Pauline groups and Judean-deity associations would be less apparent. But among the associations the avoidance of terminology simply because it was used elsewhere seems less common than has been imagined.[19]

The view that Paul's title ἐκκλησία conveys that members in Paul's groups existed in continuity with Israel needs to better account for the absence in the title of ethnic designators such as Ἰουδαῖοι, Ἰσραήλ, or Ἑβραῖοι. The term ἐκκλησία, when not accompanied by an ethnic, geographic, or institutional qualifier, simply denoted an assembly. An ἐκκλησία "of (the) god" (e.g., ἡ ἐκκλησία τοῦ θεοῦ), as Paul occasionally calls his groups (1 Cor 1:2, 2 Cor 1:1; cf. 1 Thess 1:1), does not narrow down the ethnic identity of the group's members. Rather, ἡ ἐκκλησία τοῦ θεοῦ falls within the range of titles that associations employed and so simply raises the question, which god? In Hellenistic Athens, we hear of ἡ τῆς Ἀγαθῆς Θεοῦ σύνοδος, "the assembly of the Good Goddess,"[20] and on Thera, τὸ κοινὸν τοῦ Ἀνθιστῆρος, "the association of Anthister."[21] There are many associations that designate themselves with the more common formula "the association of the god worshippers" (e.g., τὸ κοινὸν τὸ Ἀφροδισιαστᾶν Σωτηριαστᾶν; IRhodPC 7; Rhodos on Rhodes, southeastern islands; first century BCE). It is in 1 Cor 1:1-2 that Paul's address to an ἐκκλησία most resembles that particular variation of the formula, as it includes not only ἡ ἐκκλησία τοῦ θεοῦ but also refers to the group members with the substantive participle οἱ ἁγιάζοντες. But this usage is not syntactically identical to the association

---

[18] Ibid., 294.

[19] See, e.g., Tessa Rajak, "Synagogue and Community in the Graeco-Roman Diaspora," in *Jews in the Hellenistic and Roman Cities*, ed. John R. Bartlett (London: Routledge, 2002), 22–39. For usage of συναγωγή (and derivatives) by Judean-deity associations and also associations that worshiped other gods in Hellenistic Egypt, see *BGU* 4.1137 = *AGRW* 281 (Alexandria, Delta, Egypt; 6 BCE); IFayum 3.204 = *AGRW* 291 (Krokodilopolites, Fayum region; Egypt); *IEgJud* 20 = *AGRW* 283 (Alexandria, Delta region, Egypt; undated).

[20] *SEG* 56 (2006), no. 203, line 5 (Athens, Attica; third century BCE) = Ioanna Tsirigoti-Drakotou, "Τιμητικὸ ψήφισμα ἀπό την Ἱερά ὁδό," in Γενέθλιον: Ἵδρυμα Ν. Π. Γουλάνδρη Μουσείο Κυκλαδικής Τέχνης [*Genethlion: Special Volume for the 20th Anniversary of the Museum of Cycladic Art*], ed. Nicholas C. Stampolidis (Athens: Goulandris Foundation-Museum of Cycladic Art, 2006), 285–94. In this inscription, σύνοδος can mean "assembly" (lines 8–9) and also "association" (line 16). The term ἐκκλησία can also denote both concepts in the epigraphy.

[21] *IG* 12.3.329 + *IG* 12.3.Suppl. 1295, lines 1–2 (Thera, Aegean; ca. 200 BCE). For more, see the association of Zeus Hypsistos (P.Lond. 7.2193, line 4 = *AGRW* 295; Philadelphia, Fayum, Egypt; 69–58 BCE).

formula above. The association names based on verbs such as ἑρμαΐζειν that denoted participation in cult festivals form names ending in -ισταί or -ασταί.²²

To argue that Paul's title need not have included an ethnic designator because it so obviously mimicked the LXX's ἐκκλησία κυρίου ("ἐκκλησία of the Lord") would be misleading. In his extant letters, Paul *never used* that particular title for his groups. Moreover, it is not clear that ἐκκλησία κυρίου in the LXX would have been understood by Paul as anything other than what the term connotes in the Greek polis.²³ The institution of the ἐκκλησία κυρίου (when it denoted the Israelite people in the LXX) is not entirely different from the people assemblies in Greek poleis. Since Jerusalem was equipped with the institutions of a Greco-Roman polis in Paul's time, any reference to the "ἐκκλησία of the Judean people" (if indeed, ἐκκλησία τοῦ θεοῦ was meant to imply some form of this idea) might call to mind the assemblies of the people (δῆμος) in Jerusalem in the Hellenistic and Roman periods (e.g., Josephus, *J.W.* 1.457 [Herod συναγαγὼν τὸν λαόν, "Herod summoning the people"], *Ant.* 18.279–283 [Petronius συγκαλέσας δὲ εἰς τὴν Τιβεριάδα τοὺς Ἰουδαίους, "Petronius called the Judeans together in Tiberias"], 19.332–334 [Simon called together an ἐκκλησία in Jerusalem]; 1 Macc 5:16 [an ἐκκλησία μεγάλη ("great ἐκκλησία") called in Jerusalem to decide whether to go to war in the Galilee], 14:19 [an ἐκκλησία in Jerusalem]).

It is difficult to see why Greeks familiar with the LXX should have read Paul's title primarily as an allusion to the LXX's ἐκκλησία κυρίου (though this is impossible to [dis]prove). A closer reference point would be the assembly of people in Jerusalem, which functioned similarly to ἐκκλησίαι and other people assemblies in the Roman Mediterranean (Josephus, *Ant.* 15.381, 16.393–394, *J.W.* 1.150, 648–650). Even in Claudius's era, Josephus can reproduce what was apparently a letter from the emperor addressed to Jerusalem (*Ant.* 20.10), specifically, the city's ἄρχοντες ("rulers"), βουλή ("council"), δῆμος Ἰουδαίων ("Judean people"), and πᾶν ἔθνος ("whole nation").²⁴

---

[22] See L. Robert, *Monnaies grecques: Types, légendes, magistrats monétaires et géographie*, Hautes études numismatiques 2 (Geneva: Centre de recherche d'histoire et de philologie 1967), 12.

[23] See now Park, *Paul's Ekklesia*, 66. For the appearances of this phrase in the LXX, see Deut 23:2–4, 9; 1 Chr 28:8; Mic 2:5.

[24] J. Spencer Kennard, "The Jewish Provincial Assembly," *ZNW* 53 (1962): 25–51, here 35. See also the Jerusalem δῆμος in Maccabean letters of diplomacy (e.g., 1 Macc 12:6). On the issue of the Sanhedrin's authority in Jerusalem, a relevant topic in the discussion of how to classify the governance of Jerusalem in the imperial period, see Lee I. Levine, *Judaism and Hellenism in Antiquity: Conflict or Confluence?*, Samuel and Althea Stroum Lectures in Jewish Studies (Seattle: University of Washington Press, 1998), 84–95. Recently, Park has made the case that ἐκκλησία even in the "collective memory of Israel" during Hellenistic and Roman periods would have evoked images of a people's assembly actively participating in historic decisions guiding the nation through domestic and foreign affairs (*Paul's Ekklesia*, 84–91).

B. A Primarily Greek Context

Other interpreters stress Greek civic ἐκκλησίαι as models for Paul's own groups. In favor of this model is the durability of citizen assemblies in Greek poleis of the Roman East. These assemblies of voting citizens continued to be a reference point well after the first century CE.[25] At least some of the people's assemblies (δῆμος, ἐκκλησία) in Greco-Roman poleis elected their own civic magistrates into the third century CE and generally functioned in public affairs more than allowed by the old stereotype that the Greco-Roman ἐκκλησία simply issued approvals for the βουλή's proposals. Throughout the Aegean and coastal areas of Asia Minor, local assemblies of citizens oversaw other civic bodies (e.g., φυλαί, σύνεδροι), enjoyed political autonomy to make decisions independent of the local council (βουλή), and became active in civic building projects, budgetary matters, and more.[26]

Practices or features common to Paul's ἐκκλησίαι and civic ἐκκλησίαι are occasionally highlighted in the course of arguments to the effect that Paul modeled his groups after the civic institution on which he (supposedly) based their title.[27] For instance, George van Kooten proposes that the

> way in which Paul uses the term ἐκκλησία should not only be understood as a conscious adoption of the terminology of the public assembly. As it transpires from Paul's description of the Christian assembly, the actual functioning of the Christian ἐκκλησία also mirrors the operations of the civic assemblies.[28]

The common features highlighted by van Kooten and others are rather general (e.g., place of instruction, outbreaks of factions, restrictions on women's participation,

---

[25] Anna C. Miller, *Corinthian Democracy: Democratic Discourse in 1 Corinthians*, PTMS 220 (Eugene, OR: Pickwick, 2015), 40–67; Park, *Paul's Ekklesia*, 9, 17, 98–103; George H. van Kooten, "Ἐκκλησία τοῦ θεοῦ: The 'Church of God' and the Civic Assemblies (ἐκκλησίαι) of the Greek Cities in the Roman Empire; A Response to Paul Trebilco and Richard A. Horsley," *NTS* 58 (2012): 522–48, here 532–35.

[26] See Aelius Aristides, *Sacred Tales* 4.88; Dio Chrysostom, *Or.* 48.17; Plutarch, *Prae. Ger. rei publ.* 823f–825f. See also Guy MacLean Rogers, "The Assembly of Imperial Ephesos," *ZPE* 94 (1992): 224–28; Sviatoslav Dmitriev, *City Government in Hellenistic and Roman Asia Minor* (New York: Oxford University Press, 2005), 30, 67–69, 76, 87–88, 104–6, 276–77, 289, 295, 330; Giovanni Salmeri, "Dio, Rome and the Civic Life of Asia Minor," in *Dio Chrysostom: Politics, Letters and Philosophy*, ed. Simon Swain (Oxford: Oxford University Press, 2000), 53–92, here 73; Nemanja Vujčić, "Greek Popular Assemblies in the Imperial Period and the Discourses of Dio of Prusa," *EpAn* 42 (2009): 157–69; Volker Grieb, *Hellenistische Demokratie: Politische Organisation und Struktur in freien griechischen Poleis nach Alexander dem Grossen*, Historia Einzelschriften 199 (Stuttgart: Steiner, 2008), 36–45 (Athens), 150–57 (Kos), 199–210 (Miletus), 263–89 (Rhodos).

[27] Eric Peterson, *Ekklesia: Studien zum altkirchlichen Kirchenbegriff*, ed. Barbara Nichtweiß and Hans-Ulrich Weidemann, Ausgewählte Schriften: Sonderband (Würzburg: Echter, 2010) 9–83, here 20–26; van Kooten, "Ἐκκλησία τοῦ θεοῦ," 539–47; Ekkehard W. Stegemann and Wolfgang Stegemann, *The Jesus Movement: A Social History of Its First Century* (Minneapolis: Fortress, 1999), 274–76.

[28] Van Kooten, "Ἐκκλησία τοῦ θεοῦ," 539.

restrictions on the ecstatic, a public dimension, presence of officials, a religious dimension) and are characteristic not only of civic assemblies and Paul's groups but also of associations (including synagogues and philosophical groups) more generally.[29]

In recognizing the political connotations in Paul's labeling of Christ-followers' groups as the ἐκκλησίαι of given poleis, Richard Horsley attributed to the title not just the basic meaning of "assembly" but also the rhetoric of a countercultural ideological movement:

> Nor ... were Paul's communities modeled on the associations or guilds.... Paul's communities were both far more comprehensive (even totalistic) in their common purpose, exclusive over against dominant society, and parts of an intercity, international movement.... Paul's *ekklēsiai* are ... local communities of an alternative society to the Roman imperial order.... It has often been observed that Paul's communities were exclusive, separated from "the world." More than that, however, Paul's alternative society stood sharply against the Roman imperial order.[30]

Van Kooten agrees that Paul designed his ἐκκλησίαι to be "parallel, alternative organization[s] existing alongside" civic ἐκκλησίαι;[31] however, he correctly observes that Paul was not "inherently subversive to the political institutions of his time."[32] Indeed, in several passages, Paul appears to position his groups as friendly to the interests of their poleis (1 Cor 10:32–33, Rom 13:1–7).[33]

In his final analysis, van Kooten agrees that the title ἐκκλησία carried second-order meaning beyond the denotation "assembly" for Paul and also for "the Christian community," more generally.[34] The title ἐκκλησία conveyed the establishment

---

[29] Recent volumes on associations including synagogues will include mention of these features. I refer here to another illuminating recent study by van Kooten, which outlines similarities in Pauline, Platonic, and Stoic notions of dual citizenship: "Philosophical Criticism of Genealogical Claims and Stoic Depoliticization of Politics: Greco-Roman Strategies in Paul's Allegorical Interpretation of Hagar and Sarah (Gal 4:21–31)," in *Abraham, the Nations, and the Hagarites: Jewish, Christian, and Islamic Perspectives on Kinship with Abraham*, ed. Martin Goodman, George H. van Kooten, Jacques T. A. G. M. van Ruiten, TBN 13 (Leiden: Brill, 2010), 361–85, here 372–85. See below for connections between the concept of dual citizenship and Paul's usage of ἐκκλησία in van Kooten's model.

[30] Richard A. Horsley, "Building an Alternative Society: Introduction," in *Paul and Empire: Religion and Power in Roman Imperial Society*, ed. Richard Horsley (Harrisburg, PA: Trinity Press International, 1997), 206–14, here 208–10; and, in the same volume, Horsley, "1 Corinthians: A Case Study of Paul's Assembly as an Alternative Society," 242–52. See also Horsley, "Rhetoric and Empire—and 1 Corinthians," in *Paul and Politics: Ekklesia, Israel, Imperium, Interpretation: Essays in Honor of Krister Stendahl*, ed. Richard A. Horsley (Harrisburg, PA: Trinity Press International, 2000), 72–102.

[31] Van Kooten, "Ἐκκλησία τοῦ θεοῦ," 527.

[32] Ibid., 539.

[33] Ibid.

[34] Ibid., 547. Van Kooten argues that "for Paul, the phrase ἐκκλησία τοῦ θεοῦ is the recurrent

of an "alternative political structure"[35] that related peaceably to state institutions, analogous to the Platonic and Stoic idealization of the sage's dual citizenship in their town of birth and in the ideal heavenly city whose citizens are gods and humans from across regions of the earth (Plato, *Rep.* 9.592a–b; Seneca, *On Leisure* 4.1).[36]

I turn now to the assumptions that associations with civic titles, such as Paul's ἐκκλησίαι, would be modeled on their civic institutional namesakes, and that associations' selection of a civic word for its title (i.e., ἐκκλησία) would have conveyed groups' "alternative" or subversive reality. These suppositions can be tested by examining the choice and usage of titles by associations.

II. Association Titles: Common Features

For heuristic purposes, association titles can be organized into three fluid categories.

1. The "coming together" (i.e., "meeting") of different individuals (e.g., σύστημα, σύνοδος, συναγωγή, ἐκκλησία, συμβίωσις, συνέδριον).
2. Collective identity (*collegium, corpus, sodalitas, sodalicium,* φράτρα, κοινόν, ὁμότεχνον, σπεῖρα[37]).
3. Common interests among members (e.g., ἔρανος,[38] θίασος, ἑταιρεία, *cultores*) or common features (e.g., πλατεῖα, γειτνίασις, συνεργασία).

Titles in each category appeal to the ideal of cohesiveness among members but articulate cohesion from different angles. The fact that most known association titles imply a cohesive group might suggest that the claim to be a cohesive association (as opposed to an unruly one) helped groups attract recruits.[39]

The first category of titles is taken from language otherwise reserved for designating meetings or articulating the coming together of different parties. The title ἐκκλησία fits well here. Traditionally ἐκκλησία has been taken as highlighting not

---

expression of his underlying view on the two πολιτεύματα, and helps him to characterize the Christian ἐκκλησία as an alternative organization existing alongside the civic ἐκκλησίαι of the Greek cities" (ibid.).

[35] Ibid., 535; see 536–37 for the notion that this was a conscious effort.

[36] For van Kooten's development of this argument and analogy, see his "Philosophical Criticism," 373–85.

[37] For σπεῖρα, see usage of the title *spira* ("association"), in *CIL* 6.261 (Rome, Latium, Italy; 193–211 CE) and the comments on this association title in Anne-Françoise Jaccottet, *Documents,* vol. 2 of *Choisir Dionysos: Les associations dionysiaques, ou La face cachée du dionysisme,* Akanthus crescens 6 (Zurich: Akanthus, 2003), 196–97.

[38] The term ἔρανος has a complicated etymology. The decision to place it in this category is based on the work of Johannes Vondeling, *Eranos* (Groningen: Wolters, 1961), 77–159.

[39] I have included examples of association titles that fit in each category, but some of them would be appropriate in more than one spot. Categorizing the titles in this way brings out patterns and nuances that have otherwise gone unnoticed.

the coming together of different individuals but rather collective Judean identity or common political interests. As the association titles show, a host of other available designators expressed kinship (category 2) or common interest (category 3). It remains within the realm of possibility, of course, that Paul selected a title that conveyed the common kinship, ethnicity, or interests of Christ-followers at the level of second-order meaning. But it would be easier to make that case if Paul had chosen a different designator.

Since the title ἐκκλησία, as well as the other titles grouped under category 1, do not explicate the common interests of group members, it is worth considering whether heterogeneity—that is, differences in cultic practices, ethnicities, and so on—might constitute part of the character of Paul's ἐκκλησίαι. Some associations used category 1 titles but qualified them so as to clarify the basis for the group's formation. In these instances, the full titles articulate a coming together predicated on commonalities among members. For example, the σύστημα "of linen-merchants" (τῶν λημενητῶν) (MAMA 3.770 = ICiliciaHW 151; Korykos, Cilicia, Asia Minor; undated) would have been mostly homogeneous with respect to profession. The same is true of τὸ συνέδριον "of servers" (τῶν λατρευτῶν) (IEph 1247; Ephesos, Ionia, Asia Minor; third century CE). The crosses that bookend the inscription from Korykos indicate that at least some members of that occupational association were Christian.

Paul once qualified an ἐκκλησία by a city-ethnic as well as patron deity (τῇ ἐκκλησίᾳ Θεσσαλονικέων ἐν θεῷ πατρὶ καὶ κυρίῳ Ἰησοῦ Χριστῷ, "to the ἐκκλησία of the Thessalonians in God the Father and the Lord Jesus Christ"; 1 Thess 1:1). This phrase could well be the group's full name. Paul also often added to the base title ἐκκλησία a patron deity (Rom 16:16 [Christ]) or a patron deity and location (1 Cor 1:2, 2 Cor 1:1 [Corinth and God]; 1 Thess 2:14 [God, Christ, and Judea]).[40] He at least idealized these groups as cohesive with respect to their cult orientation. But when Paul named ἐκκλησίαι by province or region alone, he usually omitted the detail that these ἐκκλησίαι worshiped Christ or God (1 Cor 16:1 [Galatia], 16:19 [Asia], 2 Cor 8:1 [Macedonia], Gal 1:2 [Galatia]). There are at least three ways to account for the omission of cult identity in these cases: these ἐκκλησίαι (1) could not be defined by orientation around Christ or the Judean deity exclusively; (2) worshiped Christ but left their title ἐκκλησία unqualified; or (3) had fuller titles that Paul did not know. The third option seems unlikely in view of Paul's close relationship with some of these ἐκκλησίαι—indeed, he claims to have founded most of them. Moreover, even when Paul references the ἐκκλησίαι in Judea, with which he had a notional relationship, he always specifies their cult orientation (Gal 1:22 [Christ]; 1 Thess 2:14 [God in Christ Jesus]).

Option 2 is possible. Titles that express the act of coming together (i.e.,

---

[40] For the debated political connotations in Paul's usage of a city-ethnic, see Karl P. Donfried, *Paul, Thessalonica, and Early Christianity* (Grand Rapids: Eerdmans, 2002), 139–62; and Korner, "Before 'Church,'" 205–8.

category 1) need not be followed by qualifiers. An association in Saittai (Lydia, Asia Minor) is known from a grave inscription simply as ἡ συμβίωσις (*SEG* 29 [1979], no. 1185; 156/157 CE), and another from Rhodos (Rhodes, Aegean) is just τό κοινόν (*IG* 12.1.160; undated). Whatever the reason for this, we might speculate that by refraining from essentializing a group's identity according to a single god, the effect would be to broaden interest in these groups among potential recruits.

The first option, that some of the so-called Christian ἐκκλησίαι were polytheistic, does not imply that Paul endorsed their cult practices. A less provocative description of this possibility would be that the groups were open to individuals regardless of their cult preferences and so, it might be reasoned, excluded from their titles any information about (one of) their own, little known, patron deity (or deities). This could maximize their appeal. They were, in a sense, simply associations of different peoples (αἱ ἐκκλησίαι τῶν ἐθνῶν, Rom 16:4).

Overall, when left unqualified by a deity, ethnic identity, or other common feature of group members, titles stressing the act of coming together emphasize (relative to titles in the other categories) openness to diverse membership profiles. Associations such as ἡ συμβίωσις in Saittai, and perhaps some of Paul's ἐκκλησίαι, adopted names that would invite membership inquiries from individuals across neighborhoods, families, professions, and religious preferences. Paul's title fits very well in this category. The noun ἐκκλησία, derived as it is from ἐκκαλεῖν, "to summon," is rarely used by associations but nonetheless is archetypal of the whole category.[41]

Understanding ἐκκλησία in light of other category 1 titles suggests that the title would be useful to Christ-followers even without elaborate second-order meanings. It is conceivable that the term simply idealized the groups in question as assemblies of heterogeneous individuals who have come together and who are open to new members. Of course, hospitable dispositions need not be attributed to the actual members of the groups. At most, connotations of hospitality and openness inherent in the term ἐκκλησία might work to shape potential recruits' assumptions about Paul's ἐκκλησίαι based on the title and in light of other association titles.

The titles in category 2 differ from the ones just explored in that they emphasize corporate identity. It might be inferred that these association members are not just individuals "coming together" each month. Rather, the groups are "companionships" (*sodalicia*), "brotherhoods" (φρᾶτραι), and "partnerships" (κοινά). These titles imply a naturalness to the members' belonging in the groups, social connections prior to and beyond the periodic association meetings, or a strength in the connections between members, whereas titles such as ἐκκλησία express little other than the act of coming together.

Much has been made of Paul's usage of kinship language to naturalize

---

[41] It is noteworthy, even if coincidental, that Paul's self-understanding of his own role as an apostle also includes the concept of invitation (κλητὸς ἀπόστολος, Rom 1:1). For usage of ἐκκλησία by associations, see now Korner, "Before 'Church,'" 57–87.

companionship among Christ-followers (e.g., οἰκεῖος, ἀδελφή, ἀδελφός, τέκνον, πατήρ). It is interesting that this naturalizing discourse was not extended to the title of his groups.[42] I will not push too far the difference between titles that I have placed in different categories, but this language of kinship, apparently reserved for Paul's groups' internal communications, represents a degree of Pauline idealization, namely, the naturalness of Christ-followers' connections.

The third category consists of associations that incorporated their primary basis for group formation into their title. Occupational associations often picked names that highlighted their professional orientation, such as ἐργασία ("business") and συνεργασία ("fellow workers"). Christ-followers most likely joined occupational guilds from the earliest period.[43] In later centuries, the presence of Christians in ἐργασίαι (occupational associations) is attested.[44]

Neighborhood associations also tended to select titles that represented their social basis for coming together. Very often these associations called themselves πλατεῖαι ("streets") or γειτνιάσεις ("neighborhoods").[45] Unfortunately, the few examples of possible Christ-followers' associations that explicitly identified according to their neighborhood of residence are problematic. For instance, the third-century CE association mentioned in the Phrygian grave inscription of a certain Aristeas used to be identified as a Christian neighborhood-based association, but now there is uncertainty. The group in question called itself the γειτοσύνη of the πρωτοπυλεῖται ("neighborhood of the residents of the first gateway").[46] Aristeas assigned to the πρωτοπυλεῖται the responsibility to decorate his tomb with roses and threatened the neighborhood residents that they would "be before the justice [δικαιοσύνη] of God" if they failed to do so. William Ramsay classified this phrase as a variation of the Eumenian formula ἔσται αὐτῷ πρὸς τὸν θεόν (literally, "for him/her to be before God") and as Christian. He speculated that "we might assume in almost every case, except one or two Jewish examples, that this formula stamps the

---

[42] An early analysis of Paul's kinship language from 1979, when it could be lamented that it suffered from "unfortunate neglect" by interpreters, can be found in Robert Banks, *Paul's Idea of Community: The Early House Churches in Their Cultural setting*, rev. ed. (Peabody, MA: Hendrickson, 1994; first ed., 1979), 47–57, here 50.

[43] Richard S. Ascough, "The Thessalonian Christian Community as a Professional Voluntary Association," *JBL* 119 (2000): 311–28, https://doi.org/10.2307/3268489.

[44] For a Christian ἐργασία, see P.Stras. 4.287 (Hermopolis Magna, Upper Egypt; sixth century). For a Christian συνέργιον, see *GRA* 2.153 (Flaviopolis, Cilicia, Asia Minor; before 300 CE). See also E. L. Hicks, "Inscriptions from Eastern Cilicia," *JHS* 11 (1890): 236–54, here 236.

[45] *MAMA* 6.176 = *IPhrygR* 303 (Apameia Kelainai, Phrygia, Asia Minor; undated); *IEph* 3080 (Ephesos, Ionia, Asia Minor; 167 CE); *IMylasa* 403 (Mylasa, Caria, Asia Minor; undated); *IPrusiasHyp* 63–64 (Prusias by Hypios, Bithynia, Asia Minor; undated); *ILydiaHM* 42 (Tabilla, Lydia, Asia Minor; 13/14 CE).

[46] *IJO* 2.171 = *IPhrygR* 455–457 (Akmoneia, Phrygia, Asia Minor; 215–295 CE).

epitaph as Chr[istian]."[47] Regarding Aristeas's epitaph, Ramsay argued, "Aristeas was a Chr[istian], and we must understand that the Society to which he left his bequest was a Chr[istian] benefit and burial society."[48]

Some of the other titles grouped in this category lend themselves poorly to generalizations. For instance, the title θίασος ("religious guild") could emphasize the religious dimension of a group's character and so could vaguely reflect a common interest, though it also carried the general category 2 sense of "company," and in this way establishes the collective identity of group members. Likewise, while the title ἔρανος could emphasize banqueting activity, it may also represent an association's commitment to mutual assistance among members.

Beyond the variations in emphases among titles in different categories, most association names conveyed group cohesion and collective identity.[49] The term ἐκκλησία had an extremely limited semantic range and need not have been understood to say much more about Paul's groups than what association names announce more generally: the cohesiveness and affiliation of the group members. Moreover, since Christ-followers regularly joined associations or formed their own groups that used titles other than ἐκκλησία, it is unlikely that ἐκκλησία articulated a universally defining or essential feature of Christian collective identity.[50]

---

[47] William M. Ramsay, *The Cities and Bishoprics of Phrygia: Being an Essay of the Local History of Phrygia from the Earliest Times to the Turkish Conquest* (Oxford: Clarendon, 1897), 515.

[48] Ibid. Recent research on the inscription has illustrated that the Eumenian formula was used by both Christ-followers and also Judeans. It has been observed, moreover, that the Judean population is well represented in Akmoneia, whereas the Christian population is known from only one inscription, which itself may be Judean. See Louis Robert, "Épitaphes juives d'Éphèse et de Nicomédie," *Hell* 11–12 (1960): 381–413, here 409–12; Paul R. Trebilco, "The Christian *and* Jewish Eumeneian Formula," in *Negotiating Diaspora: Jewish Strategies in the Roman Empire*, ed. John M. G. Barclay, LSTS 45 (London: T&T Clark International, 2004), 66–89.

[49] Association titles can be obscure occasionally. The self-designator δοῦμος (Lat. *dumus*), "thorn-bush," constitutes one example. Even in these cases, though, the titles seem to articulate a common interest among group members. The title δοῦμος for instance, tends to be associated with groups that worship Cybele, an Anatolian fertility goddess associated with wild nature, but not always. See Philip A. Harland, *North Coast of the Black Sea, Asia Minor*, vol. 2 of *Greco-Roman Associations: Texts, Translations, and Commentary*, BZNW 204 (Berlin: de Gruyter, 2014), 199–202.

[50] See, e.g., the Christian σύστημα "of linen-merchants" (τῶν λημενητῶν) (*MAMA* 3.770 = ICiliciaHW 151; Korykos, Cilicia, Asia Minor; undated); and the Christian association members (οἱ συνθειασεῖται) in *IOSPE* 5.331 (Hermonassa, Bosporan region, Danube and Black Sea areas; 470–490 CE). An extensive study of these and similar groups is forthcoming in Richard Last, *The Other Christian Groups: Neighbourhood Networks, Occupational Guilds, and Scholarly Circles*, WUNT (Tübingen: Mohr Siebeck, forthcoming). For the identification of Paul's own groups as collectives of occupational colleagues and residents of the same neighborhood, see, respectively, Ascough, "Thessalonian Christian Community," 311–28; and Richard Last, "The Neighbourhood (*vicus*) of the Corinthian *Ekklēsia*: Beyond Family-Based Descriptions of the First Urban Christ-Believers," *JSNT* 38 (2016): 399–425.

III. Associations with Civic Titles

Some associations appropriated the names of governing institutions. These titles often fit best in the first two categories from section II, but they deserve focused attention in a discussion of whether Paul's title ἐκκλησία had any special political connotations. Already in 2001, Richard Ascough made the important observation that "the use of *ekklēsia* was similar to the use of other civic terms used by the associations, such as *taxis, phylē, hairesis, kollēgion, syllogos, synteleia, synedrion, systēma, synodos, koinon*."[51] Here, I would like to build on Ascough's insight and make two further observations. First, civic titles did not coincide with subversive or alternative political behavior. Second, associations did not model themselves organizationally on the civic institutions from which they took their names. The idea that Paul's ἐκκλησίαι intentionally mimicked civic ἐκκλησίαι cannot be proved or disproved by any means, but it is useful to address this proposal in light of the adoption of civic terminology by associations more broadly.

One of the most common association titles is the civic term σύνοδος ("assembly"), which was the name of various state and confederate institutions' meetings in the Greek East (Diodorus Siculus, *Bib. hist.* 15.59.1; Thucydides, *Hist.* 1.96–97, 119; *IG* 4.2/1.68, line 71 [Epidauros, Peloponnese; 302 BCE]; Aeschines 2.115), including the meetings of the βουλή and δῆμος ([Aristotle], *Ath. pol.* 4.3).[52]

Associations employing the title σύνοδος were highly diversified. The title was used by groups ranging from an association of farmers (IDelta 1.446 = *AGRW* 287 [Psenamosis, Delta, Egypt; 67 and 64 BCE]) to Dionysiac performers (e.g., ITrall 65 [Tralles, Caria, Asia Minor; first century CE]). Since there are attestations of partnerships and cooperative activities between civic institutions and σύνοδοι associations[53] and also honors paid by σύνοδοι associations to civic rulers,[54] there is no reason to suspect that σύνοδοι associations had subversive intentions in selecting this very common association designator. Although Franz Poland came close to grouping together σύνοδοι associations as a distinct subset of associations, they were so diverse in their practices that the name σύνοδος apparently carried very few connotations about a group's collective identity.[55] What these associations show is

---

[51] Richard S. Ascough, "Matthew and Community Formation," in Aune, *Gospel of Matthew in Current Study*, 96–126, here 114.

[52] Jakob A. O. Larson, *Representative Government in Greek and Roman History*, Sather Classical Lectures 28 (Berkeley: University of California Press, 1966), 66–85.

[53] *TAM* 2.1.496 = *IGR* 3.605 (Xanthos, Lycia, Asia Minor; imperial era).

[54] *IDelos* 1529 (Delos, Aegean; 145–116 BCE); Ferit Baz, "Ein neues Ehrenmonument für Flavius Arrianus," *ZPE* 163 (2007): 123–27 (Hierapolis, Cappadocia, Asia Minor; 130–137 CE); *SEG* 49 (1999), no. 697 (Dion, Macedonia; 179–168 BCE).

[55] But see the discussion of the term as a title by athletes and artists and usage of the term by all other associations (Poland, *Geschichte des griechischen Vereinswesens*, 131–51, 158–63). See also Franz Poland, "Σύνοδος," PW 5.2:1415–34.

that arguments to the effect that Paul was creating an "alternative society" of politically subversive communities can no longer rely on the a-priori assumption that the very title ἐκκλησία would convey and correlate with subversive behavior. Perhaps it did—but comparative evidence shows that this would have been an innovative function for an association title.

While political titles such as σύνοδος were common for associations, Paul selected for his groups a title from civic discourse that was less commonly attested among the associations. Would this have marked off Christ-followers as distinct from the associations with civic titles who sought to align themselves with their poleis? This possibility can be illuminated by studying associations that selected rarely attested civic titles. For instance, some associations chose the title φρατρία (and the cognate οἱ φράτορες[56] for members of these associations), but it was rare. The title φρατρία ("brotherhood") borrows, of course, from its civic namesake: Greek descent groups that were subdivisions of tribes organized on the basis of lineage and locality. Little is known about the function of the tribal social unit in Archaic and Classical periods. But in Athens membership in a phratry marked an individual as a citizen, not unlike eligibility to participate in the ἐκκλησία.[57]

Much remains unknown about the Hellenistic and Roman associations that self-designated as φρατρίαι, but evidence indicates that they pursued undertakings that fall squarely within known association practices. They did not engage in subversive political activity. Alain Bresson recently studied the practices of phratries in Neapolis (Campania, Italy), which he identified as *collegia* on the basis of their behavioral similarities to associations (as opposed to civic phratries): ownership and management of common tombs, relationships with patrons, and selection of magistrates.[58] Another possible example of a phratry association is found in an interesting inscription from Mylasa. The text attests to ἡ φρατρία τῶν Δαρρωνιστῶν. Wolfgang Blümel dates the script to the early Hellenistic era.[59] Jan-Mathieu Carbon argued persuasively that this group fell outside of the organizational structure of Mylasa.[60] As far

---

[56] In Lydia, a few associations referred to themselves as οἱ φράτορες: *TAM* 5.1148 = *AGRW* 144 (Thyatira, Lydia, Asia Minor; undated); Peter Herrmann, "Grabepigramm aus Büyükbelen in Lydien," *Arkeoloji Dergisi* 5 (1997) 171–74 = *SEG* 47 (1997), no. 1649 (Hyrkanis, Lydia, Asia Minor; second century CE); *TAM* 5.762 (Julia Gordos, Lydia, Asia Minor; first century CE); *ILydiaM* 136 (Nisyra, Lydia, Asia Minor; 48/47 BCE). See also the usage of φράτρα as a self-designation for a Zeus Hypsistos association in P.Lond. 7.2193.14 = *AGRW* 295 (Philadelphia, Fayum, Egypt; 69–58 BCE).

[57] For Kleisthenic reforms of the Athenian tribal system, see Herodotus, *Hist.* 5.66–69; and [Aristotle], *Ath. pol.* 21.1–6.

[58] Alain Bresson, "The *chōrai* of Munatius Hilarianus or Neapolitan Phratries as *Collegia*," *Mediterraneo Antico* 16 (2013): 203–22, here 204. Epigraphic attestation to the phratries of Neapolis spans from the first to the third century CE.

[59] Wolfgang Blümel, "Neue Inschriften aus Karien II: Mylasa und Umgebung," *Epigraphica Anatolica* 37 (2004): 1–42, here 17

[60] Jan-Mathieu Carbon, "ΔΑΡΡΩΝ and ΔΑΙΜΩΝ: A New Inscription from Mylasa," *Epigraphica Anatolica* 38 (2005): 1–6.

as the available evidence shows, civic tribes in Mylasa were divided into συγγένειαι, not φρατρίαι. Moreover, the name of the association (ἡ φρατρία τῶν Δαρρωνιστων) indicates that it was a phratry of "worshipers of Δάρρων," a divinity who was seemingly of Macedonian origin. In other words, the group does not appear to be a phratry formed on the basis of a common ancestor or geographic referent. Indeed, the group devised its title according to a well-known association formula: "the association of god-ισταί."[61]

Associations that chose the title φρατρία probably did not model themselves organizationally or behaviorally according to civic phratries. Poland correctly found that associations that employ phratry language (φρατρία, οἱ φράτορες) "had little or nothing to do with the division of people in phratries."[62] The phratry associations themselves do not push the analogy with civic phratries too far beyond their titles: many of them avoided self-presentation as lineage or regional collectives, instead preferring to highlight their common cult interests, as do οἱ Ἀρτεμεισίων φράτορες, "the brotherhood of Artemisioi" (*INeapolis* 44.16; Neapolis, Campania, Italy; 194 CE), and ἡ φρητρία τῆς Ἀρισταίων, "the phratry of the Aristaioi," (*INeapolis* 43.4; Neapolis, Campania, Italy; first century BCE–first century CE). Others aligned themselves with founders or benefactors, such as οἱ περὶ Αὐρ. Ἀρτέμωνα Ἑρμοκλέους φράτρα, "the phratry members around Aurelius Artemon Hermokleus" (*MAMA* 4.230 = *CMRDM* 1.127; Apameia Kelainai [Plouristreia], Phrygia, Asia Minor; third century CE), and ἡ φράτρα ἡ περὶ Διονυσόδοτον, "the phratry around Dionysodotos" (*IKyme* 39, lines 2–3 = *AGRW* 104; Kyme area, Mysia, Asia Minor; second to third century CE).[63] In short, associations with phratry names participated in practices that fall within the range of typical association activities (though some of these practices also fall within the spectrum of activities in which tribal subdivisions participated, too): funerary services,[64] monthly banquets, and passing group regulations.[65]

The phratry associations illustrate how civic terminology might be useful for expressing what most other association names do: corporate identity. Phratry ("brotherhood") language effectively describes group members as kin relations. Perhaps the clearest examples of borrowing civic language for its collectivist connotations rather than as part of a broader imitative project come from Lydia and Rhodes. The title φυλά (tribe) is very rarely attested in the association sources, but in Lydia there was a group of leather workers called ἡ ἱερὰ φυλὴ τῶν σκυτέων, "the

---

[61] See n. 21.

[62] Poland, *Geschichte des griechischen Vereinswesens*, 52.

[63] For a collection of associations employing brotherhood language (e.g., φρατρία, οἱ φράτορες) for their titles or members, see http://philipharland.com/greco-roman-associations/?s=brotherhood. For the phratries of Naples (Campania, Italy) as associations, see Bresson, "The *chōrai* of Munatius Hilarianus," 203–22.

[64] *SEG* 60 (2010), no. 1493 (Seleukeia Sidera, Pisidia, Asia Minor; imperial period); *ILydiaM* 109 (Saittai, Lydia, Asia Minor, 238/239 CE).

[65] P.Lond. 7.2193 = *AGRW* 295 (Philadelphia, Fayum, Egypt; 69–58 BCE).

sacred tribe of leatherworkers" (*IGLAM* 656.11–12; Philadelphia, Lydia, Asia Minor; second to third century CE); and an association called ἡ ἱερὰ φυλὴ τῶν ἐριουργῶν, "the sacred tribe of wool-workers" (*CIG* 3422.28 = *IGLAM* 648; Philadelphia, Lydia, Asia Minor; after 212 CE). On Rhodes, a subdivision of an immigrants' association called itself the φυλὰ Νικασιωνηΐς, "tribe of Nikasion" (*IG* 12.1.127, col. A, line 5 = *AGRW* 257; Rhodos on Rhodes, Aegean; early second century BCE).[66] These "tribes" presumably consisted not of family members but, rather, of individuals working in the same profession or, in the case of the Rhodian association, people who were part of a cultural minority association. They perhaps found tribal language to be useful for representing their groups as cohesive, natural fellowships. In any case, in these three instances, there is little reason to suspect that the civic title φυλά took on special political connotations such as communicating to the membership that their associations were alternative communities (however that term should be understood).

The argument that Paul's title ἐκκλησία functioned as part of a politically subversive program or marked the groups as modeled after civic ἐκκλησίαι is not actually based on what Paul says about the title (which is very little, indeed). Such connotations would be understood as innovative in light of naming practices in associations. In the absence of evidence from Paul concerning the function of his group title, the naming conventions of associations provide a significant control for gauging the politics of association titles.

A. Civic Titles That Convey Perceived Autonomy

In very rare instances, civic titles might be employed by associations as a way to affirm their perceived or real autonomy. One title that was possibly (and only occasionally) used this way is κοινόν, the typical name of federations of Greek states.[67] In 1924, Ernst Kornemann argued that the use of this civic title by associations of cultural minority soldiers positioned on Cyprus was designed to advertise these groups' intermediary (*Mittelding*) position in society, between associations and municipal civic institutions.[68] Kornemann offered the same assessment of the Ptolemaic πολιτεύματα associations, which were structurally similar.

The rarely employed association title πολίτευμα was also selected by an all-women's association in Stratonikeia. Here, too, it seems designed to affirm the group's place in Stratonikeia's structural organization. Our knowledge of this civic group's function in Stratonikeia is limited to three undated inscriptions from the temple of Zeus Panamaros in Panamara, located ten kilometers southeast of the

---

[66] This inscription mentions two other "tribes" as well (perhaps mimicking Rhodes's own subdivision of its citizenry into three tribes).

[67] In Ptolemaic Cyprus, the association designator κοινόν was employed by groups of cultural minority soldiers positioned on the island. See now Kruse, "Ethnic *Koina*," 292–93 nn. 71–77 for inscriptional references and discussion.

[68] Ernst Kornemann, "Κοινόν," PW 7:914–41, here 916–17.

town (*IStrat* 149, 174, 352; cf. 666 [Lagina]).⁶⁹ These inscriptions reveal only that the women's πολίτευμα held a role in the biennial women's festival, Heraia, which was celebrated at this temple complex. During this celebration, the priests typically summoned "all women both free and slaves" (πᾶσαι αἱ τε ἐλεύθεραι καὶ δοῦλαι, e.g., *IStrat* 202, lines 32–34) into the sanctuary, where the invitees received cash distributions and partook in banquets. But in the three inscriptions from Panamara referenced above (of unknown chronological relation to inscriptions using the formula quoted above), the priest invited "the women's πολίτευμα" (τὸ πολείτευμα τῶν γυναικῶν, *IStrat* 149, 174, 352) into the temple without mention of the other demographics of women participants. One possibility for reconciling the two sets of invitees is that the women referenced in the former inscriptions (i.e., free and slave) later established an association whose function was, in part, preparation for, and participation in, this festival.⁷⁰

If that reconstruction of the Stratonikeia inscriptions is correct, then the "assembly of women" (*curia mulierum*) in Lanuvium offers an analogy. This *curia*, in addition to holding the name of a civic organization, also played a role in municipal affairs.⁷¹ The Lanuvian inscription that mentions this women's *curia* reads as follows.

> C(aio) Sulpicio Victori / patri eeqq(uitum) RR(omanorum) homini / innocentissimo patrono / municipi(i) s(enatus) p(opulusque) L(anuvinus) ob in/parem

---

⁶⁹ They date anywhere from the second century BCE to the fourth century CE.

⁷⁰ This is suggested by Gert Lüderitz, who proposes that members of the πολίτευμα included the same groupings of women mentioned in the other associations: "'all the women'—free women and slaves, citizens of Stratonicaea and pilgrims (amongst whom were apparently also Roman women)" ("What Is a Politeuma?," in *Studies in Early Jewish Epigraphy*, ed. Jan Willem van Henten and Pieter Willem van der Horst, AGJU 21 [Leiden: Brill, 1994], 183–225, here 190). I find this interpretation somewhat problematic. In one of the three inscriptions, the πολίτευμα of women is *distinguished from* "the women who ascended [up to the sanctuary] with their husbands, both local residents and foreigners" (τ[αῖς] σὺν ἀνδράσιν ἀνα[βᾶσι γυ]να[ιξ]ὶν ἐντοπίο[ις καὶ] [ξέναις —] (*IStrat* 352, lines 6–9). In another inscription, this one from a different but nearby temple in Lagina (Stratonikeia), another πολείτευμα τῶν γυναικῶν is referenced. This group is distinguished from foreigners (ξένοι) and resident aliens (πάροικοι) (*IStrat* 666). On the bases of these two inscriptions, it appears that the Carian πολιτεύματα consisted of women with citizenship/elite social status and relative autonomy in comparison with the other groups from whom they are set apart.

⁷¹ Peter Thonemann, "The Women of Akmoneia," *JRS* 100 (2010): 163–78, here 175. *Curia*, which, in the civic context, designates divisions of citizens into voting districts or, in some cases, the local senate, was employed by several associations in the west. For *curiae* in Pompeii, see François Jacques, "Quelques problèmes d'histoire municipale à la lumière de la lex Irnitana," in *L'Afrique dans l'Occident romain (1er siècle av. J.C.–IVe siècle ap. J.C.)*, Collection de l'École française de Rome 134 (Rome: Ecole française de Rome, Palais Farnèse, 1990), 381–401, here 390–401; Willem M. Jongman, *The Economy and Society of Pompeii* (Amsterdam: J. C. Gieben, 1988), 289–94. For *curiae* in Spain, see Julián González, "The Lex Irnitana: A New Copy of the Flavian Municipal Law," *JRS* 76 (1986): 147–243. For examples of *curia* denoting local senates, see Pliny, *Ep.* 10.80; Apuleius, *Flor.* 16; Livy, *Hist. Rom.* 23.12.7.

obsequium et / erga se inmensam mu/nificentiam eius eques/trem ponendam cen/suerunt dedicarumq(ue) / ob cuius dedicationem / viritim divisit decuri/onibus et Augustalib/us et curis n(ummos) XXIIII et curi(a)e / mulierum epulum / duplum dedit. (*CIL* 14.2120 = *ILS* 6199; Lanuvium, Latium, Italy; late second/early third century CE)

To Gaius Sulpicius Victor, father of Roman *Equites*, a most upright man, patron of the *municipium*. The senate and the people of Lanuvium voted an equestrian (statue) to be set up, and dedicated it to him for his unparalleled service and immeasurable generosity towards them. On account of this dedication, he distributed 24 sesterces to each in the decurions, Augustales, and *curiae*, and furnished a double banquet for the women's *curia*.[72]

As the decree states, Lanuvium's civic bodies voted to award a statue to the civic patron, Gaius Sulpicius Victor. The inscription, additionally, acknowledges Victor's benefactions toward several civic groups after he had been awarded the statue. Interestingly, the *curia mulierum* is named as a recipient of Victor's generosity. Emily Hemelrijk's comments on this group are worth quoting at length:

> This *curia mulierum* must have been of some local importance since it received a double banquet (*epulum duplum*) on the dedication of his statue, whereas the decurions, the Augustales, and the members of the other (all-male) *curiae* were given handouts of money. As is apparent from the inscription, at this time Lanuvium still had *curiae*, which are often interpreted as sections of the citizen population grouped together for political purposes such as voting. The fact that a *curia* of women is added to the other, male *curiae* may mean that the associations' political function had become extinct and had perhaps been replaced by gatherings for social and religious ends. However, we should also consider another interpretation of the word *curia*: senate, or local senate. The double banquet received by the *curia mulierum*—instead of the usual, single meal—may be taken as a sign of social esteem, suggesting an association of high standing; it may have grouped together only the wealthier, well-born echelons of the female citizens. If so, the *curia mulierum* of Lanuvium may have resembled the *mulierum senatus* of Rome … and perhaps dealt with similar matters.[73]

Groupings of elite women—whether formally organized associations or informal networks—played various roles in local civic life. In the Roman West, we find women groups such as Rome's *conventus matronarum* or *mulierum senatus*

---

[72] Anna Pasqualini argued that the *curia mulierum* was an association devoted to Juno Sospita ("CIL XIV 2120, la curia mulierum di Lanuvio e l' 'associazionism' delle donne romane," in *Donna e vita cittadina nella documentazione epigrafica: Atti del II Seminario sulla condizione femminile nella documentazione epigrafica, Verona, 25–27 marzo 2004*, ed. Alfredo Buonopane and Francesca Cenerini, Epigrafia e antichità 23 [Ravenna: Fratelli Lega, 2005], 259–74), but this theory has not received much support given the lack of information from the inscription concerning the group's identity.

[73] Emily A. Hemelrijk, *Hidden Lives, Public Personae: Women and Civic Life in the Roman West* (Oxford: Oxford University Press, 2015), 206–7.

(women's senate),[74] the *matronae* in Interamnia Praetuttiorum, Italy (*CIL* 9.5071), and the *matronae municipes* in Ameria, Italy (*CIL* 11.4384; first century CE). These organizations enjoyed varying levels of independence. The council in Interamnia Praetuttiorum (Picenum, Italy) even required the consent of the local *matronae* before approving honors in one case.[75]

These groups each formed (peripheral?) parts of their city's organizational structure, unlike Paul's ἐκκλησίαι. There is logic in the calculation that selection of a civic title (e.g., *curia*, *senatus*) would reinforce such groups' actual local autonomy. But it is less obvious that associations outside the structural organization of their cities, such as any Pauline group, would deem selection of a civic title a plausible way to articulate autonomy—especially considering how commonly associations chose civic titles for themselves.

IV. Conclusions

This article explored the titles of associations as a way to generate new ideas about what might have been at stake when Paul named his groups with the title, ἐκκλησία. I proposed that association titles generally stressed one of three related connotations: (1) the act of coming together, (2) collective identity, or (3) cohesiveness among members. Paul's title ἐκκλησία fits well within the first category of the typology.

The connotation of openness or hospitality that was connected to category 1 titles is interesting in light of traditions pointing to Christ-followers in the first century who joined and formed household associations (Rom 16:11), women's groups (Acts 16:14–15, 40), neighborhood collectives, and occupational guilds.[76] Many of the groups in which Christ-followers participated were fully open to individuals with diverse cult practices (1 Cor 10:14, 2 Cor 6:14–18; Eph 5:5; 1 John 5:21; Rev 2:14–15; Polycarp, *Phil.* 11; Cyprian, *Ep.* 67.6). Conceptualizing these groups (some of which are called ἐκκλησίαι) as "churches" or "Christ groups" implies membership restrictions on the basis of cult preference (i.e., devotion to Christ) that Christ-followers themselves did not always put in place. The term "Christ-followers' groups," works better, for it is inclusive of any association (whether occupational, neighborhood-based, cult-oriented, and so on) that one or more Christ-followers joined and does not presume that the groups were defined by common cult preferences. The overlooked significance of ἐκκλησία in Pauline literature is that it too avoids essentializing Pauline groups according to a common cult preference, ethnic identity, or political orientation.

[74] Pliny, *Nat.* 37.85; Hist. Aug. Elag. 4.4; Hist. Aug. Aur. 49.6; Jerome, *Ep.* 43.3.

[75] For a discussion of various other groupings of elite women in the Roman West, see Hemelrijk, *Hidden Lives*, 207–22.

[76] For the Corinthians as a neighborhood collective, see Last, "Neighborhood (*vicus*) of the Corinthian *ekklēsia*," 399–425. For the Thessalonians as an occupational association, see Ascough, "Thessalonian Christian Community," 311–28.

Trouble with Insiders: The Social Profile of the ἄπιστοι in Paul's Corinthian Correspondence

T. J. LANG
tjl5@st-andrews.ac.uk
University of St Andrews, St Andrews KY16 9JU, United Kingdom

Conventionally translated as "unbelievers," the ἄπιστοι are usually taken to comprise an undefined class of "outsiders." The ἄπιστοι are thus viewed as the undifferentiated mass of humanity who are unworthy to be called ἀδελφοί. The actual evidence in 1 and 2 Corinthians suggests that the designation ἄπιστοι was a technical term in the community's sociolect for a group of individuals who maintained intimate social ties with the believers and could even be counted as "insiders" in the most socially serious ways. This article develops a social profile for the ἄπιστοι in which they emerge as a well-known group within the Corinth ecclesial network with intimate and even supportive ties to it—ties that are sustained by both believers and ἄπιστοι even in the face of severe social risks for both groups.

The fundamental issue animating Paul's correspondence with the Corinthian assembly is the definition of authentic Christian identity. As is the case with definitions of identity, Paul's dealings with Corinth confront questions of social and theological boundaries.[1] Who is in, and who is out? Who is genuine, and who is false? In the case of the man cohabiting with his father's wife (1 Cor 5:1–5), Paul's verdict is uncompromising: Deliver such a man to Satan! Although that man may still claim the title ἀδελφός and some may still regard him as such, he is in fact a

---

Versions of this article were presented to research seminars at St Andrews, Cambridge, and Oxford. I thank my hosts at these institutions for the invitation to share this work and all who offered feedback (and also pushback) on the argument.

[1] As John M. G. Barclay notes, "One may read the whole of 1 Corinthians as an attempt by Paul to define the boundaries of the Christian community in Corinth, and an integral part of that effort involves Paul labelling as deviant those he considers should be excluded from the church" ("Deviance and Apostasy: Some Applications of Deviance Theory to First-Century Judaism and Christianity," in *Pauline Churches and Diaspora Jews*, WUNT 275 [Tübingen: Mohr Siebeck, 2011], 123–39, here 136).

fornicator (πόρνος, 5:11), so he is a "leaven" that must be cleansed (5:6–8). In other matters of social division, the situation in Corinth is far less straightforward. The concern is often not simply to name insiders and outsiders but rather to distinguish between types of insiders, assorted degrees of deviancy, and fitting responses to untidy social circumstances. As Paul himself points out, "*There must be divisions among you* [αἱρέσεις ἐν ὑμῖν] so that those who are genuine among you [οἱ δόκιμοι ... ἐν ὑμῖν] should be recognized" (1 Cor 11:19).[2]

At the outset of 1 Corinthians Paul exhibits a wide-ranging and idiosyncratic social dialect.[3] He addresses his readers as "saints" (ἅγιοι), "brothers" (ἀδελφοί), "called" (κλητοί), "mature" (τέλειοι), and "spiritual" (πνευματικοί), but he also chastises them for the fact that there remain among them "fleshly people" (σάρκινοι) and "infants" (νήπιοι) who perpetuate innerecclesial divisions and require rudimentary instruction (3:1–4).[4] These latter individuals clearly remain deficient in Paul's eyes and problematic for the community as a whole, but they are not figured by Paul along the lines of the "natural person" (ψυχικὸς ἄνθρωπος), who is incapable of receiving the things of the Spirit of God (2:14). They are not, in other words, "outsiders," but they are also not the right kind of "insiders." The social divisions in Corinth are simply too complex to erect in every circumstance an unnuanced insider/outsider boundary. To return to the divisions (αἱρέσεις) described in 11:19: When Paul acknowledges the inevitability of schism within the church, he is not departing from his earlier lament about factionalism in the Corinthian assembly (1:10–13, 3:3–5). He is instead acknowledging that the Corinthian congregation, like any flock of two or more, is far from socially simple. Here Paul the ecclesial idealist yields to Paul the pastoral realist.

I. The ἄπιστοι among the Corinthian Believers

Further complicating any sketch of social dynamics in the Corinthian assembly is a category of individuals who had an influential social profile within the community while yet living beyond (or precariously *on*) the borders of it: the

---

[2] Barclay describes 1 Cor 11:19 as "a proto-sociological statement if ever there was one! Paul recognizes that the creation of distinction between the 'genuine' (*dokimoi*) and the 'spurious' (*adokimoi*, cf. 1 Cor. 9:27) serves to give the Christian community definition and identity" ("Deviance and Apostasy," 136–37).

[3] See esp. Barclay, "Πνευματικός in the Social Dialect of Pauline Christianity," in *Pauline Churches and Diaspora Jews*, 205–15.

[4] The key study on Christian self-designations is Paul Trebilco, *Self-Designations and Group Identity in the New Testament* (Cambridge: Cambridge University Press, 2012). See also Trebilco's "Creativity at the Boundary: Features of the Linguistic and Conceptual Construction of Outsiders in the Pauline Corpus," *NTS* 60 (2014): 185–201, esp. 187–94, which focuses explicitly on the ἄπιστοι in Corinth.

ἄπιστοι. Conventionally translated as "unbelievers,"[5] the ἄπιστοι are usually taken to constitute an undefined class of "outsiders"—or "all those who are not 'in.'"[6] The ἄπιστοι are thus viewed as the undifferentiated mass of humans who are unworthy to be called ἀδελφοί. Setting aside for the moment the problems with this understanding of the Greek word ἄπιστος (and its opposite, πιστός), the actual evidence in 1 and 2 Corinthians suggests that the designation ἄπιστοι was a technical term in the community's sociolect for a group of individuals who maintained intimate social ties with the believers and were even counted as "insiders" in certain senses.[7]

The term ἄπιστος appears fourteen times in the Corinthian correspondence and nowhere else in the undisputed letters.[8] Its prominence as a social designation within the Corinthian community is occasionally noted but rarely followed by additional comment. John Coolidge Hurd, for instance, characterizes Paul's exclusive use of the term in the Corinthian letters as "an interesting fact" and then notes that in 1 Corinthians Paul apparently had an "unusual interest in the unbeliever."[9] Hurd does not then pursue this unusual interest or probe the possibility that the ἄπιστοι had a more definable social profile. In addition to the conspicuous frequency of this particular designation in relation to this particular community is the fact that it is consistently applied by Paul to a class of individuals whose personal interactions with the Corinthian believers repeatedly prove problematic. This involves cases of legal disputes (1 Cor 6:6), marriage relations (1 Cor 7:12–15), shared meals (1 Cor 10:27), communal worship (1 Cor 14:22–24), and certain forms of ritual partnership (2 Cor 6:14–15). The corresponding πιστός is likewise prominent in 1 and 2 Corinthians, appearing seven times and otherwise only twice in the seven undisputed letters (see Gal 3:9, 1 Thess 5:24).[10] Given the prominence of the ἄπιστος/πιστός word group in relation to this particular Pauline community, it is worth exploring the possibility that it acquired a specialized sense, and one that would be important for discerning otherwise undetectable social resonances.

As Wayne Meeks points out in his analysis of early Christian speech, "Every close-knit group develops its own argot, and the use of that argot in speech among

---

[5] So ASV, CEB, ESV, KJV, NASB, NIV, NRSV/RSV, and so on. Exceptions to 1 Cor 6:6, the first reference in the letter, are the Wycliffe Bible ("unfaithful men") from the late fourteenth century and the Geneva Bible ("infidels") from the late sixteenth century under the influence of the Vulgate's *infideles*.

[6] Trebilco, *Self-Designations and Group Identity*, 83.

[7] Caroline Johnson Hodge is one scholar who has rightly raised objections to the translation of ἄπιστος as "unbeliever" in the Corinthian letters ("Married to an Unbeliever: Households, Hierarchies, and Holiness in 1 Corinthians 7:12–16," *HTR* 103 [2010]: 1–25, here 2 n. 5).

[8] The term is also found in 1 Tim 5:8 and Titus 1:15.

[9] John Coolidge Hurd, *The Origins of I Corinthians* (London: SPCK, 1965), 221.

[10] For πιστός, see 1 Cor 1:9; 4:2, 17; 7:25; 10:13; 2 Cor 1:18; 6:15. It appears frequently in the disputed letters of Ephesians, Colossians, 2 Thessalonians, and the Pastoral Epistles.

members knits them more closely still."[11] A common trait of any sociolect is the specialized use of particular words. As John Barclay explains, "the characteristic linguistic innovation in early Christianity was not the coining of neologisms, but the special frequency and emphasis with which Christians deployed perfectly acceptable terms which were used otherwise quite rarely, or rather differently, outside the circle of believers." Barclay explores how the adjective πνευματικός functioned this way in 1 Corinthians, where fifteen of the twenty-four Pauline uses of that word occur. For Barclay, such lexical accumulation suggests that "the term has become an important item in the social idiom of this particular network." But, as Barclay shows, the term was much more than just a *Lieblingswort* in the community's collective vocabulary. Rather, by introducing a new category for dividing the world, the term provided "an important linguistic tool by which to interpret social reality, a tool which is fully comprehensible only within its own patterns of discourse."[12] The equally conspicuous lexical data for ἄπιστος in the Corinthian letters, when coupled with the facts that (1) it is used by Paul exclusively in relation to Corinth, and (2) it is applied repeatedly to individuals with intimate social ties to the believers, are prima facie evidence that this social designation, like πνευματικός, attained special meaning in the community's social idiom and perhaps also some localized sense. And as with the use of πνευματικός in the Corinthian sociolect, determining a specialized sense for ἄπιστος requires attention to the patterns of discourse in which the word participates and to the complexities that attend the social divisions it creates. In other words, it is necessary to ask, In what sorts of social circumstances does the repeated use of this designation intervene, and what sort of social world does it instantiate?

To be clear: In arguing that this social designation must be comprehended within the community's sociolect, I am not suggesting it is necessarily a label the Corinthians created internally, nor that all within the community would have been pleased with it or been in agreement with those to whom Paul appends it. This is where the conflict between Paul's rhetoric and the Corinthian social reality lies. I suspect the ἄπιστος label is one Paul himself has developed in relation to the ἐκκλησία, even imposed upon it, in order to shape his readers into his desired social formation. But whatever the case, my claim is that the specific profile of an ἄπιστος—and, indeed, the specific people so labeled—is something the Corinthians would have detected natively, even if subsequent readers of Paul's letters have not.

In what follows I develop a social profile for the ἄπιστοι in which they emerge as a well-known group within the Corinth ecclesial network with intimate and even supportive ties to it—ties that are sustained by both believers and ἄπιστοι even in the face of severe social risks for both groups. The ἄπιστοι thus remain in marriages with believers despite the challenges accompanying domestic disharmony,

---

[11] Wayne A. Meeks, *The First Urban Christians: The Social World of the Apostle Paul* (New Haven: Yale University Press, 1983), 93.

[12] Barclay, "Πνευματικός in the Social Dialect of Pauline Christianity," 207, 210.

particularly in cases of domestic piety (1 Cor 7); they socialize with believers in ritually sensitive contexts, again tempting circumstances for public shame (1 Cor 10); they participate in the community's worship life with enough frequency that Paul calls upon the believers to be more mindful as to how they might best win their conversion (1 Cor 14); they had even been called upon to intervene in intraecclesial legal affairs (though Paul contends they should not) (1 Cor 6). In sum, although the ἄπιστοι are unquestionably "outsiders" in terms of exclusive loyalty to Christ, they are also unquestionably "insiders" in the most socially serious ways.

II. Ἄπιστος: The Lexical Data

The place to begin is with the lexical data for the ἄπιστος/πιστός word group. Despite the preference of modern translations, there is simply no lexical precedent for translating ἄπιστος as "unbeliever" in the sense of categorical outsider. Even Paul Trebilco, the most sophisticated analyst of this word group and proponent of the conventional translation, concedes, "Pauline usage where 'the unbelievers' is a label for *all outsiders* ... is quite distinct. As far as we know then, οἱ ἄπιστοι is not used in a Jewish or Greco-Roman context in the way that Paul uses it, that is, as a designation for all outsiders in general."[13] Trebilco defends his own reading of the ἄπιστοι as generic "unbelievers" primarily on the contrast with "the believers" (οἱ πιστεύοντες) in 1 Cor 14:22.[14] The juxtaposition of οἱ ἄπιστοι and οἱ πιστεύοντες here is indeed significant, but so is its asymmetry. Paul does not contrast those who believe (οἱ πιστεύοντες) with those who do not believe (οἱ μὴ πιστεύοντες or οἱ ἀπιστοῦντες).[15] Paul instead contrasts the participle (οἱ πιστεύοντες) with the adjective (οἱ ἄπιστοι). While Trebilco reads this as proof that Paul's use of ἄπιστοι "is comprehensive and includes all outsiders,"[16] the imparity in the juxtaposition may instead correspond to the fact that the ἄπιστοι here are something more like what the word usually means.[17] Furthermore, the likelihood that Paul's use of the designation had a specific social referent within its ordinary lexical range is supported

---

[13] Trebilco, "Creativity at the Boundary," 188.

[14] Ibid., 187.

[15] See οἱ μὴ πιστεύοντες in John 6:64 and Acts 9:26. Cf. οἱ μὴ πιστεύσαντες in 2 Thess 2:12. For ἀπιστέω, see esp. Rom 3:3, 2 Tim 2:13.

[16] Trebilco, "Creativity at the Boundary," 187.

[17] Trebilco is following John Taylor, "Paul's Understanding of Faith" (PhD thesis, University of Cambridge, 2004). As Taylor concludes, "It does not appear that ἄπιστος was used to indicate religious, philosophical or ethnic outsiders before its appearance in 1 Corinthians.... It seems most likely that Pauline use of οἱ πιστεύοντες, designating those who have received the gospel as believers, generated its own logical opposite" (cited in Trebilco, *Self-Designations and Group Identity*, 83). I simply point out that οἱ ἄπιστοι, in its ordinary sense, is not necessarily the logical opposite of οἱ πιστεύοντες. Nothing requires us to read Paul as using ἄπιστος in ways in which it had otherwise never been used.

not only by Paul's exclusive use of ἄπιστος in relation to Corinth but also by the fact that in the fifteen other times Paul uses οἱ πιστεύοντες as a substantival participle, it is never contrasted with οἱ ἄπιστοι. Paul employs a host of "outsider" designations in his other letters to stand in contrast to οἱ πιστεύοντες, but οἱ ἄπιστοι is never one of them. As Trebilco himself observes, "There were a number of occasions when Paul could have called outsiders οἱ ἄπιστοι ... but he does not."[18] Rather than appeal forthwith to "a new and innovative use of language,"[19] it is worth considering the possibility of a specialized application within the word's ordinary semantic range.

To return to the πιστός word group: In Jewish, Christian, and pagan literature surrounding the New Testament, the adjective πιστός describes a person (or god) who is "trustworthy, faithful, dependable, inspiring trust/faith" (BDAG, s.v. "πιστός") or "genuine" (LSJ, s.v. "πιστός").[20] So, by contrast, an ἄπιστος is someone who is viewed either passively as "not to be trusted," "unreliable," or actively as "mistrustful," "suspicious," "disobedient," or "disloyal" (LSJ, s.v. "ἄπιστος"). To render ἄπιστος as "unbeliever"—and thereby to understand such an individual as a nonspecific outsider in terms of "belief"—is simply not in keeping with the semantic data. It is also not in keeping with Paul's use of πιστός in 1 and 2 Corinthians, which, as one might expect, is repeatedly applied in its standard sense of "loyalty" or "fidelity."[21] Hence, when Paul characterizes God as πιστός, he is acclaiming God's ongoing "faithfulness" to sustain those who are called (1 Cor 1:8–9), not to let Christians be tempted beyond what they can bear (1 Cor 10:13), and never to waver in his word (2 Cor 1:18). So also, a πιστός person is a "faithful" administrator (1 Cor 4:2), or the "faithful" Timothy sent by Paul to remind the Corinthians of Paul's ways in Christ (1 Cor 4:17), or Paul himself, who is "trustworthy" in giving his opinion on marriage matters without explicit traditions from the Lord (1 Cor 7:25).

The use of ἄπιστος within the Corinthian church, like the use of πιστός, need not depart from established semantic conventions. The case to be made is that Paul reserves this designation for a special class of affiliates, even sympathizers, of the Corinthian ἐκκλησία. These individuals are in significant ways internal to the community's life, yet they resist exclusive loyalty to Christ-devotion, even if they may perhaps be attracted to it. The social profile of the ἄπιστοι in Corinth is thus one of deviant insiders who sustain thick social bonds with the community but, because they fail to extract themselves from pagan ritual life, remain outside the "temple of God" (1 Cor 3:16–17, 2 Cor 6:16). Although they are still welcome in worship, they are not counted as siblings in the ecclesial family.

---

[18] Trebilco, "Creativity at the Boundary," 189.

[19] Ibid., 190.

[20] The word can of course be used for things hard to believe or for people characterized by disbelief (John 20:27, Acts 26:8), but this is not what it means in the context of the Corinthian letters.

[21] So Trebilco: "Paul generally uses πιστός with the meaning 'reliable' or 'faithful'" (*Self-Designations and Group Identity*, 86).

To develop this profile of the ἄπιστοι it is necessary to track their emergence throughout the Corinthian letters while attending closely to the social implications of their interaction with the community. I begin with the instance in which the precise nature of their relation with believers is most evident.

III. The ἄπιστοι in the Corinthian Correspondence

Mixed Marriages: 1 Corinthians 7:12–16

Paul's ruling on relationships between the ἄπιστοι and the Corinthian believers in 1 Cor 7 is uncomplicated: as long as the ἄπιστος partner willingly agrees to cohabit (συνευδοκεῖ οἰκεῖν),[22] the two are united in a marriage that need not be dissolved (vv. 12–13). Paul's full reasoning on this matter is less lucidly expressed. Uncertainty begins with the "real life" identity of a given ἄπιστος and her or his history with the Corinthian assembly and Christ-devotion.[23] Given the fact that the ἄπιστος in 1 Cor 10:27–28 is associated with idol food, it can be assumed that the ἄπιστοι envisioned in chapter 7 also remain ensconced in such activities. But what could possibly account for such a person tolerating the Christ-devotion of a believing spouse given the disruptions to domestic life such devotion would entail?

It is important to stress that for a spouse to desist from ordinary ritual life in Roman Corinth would have been no small matter. As Barclay explains, "the disdain with which believers learned to speak of their past 'idolatry' ... could cause deep social offense. Gentile converts here broke with their ancestral customs and fractured the familiar habits which united their households."[24] Ritual life was just *life* in the Roman world. For one spouse to defect from household piety, especially a subordinate female spouse, would have destabilized the functioning of the home and risked social disgrace. Since the loyalty of an entire household to the newly acquired deity of the master of an οἶκος/*domus* would have been the expectation of a paterfamilias in Roman Corinth,[25] how then are we to account for the active

---

[22] The verb συνευδοκέω suggests not resigned toleration but active consent and approval by both parties. Cf. Rom 1:32, Luke 11:48, Acts 8:1, 22:20. Wolfgang Schrage, *Der Erste Brief an die Korinther*, 4 vols., EKK 7 (Zurich: Benziger; Neukirchen-Vluyn: Neukirchener Verlag, 1991–2001), 2:104.

[23] Although it is possible that the issue in these verses is marital infidelity, this is unlikely given the use of ἄπιστος elsewhere in the letter.

[24] Barclay, "Pauline Churches, Jewish Communities and the Roman Empire," in *Pauline Churches and Diaspora Jews*, 3–33, here 24.

[25] See Johnson Hodge, "Married to an Unbeliever." For the broader Roman concept of the household, see Richard P. Saller, *Patriarchy, Property, and Death in the Roman Family*, Cambridge Studies in Population, Economy, and Society in Past Time 25 (Cambridge: Cambridge University Press, 1994), 71–154. The responsibility of the head of household to convert (ἵνα τὸν οἶκόν σου ... ἐπιστρέψῃς) all members of the οἶκος is nicely illustrated in Herm. Vis. 1.3 (3).

consent of the ἄπιστοι in such disruptive marital arrangements? The answer lies in the social embeddedness of the ἄπιστοι within the ecclesial network and also in a shared sympathy for Christ-devotion.

The key exegetical gain in this understanding of the ἄπιστοι in the context of chapter 7 is that it helps account for the twofold implausibility of such a marital arrangement: (1) the implausibility of a *converted head of household not imposing* Christ-devotion on all his subordinates, thereby reorienting the entirety of domestic space and cleansing all forms of pagan religiosity; and (2) the implausibility of a *pagan head of household tolerating* the domestically rebellious Christ-devotion of a subordinate spouse.[26]

As for the latter implausibility, Plutarch's comments on a woman's place in domestic religion in his *Advice to the Bride and Groom* highlight the oddity of a pagan head of household tolerating the religious noncompliance of a spouse:

> A married woman should therefore worship and recognize the gods whom her husband holds dear, and these alone. The door must be closed to strange cults and foreign superstitions. No god takes pleasure in cult performed furtively and in secret by a woman.[27] (*Conj. praec.* 19 [140d])

The fact that Plutarch gives this admonition betrays the reality that women did in fact abandon a husband's piety by attaching themselves to foreign deities,[28] and perhaps some had in Corinth, devoting themselves to Christ. But if this did occur, and a paterfamilias deigned to allow it, severe challenges and even dangers would have ensued. The home was highly visible to neighbors and passersby, and a wife's refusal to participate in the day-to-day ritual life of the paterfamilias would have been to the eyes of onlookers "a slap at her husband's authority over her."[29] There was nothing like a public/private dichotomy in Roman society. As Andrew Wallace-Hadrill explains, in Roman culture "the home was a locus of public life. A public figure went home not so much in order to shield himself from the public gaze, as to present himself to it in the best light."[30] The home in Roman society was "deliberately designed for the performance of social rituals" and, hence, "the basic

---

[26] David E. Garland, *1 Corinthians*, BECNT (Grand Rapids: Baker, 2003), 284–86. So Johnson Hodge notes, "Paul's advice here (to stay with the unbelieving spouse) glosses over a variety of complicated issues that a mixed household might produce, especially for the believing wives" ("Married to an Unbeliever," 5). Cf. Schrage, *Der Erste Brief an die Korinther*, 2:104.

[27] This translation is from *Plutarch's Advice to the Bride and Groom and A Consolation to His Wife: English Translations, Commentary, Interpretive Essays, and Bibliography*, ed. Sarah B. Pomeroy (Oxford: Oxford University Press, 1999), 7.

[28] See, for instance, Justin's account of the female convert and her unconverted husband in *2 Apol.* 2.1–6.

[29] Garland, *1 Corinthians*, 284. For further elaboration of the complications embedded in such a relationship, see Johnson Hodge, "Married to an Unbeliever," 4–9.

[30] Andrew Wallace-Hadrill, "The Social Structure of the Roman House," *PBSR* 56 (1988): 43–97, here 46. For more on the visibility of Roman homes and the performative dimension of

structures [of the Roman house] are determined by the (to us) astonishingly public nature of domestic life, and how little weight contemporary western preoccupations of privacy and family life carry."[31] A wife's domestic insubordination and newfound attraction to an executed foreign deity would not have been without extraordinary risks of societal shame. From its furniture to its food, the ancient Roman home was a spiritually suffused space with reverence for the household gods integral to daily life.[32] For either spouse to abandon ritual life in the home would have been a widely observable and embarrassing disruption—for a wife to withdraw from the gods of her husband and to adopt a new and aberrant form of piety even more so.[33] If, however, the ἄπιστοι are Christian sympathizers with strong and preexisting social ties to other believers, the acceptance of religious difference within the home becomes more understandable. A spouse unsympathetic to Christ-devotion would not be inclined to tolerate the embarrassment and complications a mixed marriage would entail.

As implausible as an unconverted, unsympathetic head of household allowing the ritual noncompliance of a believing wife is a believing paterfamilias permitting a wife's refusal to adhere to his new Christian piety.[34] The conventional reading of the γυναῖκα ἄπιστον in 1 Cor 7:12 presupposes just this. Far more plausible is that Paul is addressing a specific class of individuals embedded within the social life of the Corinthian assembly who retain sympathies for Christ-devotion yet desist from exclusive adherence to it. Although the precise nature or degree of their sympathy to Christ-devotion is unknown, it was at least such that they would embrace the risks and disruptions of mixed marriages and other social engagements, and even join the believers in corporate gatherings.

But what of Paul's apparent endorsement of believers engaging in sex with ἄπιστοι? The problem here is that Paul must account for why the standing of the ἄπιστοι vis-à-vis believers in matters of sex is not like that of a prostitute (6:15–20).

---

domestic life, see Kate Cooper, "Closely Watched Households: Visibility, Exposure and Private Power in the Roman *Domus*," *PaP* 197 (2007): 3–33.

[31] Wallace-Hadrill, "Social Structure of the Roman House," 96.

[32] As Kathy Ehrensperger explains, "Most members of the Corinthian ἐκκλησία were accustomed to a context in which numerous deities and spiritual beings were seen as responsible for diverse aspects of daily life. Entrenched in their *habitus* was the perception that each and every aspect of life required the appropriate relationship to a specific deity or spiritual being. This permeated public life but *to an even greater and more significant extent kin group and household on an everyday basis*" ("Between Polis, Oikos, and Ekklesia: The Challenge of Negotiating the Spirit World [1 Cor 12:1–11]," in *Roman Corinth*, vol. 2 of *The First Urban Churches*, ed. James R. Harrison and L. L. Welborn, WGRWSup 8 (Atlanta: SBL Press, 2016]), 105–32, here 105 (emphasis mine).

[33] As Margaret Y. MacDonald puts it, "the illicit religious activities of women were considered to be far more than annoying; they were an assault on the social order of the family" ("Early Christian Women Married to Unbelievers," *SR* 19 [1990]: 221–34, here 230).

[34] See ibid., 222.

In Paul's nimble reasoning, he declares that sexual relations between believers and ἄπιστοι communicate *cleansing* to the ἄπιστοι rather than *contagion* to the believer—otherwise the children of such relations would be unclean; but as it is they are holy (7:14).[35] Paul may very well here be reapplying halakic principles of transferable sanctity, but if he is, he nowhere explains this Jewish logic to his readers.[36] Whatever the case may be, Paul is seriously grappling with two clashing social givens: the impure, "outsider" status of the ἄπιστοι in relation to the ecclesial body and their sanctioned, "insider" status in matters of marriage.[37] He concludes that the former neither countermands nor contaminates the latter. But in other relational matters, it does.

Social Relations: 1 Corinthians 10:27–29

The social proximity of the ἄπιστοι and the Corinthian believers again occasions a matter of practical concern. Paul writes, "If one of the ἄπιστοι invites you to dinner [εἴ τις καλεῖ ὑμᾶς τῶν ἀπίστων][38] and you want to attend, eat everything placed before you, not adjudicating on account of conscience" (10:27). Paul does not object to believers accepting invitations to dine with the ἄπιστοι.[39] He even assures believers that they need not have misgivings about any sacrificial food (ἱερόθυτος) placed before them (see the arguments in vv. 23a, c; 25–26; cf. 8:1–6).[40] But, although such food is innocuous in principle, this is not a license to ignore the

---

[35] For further consideration of this dynamic, see Dale B. Martin, *The Corinthian Body* (New Haven: Yale University Press, 1995), 218–19.

[36] See Benjamin D. Gordon, "On the Sanctity of Mixtures and Branches: Two Halakic Sayings in Romans 11:16–24," *JBL* 135 (2016): 355–68, esp. 364, https://doi.org/10.15699/jbl.1352.2016.2783; Yonder Moynihan Gillihan, "Jewish Laws on Illicit Marriage, the Defilement of Offspring, and the Holiness of the Temple: A New Halakic Interpretation of 1 Corinthians 7:14," *JBL* 121 (2002): 711–44, https://doi.org/10.2307/3268578.

[37] It is also worth pointing out Paul's hope for evangelistic success. See Joachim Jeremias, "Die missionarische Aufgabe in der Mischehe (1. Kor. 7,16)," in *Neutestamentliche Studien für Rudolf Bultmann zu seinem 70. Geburtstag am 20. August 1954*, ed. Walther Eltester, BZNW 21 (Berlin: Töpelmann, 1954), 255–60.

[38] The use of τὶς here is at least worth noting; a definite person could stand behind it. For the use of τὶς "with suggestion of non-specificity in a context where an entity is specified to some extent," see BDAG s.v. "τὶς" 1aב; or "in reference to a definite person, whom one wishes to avoid naming," see LSJ s.v. "τις" II.3.

[39] Paul has already indicated that he has no problem with the believers associating in general with "immoral" people. The problem is when they allow immorality among their own ranks (1 Cor 5:9–13).

[40] This is probably an invitation to a host's home. Some have interpreted it as an invitation to dine in temple precincts, perhaps a dining room attached to a sanctuary. This is not impossible, but it would perhaps make the informant's remarks in verse 28 about the food being ἱερόθυτος ridiculous. It is again worth pointing out that a purported division between "sacred" temple space and neutral or "nonsacred" domestic space is simply false. Domestic space is always sacredly

qualms of a fellow believer for whom such food may present challenges of conscience. If another believer with a vulnerable conscience is troubled by the presence of such food (v. 28), then neither believer should partake of it (v. 29a). Admittedly, the person raising the objection in vv. 28–29a is not explicitly identified as a fellow believer, and some have proposed that a pagan guest or even the host is in view.[41] But since the hypothetical informant takes the initiative to raise the issue with the Christian and since the informant's conscience is the one in question, a fellow believer with a "weak" conscience is more likely.[42]

The problem of idol food is a subject Paul already treated at length in 8:1–13. Paul returns again to that same issue in 10:27–29, but now specifically as it relates to the believer's dealings with the ἄπιστοι in social contexts. Paul's counsel is the same. Whether in temple precincts or a host's home, eat whatever is served unless it compromises the weaker conscience of a fellow believer.[43] The ethical imperative to protect a neighbor's conscience surpasses any dietary freedom afforded by theological principle.[44]

As for the profile of the ἄπιστοι here, their ongoing integration with the believers is again highlighted. They appear to maintain convivial ties with multiple members of the community, if not the entire community. A key aspect of their deviancy also emerges in their relation to sacrificial food,[45] which indicates an ongoing participation in pagan ritual life. Even so, it is not impossible to imagine that, as resourceful and devout pagans, they had attempted to integrate Christ-piety into their preexisting cultic framework. Perhaps Christ was simply for them another deity to be incorporated into something like the household lares or penates.[46] There

---

charged. See David G. Horrell, *Solidarity and Difference: A Contemporary Reading of Paul's Ethics* (London: T&T Clark, 2005), 145–50.

[41] Since Paul always elsewhere uses the term εἰδωλόθυτος, which has pejorative connotations, the use of ἱερόθυτος is sometimes taken as indicating a pagan informant. If, however, Paul is assuming the voice of a gentile Christian, the use of the ἱερόθυτος is unproblematic. It was the term such a person had always used.

[42] So Archibald Robertson and Alfred Plummer: "That a heathen would do it out of malice, or amusement, or good-nature ('I dare say, you would rather not eat that'), is possible, but *his* conscience would hardly come into consideration" (*A Critical and Exegetical Commentary on the First Epistle of St. Paul to the Corinthians*, 2nd ed., ICC [Edinburgh: T&T Clark, 1914], 221). See also Schrage, *Der Erste Brief an die Korinther*, 2:469–70.

[43] The rhetorical question at the end of verse 29 and then leading to verse 30 is indeed "sehr schwierig" (Schrage, *Der Erste Brief an die Korinther*, 2:471). It is probably best to see this as picking up Paul's reasoning from verse 27. What lies between (vv. 28–29a) thus becomes parenthetical—but no less critical!

[44] For an excellent account of the "christological praxis" driving Paul's reasoning here, see David G. Horrell, "Theological Principle or Christological Praxis? Pauline Ethics in 1 Corinthians 8.1–11.1," *JSNT* 67 (1997): 83–114.

[45] The use of the nonpejorative ἱερόθυτος in verse 28 is significant. This is neutrally viewed sacrificial food, not stigmatized idol food (εἰδωλόθυτος).

[46] I say "something like" because it is extremely difficult to know what ritual practices or

is ample ancient evidence of pagan attraction to Judaism apart from any concern for what we might call monotheism.⁴⁷ This was simply part and parcel of the religious eclecticism of the ancient Mediterranean world. Whatever the case may be in Corinth, the ἄπιστοι clearly retain their customary cultic rituals while also maintaining (indeed, risking) social ties with believers.

It is worth underscoring again the remarkable leniency the ἄπιστοι would potentially be required to extend to the believers in the case of shared meals. Given that the meal Paul is imagining is one taking place in a pagan home (or even in a temple if the occasion required [see 8:10]), the believer, in denying the very gods of the household,⁴⁸ would have been obliged to withdraw from any number of ritual acts—and even, if conscience required it, the meal itself. This is no minor social matter. In his detailed description of the numerous ritual customs that accompanied ordinary household meals—such as burning any morsel of food that fell to the ground on the household *lar* as an act of expiation (*adolerique ad Larem piatio est*) (*Nat.* 28.28)—Pliny the Elder explains the importance of such acts: "These customs were established by those of old, who believed that gods are present on all occasions and at all times" (*Nat.* 28.27; Jones, LCL).⁴⁹ For the Christ-believer there were no such gods; no such customs to rehearse. Though idol food could be consumed without personal worry, a believer could not have joined the prayers, offerings, libations, hymns, and gestures that also would have attended such gatherings. The believer must flatly reject the idol worship offered by her host (10:14)— "for we know that an idol is nothing in the world and that there is no God but one" (8:4). Apparently, however, the social bonds were such that the ἄπιστοι continued to permit this highly visible antisocial and atheistic behavior even in their own homes.⁵⁰ This tolerance afforded to believers is not what one would expect from unsympathetic outsiders.

---

divine figures would have been common in Corinthian domestic life at this time. We can assume that the city provided an à la carte cultural matrix, with mixtures of Roman, Greek, and additional "foreign" or eastern traditions. What we can say confidently is that the aggregate of evidence from the first-century Roman world points to the richness and pervasiveness of domestic religious life. For more on these matters, see Alexandra Sofroniew, *Household Gods: Private Devotion in Ancient Greece and Rome* (Los Angeles: J. Paul Getty Museum, 2015). In relation to Corinth in particular, see Ehrensperger, "Between Polis, Oikos, and Ekklesia," 112–17.

⁴⁷ Nero's second wife, Poppaea Sabina, is one likely and well-known example of this. See Margaret H. Williams, "'Θεοσεβὴς γὰρ ἦν'—The Jewish Tendencies of Poppaea Sabina," *JTS* 39 (1988): 97–111.

⁴⁸ For the lares as protectors of the household, see Ovid, *Fast.* 5.129–146.

⁴⁹ For further analysis of such rituals, see Peter Foss, "Watchful Lares: Roman Household Organization and the Rituals of Cooking and Dining," in *Domestic Space in the Roman World: Pompeii and Beyond*, ed. Ray Laurence and Andrew Wallace-Hadrill, JRASup 22 (Portsmouth, RI: JRA, 1997), 196–216.

⁵⁰ Ehrensperger also emphasizes that, "given the all-permeating nature of cult practices at all levels and in all and every context of life, to abstain from any such activity was an enormously

Christian Worship: 1 Corinthians 14:20–25

The assumption that the ἄπιστοι in Corinth are generic "unbelievers" meets further difficulties in the fact that they show up in ecclesial gatherings with enough regularity that Paul advises the congregants on how to behave when they are present so as to secure their salvation (cf. 1 Cor 7:16). Paul also in this passage differentiates the well-known ἄπιστοι from what I do take to be a generic class of outsiders: the ἰδιῶται, or common people (vv. 16, 23, 24; 2 Cor 11:6).[51] The distinction between ἄπιστοι and ἰδιῶται is worth respecting.[52] That Paul sets the ἄπιστοι apart from ἰδιῶται (a social designation that *is* usually applied to generic individuals or common people not initiated as members) reinforces the possibility that the label ἄπιστοι obtained a special sense within the Corinthian community.[53]

Taken as a whole, 1 Cor 14:20–25 is an old exegetical enigma. The challenge is in relating the apparent claim in verse 22 that tongues are a sign for the ἄπιστοι, while prophecy is for believers (τοῖς πιστεύουσιν), with the scriptural citation in verse 21 and then the examples in verses 23–25, which seem to indicate that what the ἄπιστοι really need is, in fact, not tongues but rather the intelligible speech of prophecy.

In verse 20 Paul again exhorts the Corinthians to be mature in their thinking, which is to say, mature in promoting intelligible speech instead of uninterpreted glossolalia. In verse 21 he appeals to a scriptural prooftext for clarifying one function of tongues.[54]

> In the law it has been written, "In other tongues and with the lips of foreigners I shall speak to this people, and even then they will not listen to me," says the Lord.
>
> ἐν τῷ νόμῳ γέγραπται ὅτι ἐν ἑτερογλώσσοις καὶ ἐν χείλεσιν ἑτέρων λαλήσω τῷ λαῷ τούτῳ καὶ οὐδ' οὕτως εἰσακούσονταί μου, λέγει κύριος. (Isa 28:11–12)[55]

---

challenging and possibly dangerous endeavor. It would have been challenging in that daily cult practices in the domestic realm had to be given up, including the security they provided. It would have been difficult in a context of multiple small shrines, niches, and altars dedicated to Lares and Penates or Greek domestic deities in every house. It is difficult to imagine how this requirement could have been fulfilled if an entire household had not joined the Christ-movement" ("Between Polis, Oikos, and Ekklesia," 119–20).

[51] This is another social designation Paul uses exclusively in the Corinthian correspondence.

[52] The τις in the τις ἄπιστος ἢ ἰδιώτης in verse 24 may again have a specific ἄπιστος in view, whereas ἰδιώτης does not. Cf. τις … τῶν ἀπίστων in 10:27.

[53] On the distinction of two classes here, see Johannes Weiss: "von den ἄπιστοι verschiedene Klasse von Menschen bezeichnet werden" (*Der Erste Korintherbrief*, rev. ed., KEK [Göttingen: Vandenhoeck & Ruprecht, 1910], 329).

[54] Isaiah 28 is a text Paul returns to elsewhere (cf. Rom 9:33, 10:11). Translations of biblical passages are my own unless otherwise noted.

[55] Differences between this citation, the extant Greek traditions, and the MT are substantial.

It is likely that the word ἑτερόγλωσσος ("other-tongues") is what attracts Paul's attention to this text from Isaiah.[56] This passage is part of an oracle against Ephraim and Judah. In 28:7 the prophet turns to the leaders of Judah, whom he chastises for their drunkenness and unwillingness to heed Isaiah's counsel (vv. 7–10). Since these leaders would not listen to the Lord through the message of Isaiah, the Lord will then address them through the alien speech of an invading Assyrian force (vv. 11–12).

In this context, the sign function of incomprehensible tongues is to confirm judgment on individuals who refuse to mind God's message. The sign function of tongues is disciplinary; it is reserved not for generic outsiders but for *unfaithful insiders* who incite divine judgment. Extended to the ἄπιστοι in 1 Cor 14:22, the sign function of tongues is again to demonstrate that the ἄπιστοι, in the presence of the worshiping community, are similarly resistant to God's demands and so stand under judgment. Although they join the community in worship and may even express forms of Christ-piety, they remain disloyal insofar as they resist exclusive worship of God. What, then, should the Corinthian believers do?

In verses 23–25, Paul advances his case for curtailing glossolalia in communal worship by explaining that since prophecy, and not tongues, is the fitting sign for believers, it is prophecy that will lead the ἄπιστοι to repentance. Whereas tongues leave the unfaithful under judgment, prophecy holds out hope for their confession of allegiance to God. In other words, whereas tongues, as a sign of judgment, convert unfaithful insiders into outsiders, prophecy, as an instrument of edification, has the potential to turn infidelity into loyalty. The nature of the confession in verse 25 is also significant: "Truly God is among you" (ὄντως ὁ θεὸς ἐν ὑμῖν ἐστιν). This confession evokes scriptural passages such as 3 Kgdms 18:39 (ἀληθῶς κύριός ἐστιν ὁ θεός αὐτὸς ὁ θεός, "Truly the Lord is God; he is God" [NETS]), Dan 2:47 (ἐπ' ἀληθείας ἐστὶν ὁ θεὸς ὑμῶν θεὸς τῶν θεῶν, "It is certain; your God is God of gods" [NETS]), and Zech 8:23 (ἀκηκόαμεν ὅτι ὁ θεὸς μεθ' ὑμῶν ἐστιν, "we have heard that God is with you" [NETS]), all of which portray non-Israelites acknowledging the truth of Israel's God. What these passages together underscore is the identity of Israel's God as *exclusively* God and *exclusively* present with God's people. Such is the emphasis in Isa 45:14, which is the scriptural text most similar to 1 Cor 14:25: "Truly God is with you, and there is no other, no God besides him" (אך בך אל ואין עוד אפס אלהים; ἐν σοὶ ὁ θεός ἐστιν καὶ ἐροῦσιν οὐκ ἔστιν θεὸς πλὴν σου). If the ἄπιστοι are a group of individuals in Corinth who are sympathetic to Christ-piety but refuse exclusive devotion to Christ, then this is just the sort of confession Paul would demand of them.[57]

---

[56] This term is not found in any extant Greek traditions of Isaiah and so could have been Paul's own gloss.

[57] The fittingness of this confession for the ἄπιστοι stands out all the more when placed alongside a christologically focused confession such as that in Rom 10:9.

Internal Litigation: 1 Corinthians 6:1–8

The first appearance of the ἄπιστοι in this letter occurs in 1 Cor 6:6. The key contribution of this text to their identity is, however, the reference in verse 4 to "those who have no standing in the church" (τοὺς ἐξουθενημένους ἐν τῇ ἐκκλησίᾳ [NRSV]). This is almost certainly a reference to the ἄπιστοι and, when read in relation to Paul's other uses of the verb ἐξουθενέω (reject, despise, disregard, marginalize), it supplies crucial information about how they were viewed within the community. The dative phrase ἐν τῇ ἐκκλησίᾳ, which is always used locatively by Paul ("in the church"), also has implications for envisaging their social location.[58]

Who, then, are these individuals "who have no standing in the church" (v. 4) but have been tasked with arbitrating intraecclesial disputes? The solution is to be found in Paul's use of the verb ἐξουθενέω elsewhere. In 1 Cor 1:28 he again applies the participial form of the verb, but this time to the Corinthians themselves ("God chose what is low in this world and disdained [τὰ ἐξουθενημένα]"). In 1 Cor 16:11 he applies the term to Timothy, whom the Corinthians are instructed not to dismiss (μή τις οὖν αὐτὸν ἐξουθενήσῃ). In 2 Cor 10:10 Paul uses the verb to describe how he himself is viewed by some in Corinth ("his bodily presence is weak and his message has been disparaged [καὶ ὁ λόγος ἐξουθενημένος]"). The sense of interpersonal dismissal or marginalization is found also in Gal 4:14 ("and you did not reject [οὐκ ἐξουθενήσατε] or disdain me, but received me as an angel of God").[59] This is the case also in the two occurrences of the verb in Rom 14:3, 10, where it takes on a more precise sociological sense, and one particularly relevant to 1 Cor 6. Here Paul applies ἐξουθενέω to marginalized individuals within the assembly on grounds of dietary dispute.

> Rom 14:3
> Let not the one who eats marginalize the one not eating [ὁ ἐσθίων τὸν μὴ ἐσθίοντα μὴ ἐξουθενείτω], and let not the one not eating judge [μὴ κρινέτω] the one who eats, for God has accepted [προσελάβετο] him.

> Rom 14:10
> And you, why do you judge [τί κρίνεις] your brother? Or then, why do you marginalize [τί ἐξουθενεῖς] your brother? For we shall all stand before the judgment seat of God.

The verb here thus again describes a form of social marginalization, and specifically one that the so-called strong impose upon the weak, to the detriment of communal harmony and edification (14:19). How this marginalization was expressed is unclear.

---

[58] The καθίζετε in verse 6, and the whole of the verse with it, can be read as (1) an indicative ("you are appointing …"), (2) an interrogative ("why are you appointing …?"), or (3) an imperative ("appoint …!"). Since Paul says this to their shame and chastises them for their failure in judgment in verse 5, the indicative and the interrogative are the best options.

[59] The verb occurs one other time, in 1 Thess 5:20 ("Do not reject prophecy" [προφητείας μὴ ἐξουθενεῖτε]). This is the only instance that does not involve people.

Whereas ἐξουθενέω indicates how the "strong" perceive the "weak" on these matters of eating, the verb κρίνω describes the feelings of the "weak" toward the "strong." Whether there is a distinction at work in these two verbs is also unclear, though Paul's infrequent use of κρίνω suggests there might be. Since the command to "receive" (προσλαμβάνω) the weak in 14:1 may refer to an expression of formal recognition or fellowship, this may be what the "strong" are denying to the "weak."[60] Whatever the case may be, what both verbs name is the perception of deviancy. The "strong" marginalize or reject the "weak" because they view their dietary abstention as aberrant behavior.

This use of ἐξουθενέω in relation to intracommunal definitions of deviancy should inform the usage in 1 Cor 6:4. "Those who have no standing in the church" are the ἄπιστοι who, while remaining "in the assembly" in terms of shared social space, are nonetheless not regarded as ἀδελφοί. As in Rom 14, the tangible expressions of this marginalization are not detailed beyond the recommendation that the ἄπιστοι not arbitrate internal ecclesial disputes. The main contrast with Rom 14, however, is that, whereas the marginalization of others in matters of food is misguided, in 1 Cor 6 the denial to the ἄπιστοι of proper membership in the assembly is entirely appropriate.

This understanding of the ἄπιστοι as a group of individuals whose *social* marginalization does not translate into *physical* exclusion from ecclesial space finds corroboration in Paul's other uses of the phrase ἐν [τῇ] ἐκκλησίᾳ. This expression occurs nine times in the Pauline corpus, seven of which are in 1 Corinthians. In every instance the phrase is used locatively.

> 1 Cor 4:17
> Therefore I sent to you Timothy ... to remind you of my ways in Christ, as I teach them everywhere **in every church** [ἐν πάσῃ ἐκκλησίᾳ].
>
> 1 Cor 11:18
> For first of all I hear that when you come together **in the church** [ἐν ἐκκλησίᾳ], there are schisms among you ...
>
> 1 Cor 12:28
> And God has appointed **in the church** [ἐν τῇ ἐκκλησίᾳ] first apostles ...
>
> 1 Cor 14:19
> But **in church** [ἐν ἐκκλησίᾳ] I would rather speak five words with my understanding ...
>
> 1 Cor 14:28
> But if there is no one to interpret, let each of them keep silent **in church** [ἐν ἐκκλησίᾳ] ...

---

[60] The verb προσλαμβάνω appears in Paul only in Rom 14:1, 3; 15:7; and Phlm 17. At the very least it expresses a more intense form of welcoming.

1 Cor 14:35
For it is shameful for a woman to speak **in church** [ἐν ἐκκλησίᾳ].

Eph 3:21
... to him be glory **in the church** [ἐν τῇ ἐκκλησίᾳ] and in Christ Jesus to all generations, for ever and ever.

Col 4:16
... and when this letter has been read among you, have it read also **in the church of the Laodiceans** [ἐν τῇ Λαοδικέων ἐκκλησίᾳ].

Though they are barred from full membership, the fact that the ἄπιστοι can be described as "those who have no standing *in the church*" demonstrates the degree to which they maintain a form of insider status. This is evident also from 1 Cor 14:22–24. What Paul finds shameful in 6:4–6 is, therefore, not the fact that some members of the Corinthian assembly associate socially with the ἄπιστοι or even participate with them in worship. The problem is that they have submitted themselves to the judgment of the ἄπιστοι in intraecclesial affairs when they should be competent to judge themselves, if judge they must (see vv. 7–8).

Partnership with Idolatry: 2 Corinthians 4:4, 6:14–15

The appearance of the ἄπιστοι in 2 Corinthians again supports their profile as individuals closely related to the Corinthian assembly, even "insiders" in some sense, though they remain embroiled in idolatrous activity. The potential threat they pose to the community also comes to the fore. If 2 Cor 6:14–7:1 is an interpolation, then its contribution to the profile of the ἄπιστοι in Corinth is less certain. But whether an interpolation or not, the passage remains significant because the ἄπιστοι here are frequently read as disloyal Christians or even rivals to Paul's mission. Michael Goulder, for instance, has argued that the ἄπιστοι in this passage are not generic pagans or "unbelievers" but rather "faithless Christians."[61] He bases his argument on the ordinary sense of πιστός/ἄπιστος and on the fact that Paul elsewhere clearly permits Christian interaction with pagan idolaters (see esp. 1 Cor 5:9–13). Several scholars in more recent years have connected the ἄπιστοι in this passage with Paul's opponents in Corinth, particularly as they emerge in chapters 10–13.[62] On this reading of 6:14–16, Paul is depicting those ψευδαπόστολοι as worse

---

[61] Michael Goulder, "2 Cor. 6:14–7:1 as an Integral Part of 2 Corinthians," *NovT* 36 (1994): 47–57, here 47. Goulder also describes them as "immoral/non-Pauline Christians" (54).

[62] See esp. the inventory of scholarship provided by David Starling, "The ἄπιστοι of 2 Cor 6:14: Beyond the Impasse," *NovT* 55 (2013): 45–60; see 50 n. 25. Prominent and early representatives of this position include Jean-François Collange, *Enigmes de la Deuxième Épître de Paul aux Corinthiens: Étude exégétique de 2 Cor. 2:14–7:4*, SNTMS 18 (Cambridge: Cambridge University Press, 1972), 282–306; D. Rensberger, "2 Corinthians 6:14–7:1—A Fresh Examination," *Studia Biblica et Theologica* 8 (1978): 25–49. More recently, Volker Rabens reads the passage as "a double

than idolaters. They are equivalent to Beliar himself (v. 15). On any reading, the ἄπιστοι described in 2 Cor 6 are close enough in their relations with the Corinthian "faithful" to tempt them into partnerships that involve idolatry.[63] The nature of these partnerships (ἑτεροζυγοῦντες) is not defined (cf. Lev 19:19), but it must differ from the other forms of social interaction between believers and outsiders that Paul permits, such as marriage relations, wherein believers overcome the impurity of the ἄπιστοι rather than being polluted by it (1 Cor 7:14). What is envisioned in 2 Cor 6 is some specific formal relationship with the ἄπιστοι that faithful believers currently do not and should not maintain.[64] Given the climactic rhetorical question in verse 16—"What concord has the temple of God with idols?"—the partnership envisioned by the verb ἑτεροζυγέω presumably involves something along the lines of "covenant-like relationships with pagans which in turn violate the church's existing covenant with God."[65]

If the ἄπιστοι here are the same as elsewhere, then the contrast between πιστός and ἄπιστος in 6:15 is between the person who remains loyal to the "living God" (v. 16) and the disloyal sympathizer who still persists in idolatrous devotion.[66] A loyal versus disloyal contrast is precisely how one would normally understand the πιστός versus ἄπιστος contrast. The problem Paul is addressing here, then, is partnership not with generic outsiders but with a problematic class of deviant affiliates of the Corinthian community who are corrupted by idolatrous influences and seek to recruit the believers into these practices. As Regina Plunkett-Dowling concludes, the problem Paul is addressing in 6:14–7:1 is one of "internal pollution" that constitutes "disloyalty to Paul, and by extension, to God."[67] The ἄπιστοι in this passage

---

entendre referring first to demarcation from idolatrous people outside the church (= unbelievers), and second to demarcation from false apostles (= unbelievers)" ("Inclusion of and Demarcation from 'Outsiders': Mission and Ethics in Paul's Second Letter to the Corinthians," in *Sensitivity towards Outsiders: Exploring the Dynamic Relationship between Mission and Ethics in the New Testament and Early Christianity*, ed. Jakobus (Kobus) Kok et al., WUNT 2/364 [Tübingen: Mohr Siebeck, 2014], 290–323, here 298).

[63] Gordon D. Fee also has emphasized the importance of idolatry in this passage ("II Corinthians vi. 14–vii. 1 and Food Offered to Idols," *NTS* 23 [1977]: 140–61).

[64] So Thomas Schmeller: "Das Verbot, sich mit Ungläubigen einzulassen, ist sprachlich so formuliert, als werde vor einer Änderung des bisherigen getrennten Zustands gewarnt, den γίνεσθε mit Partizip Präsens impliziert den Beginn eines neuen Zustands" (*Der Zweite Brief an die Korinther*, 2 vols., EKKNT 8 [Neukirchen-Vluyn: Neukirchener Verlag, 2010], 1:373).

[65] Rabens, "Inclusion of and Demarcation from 'Outsiders,'" 305.

[66] Regardless of whatever forms of "yoking" Paul would deem inappropriate, the focus in this passage is on idolatry and association with demonic forces. Again, see the argument of Fee, "II Corinthians vi. 14–vii. 1." Cf. also the remarks of Margaret E. Thrall, who notes that the final rhetorical question concerning idolatry in verse 16 is "the only one to contain a specific reference to the kind of moral danger which association with unbelievers might bring with it. There can be no compromise with idolatry" (*The Second Epistle to the Corinthians*, 2 vols., ICC [London: T&T Clark, 1994–2000], 1:475).

[67] Regina Plunkett-Dowling, "Reading and Restoration: Paul's Use of Scripture in 2 Corinthians 1–9" (PhD diss., Yale University, 2001), 155.

must, then, be current or former congregants "who have proved, or will prove, live candidates for defection from Paul's gospel."[68]

The reference to the ἄπιστοι in 4:4 has also been read along the lines I am proposing. Goulder describes the ἄπιστοι in this verse as "Christians who are perishing," that is, "faithless" individuals associated with Christ yet whose minds are now being blinded by the god of this age.[69] The key point is that the ἄπιστοι, not humanity as a whole, are singled out as a special class of individuals for whom misperception is attributed to satanic agency. This is quite similar to the additional "Pauline" use of ἄπιστος in Titus 1:15–16—"To the pure all things are pure, but to the defiled and disloyal [μεμιαμμένοις καὶ ἀπίστοις] nothing is pure; their very minds and consciences are defiled [μεμίανται αὐτῶν καὶ ὁ νοῦς καὶ ἡ συνείδησις]. They profess to know God, but they deny him by their deeds; they are detestable, disobedient, unfit for any good deed." Like the ἄπιστοι in Titus 1:15, the ἄπιστοι in 2 Cor 4:4 may very well boast of knowledge of God but, according to Paul, their inability to submit to Paul's gospel is, in fact, the consequence of satanic intervention.

The status of the ἄπιστοι in verse 4 as a subset of some larger group is seen in the relative clause beginning "among whom" (ἐν οἷς), which defines the ἄπιστοι as a subgroup within "those who are being destroyed" (ἐν τοῖς ἀπολλυμένοις) from verse 3.[70] The ἄπιστοι are not the whole mass of unbelieving humanity but a specific subcategory of it. As for the agent responsible for blinding the ἄπιστοι, "the god of this age" must be synonymous with Beliar (6:15). The blinding of the ἄπιστοι may also be the consequence of engagement with idolatry, a betrayal of loyalty to the living God (6:16). The association of idol worship and blindness is a common trope.[71] Especially close to the language of "blinded minds" in 2 Cor 4:4 is the depiction in Isa 44:18 of idol makers as simultaneously blind and uncomprehending: "They do not know, nor do they comprehend; for their eyes are shut, so that they cannot see, and their minds as well, so that they cannot understand" (NRSV). As Plunkett-Dowling explains, "in their defective condition, these perishing, blinded unbelievers share the typical defect of idolaters, the ones deprived of their senses when they turn away from the living God."[72] This is also the type of language one might use of those who have been instructed on how they ought to believe and act but do not. There are, then, once again good reasons for associating the ἄπιστοι

---

[68] Ibid., 168.

[69] Goulder, "2 Cor. 6:14–7:1," 57.

[70] The relative clause at the beginning of verse 4 is frequently deemed "awkward" (Thrall, *Second Epistle to the Corinthians*, 1:305) and as having "no logical sense" because it would seem to indicate "a smaller group of unbelievers" (306 n. 805). See also Schmeller, *Die Zweite Brief an die Korinther*, 1:243. This presumed logical awkwardness stems from the assumption the ἄπιστοι are generic unbelievers. This is simply not necessary.

[71] See esp. Isa 44:9, 18. See also the references in Plunkett-Dowling, "Reading and Restoration," 89 n. 178.

[72] Plunkett-Dowling, "Reading and Restoration," 104–5.

in 4:4 with idolatrous practices, as in 6:14–16. There are also good reasons why Paul's language here is so sharp. The risk the ἄπιστοι pose is so severe. And the risk is so severe precisely because of their social proximity.

IV. Conclusion

Paul's struggle with the ἄπιστοι in Corinth is political. Since "idolatrous error is an error about the management of society (a political error),"[73] to name the deviancy of the ἄπιστοι is to fortify the societal integrity of the ἐκκλησία. But even though in 2 Cor 6:14–7:1 (if it is authentic) Paul places strict parameters on the types of relations believers ought not maintain with the ἄπιστοι, the evidence from 1 Corinthians otherwise reveals a surprising permissiveness when it comes to social interaction between ἐκκλησία and ἄπιστοι. If "Paul thinks the Corinthians are far too comfortable in their social integration, and he spends much of the letter erecting barriers where the Corinthians presently see none,"[74] then the ἄπιστοι represent a stark exception in Paul's broader social strategy, if not a surd in his social vision. Like irrational numbers, the ἄπιστοι repeatedly unsettle any neat social fractioning. Note again the contrasts: Whereas Paul is unbending on sex with prostitutes because of the "oneness" it entails (6:16–18), he permits ongoing sexual activity between ἄπιστοι and believers (7:12–15); he even inverts his argument about purity to accommodate it. Although in one breath he roundly condemns any flirtation with idolatry (10:14–22)—"you cannot partake of the table of the Lord and the table of demons" (10:21)—he nonetheless authorizes believers to dine at the tables of ἄπιστοι and partake of their idol food (10:27). While the man cohabiting with his father's wife is to be delivered over to Satan by the gathered assembly with Paul's spirit present (5:1–13), the ἄπιστοι appear to frequent community worship with enough regularity that Paul encourages liturgical alterations to accommodate them (14:22–25).[75]

As Trebilco similarly notices, although by the label ἄπιστοι these individuals "are 'defined out' by a very strong boundary," in actual fact Paul's statements about them "are often surprisingly positive, demonstrating a prominent degree of

---

[73] Moshe Halbertal and Avishai Margalit, *Idolatry*, trans. Naomi Goldblum (Cambridge: Harvard University Press, 1992), 163.

[74] Barclay, "Deviance and Apostasy," 137.

[75] As Trebilco observes, Paul applies "the same principle to the 'unbeliever'—that of 'other-regard'—that he applies elsewhere to the 'weaker brother or sister'. An activity of the believer should be curbed if its impact on the unbeliever who is present is deleterious, just as the activity of the strong (believer) should be curbed if it has an adverse impact on the weaker believer. This is to accord a very significant status to the ἄπιστοι, and to apply the overarching principle of 'the love of the brother or sister' to 'the love of the unbeliever', even if Paul does not state it in these terms" ("Creativity at the Boundary," 192–93).

openness to these outsiders who are so labelled."[76] Paul thus "encourages social differentiation from these clearly labelled 'outsiders' but without a corresponding social distance." This is unquestionably the case. But unanswered is the question of why what is "said about the unbelievers … belies the negativity that seems to be inherent in the designation." Trebilco maintains that one of the primary issues Paul was facing was weak or unenforced boundaries for defining the believers as a group; consequently, "the necessity for stronger group boundaries has led to the *use of* οἱ ἄπιστοι in 1 Corinthians. One way in which he creates this stronger boundary is through this label." Paul thus exercises "creativity at the boundary" through his "new and innovative use of language," whereby the term ἄπιστοι takes on a sense it never otherwise had. But this appeal to linguistic novelty does not address the contradiction of Paul reinforcing social boundaries by labeling as ἄπιστοι a group of people who continue to problematize such boundaries by their very location within them. Trebilco is correct to identify Paul's creativity here and its position *at the boundary*, but it is not the creativity of linguistic novelty. Paul's creativity is instead expressed in the tactful social control he exhibits by defining "out" a class of individuals whose ongoing presence defines them as "in." In Paul's eyes, as attracted to Paul's Christ as they may be, and as tightly braided with the lives of Christ's people in Corinth as they clearly are, the ἄπιστοι remain as the word usually means, disloyal insiders.

---

[76] Trebilco, "Creativity at the Boundary," 191; quotations in this paragraph come from 190, 191, and 193.

SBL PRESS

New and Recent Titles

JEWISH FICTIONAL LETTERS FROM HELLENISTIC EGYPT
The Epistle of Aristeas and Related Literature
L. Michael White and G. Anthony Keddie
Paperback $56.95, 978-1-62837-185-7   490 pages, 2018 Code 061643
Hardcover $76.95, 978-0-88414-240-9   E-book $56.95, 978-0-88414-239-3
Writings from the Greco-Roman World 37

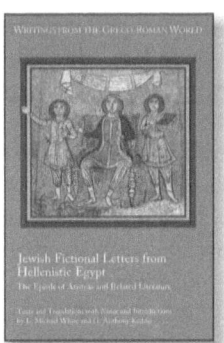

NEGOTIATING THE DISABLED BODY
Representations of Disability in Early Christian Texts
Anna Rebecca Solevåg
Paperback $29.95, 978-1-62837-221-2 206 pages, 2018 Code: 064524
Hardcover $44.95, 978-0-88414-325-3   E-book $29.95, 978-0-88414-326-0
Early Christianity and Its Literature 23

THE WAYS THAT OFTEN PARTED
Essays in Honor of Joel Marcus
Lori Baron, Jill Hicks-Keeton, and Matthew Thiessen, editors
Paperback $61.95, 978-1-62837-216-8 460 pages, 2018   Code: 064525
Hardcover $81.95, 978-0-88414-315-4   E-book $61.95, 978-0-88414-316-1
Early Christianity and Its Literature 24

BOOKS AND READERS IN THE PREMODERN WORLD
Essays in Honor of Harry Gamble
Karl Shuve, editor
Paperback $32.95, 978-1-62837-223-6   234 pages, 2018 Code: 064213
Hardcover $47.95, 978-0-88414-329-1   E-book $32.95, 978-0-88414-331-4
Writings from the Greco-Roman World Supplements 12

THE FIRST URBAN CHURCHES 4
Roman Philippi
James R. Harrison and L. L. Welborn, editors
Paperback $49.95, 978-1-62837-226-7 424 pages, 2018 Code: 064216
Hardcover $64.95, 978-0-88414-336-9   E-book $49.95, 978-0-88414-337-6
Writings from the Greco-Roman World Supplements 13

SBL Press • P.O. Box 2243 • Williston, VT 05495-2243
Phone: 877-725-3334 (toll-free) or 802-864-6185 • Fax: 802-864-7626
Order online at www.sbl-site.org/publications

A Precedented Approach: Paul's Use of the Law of Witnesses in 2 Corinthians 13:1

J. DAVID WOODINGTON
jwooding@nd.edu
University of Notre Dame, Notre Dame, IN 46556

Much debate has surrounded Paul's reason for citing the law of witnesses from Deut 19:15 in 2 Cor 13:1. Despite the existence of alternative theories, the best explanation remains a metaphorical interpretation of the witnesses as Paul's visits to Corinth. This view has been critiqued for being too far from the original intention of Deut 19:15, but an examination of the law's appearances in other texts shows that Paul is not alone in his adaptation of this Deuteronomic law. Regulations from rabbinic sources, Qumran, and elsewhere in the New Testament strongly parallel Paul's own aims, and the seemingly novel aspects of Paul's citation are mirrored in other texts. Paul admonishes the Corinthians to cease their sinful behavior because his upcoming visit to the city will serve as the third and final witness against their immorality and grant him the authority to administer punishment against them.

In 2 Cor 13:1, Paul directly cites Deut 19:15: "Let every charge be established by the testimony of two or three witnesses."[1] Paul identifies his words as a quotation of Scripture, and this text matches the Septuagint aside from the omission of three superfluous words.[2] Scholars have offered different explanations for what exactly Paul seeks to accomplish by employing this biblical rule. Most prominent has been a metaphorical interpretation of Paul's intentions, but this position has been routinely scrutinized by those who prefer a more literal understanding of the law and its role in 2 Cor 13:1. I seek to defend the metaphorical reading, but I will do so by comparing what we find in Paul with other passages that make use of Deut 19:15 both inside and outside the New Testament. The stipulation of "two or three

---

[1] Unless noted otherwise, all translations are my own.
[2] See Christopher D. Stanley, *Paul and the Language of Scripture: Citation Technique in the Pauline Epistles and Contemporary Literature*, SNTSMS 69 (Cambridge: Cambridge University Press, 1992), 33, 66 n. 8. Deuteronomy 19:15 LXX: ἐπὶ στόματος δύο μαρτύρων καὶ ἐπὶ στόματος τριῶν μαρτύρων σταθήσεται πᾶν ῥῆμα. Paul removes the underlined words from his version, but this does not disrupt the meaning.

witnesses" found in 2 Cor 13:1 appears regularly in Jewish and early Christian literature, and rather than being idiosyncratic, Paul takes his place among a series of interpreters who adapted the principle of Deut 19:15 to suit their own purposes. I will argue that proponents and detractors alike of the metaphorical interpretation have failed to notice that every element of 2 Cor 13:1 has a counterpart elsewhere in non-Pauline writings. This article fleshes out previous summary discussions of the relationship between 2 Cor 13:1 and these other citations of the law of witnesses, and it rebuts the misconception shared on both sides of the debate that everything Paul has to say is altogether unique. Once one recognizes that nothing in Paul's statement is entirely novel, there remains no compelling argument against the metaphorical interpretation of this verse.

I. Scholarly Theories about 2 Corinthians 13:1

The majority of modern scholars, like some of the early church fathers (e.g., John Chrysostom, *Hom. 2 Cor.* 29.1), consider Paul's application of Deut 19:15 in 2 Cor 13:1 to be metaphorical. Immediately following and preceding his citation of the law, Paul mentions his previous second visit to Corinth (13:2) and his upcoming third visit (13:1). Many commentators see this as too perfect a correspondence to be mere coincidence and argue that the Deuteronomic quotation should be interpreted in light of these visits. In their view, Paul's visits to the Corinthians are the witnesses to which he refers.[3] Paul is not referring to actual human witnesses but to his three separate trips as providing the evidence needed to punish them for their sins (13:2).[4] While Paul hopes that it will not be necessary, the citation serves

---

[3] E.g., Alfred Plummer, *A Critical and Exegetical Commentary on the Second Epistle of St Paul to the Corinthians*, ICC (Edinburgh: T&T Clark, 1915), 372; Hans Windisch, *Der zweite Korintherbrief*, KEK (Göttingen: Vandenhoeck & Ruprecht, 1924), 413; C. K. Barrett, *The Second Epistle to the Corinthians*, HNTC (New York: Harper & Row, 1973), 333; Margaret E. Thrall, *A Critical and Exegetical Commentary on the Second Epistle to the Corinthians*, 2 vols., ICC (New York: T&T Clark, 1994–2000), 2:876; Raymond F. Collins, *Second Corinthians*, Paideia (Grand Rapids: Baker Academic, 2013), 254; Jan Lambrecht, *Second Corinthians*, SP 8 (Collegeville, MN: Liturgical Press, 1999), 211; Hendrik van Vliet, *No Single Testimony: A Study on the Adoption of the Law of Deut. 19:15 Par. into the New Testament*, STRT 4 (Utrecht: Kemink & Zoon, 1958), 96 n. 8.

[4] There are variations on this general position in scholarship. Murray J. Harris sees the witnesses as representative of not just Paul's visits but "both visits and warnings, or, rather, warnings that are associated with visits" due to "the τρίτον–τριῶν and δύο–δεύτερον associations in vv. 1–2 and to the notion of warning that dominates v. 2" (*The Second Epistle to the Corinthians: A Commentary on the Greek Text*, NIGTC [Grand Rapids: Eerdmans, 2005], 908). Other commentators see the three witnesses as the second visit, the letter that Paul is currently writing, and the upcoming third visit. Proponents of this theory argue that Paul would not have considered his original founding visit to Corinth as a witness against the Corinthians' sins. The foundational trip would

as a warning that he will have sufficient grounds to use his apostolic authority upon his third arrival in Corinth (13:10). Several supporters of this theory note that the regulation of having two or three witnesses was widely known by this point and could have served as a general principle or even a "proverb," making the somewhat strained relationship between 2 Cor 13:1 and the original law of Deut 19:15 more explicable.[5]

An alternative view takes a literal understanding of Paul's citation of Deut 19:15 and assumes that he will call witnesses against sinners in the Corinthian community when he returns to the city. According to this view, Paul plans to hold court in Corinth, put those misbehaving on trial, and bring forward those who can provide testimony of their transgressions.[6] The specific details of this general position vary from author to author. For instance, David Garland argues that Paul's quotation of Deut 19:15 indicates a shift of private matters into the public arena so that "Paul will take disciplinary action according to the biblical principles governing a judicial proceeding" when he returns.[7] Mathias Delcor claims that Paul will act as a supreme judge in a role analogous to that of the *məbaqqēr* described in the Damascus Document.[8] Minor differences notwithstanding, all of these views assume

---

have been an occasion for spreading the gospel and evangelizing the Corinthians, not rebuking their misbehavior or gathering evidence against them; see, e.g., Rudolf Bultmann, *Der zweite Brief an die Korinther*, KEK (Göttingen: Vandenhoeck & Ruprecht, 1976), 243; Victor Paul Furnish, *II Corinthians*, AB 32A (Garden City, NY: Doubleday, 1984), 575; Frank J. Matera, *II Corinthians: A Commentary*, NTL (Louisville: Westminster John Knox, 2003), 305–6; Paul Han, *Swimming in the Sea of Scripture: Paul's Use of the Old Testament in 2 Corinthians 4.7–13.13*, LNTS 519 (London: Bloomsbury T&T Clark, 2014), 178. One could point to the flow of Paul's words in 2 Cor 13:2 (warned on second visit, warning now with the letter) to give additional credence to this theory. As Thrall rightly notes, this theory is "over-complicated" and overburdens the metaphor (*Second Epistle*, 2:876). Furthermore, such a move seems rather unnecessary as we can readily include the denouncing of sins as an integral part of Paul's spreading the gospel in the first place (cf. 1 Cor 6:9–10, Gal 5:19–21).

[5] E.g., van Vliet, *No Single Testimony*, 88; Furnish, *II Corinthians*, 574–75; Lambrecht, *Second Corinthians*, 221; Barrett, *Second Epistle*, 333; cf. W. D. Davies and Dale C. Allison Jr., *A Critical and Exegetical Commentary on the Gospel according to Saint Matthew*, 3 vols., ICC (Edinburgh: T&T Clark, 1988–1997), 2:784; R. T. France, *The Gospel of Matthew*, NICNT (Grand Rapids: Eerdmans, 2007), 693.

[6] E.g., Philip Edgcumbe Hughes, *Paul's Second Epistle to the Corinthians: The English Text with Introduction, Exposition and Notes*, NICNT (Grand Rapids: Eerdmans, 1962), 474–75; E. Bernard Allo, *Saint Paul: Seconde Épître aux Corinthiens*, 2nd ed., EBib (Paris: Gabalda, 1956), 335; Han, *Swimming in the Sea*, 178.

[7] David E. Garland, *2 Corinthians*, NAC 29 (Nashville: Broadman & Holman, 1999), 541; cf. A. E. Harvey, *Renewal through Suffering: A Study of 2 Corinthians*, SNTW (Edinburgh: T&T Clark, 1996), 108.

[8] Mathias Delcor, "The Courts of the Church of Corinth and the Courts of Qumran," in *Paul and Qumran: Studies in New Testament Exegesis*, ed. Jerome Murphy-O'Connor (London: Geoffrey Chapman, 1968), 69–94, here 76.

that Paul's words in 2 Cor 13:1 should be taken literally in reference to an actual court that will prosecute members of the Corinthian community for their sins.

One can understand the impetus to read the verse in this way, but there are several problems with this line of thinking. Most obviously, Paul never mentions human witnesses or this kind of court in 2 Corinthians.[9] Many point to 1 Cor 6:1–6 as a parallel, but this overlooks Paul's "scathing condemnation of lawsuits between community members" that follows immediately afterwards in 6:7.[10] Paul denounces precisely the kind of legal divisiveness that such a court would inevitably stir up. If there is a solution for sinful members of the community, it is to dissociate from them, not bring lawsuits against them (1 Cor 5:9–13). Furthermore, many of the Corinthians do not seem to be concealing their sinful actions; there would be no reason to call witnesses for deeds that were already public knowledge.[11] Lastly, it seems unlikely that Paul would have the Corinthians testify against one another, given the disruptive tensions within the community (12:20). This would seem to counter much of the work he has been trying to accomplish there.[12] When considered together, the cumulative weight of these points is sufficient to cast doubt on a rigorously literal utilization of Deut 19:15.

A third option keeps the idea of court and witnesses in play, but now the one on trial is Paul rather than the sinful Corinthians. According to this interpretation, Paul cites the rule of witnesses to defend himself and to show that he has legal proof of his apostolic credentials.[13] The identity of these witnesses (God and Christ? Timothy and Titus? members of the Corinthian community?) remains unclear, but the citation is decidedly apologetic. In a recent article, Laurence Welborn defends a reconstruction along these lines but with an added wrinkle: Paul's citation of Deut 19:15 happened *previously* when he was in Corinth, and his words in 2 Cor 13:1–2

---

[9] Collins, *Second Corinthians*, 254; Thomas Stegman, *The Character of Jesus: The Linchpin to Paul's Argument in 2 Corinthians*, AnBib 158 (Rome: Pontifical Biblical Institute, 2005), 371.

[10] Stegman, *Character of Jesus*, 371. For more on the legal background of 1 Cor 6:1–11, see Bruce W. Winter, "Civil Litigation in Secular Corinth and the Church: The Forensic Background to 1 Corinthians 6.1–8," *NTS* 37 (1991): 559–72; and Alan C. Mitchell, "Rich and Poor in the Courts of Corinth: Litigiousness and Status in 1 Corinthians 6.1–11," *NTS* 39 (1993): 562–86.

[11] Harris, *Second Epistle*, 907; Plummer, *Second Epistle*, 372; Thrall, *Second Epistle*, 2:874; George H. Guthrie, *2 Corinthians*, BECNT (Grand Rapids: Baker Academic, 2015), 631.

[12] Stegman, *Character of Jesus*, 370–71; Thrall, *Second Epistle*, 2:873. Han attempts to rebut this point by arguing that Paul's concern for holiness in the church would outweigh his concern for "superficial peace among the Corinthians" (*Swimming in the Sea*, 179).

[13] E.g., R. V. G. Tasker, *The Second Epistle of Paul to the Corinthians: An Introduction and Commentary*, TNTC (London: Tyndale, 1958), 186; Calvin J. Roetzel, *2 Corinthians*, ANTC (Nashville: Abingdon, 2007), 118. Bernard S. Jackson also supports this apologetic sense of the citation, but he mixes this view with the metaphorical interpretation of the visits as witnesses ("*Testes Singulares* in Early Jewish Law and the New Testament," in *Essays in Jewish and Comparative Legal History*, SJLA 10 [Leiden: Brill, 1975], 172–201, here 193–96).

are a reminder of what he said at that time.[14] Welborn hypothesizes that an individual charged Paul with financial wrongdoing during a community assembly, and in the midst of a raucous crowd he invoked this legal precedent to prove his innocence and out his accuser as a false witness.[15] He further argues that the concerns about Paul's weakness in this section (13:3–4) arise from his prior choice not to punish his malicious accuser, as was his right by law.[16]

Although proof of Paul's authenticity as an apostle is indeed a prominent issue in 2 Cor 10–13, this sort of apologetic reading overlooks other noteworthy aspects of the immediate context of the pericope. In particular, it fails to account for the emphasis Paul places on the Corinthians' sins immediately before (12:29) and after (13:2) he quotes the law, and it does not fit well with the threatening tone so apparent in the citation. Welborn attempts to meet these problems by asserting that Paul's appeal to the law brings to mind the harsh penalties inflicted on false witnesses mentioned in the same section of Deuteronomy (Deut 19:19–21). Paul's quotation, therefore, serves not only as a defense but also as "a warning for anyone familiar with the context of the statute" that punishment awaits "anyone involved in false witness against Paul."[17] Welborn also notes numerous verbal parallels between Deut 19:19–21 and Paul's words to the Corinthians, further strengthening this connection.[18]

Nevertheless, even if one accepts that Paul has the entire pericope of Deut 19:15–21 in mind, his claim that self-defense is not his primary goal at this point in the letter (12:19) speaks against such a theory. To be sure, Paul has been mounting a defense of his apostolic ministry in 2 Cor 10–13, but these chapters are "not simply an apology made to the Corinthians."[19] Instead, the apology is part of Paul's larger appeal (cf. 10:1–2) "to persuade the Corinthians" that he "is God's approved apostle (10:18)—that Christ does indeed speak in him (13:3)."[20] In addition to defending himself, Paul also gives the Corinthians "an ultimatum that carries a threat (2 Cor 10:6, 13:2), a *Drohrede* that carries with it a call for repentance," and it is to this purpose that Paul turns his attention in 2 Cor 12:19.[21] As his own words

---

[14] Laurence L. Welborn, "'By the Mouth of Two or Three Witnesses': Paul's Invocation of a Deuteronomic Statute," *NovT* 52 (2010): 207–20, here 218. Welborn's argument can also be found in his later monograph, *An End to Enmity: Paul and the "Wrongdoer" of Second Corinthians*, BZNW 185 (Berlin: de Gruyter, 2011), 182–94.

[15] Welborn, "'By the Mouth,'" 218.

[16] Ibid., 219.

[17] Ibid., 215.

[18] Ibid., 216–17.

[19] John T. Fitzgerald, "Paul, the Ancient Epistolary Theorists, and 2 Corinthians 10–13: The Purpose and Literary Genre of a Pauline Letter," in *Greeks, Romans, and Christians: Essays in Honor of Abraham J. Malherbe*, ed. David L. Balch, Everett Ferguson, and Wayne A. Meeks (Minneapolis: Fortress, 1990), 190–200, here 198.

[20] Ibid., 194.

[21] Ibid., 195.

indicate, Paul here shifts his focus away from himself and onto the plight of the Corinthians and the imminent threat that their sins pose to them. He switches from defense to offense, from apology to accusation.[22] Condemning the false witness(es) against him could perhaps scare the rest of the Corinthians straight, but such a picture does not fit with the kinds of misdeeds specified in the verse immediately preceding the citation: impurity, sexual immorality, and sensuality (12:21). Second Corinthians 12:19–13:4 decries the immorality of a community, not the wrongful testimony of Paul's opponent(s) therein. The decidedly ambiguous nature of the supposed two or three witnesses makes the picture murkier still. In the end, then, these theories also fall short in explaining the background of 2 Cor 13:1.

Despite the occasional support for other explanations of 2 Cor 13:1, the metaphorical interpretation of Paul's visits as witnesses fits best with the surrounding context and provides the most convincing reading of the Deuteronomic citation.[23] The correlation between the number of visits and the number of witnesses is simply too compelling to ignore.[24] Those who oppose this view do so primarily on the grounds that Paul could not be applying this law in a way that diverges so dramatically from its original use in Deuteronomy.[25] What Paul is doing in 2 Cor 13:1, however, is not entirely unprecedented. Several Jewish writings use the principle of two or three witnesses in ways that parallel Paul's own use quite closely. Even the New Testament itself provides evidence of the multifaceted manner in which this law was employed. By turning to these Jewish and Christian sources, we can note several similarities in how Paul and these other writers altered Deut 19:15 to suit their own purposes.

[22] Cf. ibid., 199; Guthrie, *2 Corinthians*, 631.

[23] Stegman proposes a fourth option, arguing that the witnesses should be understood "not in a strict judicial sense" but rather as "witnesses to a mode of existence lived out of love for the sake of others, in obedience to God" (*Character of Jesus*, 375). Removing any forensic sense in the pericope, Stegman emphasizes Paul's statement about speaking "in Christ" (13:3; cf. 2:17, 12:19); the testimony Paul is concerned with here is that which verifies "the life, sufferings, death, and resurrection of Jesus" (372). Because of this, Stegman interprets the first witness as Christ, the faithful μάρτυς par excellence, the second witness as Paul, the one who embodies Christ's ethos, and the third (potential) witness as the Corinthians themselves, who have the opportunity to follow Christ in the same way Paul does. While he is right to emphasize the importance of being "in Christ," this detail can be explained in other, simpler ways (e.g., Furnish, *II Corinthians*, 576). Stegman criticizes scholars for focusing too closely on the local context of 2 Cor 13:1 and ignoring the wider message of the letter as a whole (*Character of Jesus*, 375), but his exegesis seems to suffer from an overcorrection in the opposite direction as his explanation makes little sense in the flow of the passage. This suggestion does not fit with the threatening and aggressive character of the apostle's words, nor can it explain the emphasis Paul places on his visits.

[24] Cf. Harris, *Second Epistle*, 908.

[25] E.g., Welborn, "'By the Mouth,'" 208–10. Han claims that the correlation of visits with witnesses would entail Paul's "using the verse [Deut 19:15] in such a highly metaphorical and strange way that it is doubtful whether the Corinthians would have understood him" (*Swimming in the Sea*, 178).

II. Deuteronomy 19:15 and Its Use in Later Sources

To begin our exploration into the rule of witnesses in ancient Judaism, we should first look at Deut 19:15 in its biblical context. The verse states that "a single witness shall not suffice to convict a person of any crime or wrongdoing in connection with any offense that may be committed. Only on the evidence of two or three witnesses shall a charge be sustained" (NRSV).[26] Occurring in the midst of a list of Deuteronomic laws in chapters 19–22, Deut 19:15 begins a section detailing regulations concerning witnesses (19:15–21). The passage is concerned with the problem of false witnesses and what their penalty should be and concludes that they should receive whatever punishment would have been given to the one wrongly accused (19:19–21). The reason for insisting on multiple witnesses is straightforward: it prevents a single person from maliciously and falsely accusing someone of a crime.[27] This concern with false testimony is present elsewhere in the Pentateuch, as is the precautionary measure of having more than one witness, as in Deut 17:6 and Num 35:30.[28] These two instances, however, diverge from Deut 19:15 in that they apply only to situations where the false witness is being put to death. Deuteronomy 19:15, by contrast, broadens the concept to include "every charge."[29] What began as an additional legal prerequisite in cases of capital punishment has been extended to apply to all criminal disputes.[30] In Deut 19:15 itself, then, we already

---

[26] As with the Greek of Deut 19:15/2 Cor 13:1, several of the Hebrew terms are rendered in a legal fashion due to the context of the verse: "to convict a person" (lit., "to rise up against a man," יקום באיש), "crime" ("iniquity," עון), "wrongdoing" ("sin," חטאת), "offense" ("sin," חטא), "may commit" ("may sin," יחטא), "evidence" ("mouth," פי), and "be sustained" ("rise up" or "stand," יקום).

[27] See Richard D. Nelson, *Deuteronomy: A Commentary*, OTL (Louisville: Westminster John Knox, 2002), 242; Jeffrey H. Tigay, *Deuteronomy* דברים: *The Traditional Hebrew Text with the New JPS Translation*, JPSTC (Philadelphia: Jewish Publication Society, 1996), 183. Shlomo Naeh and Aharon Shemesh have suggested an alternative reading of Deut 19:16–19, arguing that these verses should be considered separately from Deut 19:15 and that they present a second kind of legal procedure ("Deuteronomy 19:15–19 in the Damascus Document and Early Midrash," *DSD* 20 [2013]: 179–99, here 180–83). In this second type, evidence from a single witness, along with rigorous inquiry by the judge to confirm the individual's testimony, can be sufficient to charge someone.

[28] Jack R. Lundbom, *Deuteronomy: A Commentary* (Grand Rapids: Eerdmans, 2013), 573; J. G. McConville, *Deuteronomy*, ApOTC 5 (Leicester: Apollos, 2002), 313; Calum M. Carmichael, *The Laws of Deuteronomy* (Ithaca, NY: Cornell University Press, 1974), 115. For more on the law of two or three witnesses in the Hebrew Bible and the ancient Near East, see Jackson, "Two or Three Witnesses," in *Essays in Jewish and Comparative Legal History*, 153–71.

[29] S. R. Driver, *A Critical and Exegetical Commentary on Deuteronomy*, 3rd ed., ICC (Edinburgh: T&T Clark, 1902), 235.

[30] A. D. H. Mayes, *Deuteronomy*, NCB (Grand Rapids: Eerdmans, 1979), 289.

see evidence of the rule being altered and expanded, a theme that will continue in later texts as well.

Rabbinic Literature

Although it appears elsewhere, the law of witnesses factors most prominently in two areas of Jewish literature.[31] First, it is often found in the writings of the rabbis, who cite Deut 19:15 quite regularly during their legal debates. In general, this verse acts as justification for forewarning someone suspected of wrongdoing about the possibility of being punished for the offense.[32] As a representative example, consider Mekilta de R. Ishmael on Exod 21:12:

> *Shall surely be put to death.* Provided there was a forewarning by the witnesses. You interpret it to mean: only if there was no forewarning. Perhaps this is not so, but it means: even if there was no forewarning by the witnesses? But Scripture says: "At the mouth of two witnesses" etc. Hence when saying here "Shall surely be put to death," Scripture must mean: only if there was a forewarning by the witnesses.[33]

Here the role of the witnesses' testimony has switched from a requirement to charge someone with a crime to a warning of an impending charge. Only if someone has been properly forewarned by multiple persons can that person later be punished for the misdeed. Similar references abound throughout rabbinic discussions (e.g., m. Sanh. 5:1; 8:4; 10:4; m. Mak. 1:8–9; m. Soṭah 1:1–2). In practice, Deut 19:15 appears to have served as a way of making it more difficult to prosecute someone for a crime, especially in cases that would be subject to capital punishment (e.g., t. Sanh. 8.3).[34]

In some sense, this rabbinic trend continues the Pentateuch's theme of protecting someone wrongly accused from being unjustly punished, but the application of the law has drastically changed. The role of the witnesses now involves forewarning the accused about the legal charges coming against them in the future. Some

---

[31] E.g., Susanna, passim; T. Ab. 13:8; Philo, *Spec.* 4.41–77; Josephus, *Life* 256–257. For more on the law of witnesses in these texts, see Han, *Swimming in the Sea*, 176–77.

[32] Van Vliet, *No Single Testimony*, 52–62; Ulrich Luz, *Matthew: A Commentary*, trans. James E. Crouch, 3 vols., Hermeneia (Minneapolis: Fortress, 2001), 2:452; Thrall, *Second Epistle*, 2:873; Furnish, *II Corinthians*, 575.

[33] Trans. van Vliet, *No Single Testimony*, 54.

[34] Not surprisingly, there are exceptions to this general rule, especially in circumstances such as that of a repeat offender. For more on this, see N. Rabinovitch, "Damascus Document IX, 17–22 and Rabbinic Parallels," *RevQ* 9 (1977): 113–16. Debates surrounding witnesses extend beyond the problem of forewarning as well; see Jacob Neusner, "'By the Testimony of Two Witnesses' in Damascus Document IX, 17–22 and in Pharisaic-Rabbinic Law," *RevQ* 8 (1973): 204–16; Bernard S. Jackson, "Damascus Document IX, 16–23 and Parallels," *RevQ* 9 (1978): 447–50; Lawrence H. Schiffman, "The Qumran Law of Testimony," *RevQ* 8 (1975): 603–12; Jackson, "*Testes Singulares*," 183–93.

scholars have argued that these rabbinic texts are too late or "recherché" to be of any relevance to 2 Corinthians, but this seems to be a rather hasty dismissal of noteworthy points of comparison with the Pauline material.[35] The problems surrounding the dating of rabbinic materials and their relation to the New Testament are undeniable, but ignoring them altogether seems imprudent, especially when we have such widespread evidence for the use of Deut 19:15 among the rabbis. Even if these rabbinic texts are later, their parallels with Paul are still worth considering. As we shall see, the rabbinic concept of forewarning generated from this regulation bears a striking resemblance to the situation in 2 Cor 13:1.

Qumran Rules

In addition to rabbinic sources, the law of witnesses forms a part of the communal rules recorded at Qumran. Undoubtedly impacted by Deut 19:15 as well as Lev 19:17; 1QS V, 25—VI, 1; CD IX, 2–8 and 16–22 all depict instructions for the reproof of members who have sinned.[36] There is much that could be discussed in these passages, but what matters most for our purposes is a repeated concern that reproof take place before multiple witnesses so as to be admissible in the judicial court of the community.[37] Once again, the function of the witnesses has shifted from what we observed in Deuteronomy, turning regulations for testimony about a crime into testimony about the reproof itself. In tandem with this is another notable alteration. Similar to Deut 19:15, CD IX, 16–22 says that two witnesses to an individual's sin are sufficient to prove his or her guilt, but now this is true even if they each saw separate instances of the person sinning at different times; it no longer has to be multiple witnesses to the same single act.[38] Both of these developments mark clear divergences from their original source for the law in Deut 19:15.

---

[35] Garland, *2 Corinthians*, 541; cf. Welborn, "'By the Mouth,'" 209–10.

[36] Timothy R. Carmody, "Matt 18:15–17 in Relation to Three Texts from Qumran Literature (CD 9:2–8, 16–22; 1QS 5:25–6:1)," in *To Touch the Text: Biblical and Related Studies in Honor of Joseph A. Fitzmyer, S.J*, ed. Maurya P. Horgan and Paul J. Kobelski (New York: Crossroad, 1989), 141–58; Furnish, *II Corinthians*, 569.

[37] Carmody, "Matt 18:15–17," 149–50. For more on this, see Charlotte Hempel, *The Laws of the Damascus Document: Sources, Tradition, and Redaction*, STDJ 29 (Leiden: Brill, 1998), 93–100; Schiffman, "Qumran Law of Testimony," 603–12; Neusner, "'By the Testimony of Two Witnesses,'" 199–204; Jackson, *"Testes Singulares,"* 172–83.

[38] David Lincicum, *Paul and the Early Jewish Encounter with Deuteronomy*, WUNT 2/284 (Tübingen: Mohr Siebeck, 2010), 76; Carmody, "Matt 18:15–17," 144–45. CD IX, 16–22 is a complicated text, and scholars have struggled to harmonize its details about the number and type of witnesses needed to mete out two different kinds of punishments (death/payment or removal from purity) in two different kinds of cases (capital or property). Naeh and Shemesh provide a helpful summary of this debate alongside their own interpretation based on a new reconstruction of the text ("Deuteronomy 19:15–19," 185–96). Solving these difficult problems is beyond our scope here, but as Naeh and Shemesh themselves reiterate, even their reconstruction does nothing to change the basic fact that "cumulative testimony is the essential innovation of the sectarian law

As scholars have routinely remarked, these community rules from Qumran are paralleled in Matt 18:15–17.[39] Here too we find guidelines for how to deal with the admonition of members of the congregation for their sins, and once again the principle of witnesses is invoked to ensure the validity of this process.[40] If someone confronts a sinner about his or her misbehavior one-on-one and is ignored, the next step is to try again but this time "take along with you one or two [others], so that every charge may be established by the testimony of two or three witnesses" (Matt 18:16). If this also fails, then the matter should be brought before the entire church, after which there are no more options. A recalcitrant sinner who resists all of these attempts to bring him or her back into line is to be considered like a "gentile or a tax collector" (Matt 18:17).[41] Of course, our interest lies in the second phase of this gradual process where Matthew quotes the Deuteronomic law almost verbatim. As it was in Qumran, the concern here is not witnessing the sin itself but rather the reproof of it.

While not identical, the regulations in the Damascus Document, the Community Rule, and Matthew all connect the law of two or three witnesses with the reproof of sinful members in the community.[42] In the rabbinic sources, the regulation serves as a form of protection for those who have been accused, but the three

---

of testimony" (ibid., 194; cf. 186–87). In their view, however, such cumulative testimony "is limited to capital cases only" (ibid., 194).

[39] See, e.g., John P. Meier, *Matthew*, NTM 3 (Wilmington, DE: Glazier, 1980), 205; Maarten J. J. Menken, "Deuteronomy in Matthew's Gospel," in *Deuteronomy in the New Testament: The New Testament and the Scriptures of Israel*, ed. Steve Moyise and Maarten J. J. Menken, LNTS 358 (London: T&T Clark, 2007), 42–62, here 54–55.

[40] A textual variant potentially alters the meaning of Matt 18:15 quite significantly. Several versions of Matt 18:15 lack εἰς σέ, a change that causes someone to reprove another community member not just for a sin specifically against that person but rather for any sin whatsoever. The impact of these regulations obviously increases dramatically in the latter scenario. Regardless, the main takeaway for our purposes is the utilization of the law of witnesses in a system meant for reproving sinners. For more on this textual issue in Matt 18:15, see Bruce M. Metzger, *A Textual Commentary on the Greek New Testament*, 2nd ed. (Stuttgart: Deutsche Bibelgesellschaft, 1994), 36; Davies and Allison, *Critical and Exegetical Commentary*, 2:782; France, *Gospel of Matthew*, 689 n. 3

[41] For more on this passage and its meaning in Matthew, see Davies and Allison, *Critical and Exegetical Commentary*, 2:781–87; France, *Gospel of Matthew*, 689–94; Luz, *Matthew*, 2:447–54; Daniel J. Harrington, *The Gospel of Matthew*, SP 1 (Collegeville, MN: Liturgical Press, 1991), 269–71.

[42] For a more detailed comparison between the regulations found at Qumran and those in Matthew, see Carmody, "Matt 18:15–17," 150–58; David Catchpole, "Reproof and Reconciliation in the Q Community: A Study of the Tradition-History of Mt 18,15–17.21–22/Lk 17,3–4," in *SNTSU* 8 (1983): 79–90. For more on the relationship between the structure of the Qumran community and the early church, see Joseph Schmitt, "L'organisation de l'Église primitive et Qumrân," in *Le Secte de Qumrân de les origines du Christianisme*, RechBib 4 (Brussels: Desclée de Brouwer, 1959), 217–31.

documents treated here utilize the law in a more hostile and aggressive sense. The witnesses provide verification in the midst of a process that assertively calls out immorality and, if necessary, brings those faults before the entire community for judgment. Even if the accused is being partially safeguarded by the requirement of multiple witnesses for legally sanctioned admonition, the law now carries the connotation of a threat. In this context, the rule of witnesses is closely connected with the consequences that can follow now that the offender has officially been warned.

New Testament

The law also makes several appearances in the New Testament outside of 2 Cor 13:1 and Matt 18:16. Scholars typically mention these other instances only in passing, if at all. Nevertheless, these passages provide further fruitful points of comparison with the Pauline citation. In John 8:17–18, Jesus argues with the Pharisees about the validity of his judgments, and he justifies his position by recourse to the Jewish law of two witnesses, saying that he and the Father fulfill this requirement.[43] First Timothy 5:19 reflects the protective aspect of Deut 19:15 by asserting that elders in the church can be accused only "on the evidence of two or three witnesses." The following verse then speaks about publicly rebuking elders who persist in their sins, an unsurprising move given what we have previously observed at Qumran and in Matthew.[44] Hebrews 10:28–29 brings up the law to emphasize the harsh eschatological punishment in store for believers who forsake their faith.[45] Lastly, 1 John 5:8 claims that the three entities of "the Spirit, the water, and the blood" all testify together to the truth of Jesus Christ. In the New Testament alone, this law has been utilized by an array of authors to serve a wide range of purposes.[46]

III. Interpreting 2 Corinthians 13:1

With this background in mind, we now return to 2 Cor 13:1. Starting at 2 Cor 12:19, Paul proclaims that he speaks not merely out of self-defense but in order to

---

[43] For more on the role of the Deuteronomic law in this pericope, see Michael Labahn, "Deuteronomy in John's Gospel," in Moyise and Menken, *Deuteronomy in the New Testament*, 82–98, here 84–86; Severino Pancaro, *The Law in the Fourth Gospel: The Torah and the Gospel, Moses and Jesus, Judaism and Christianity according to John*, NovTSup 42 (Leiden: Brill, 1975), 275–78.

[44] See Davies and Allison, *Critical and Exegetical Commentary*, 2:785. For more on Deut 19:15 in this passage, see Gerd Häfner, "Deuteronomy in the Pastoral Epistles," in Moyise and Menken, *Deuteronomy in the New Testament*, 136–51, here 144–47.

[45] For more on Deut 19:15 in these verses, see Gert J. Steyn, "Deuteronomy in Hebrews," in Moyise and Menken, *Deuteronomy in the New Testament*, 152–68, here 159–60.

[46] Other passages in the New Testament (e.g., Matt 26:59–61) and early Christianity (e.g., Tertullian, *Bapt.* 6.2) indicate the prominence of this principle in Christian society.

build the Corinthians up. He is greatly concerned about the state in which he might find the community when he arrives, saying that there could be a host of problems among them (12:20). He might have to mourn for "many of those who have sinned previously and did not repent of the impurity, sexual immorality, and sensuality that they have practiced" (12:21). It is immediately following this bemoaning of the Corinthians' sins that Paul reiterates that he is soon coming for his third visit to Corinth (13:1; cf. 12:14) and quotes the law from Deuteronomy. Driving the point home, Paul follows his citation by reminding the Corinthians of the previous warnings he gave them about their sins, including the occasion of his second visit to the city, and by issuing the same warning again: on his next visit, he "will not spare them" (13:2).[47] Paul goes on to tell the Corinthians how he hopes for their restoration and their place "in the faith" (13:5–9). According to Paul, this is his purpose writing to the Corinthians. He does not want to use the apostolic authority given to him by God to reprimand the Corinthians but instead desires to build up the church there (13:10; cf. 10:8).[48]

Paul is explicit about his main concerns in 2 Cor 12:19–13:10: the sinfulness of the Corinthians and the moral improvement he longs for them to make. Statements regarding their sins bracket 2 Cor 13:1 on both sides, and 13:5–10 is focused upon their behavior. Paul's final words in this pericope underline his desired outcome for the situation, simultaneously reminding the Corinthians of his ability to discipline them for their wrongdoing yet encouraging them with his ardent hope that such a thing will not be necessary (13:10). "Paul is coming to the Corinthians in any case," but "*how* he comes depends on them" (12:4, 20; 13:1; cf. 1 Cor 4:19–21).[49] Although he does not wish to, he is "ready to punish every disobedience" (10:6) if he must do so.[50] It is in the midst of this discussion that he chooses to bring up Deut 19:15. Previously, we settled on the idea that this law should be understood metaphorically, with Paul's three visits (two past, one future) acting as the analogue for the three witnesses. Despite claims of some scholars to the contrary, the close proximity in which Paul mentions his second and third visits and the two or three witnesses cannot be coincidental; there must be a connection between the two.

To understand Paul's message in this metaphor, our first interpretive key is the main issue at hand: the sins of the Corinthians and Paul's attempts at correcting

---

[47] As Welborn notes, Paul's warning that he will not "spare" the Corinthians could be another allusion to Deut 19, which uses the same Greek word in the LXX (φείδομαι, 19:21) to describe the punishment of false witnesses ("'By the Mouth,'" 216).

[48] See Scott Hafemann, "Paul's Use of the Old Testament in 2 Corinthians," *Int* 52 (1998): 246–57, here 254. This reluctance by Paul to punish the Corinthians exemplifies his leniency throughout chapters 10–13 (cf. 10:1). For more on this topic, see Donald Dale Walker, *Paul's Offer of Leniency (2 Cor 10:1): Populist Ideology and Rhetoric in a Pauline Letter Fragment*, WUNT 2/152 (Tübingen: Mohr Siebeck, 2002).

[49] Fitzgerald, "Paul, the Ancient Epistolary Theorists," 194.

[50] Ibid.

them. As we have already seen, Jewish and Christian writers roughly contemporaneous with Paul are doing remarkably similar things with this Deuteronomic law, and these other examples are extraordinarily helpful in illuminating Paul's own purposes in 2 Cor 13:1.[51] For instance, the rabbis utilized the law as a way of forewarning those guilty of misbehavior that they would be prosecuted for their crimes. Once the requisite two or three witnesses have completed this process, the accused can legally be punished. This rabbinic principle fits the situation in 2 Cor 13:1.[52] Paul not only emphasizes the sins of the Corinthians but also reminds them that he has previously warned them about the repercussions of their actions (13:2). As the third witness, Paul's upcoming third visit will fulfill the requirement needed to discipline the Corinthians for their sins to the fullest extent possible. By citing Deut 19:15, Paul is serving notice that, upon his arrival, he can and, if necessary, will penalize those in the community who continue to practice immorality despite the two warnings given to them previously.

Paul's forewarning is thus reminiscent of the rabbinic discussions, but his words carry a far more threatening and ominous tone in 2 Corinthians than those of later rabbinic authorities. This difficulty is overlooked by commentators who favor the metaphorical reading but do so with recourse to the rabbinic sources alone. Whereas the rabbis' invocation of this principle prolongs the process of prosecution, Paul wants the Corinthian community to know that consequences for their sins are imminent. To find a suitable comparison for this aspect of 2 Cor 13:1, we can look to the techniques of reproof reported at Qumran and in Matthew. Although these texts address the people at large rather than the sinners themselves, their regulations call for offenders to be repeatedly admonished for their sins. A continued refusal to take these reproofs to heart results in negative consequences, often in the form of ostracism from the community. Elsewhere in the Corinthian correspondence (1 Cor 5:1–13), Paul speaks of dissociation from community members on the basis of sins, but it is probably going too far to see that idea in play here as well. Instead, the point is simply that Paul's first two visits served as a means of a reproof for sinful Corinthians, and with the third and final reproof will come the deserved punishment. In contrast to the protective impetus of the rabbinic regulations, the rules of reproof warn the offenders about what will happen to them if they do not stop their sinful behavior, and Paul's visits do precisely the same. The procedures in the Damascus Document, the Community Rule, and Matthew give

---

[51] This is not to say that Paul was directly drawing on or even familiar with these other texts. The point is the evident use of Deut 19:15 in ways reminiscent of Paul in literature from before and after his own time. The prevalence of similar traditions involving the law of two or three witnesses shows the cultural currency of these ideas in ancient Judaism and Christianity more broadly. The fact that Paul is sometimes the first to exhibit a specific tendency is not grounds to dismiss a reading as impossible a priori (*pace* Welborn, "'By the Mouth,'" 209–10).

[52] See, e.g., Furnish, *II Corinthians*, 575; van Vliet, *No Single Testimony*, 96 n. 8; Harris, *Second Epistle*, 908.

us a way to understand the threatening edge so evident in Paul's words in 2 Cor 13:1.

These instances of forewarning and reproof are helpful in interpreting Paul's citation of the Deuteronomic law, but not everything he does is paralleled directly by the rabbinic and Qumranic texts. Most obvious in this regard is Paul's use of metaphor. Whereas the rabbinic and Qumran texts both involve human witnesses providing testimony, Paul turns this human element into visits to a city. One can minimize this difference by noting that Paul would actually have witnessed the sins during his visits, but the statement remains striking. Even more, this explanation still leaves Paul making the rather bold claim that his own testimony can meet the demands of this law by itself. Every other instance of this principle in action involves the participation of multiple witnesses, but Paul thinks that he alone is sufficient to accomplish this.[53]

Proponents of the metaphorical interpretation have willingly conceded these points. Even those who acknowledge that "Paul is still operating within a tradition of interpretation concerning the law of witnesses" in 2 Cor 13:1 nevertheless accept that there is "some innovative apostolic halakhah behind his warning here."[54] In their view, the logical sense provided by understanding the three trips as witnesses outweighs the problem of Paul's novelty. The fact that no one before Paul has utilized the Deuteronomic law in such an abstract fashion should not deter us from accepting that he did so. After all, we see him taking similar liberties elsewhere in his writings. He is often imaginative in his reading of the Scriptures (e.g., Gal 3:5–9, 13–14, 16–18), nor does he shy away from nonliteral interpretations that make the text relevant for Christ-confessors (e.g., Gal 4:21–31). This willingness to interpret creatively extends even to the laws of the Torah, as evidenced earlier in his correspondence with the Corinthians (1 Cor 9:8–12).[55] If Paul can adapt a statute concerning muzzling oxen into a lesson about the material support of an apostle, surely it would be little problem for him to turn human witnesses into his own visits.

I find these arguments compelling, but there is more that can be offered in defense of the metaphorical interpretation. Even if I would concur with their ultimate conclusions, I do not agree with supporters of the metaphorical view (as well as its detractors) who portray Paul's words as exceedingly eccentric. It is incorrect to characterize 2 Cor 13:1 as an unparalleled application of the law of witnesses. We have seen that Jewish and Christian authors alike showed little hesitation in creatively modifying the original Deuteronomic law. By putting his own personal touches on his citation of Deut 19:15 and fitting it to the specifics of his relationship with the Corinthians, Paul joins a long line of writers who did the same as a means

---

[53] Cf. Welborn, "'By the Mouth,'" 208.
[54] Lincicum, *Paul and the Early Jewish Encounter*, 135.
[55] Thrall, *Second Epistle*, 2:875.

of responding to their respective situations. In short, Paul's willingness to adapt Deut 19:15 is not exceptional.

But we can say more than this. Upon further inspection, the "unique" aspects of 2 Cor 13:1 are not as unprecedented as they have been portrayed. Many of the initially surprising elements of Paul's statement have counterparts in other texts that correspond to the details of 2 Cor 13:1 quite closely. As mentioned previously, David Lincicum has correctly pointed out that the verse shares a modification of Deut 19:15 with CD IX, 16–22.[56] While still involving the presence of multiple witnesses, the regulations from Qumran allow them to observe separate occurrences of a person sinning at different times. This is exactly what Paul does with his visits to Corinth. Just as the protocols of the Damascus Document enable a single individual to fulfill the law's requirement by catching the guilty party in the act three separate times, Paul maintains that he can punish the Corinthians if he personally witnesses their sinfulness for a third time.

Similarly noteworthy are some correspondences between 2 Cor 13:1 and other New Testament texts. We have already mentioned Matt 18:15–17 in conjunction with the regulations from Qumran, but two significant parallels exist between 2 Cor 13:1 and other passages as well. First, when Jesus provides two witnesses to verify the validity of his judgment in John 8:17–18, he names (in addition to the Father) *himself* as his own witness. Paul does much the same when he declares that he serves as a witness on his own behalf against the sins of the Corinthians. Combining (a) the applicability of a single witness's testimony on three separate occasions from CD IX, 16–22 with (b) the possibility of calling oneself as a witness from John 8:17–18 yields the exact situation described in 2 Cor 13:1. The individuality of Paul's application of the law is therefore not without precedent. Second, 1 John 5:7–8 claims that the three witnesses that testify to the truth of Jesus Christ are the Spirit, the water, and the blood. While the inclusion of the Spirit is less surprising, the citation of water and blood as witnesses is striking and, most pertinently for our purposes, obviously metaphorical. The notion that blood and water can serve as witnesses is far more abstract than Paul's contention that the same could apply to his visits, during which he would actually have seen the actions of the Corinthians.

These similarities remove any last vestiges of the supposed novelty of 2 Cor 13:1. No other text has a person invoke himself as his own witness in three separate instances, but the constituent elements of this stance are reflected in the Damascus Document and the Gospel of John. Additionally, 1 John shows that Paul was not the only epistolary author to adopt an abstract approach to the nature of the law's witnesses. Indeed, his liberties with the Deuteronomic law pale in comparison to those taken in 1 John. In light of the evidence provided by these parallels, there is

---

[56] Lincicum, *Paul and the Early Jewish Encounter*, 134–35.

no compelling reason to reject the metaphorical identification of Paul's three visits to Corinth with the three witnesses of 2 Cor 13:1.

IV. Conclusion

Despite the proliferation of scholarly views on how to interpret 2 Cor 13:1, the option that fits the surrounding context best remains the metaphorical equation of Paul's three visits with the three witnesses of the law from Deut 19:15. Other Jewish and Christian texts that cite this Deuteronomic principle provide a fruitful point of comparison to 2 Cor 13:1 and can illuminate Paul's meaning. Paul warns the Corinthians to correct their sinful behaviors before his arrival, lest he be forced to discipline them. Having pointed out their sins and forewarned them of their consequences twice before, his subsequent visit will act as the third and final witness against their wrongdoing and grant him the authority to administer punishment against them. Technically speaking, Paul employs the well-known principle of Deut 19:15 in a new way, but no aspect of his application of the law of witnesses is without precedent. Texts outside of the writings of Paul can be found validating the testimony of a single witness on three occasions, calling oneself as a witness, and taking a metaphorical approach to the identity of the witnesses. What at first glance appears to be an entirely novel interpretation of Deut 19:15 turns out to be only one of many comparable examples of this law being adapted by later authors.

Is It Valid? A Case for the Repunctuation of Hebrews 9:17

DANIEL STEVENS
djs233@cam.ac.uk
University of Cambridge, Cambridge CB2 1TN, United Kingdom

Traditionally in translation and edited Greek texts, Heb 9:17 has been punctuated and understood as a declarative statement. I argue, however, that 9:17, particularly 9:17b, should be understood as a rhetorical question, not as a declaration. One possible translation would be "For a testament is made sure upon death. After all, is a testament ever valid while the one who made it lives?"

In nearly all editions and translations of Heb 9:17b, the passage is presented as a declarative statement.[1] This manner of translation has been common since the sixteenth century and has remained the default reading. I argue, however, that 9:17b is best understood as a question, not a statement.

The Greek text of 9:17, διαθήκη[2] γὰρ ἐπὶ νεκροῖς βεβαία, ἐπεὶ μήποτε ἰσχύει ὅτε ζῇ ὁ διαθέμενος, is usually translated along the lines of, "For a testament is made sure upon death, since it is never in force while the one who made it lives." In this

---

I would like to thank the Gates Cambridge Trust, which funded the research behind this article.

[1] For example, in Greek editions: UBS[5], NA[28], SBL; in English editions: Geneva, Bishop's, Douay, KJV, NRSV, NASB, ESV, NIV, NET; in German: Schlachter, Luther 1984; in French: Genève 1979, Segonde; in Spanish: NRV. Although some translators have suggested an interrogative reading, they tend not to state why, and their suggestions have not generally been heeded. See, e.g., a marginal note in WH; Jean Héring, *The Epistle to the Hebrews*, trans. A. W. Heathcote and P. J. Allcock (London: Epworth, 1970), 80; and F. F. Bruce, *The Epistle to the Hebrews*, rev. ed., NICNT (Grand Rapids: Eerdmans, 1990), 219. Most current scholars and commentators do not mention the possibility at all.

[2] It is not within the scope of this note to contribute to the ongoing debate as to whether διαθήκη in this passage is best understood in the sense of "will" or "covenant." I will use the term *testament* to translate διαθήκη, not because it falls on the side of "will" but because (1) by itself it is hardly used in modern English and therefore has fewer connotations ascribed to it by the reader, (2) modern interpretations of the Old Testament and New Testament import a religious ambiguity that mitigates the legal sense of *testament*, and (3) in a sense *testament* is a nonchoice, in that it simply carries over the Latin translation of διαθήκη, *testamentum*.

1019

context, μήποτε followed by an indicative verb (ἰσχύει) is claimed to be an inconsistent application of negation rules that were normative in the Koine period.[3] On the contrary, taking 9:17b as a declarative statement is neither the natural way of interpreting μήποτε (or any negation with μή) followed by an indicative in Koine (at least that of the first century CE), nor is it the best explanation of the data provided by Hebrews or the New Testament as a whole. On the contrary, I propose that Heb 9:17b is completely understandable as a question within the general negation practices of Koine.

I. Positive Evidence

While it is generally agreed that Koine Greek, particularly in the varieties that appear in the New Testament, does not follow the complex Attic rules governing the usage of οὐ and μή, that is not the same as saying that there is no internal consistency whatsoever, or that the authors of the texts in question used the various negatives in a haphazard manner. Friedrich Blass's canon, "In the κοινή of the N.T. all instances may practically be brought under the single rule, that οὐ negatives [sic] the *indicative*, μή the *other moods*, including the *infinitive* and *participle*,"[4] still generally holds within the confines of the New Testament. The exception to this, as in Classical Greek, that either οὐ or μή can be used with questions in the indicative is readily acknowledged by all grammars (e.g., BDF §§426–27; Smyth §§2651, 2676, 2688, 2703). These general rules apply to both οὐ and μή simplex and to their various derivatives.

---

[3] In referring to the rules of grammar of the Koine period, and of the New Testament in particular, I do not mean to suggest that there were iron-clad rules by which speakers and writers of ancient Greek felt that they had to abide. At best, grammatical rules are descriptions of the most common ways of making meaning with language at a given point of time. Any author, no matter how learned, is free to be "ungrammatical," but the more one does so, the more one risks either being misunderstood or judged for having poor style. In referring to the rules of grammar or the natural reading, I simply mean that a given passage can be understood within the normal ways of making meaning within the cross-sections of the Greek of the Koine period that we see in the New Testament. Although this note focuses on a relatively minor issue of punctuation, it is also in part a push-back against tendencies to dismiss Koine Greek as inconsistent to the point that meaningful variation is dismissed.

[4] Friedrich Blass, *Grammar of New Testament Greek*, trans. Henry St. John Thackeray (London: Macmillan, 1898), 253 (emphasis original). Later editions kept the rule with slight modifications of phrasing, such that the most recent edition says, "Essentially everything can be subsumed under one rule for the Koine of the NT: οὐ negates the indicative, μή the remaining moods including the infinitive and participle" (BDF §426). I refer to the older form of his grammar in this note because the majority of the extant scholarly discussion of whether to punctuate this passage as a statement occurred about a century ago and made reference to the early editions of Blass's grammar.

In the New Testament, it is very hard to find μή negating an indicative in a normal, declarative, speech.⁵ The natural rendering of μή followed by a present indicative is a question along the lines of, "Is it really the case that …?"⁶ While contextual factors can shift the interpretation of the formula, there would need to be some clue in the context that the author did not intend the usual interrogative meaning of the phrase.

Two lines of external evidence testify to the interrogative nature of 9:17b. First is the reading of several patristic sources. Ps.-Oecumenius is clear on the passage, instructing his readers, κατ' ἐρώτησιν ἀνάγνωθι, that is, "Read this as a question" (*Comm. in Epist. ad Heb.* ch. IB [12] on Heb 9:11–10:4 [PG 119:380a]). Similarly, Theophylact also comments, Ἐρωτηματικῶς τοῦτο καὶ ἀνάγνωθι καὶ νόησον, "Both read and think of this as a question" (*Expos. in Epist. ad Heb.* on Heb 9:17 [PG 125:309b]). Both of these witnesses show an awareness that by their period, when the growth of μή had spread even further, there was a potential ambiguity in reading the passage. Yet, without argument, both asserted that the right way to read 9:17b was as a question. Isidore of Pelusium's witness is less explicit but does further indicate that 9:17b is best received as a question. While he prefers a variant reading of μὴ τότε, he seems to assume that the passage is best taken as a question.⁷

Second, a textual variant and its interpretation lead toward reading 9:17b as a question. In ℵ* and D*, the text reads μὴ τότε. While this is commonly taken as a corruption of μήποτε, it is significant that this variant is universally interpreted as a question.⁸ Yet, unless one assumes a stereotyped μήποτε, there is no reason why μὴ τότε should be any more interrogative, since it is not the τότε but the μή that

---

⁵ Instances where μή with an indicative is expected/allowed are (1) questions, (2) negation of contrafactuals in conditional clauses, (3) negation of future indicative as imperative, (4) emphatic negation of future using the formula οὐ μή + indicative, and (5) introduction of a fear/lest clause.

⁶ So with 64 (65 if Heb 9:17b is counted) of 104 instances of μή-derivatives negating indicative verbs in the New Testament. For most of the other instances, see n. 15 below.

⁷ Isidore of Pelusium, *Ep.* 4.113 (PG 78:1184c–1185a). «ἐπεὶ μή ποτε ἰσχύει ὅτε ζῇ ὁ διαθέμενος;» ἀντεπιστέλλω, ὅτι τὸ μή ποτε, τότε ἐστί, [sic] μιᾶς κεραίας ἑνὶ στοιχείῳ, ὑπό τινων ἴσως ἀμαθῶς προστεθείσης· οὕτω γὰρ εὗρον καὶ ἐν παλαιοῖς ἀντιγράφοις, "'After all, is it ever in force while the one who made it still lives?' I write instead that 'μή ποτε' is 'τότε' where one stroke has been added, perhaps ignorantly by someone, to one letter. For I find the text like this (with τότε) in the old copies." While not directly commenting on the interrogative or declarative nature of the sentence, this—along with all readings with τότε—is generally read as on the side of an interrogative interpretation since μὴ τότε never became a stereotyped conjunction or adverb, unlike μήποτε. Thus, the only possible readings of it are an awkward use of μή with the indicative, which is unaccounted for, or an interrogative.

⁸ The NASB's translation footnote on the passage reads this variant as a question. Further, Isidore of Pelusium's preference for this reading is viewed as an argument for taking the statement as an interrogative in James Moffatt, *A Critical and Exegetical Commentary on the Epistle to the Hebrews*, ICC (Edinburgh: T&T Clark, 1924), 128, though Moffatt refers to the interrogative interpretation as a "needless [difficulty]," and in Franz Delitzsch, *Commentary on the Epistle to the Hebrews*, trans. Thomas L. Kingsbury, 2 vols. (Edinburgh: T&T Clark, 1887), 2:108.

lends the clause its nature as a question.⁹ That is, if μὴ τότε is interrogative in this context, which none dispute, μήποτε should be interrogative as well, unless some clear contextual factor argues against it.

While it is not clear how Heb 9:17b was received by the earliest church, the weight of the internal evidence and of the patristic authors who do comment on how to read the verse falls on the side of interpreting it as a question. There is no significant reason, beyond interpretive momentum, for overruling the lines of evidence mentioned above and reading Heb 9:17b as a declarative statement.

II. Opposed Claims

Those who comment on this passage offer two main arguments for why 9:17b should be taken as a declarative statement. The first is that, in the Koine period, οὐ and μή became generally confused as the usage of μή broadened, leading to general inconsistency.¹⁰ Along these lines, some seem to suggest that it is unnecessary to find a consistent distinction between μή and οὐ.¹¹ The second argument is that, as a careful and literary author, the author of Hebrews sought to avoid hiatus as much as he could, which led him to look for an alternative to the phrase ἐπεὶ οὔποτε. Support for this is often adduced from Lucian and the Pseudo-Clementine Homilies, in which ἐπεὶ μήποτε does occur.¹²

---

⁹Without explanation, Harold Attridge, in connection with this reading, describes taking the clause as a question as "the awkward patristic construal of the clause as interrogative" (*The Epistle to the Hebrews: A Commentary on the Epistle to the Hebrews*, Hermeneia [Philadelphia: Fortress, 1989], 253). I hope to demonstrate that such a reading is in fact not awkward but natural and sensible.

¹⁰For example, Ceslas Spicq rejected the interrogative reading, saying, "Avec le verbe à l'indicatif dans une phrase temporelle on attendrait la particule οὐ, mais la *Koiné* tend à substituer μή à οὐ après ὅτι" (*L'Épître aux Hébreux*, 2 vols., EBib [Paris: Gabalda, 1953], 2:262). However, the text is not "after ὅτι" in this clause. Similarly, William Lane, *Hebrews 9–13*, WBC 47b (Dallas: Word, 1991), 232: "But in later Gk. μή is found in causal clauses where οὐ would be expected; μήποτε with the indicative is simply a strong negative particle meaning 'never.'" Although these linguistic elements became more and more prevalent as Greek developed, they do not reflect the actual data of the New Testament.

¹¹Commenting on the tendency of some patristic authors, as well as Delitzsch and Héring, to read this passage as an interrogative, Erich Gräßer responds, "Aber das ist weder grammatisch zwingend … noch dem Duktus der Aussage angemessen" (*An die Hebräer*, 3 vols., EKKNT [Zurich: Benziger, 1993], 2:174 n. 80). On the contrary, the interrogative reading is both most in line with the grammar and does not disrupt the flow of the passage at all.

¹²Even then, however, a *TLG* search yields only fifteen instances in the Lucianic corpus (eleven of which do seem to be negating indicatives, though usually in conjunction with an infinitive of a verb alleging that this is what another character in a dialogue would say) in which a derivative of μή occurs immediately after a derivative of ἐπεί. A similar search produces twenty-two instances in which a derivative of οὐ follows one of ἐπεί. This is out of the total 2,963 usages

As far as the charge of inconsistency goes, while it is true that Koine Greek did not exhibit the same nuances in its usage of the various negations as Attic, there is little evidence at this period for the claim that there was no, or even low, consistency in the usage of negations. In fact, the weight of the evidence, while supporting a gradual broadening of μή, does testify to the general validity of Blass's canon mentioned above.[13] Further, within the text of Hebrews itself, there are no other disputed cases of negation, and it seems that the author used the various negative adverbs consistently. In addition to this, the older commentaries and grammatical works usually cited by modern proponents of reading 9:17b as a statement do not support the claims they make.[14] As a general rule, most modern studies do not interact with the possible interrogative in 9:17. At most they refer to earlier conclusions in favor of a declarative sentence, with varying degrees of accuracy in reflecting what the earlier studies in fact say.

Regarding hiatus, the author of Hebrews is more careful than other New Testament authors in avoiding hiatus, but he is by no means fastidious in this regard.[15]

---

of forms of μή in Lucian. While this does show that an author who wrote seventy or more years after the composition of Hebrews could use μή in this way, it hardly speaks for the existence of a set form involving ἐπεί μή.

[13] Of the 103 instances in the New Testament of μή negating an indicative apart from Heb 9:17, 95 of them appear according to expected patterns (64 are in questions, 12 are in emphatic negation with οὐ, 9 negate contrafactuals/hypothetical conditions, 8 introduce fear clauses, and 2 negate the future indicative used as an imperative). Only the remaining eight (John 3:18; 1 Cor 4:6; 1 Tim 6:3; Titus 1:11; 2 Pet 1:9; 1 John 4:3; Rev 9:4, 20) are not easily categorized. Many of these, however, have contextual factors that could have led to the shift, such as a correct μή within the same sentence (John 3:18), or a negated purpose clause with an ungrammatical indicative verb (1 Cor 4:6; Rev 9:4, 20). These last three verses could be an example of the classical pattern of retaining an indicative verb in purpose clauses of frustrated result, but that does seem unlikely, especially in the case of Revelation.

[14] For example, Moffatt (*Critical and Exegetical Commentary*, 128) cites J. H. Moulton (*Prolegomena*, vol. 1 of *A Grammar of New Testament Greek* [Edinburgh: T&T Clark, 1908], 239–40, note to p. 171), himself citing a papyrus (*BGU* 530), to demonstrate the broadening of μή in the relevant period. That instance, however, is μή followed by a participle, an example of the general rule given above for Koine Greek, and is irrelevant for the usage of μή with the indicative.

[15] No comprehensive studies on hiatus in the New Testament have been done, but there are some smaller-scale comparisons of literary style including hiatus. Recently, Dan Nässelqvist analyzed the beginning of Hebrews in light of ancient conceptions of literary style, finding only one instance of hiatus ("Stylistic Levels in Hebrews 1.1–4 and John 1.1–18," *JSNT* 35 [2012]: 31–35). Daniel A. Penick undertook an analysis of hiatus throughout the whole of Hebrews but only after μή, διό, and forms of the article ("Paul's Epistles Compared with One Another and with the Epistle to the Hebrews," *AJP* 42 [1921] 58–72, esp. 69–71). His conclusion (though with what seems to be a flawed statistical methodology for the Pauline letters) reads, "I cannot contend that either the author of Hebrews or Paul studiously avoided hiatus, tho [sic] one gets that feeling for both at times when looking for examples of its occurrence" (71). Blass, to whom Penick was somewhat responding, comments, "The Epistle to the Hebrews is the only piece of writing in the N.T., which in structure of sentences and style shows the care and dexterity of an artistic writer, and so it

While it would be tedious to rehearse every instance of hiatus in Hebrews, it is valuable to compare the context in which hiatus is allegedly avoided by resorting to μήποτε in 9:17b.[16] Of the nine instances of ἐπεί in Hebrews (2:14; 4:6; 5:2, 11; 6:13; 9:17, 26; 10:2; 11:11), five are without hiatus (5:2, 11; 6:13; 9:17; 11:11). This suggests that the author was not overly concerned with hiatus after ἐπεί and therefore would not need to adjust his grammar to avoid it.[17] This is made especially clear by the fact that three of the instances of hiatus after ἐπεί in Hebrews occur in the sound cluster that it is suggested the author attempted to avoid in 9:17b, with ἐπεὶ οὖν (2:14, 4:6) and, most significantly, ἐπεὶ οὐκ (10:2).[18] Because of this ready willingness to bear hiatus involving this exact sound cluster, it is unnecessary to look for stereotyped phrases from writers who wrote at a later point in the gradual broadening of μή within Greek.

III. Conclusion

While there is scholarly momentum behind understanding Heb 9:17b as a declarative statement, this reading simply does not fit the data of Hebrews itself. Further, since the sources often cited as support for taking Heb 9:17b as a declaration do not all actually support that claim, the consensus, inasmuch as it is thought about at all, rests on shaky foundations. There are no evident reasons within Hebrews itself to view 9:17b as anything other than a question, and it makes fine sense to view it as such.

Hebrews 9:17 should be punctuated as follows: διαθήκη γὰρ ἐπὶ νεκροῖς βεβαία. ἐπεὶ μήποτε ἰσχύει ὅτε ζῇ ὁ διαθέμενος; A possible translation would then be, "For a testament is made sure upon death. After all, is a testament ever valid while the one who made it lives?" While this change does not greatly alter the meaning of the passage, it does affect the flow and argumentation of chapter 9. First, by phrasing this as a rhetorical question, the author casts aspersions on the thought that such

---

cannot be wondered at, if it is in this work alone that the principle of avoiding **hiatus** is, to some extent, taken into account.... On the other hand, instances of the harsher hiatus mentioned above, while certainly rarer than elsewhere, are not absolute rarities and cannot be set aside; it appears, then, that the author had not, as others had, been taught to regard the rule as a categorical one" (§82.2; emphasis original).

[16] That is, hiatus after ἐπεί at the beginning of a clause.

[17] Potentially this minor hiatus was less than troubling to the author because of the possibility of supplying a y-glide semivowel between the words, making [εpeju] or [εpiju] depending on the progress of itacism. Thanks to Simon Gathercole at Cambridge for suggesting this to me.

[18] Here, if anywhere in Hebrews, had the author wanted to avoid hiatus by substituting a derivative of μή for one of οὐ, he could easily have done so. In this passage, the author is negating a contrafactual indicative with ἄν, which is one of the main circumstances in which μή encroached on οὐ in the Koine period. If anything, this shows evidence that the author of Hebrews somewhat resisted the broadening usage of μή.

a testament could be executed while the testator lived, thus further strengthening the sense of necessity of the death of Jesus for its enactment.

Second, this change may have implications for how we read διαθήκη in Heb 9. A rhetorical question, by nature, draws upon shared knowledge or assumptions between the author and the audience. Even with μή suggesting that the author expects an answer of no, if he were not appealing to something that seemed commonsense to the audience, the rhetorical question would not work. If the audience was predominantly ethnically Jewish, they would have had a developed concept of covenant, but the intervening centuries make it highly unlikely that they would have had a familiarity with the covenantal procedures of ancient Israel and the various other ancient Near Eastern civilizations that influenced the texts of the Jewish Scriptures. Rather, they would have had intuitive or commonsense knowledge of contemporary testamentary procedures. Thus, even if the author draws also from the biblical concept of covenant, he draws as well from his contemporary understanding of a will.

Wabash Center
for Teaching and Learning in Theology and Religion

Fully funded by Lilly Endowment Inc.
Located at Wabash College

2018-19
Workshops & Colloquies
- Early Career Theological School Faculty
- Early Career Faculty Teaching Undergraduates
- Colloquy on Writing the Scholarship of Teaching
- Teaching with Digital Media

Application Deadline:
January 15, 2019

Grants up to $30,000
Application Deadline:
February 15, 2019

Resources
- *Journal on Teaching*
- Teaching Resources
- Book Reviews
- Syllabi
- Blogs

wabash.center

The Prayer of Elijah in James 5: An Example of Intertextuality

MARIAM KAMELL KOVALISHYN
mkovalishyn@regent-college.edu
Regent College, Vancouver, BC V6T 2E4, Canada

The structure of James, particularly the conclusion, remains contested. In this article, I contend that the example of Elijah in Jas 5:17–18 ties the conclusion to the single-minded worship of God in faithfulness (cf. 1:27) as the central theme of the epistle. To support this claim, I will examine the way in which the author uses 1 Kgs 17–18, encapsulated in the succinct phrases "he prayed fervently that it might not rain.… Then he prayed again, and the heaven gave rain" (Jas 5:17– 18). When read intertextually with the narrative of 1 Kgs 17–18, the confusion surrounding the use of Elijah in its Jas 5 location disappears. This example concludes the epistle, highlighting the main theme of faithfulness, as well as the supporting topics of prayer, community worship, and accountability.

Commentators have long noted that the flow of logic in the conclusion of the Epistle of James is well-nigh impossible to discern.[1] Indeed, establishing how the final verses function as a conclusion remains elusive.[2] Among its perplexing

---

[1] Martin Dibelius most famously argued for a lack of structure, positing instead that the instructions were placed together without a coherent logical argument (*James: A Commentary on the Epistle of James*, trans. Michael A. Williams, Hermeneia [Philadelphia: Fortress, 1975], 1–7). This article continues the push-back against such a minimalist reading. The question of authorship is not pertinent to this article, and I use "James" simply to refer to the text's presented author.

[2] Also questioned is where one would begin a conclusion, with suggestions from 5:7 (Fred O. Francis, "The Form and Function of the Opening and Closing Paragraphs of James and 1 John," *ZNW* 61 [1970]: 110–26, esp. 124–26; Christoph Burchard, *Der Jakobusbrief*, HNT 15/1 [Tübingen: Mohr Siebeck, 2000], 197); 5:12 (e.g., Luke Timothy Johnson, *The Letter of James: A New Translation with Introduction and Commentary*, AB 37A [New York: Doubleday, 1995], 326; Sophie Laws, *A Commentary on the Epistle of James*, BNTC [London: Black, 1980], 218; Dale C. Allison, "A Liturgical Tradition behind the Ending of James," *JSNT* 34 [2011]: 3–18); 5:13 (P. B. R. Forbes, "Structure of the Epistle of James," *EvQ* 44 [1972]: 147–53; Robert W. Wall, *Community of the Wise: The Letter of James*, New Testament in Context [Valley Forge, PA: Trinity Press International, 1997], 248); or 5:19 (e.g., R. B. Crotty, "The Literary Structure of the Letter of James," *ABR* 40 [1992]: 45–57).

1027

features is the example of Elijah in 5:17. In Jas 5:12–16, the author begins his concluding guidelines for life in the community: oath taking, responses to joy and sadness, prayer for the sick, the role of confession and the elders, and the power of prayer by a righteous person. To illustrate this last point, James highlights Elijah and his prayers to bring drought and then rain to Israel. Yet this example sits oddly. From the context, one might perhaps expect that the letter would end with a healing prayer; instead the author claims that the prophet Elijah was "like us" and cites a prophetic miracle that does not seem to involve healing. The epistle then ends abruptly with an elusive saying about calling sinners back from the error of their ways. Surely no one would dispute that the drought of Elijah is a profound example of the power of prayer, but Elijah does not seem ὁμοιοπαθής (of the same nature), and the incident does not illustrate prayer for healing. Likewise, the example of Elijah appears disconnected from the final summons of the epistle to "bring back a sinner from wandering."

I contend that the example of Elijah works as a summative illustration to highlight a key theme of the letter and to draw together the conclusion. An intertextual examination of the context of 1 Kgs 17–18 illuminates this concluding passage. First, reading the narrative of 1 Kgs 17–18 will establish a basis for comparison. Second, I will examine Jewish interpreters on the example of Elijah. Third, I will briefly survey several common interpretations of Jas 5:17–18 before suggesting a comprehensive way to understand why James inserts this example into this location. Finally, I seek to show how intertextual awareness unites several themes of the epistle and provides a fitting conclusion to its argument.

I. Elijah in 1 Kings 17–18

First Kings 17–18 recounts the story of Elijah and the famine. The narrative begins with Elijah's bold pronouncement to Ahab: "As the LORD the God of Israel lives, before whom I stand, there shall be neither dew nor rain these years, except by my word" (17:1).[3] This declaration initiates a two-chapter cycle dealing with Israel's famine and Elijah's confrontation with the prophets of Baal.[4] After his declaration, the reader eavesdrops on God telling Elijah to flee from Ahab and hide

---

[3] Quotations from the Hebrew Bible, the Apocrypha, and the New Testament are from the NRSV throughout.

[4] Marsha White defends the drought legend ("I Kgs 17:1, 17:7, 18:1, and 18:41–46"), which she argues was "originally independent of the inserted material" (*The Elijah Legends and Jehu's Coup*, BJS 311 [Atlanta: Scholars Press, 1997], 31). She concludes, "we may posit that the historical Elijah was a legendary rain-inducer" (32). Whether the narrative of chapters 17–18 is of one piece originally is unimportant to my argument, as I am examining the final form that would have been available to James. White's argument is, however, of interest in that she concludes the (relative) historicity of the same narrative frame that James highlights.

in the wilderness, where he is fed by birds. The first miracle story lasts just until the famine is severe enough to dry up his water supply (17:5–7). At that point God sends him into exile: "Go now to Zarephath, which belongs to Sidon, and live there" (17:9a). In an interesting twist on biblical commands to care for widows and orphans (cf. Jas 1:27), God says, "I have commanded a widow there to feed you" (17:9b). Elijah's presence, however, ensures that the widow and her son continue to have food. In this story, we also see the scope of the famine. Israel's covenant unfaithfulness under Ahab affected not only Israel but also the surrounding nations (17:14).

When the widow's son becomes ill and dies, she exclaims, "What have you against me, O man of God? You have come to me to bring my sin to remembrance, and to cause the death of my son!" (1 Kgs 17:18). In this first mention of her sin, the widow associates this sickness and death with her unconfessed sin (cf. Jas 5:15–16).[5] Elijah does not engage as prosecutor; rather, he acts to revive the boy, crying out to the Lord in prayer and intercession. This narrative illustrates James's command in chapter 5 that believers intercede for one another for healing, along with its implication that some illness is caused by sin, which requires confession. This is not, however, the part that James highlights.

After the mother's confession of faith, the narrative returns to Israel in chapter 18.[6] First, Elijah faces Obadiah, who, though a leader in the king's court, also quietly defies the king and alerts Elijah that he is not as alone in faithfulness as he presumes (vv. 7–16). Elijah swears himself bound to face Ahab, which comforts the troubled Obadiah. Elijah here uses a military title for YHWH (יהוה צבאות, 18:15; cf. Jas 5:4), a "title [that] was particularly associated with Yahweh as the covenant God of Israel," signifying that he is ready to fight for Israel's covenant.[7] When Ahab encounters Elijah, they engage in verbal sparring over who has troubled (עכר; vv. 17, 18) Israel—Elijah through the famine or Ahab through his leadership: "Elijah's indictment is

---

[5] James A. Montgomery notes that the mother's cry is an "expression of ancient religion, the 'Scheu vor Heiligkeit.' What had escaped divine notice before is now revealed by the discovery of a divine in her house, who has acted as detective of holiness" (*A Critical and Exegetical Commentary on the Books of Kings*, ICC [Edinburgh: T&T Clark, 1951], 295). See also J. Robinson, *The First Book of Kings*, CBC (Cambridge: Cambridge University Press, 1972), 202.

[6] Raymond Westbrook notes that, on the basis of Obadiah's statement in 18:10 and extradition laws, it was necessary for Elijah to flee the country, but remaining with a lowly widow may have helped to hide him from the political machinations of his day ("Law in Kings," in *The Books of Kings: Sources, Composition, Historiography and Reception*, ed. André Lemaire and Baruch Halpern, VTSup 129 [Leiden: Brill, 2010], 445–66, here 461).

[7] Robinson, *First Book of Kings*, 206. He adds, "this is the first time that this title has been used in Kings. LORD of Hosts expressed therefore the character and demands of Yahweh the God of Israel, and embodied the emotional force of the loyalty which Israel felt to her own history, tradition, and forefathers. It is in subtle touches such as this rather than in direct explanation that the narrative makes plain the full significance of the confrontation that Elijah was seeking." See also Patricia J. Berlyn, "Elijah's Battle for the Soul of Israel," *JBQ* 40 (2012): 52–62.

characteristically deuteronomic."[8] Rhetorically, Elijah dominates the conversation with Ahab, who asks only one question. From this point, Elijah drives the narrative. He has invoked the Lord of Hosts as the one for whom he mediates and rests this confrontation wholly in the Lord's hands as he issues his challenge to the 850 prophets of Baal and Asherah (18:19).

Ahab obeys Elijah, acceding to the confrontation to Elijah's control. As the narrative draws toward its climax, Elijah issues his challenge to the Israelites: "How long will you go limping with two different opinions? If the LORD is God, follow him; but if Baal, then follow him" (1 Kgs 18:21). The Israelites refuse to answer.[9] After pleading that he stands alone (despite Obadiah's statement to the contrary just before),[10] Elijah issues his challenge. Patricia J. Berlyn comments, "Elijah had given [the prophets of Baal] every advantage: First turn, first choice of sacrificial beast, a good part of the day for their efforts. They had no excuse for the fiasco watched by the assembled Israelites."[11] Charles E. Baukal adds that the elapsed time is the key to the impact of the narrative:

> The prophets of Baal prayed loudly and even cut themselves for hours with no answer from their god. Elijah prayed a short prayer to Yahweh and received an immediate response.… Elijah deliberately challenged Baal's prophets in the morning to give them plenty of time to contact their god and leave them with no excuse for Baal's failure to respond.… After hours of frenetic activity by hundreds of prophets of Baal, Elijah calmly made his preparations for the miracle so that it occurred at the time of the evening sacrifice.[12]

---

[8] Havilah Dharamraj, *A Prophet like Moses? A Narrative-Theological Reading of the Elijah Stories*, PBM (Milton Keynes: Paternoster, 2011), 25. Given that Baal was the deity who brought rain, she adds, "A likely possibility is that the Baalist Ahab believes that Elijah's intransigent stance re the LORD has offended Baal and caused him to withhold Israel's rain." Iain Provan notes that Elijah's challenge serves to upset the polytheistic worldview of Baal, god of rain, who must occasionally submit to Mot, the god of death. He argues that "it is the Lord's *presence in judgment* that leads to infertility, rather than his *absence in death*" (*1 and 2 Kings*, Understanding the Bible [Grand Rapids: Baker, 2012], 132; emphasis original).

[9] Dharamraj, *Prophet like Moses?*, 27, observes, "Walsh correctly evaluates the situation thus: 'Since Yahweh is on the side of exclusivism and Baal is not, even a willingness to consider choosing moves one toward Yahweh.' Thus, Israel's silence communicates not only their refusal to be drawn into choice, but also their inability to see the two deities as rivals." See Jerome T. Walsh and David W. Cotter, *1 Kings*, Berit Olam (Collegeville, MN: Liturgical Press, 1996), 245–46.

[10] Montgomery notes that he is "contrasting himself with the hundreds of Baal prophets; but his sense of utter loneliness is expressed again at 19:14" (*Critical and Exegetical Commentary*, 301). This sense of standing alone on YHWH's side, exacerbated by his time in the wilderness, appears as a common theme of Elijah.

[11] Berlyn, "Elijah's Battle," 57. Several articles focus on the context for the prophetic frenzy and Elijah's mockery of it, e.g., J. J. M. Roberts, "A New Parallel to 1 Kings 18:28–29," *JBL* 89 (1970): 76–77, https://doi.org/10.2307/3263640; Gary A. Rendsburg, "The Mock of Baal in 1 Kings 18:27," *CBQ* 50 (1988): 414–17.

[12] Charles E. Baukal, "Pyrotechnics on Mount Carmel," *BSac* 171 (2014): 293.

It is not simply that Elijah had to wait all day for the prophets of Baal to exhaust themselves but that the timing "coincided with what should have been the time of the evening sacrifice (1 Kings 18:36), had the Israelites been faithfully practicing the commands prescribed by God."[13] Berlyn adds that, in building the twelve-stone altar, Elijah likely rebuilt one that had been knocked down (cf. 18:30, 19:14), and in so doing "took care that all the tribes ... were represented, ... including those now in the Kingdom of Judah; another instance of the prophetic tradition clinging to the idea of a single peoplehood regardless of political schism. Invoking the memory of their Patriarchs would stir emotion in the assembly, a reminder of an origin and historic identity."[14]

Elijah controls the scene to restore Israel to its religious loyalty to YHWH. This is, in Terence Fretheim's words, "a dramatized form of the First Commandment."[15] If, before the contest, Israel refused to be drawn into even acknowledging the contest, at this moment of fire and wonder, the Israelites "fell on their faces and said, 'The LORD indeed is God; the LORD indeed is God'" (יהוה הוא האלהים; 18:39), finally reiterating the Shema (Deut 6:4: יהוה אלהינו) and declaring their covenant fidelity. Elijah, speaking in the name of the Lord (cf. Jas 5:10), restores Israel to its rightful worship of God alone, no longer wavering between two opinions (1 Kgs 18:21; cf. Jas 4:4–10). The prophets of Baal (and presumably Asherah) are executed for their role in leading Israel in false worship, and Ahab is invited to "Go up, eat and drink" (18:41). Kathryn L. Roberts argues that this odd command is an invitation to the king to restore covenant relations with YHWH in the place where YHWH had just provided a clear sign of presence.[16] She concludes, "Yahweh's acceptance of Ahab in the renewal of covenant is visibly confirmed when the rain

---

[13] Ibid. See also W. Phillip Keller, *Elijah: Prophet of Power* (Waco, TX: Word, 1980), 78.

[14] Berlyn, "Elijah's Battle," 58.

[15] Terence E. Fretheim, *First and Second Kings*, WeBC (Louisville: Westminster John Knox, 1999), 102–3.

[16] Kathryn L. Roberts, "God, Prophet, and King: Eating and Drinking on the Mountain in First Kings 18:41," *CBQ* 62 (2000): 632–44. She argues this based on parallels with Moses and the exodus account at Sinai: "in the older tradition found in Exod 24:1–2, 9–11 the covenant is ratified by a meal on the sacred mountain in the presence of the deity. In Exod 24:1–2 Yahweh commands Moses and the elders of Israel to come up onto the mountain; this command is echoed by Elijah's 'Go up!' in 1 Kgs 18:41. Ahab responds by going up, just as Moses and the elders of Israel go up onto the mountain to eat and to drink in Exod 24:9–11.... After the terrifying display ..., the eating and drinking on the mountain served to reassure the participants that a true covenantal relationship had been established between them and God. The meal signified not merely that the people of Israel had accepted the covenant with God but, more importantly, that this dangerous god [sic] was affirming relationship with Israel" (637–38). In contrast, Montgomery (*Critical and Exegetical Commentary*, 306) interprets verse 41 as "Elijah courteously bids his monarch to refresh himself," which follows Josephus (*Ant.* 8.343): ἔφη δὲ καὶ τῷ βασιλεῖ πορεύεσθαι πρὸς ἄριστον μηδὲν ἔτι φροντίσαντα, "He also told the king to go to his midday meal without further care" (Thackeray, LCL). Roberts's proposition seems to be accepted among modern commentators; see Marvin A. Sweeney, *I and II Kings: A Commentary*, OTL (Louisville: Westminster John Knox, 2007), 229; or

comes and the drought ends. Rain and blessing, abundance and growth are Yahweh's promised results for obedience to the commandments of the covenant."[17] Throughout, Ahab is a man swayed by the strongest personality around him, vacillating between Jezebel and Elijah regarding who will influence Israel through him. At this point, Ahab continues to follow Elijah (as he has throughout the chapter), persuaded by the dramatic events that have occurred. Once he returns to Jezebel, however, he exemplifies a double-minded person "like a wave of the sea, driven and tossed by the wind … unstable in every way" (Jas 1:6–7). Ahab immediately blames Elijah for all the events that led to the death of the prophets of Baal (1 Kgs 19:1).

Elijah, meanwhile, bows to the ground at the summit of Mount Carmel. The reader infers that he is interceding on behalf of Israel that YHWH would end the drought. Indeed, in contrast to the wavering king Ahab, Elijah demonstrates what it means to pray "in faith, never doubting" (Jas 1:6) that God would restore Israel on the basis of their covenant reaffirmation in 1 Kgs 18:39. Elijah sends his servant seven times, confident that by the seventh a sign of God's faithfulness would appear, and it does (1 Kgs 18:43–44).[18] Elijah returns to Ahab and runs as herald before him. James A. Montgomery observes, "Elijah assumes this office of herald because he had to all appearance won the king and all the people over to the cause of the nation's God."[19]

Thus, the narrative arches from covenant pronouncement of drought, to God's directive to Elijah to hide, to the miracle healing story outside of Israel, and finally to the miracle story of restoration of Israel and its king. Recurrences of Elijah's insistence that he is all alone crop up in these chapters, making his self-pitying remarks in chapter 19 unsurprising.[20] Nonetheless, he remains faithful and obedient to the work of calling Israel back from its double-minded ways to covenant worship of YHWH alone.

Lissa M. Wray Beal, *1 and 2 Kings*, ApOTC (Nottingham: Apollos; Downers Grove, IL: InterVarsity Press, 2014), 245.

[17] K. L. Roberts, "God, Prophet, and King," 643.

[18] Paul R. House comments, "Rain is not just rain here but evidence of the Lord's absolute sovereignty over nature and human affairs" (*1, 2 Kings*, NAC [Nashville: Broadman & Holman, 1995], 221).

[19] Montgomery, *Critical and Exegetical Commentary*, 307.

[20] Robert J. Foster argues that we should include 1 Kgs 19, when Elijah flees to the desert and pleads to die, as part of James's narrative background, because this narrative further draws out how ὁμοιοπαθής Elijah truly was with us (*The Significance of Exemplars for the Interpretation of the Book of James*, WUNT 376 [Tübingen: Mohr Siebeck, 2014], 184–89). For this article, however, I am working within the bounds of the three-and-a-half year drought/rain miracle that James outlines, but I would argue that the seeds of Elijah's later loneliness and despair are evident in chapters 17–18.

II. Elijah in Early Jewish Literature

Wiard Popkes observes that Elijah "was a very popular figure in Judaism and early Christianity, as a man of God endowed with miraculous power, as an eschatological figure, and as a firm, unshakeable fighter for the Lord."[21] In early Jewish literature, there is very little sense that Elijah was an ἄνθρωπος ... ὁμοιοπαθὴς ἡμῖν. For instance, in the Praise of the Ancestors (Sir 44–50), the poem of Elijah (48:1–11) is one of the longest, surpassing even Moses's account (44:23c–45:5).[22] James M. Darlack notes that, in Sirach, "Elijah's ministry is characterized by judgment and fire."[23] Indeed, in verse 4, the author asks a rhetorical question that sets this text in direct opposition to how James reads the Elijah story: "How glorious you were, Elijah, in your wondrous deeds! Whose glory is equal to yours?" (ὡς ἐδοξάσθης, Ηλια, ἐν θαυμασίοις σου· καὶ τίς ὅμοιός σοι καυχᾶσθαι; 48:4). One might wonder whether James's expression Ηλίας ἄνθρωπος ἦν ὁμοιοπαθὴς ἡμῖν is a response to Sirach's question. Throughout Sirach's recitation of his history, Elijah towers over his fellow Israelites. His defining act is that "by the word of the Lord he shut up the heavens" (Sir 48:3; see v. 2), the incident James also highlights. Sirach's illustration of Elijah's startling deeds, however, is that he "raised a corpse from death" (48:5). This story of the widow's son, which James seemingly ignores, is one of the primary demonstrations for why no one can equal Elijah's glory.[24] Elijah, in Sir 48:5–6 at least, has power over life and death. He raises kings and overthrows powers, even while himself bears rebuke (v. 7a) and rebukes Israel (vv. 2–3). The poem ends with

---

[21] Wiard Popkes, "James and Scripture," *NTS* 45 (1999): 227–28.

[22] This is of note, given that Deut 34:10–12 concludes the Pentateuch with "Never since has there arisen a prophet in Israel like Moses, whom the Lord knew face to face. He was unequaled for all the signs and wonders that the Lord sent him to perform in the land of Egypt, against Pharaoh and all his servants and his entire land, and for all the mighty deeds and all the terrifying displays of power that Moses performed in the sight of all Israel." Yet in Sirach's narration, Elijah is given more weight. Dharamraj argues that, narratively at least, Elijah is presented in the stories in 1 Kgs 17–2 Kgs 2 as a prophet like Moses (*Prophet like Moses?*, 218–25). This is not a new argument, as she includes in her appendix a rabbinic text of Pesiq. Rab. Piska 4.2 that argues, "You find that Moses and Elijah were alike in every respect."

[23] James M. Darlack, "Pray for Reign: The Eschatological Elijah in James 5:17–18" (MA thesis, Gordon-Conwell Theological Seminary, 2007), 29.

[24] Intriguingly, Liv. Pro. 10:4–5 appears to view the raising of the widow's son as a prophetic witness to Jonah: "At that time [while Jonah was living in self-imposed exile for having falsely prophesied in Nineveh] Elijah was rebuking the house of Ahab, and when he had invoked famine upon the land he fled. And he went and found the widow with her son, for he could not stay with uncircumcised people; and he blessed her. And when her son died, God raised him again from the dead through Elijah, for he wanted to show him that it is not possible to run away from God" (trans. D. R. A. Hare, *OTP* 2:392). Note 10.d adds, "the narrative assumes familiarity with the widespread tradition that Jonah was the son of the widow of Zarephath."

the prophecy of Elijah's return at the end of times to help again with restoring Israel (v. 10).[25] This poem focuses on the deeds of Elijah in transforming Israel and in judging kings and leaders.

Alongside his deeds, there are also "eschatological implications of using Elijah as an example of faithful, righteous prayer."[26] This tradition emphasizes the themes of repentance and restoration mediated by an intercessor amid dramatic events. Giovanni Bottini notes a broadening of the theme of intercessors throughout the early Jewish period, saying of 4 Ezra (2 Esdras) that "it testifies that the circle of intercessors in late Judaism had widened, multiplying the figures and agents of intercession,"[27] something we can see from the multitude of intercessors such as angels and martyrs in texts like 1 Enoch as well. In 2 Esd 7:106–11 [36–41], a list of those who have interceded on behalf of God's people despite the people's covenantal unfaithfulness concludes with an appeal for all the righteous to pray for the ungodly. Included in this list is Elijah, who prayed "for those who received the rain, and for the one who was dead, that he might live" (7:109). Here, the two illustrations of Elijah's intercessions represent dramatic transformations of the two major events of his mighty deeds in Sirach.[28] These two incidents typify how Elijah's story was summarized in early Jewish literature. Significantly for our passage in James, this text from 2 Esdras highlights two incidents, the rain and the raising of the dead child, suggesting that, if James had wished to illustrate the power of prayer for healing, he could have selected the latter incident from the common narrative of Elijah's great deeds and prayers. These retellings of Elijah's story concentrate on both his drought/rain miracle and the healing miracle and emphasize his exaltation as a prophet distinct from the average person.

---

[25] Jeremy Corley, "Sirach 44:1–15 as Introduction to the Praise of the Ancestors," in *Studies in the Book of Ben Sira: Papers of the Third International Conference on the Deuteroncanonical Books, Shime'on Centre, Pápa, Hungary, 18–20 May, 2006*, ed. Géza Xeravits and József Zsengellér, JSJSup 127 (Leiden: Brill, 2008), 180. While Sirach largely "lacks the hope of an afterlife for his deceased predecessors, … interpreting the Book of Malachi, Ben Sira has an expectation of Elijah's return (48:10–11), so the implication is that the prophet escaped death and will return to earth in the future."

[26] Darlack, "Pray for Reign," abstract. According to Darlack, the text of Sirach points to a future return of Elijah, when he will "calm the wrath of God before it breaks out in fury, … turn the hearts of parents to their children, and … restore the tribes of Jacob," thereby "[associating] the mission of the eschatological Elijah with the mission of the Servant of the Lord" (30).

[27] Giovanni Claudio Bottini, *La Preghiera di Elia in Giacomo 5,17–18: Studio della tradizione biblica e giudaica*, SBFA 16 (Jerusalem: Franciscan Printing Press, 1981), 80: "Esso testimonia inoltre che il cerchio degli intercessori nel tardo Giudaismo si era allargato moltiplicando le figure e gli operatori di intercession" (my translation). Some texts also indicate that intercession can be done by righteous commoners, although 2 Esdras, which lists Abraham, Moses, Joshua, Samuel, David, Solomon, Elijah, and Hezekiah (7:106–11), does not clearly move in that direction.

[28] Given this development, Sophie Laws's complaint that "it is at first sight surprising to find Elijah, commonly thought of as the archetypal prophet, appealed to as the exemplary man of prayer" becomes less of a surprise (*Commentary on the Epistle of James*, 237).

Sirach ends with the awareness that Elijah was taken up to heaven bodily, and this developed into a theme that he was the ultimate righteous man, a theme that James might have referenced in the statement "the prayer of the δίκαιος is effective" (Jas 5:16). In its list of Israel's faithful ancestors, 1 Macc 2:58 comments that "Elijah, because of great zeal for the law, was taken up into heaven."[29] His righteousness accounts for both God's assumption of him and his promised return in Mal 4:5–6 to again set Israel right. Elijah's zeal for the law is reflected in a later rabbinic tradition wherein Elijah would appear and moderate disputes about legal interpretation, whether by showing up in the present[30] or the future[31] to mediate legal disputes or affirm another person's righteousness.

Building on the elusive statement in Mal 4:5–6 ("I will send you the prophet Elijah before the great and terrible day of the LORD comes"), Second Temple literature and early Christian and rabbinic writings focused on the return of Elijah as a sign of the end of time. For instance, the second Sibylline Oracle includes Elijah as one of the key characters who will return with Moses and Abraham at the time of final and fiery judgment (Sib. Or. 2:247).[32] These eschatological interpretations

---

[29] Josephus (*Ant.* 9.28) is less confident of Elijah's end: κατ' ἐκεῖνον δὲ τὸν καιρὸν Ἠλίας ἐξ ἀνθρώπων ἠφανίσθη καὶ οὐδεὶς ἔγνω μέχρι τῆς σήμερον αὐτοῦ τὴν τελευτήν· μαθητὴν δὲ Ἐλισσαῖον κατέλιπεν, ὡς καὶ πρότερον ἐδηλώσαμεν. περὶ μέντοι γε Ἠλία καὶ Ἐνώχου τοῦ γενομένου πρὸ τῆς ἐπομβρίας ἐν ταῖς ἱεραῖς ἀναγέγραπται βίβλοις, ὅτι γεγόνασιν ἀφανεῖς, θάνατον δ' αὐτῶν οὐδεὶς οἶδεν, "Now about that time Elijah disappeared from among men, and to this day no one knows his end. He left behind him a disciple Elisha, as we have already related. However, concerning Elijah and Enoch, who lived before the Flood, it is written in the sacred books that they became invisible, and no one knows of their death" (Thackeray, LCL).

[30] See b. Ber. 6b: "There was once a man who prayed at the rear of a Synagogue and did not turn his face towards the Synagogue. Elijah passed by and appeared to him in the guise of an Arabian merchant. He said to him: Are you standing with your back to your Master? and drew his sword and slew him"; b. Taʿan. 22a, "R. Beroka Hozaʾah used to frequent the market at Be Lapat where Elijah often appeared to him. Once he asked [the prophet], is there any one in this market who has a share in the world to come? He replied, No. Meanwhile he caught sight of a man wearing black shoes and who had no thread of blue on the corners of his garment and he exclaimed, This man has a share in the world to come"; b. Sukkah 52a , "'If it were I', said Abaye, 'I could not have restrained myself', and so went and leaned in deep anguish against a doorpost, when a certain old man came up to him and taught him: The greater the man, the greater his Evil Inclination." According to the Soncino edition, tradition identifies the anonymous old man with Elijah. Translations of the Babylonian Talmud are from I. Epstein, ed., *The Babylonian Talmud*, 18 vols. (London: Soncino, 1935–1952; repr., 1978).

[31] See b. Pesaḥ 20b: "But how can we burn even that which is doubtful together with that which is unclean: perhaps Elijah will come and declare it clean!"; b. Ber. 35b: "He replied: When Elijah comes he will tell us whether it can really serve as a basis; at present, at any rate, no man thinks of such a thing."

[32] One rabbinic tradition also picks up on this and urges Sabbath law observance as the right course of action to avoid the threat of Elijah's return. See b. Šabb. 118a: "R. Simeon b. Pazzi said in the name of R. Joshua b. Levi in Bar Ḳappara's name: He who observes [the practice of] three meals on the Sabbath is saved from three evils: the travails of the Messiah, the retribution of

raise the possibility that James uses Elijah to conclude the epistle based on the Malachi tradition, since Elijah will "turn the hearts of parents to their children and the hearts of children to their parents, so that I will not come and strike the land with a curse" (Mal 4:6; cf. Jas 5:19–20). In the tradition, Elijah was not only a historical prophet who called the people to repentance but one who *will* call the people to repentance again (see Matt 17:10–12).

Given these various strands, we can affirm that Elijah was viewed as anything but ὁμοιοπαθὴς ἡμῖν. He was a great and glorious heroic figure, righteous beyond his contemporaries and his successors, and expected to return to prepare humanity for the end, restoring the faithful so that they do not face God's judgment. The author of James follows some of these threads and yet also deviates from fellow Jews in his interpretation of Elijah. The context of prayer for healing by a righteous person may have triggered the use of Elijah as a model. The author refuses, however, to join in the idealization of Elijah as a faultless hero of the faith. Instead, drawing on the tradition recorded in Kings and in contrast to early Jewish literature, James follows his own path.

III. Elijah in Modern James Scholarship

The most common interpretation of Jas 5:17–18 has been through the line, Ἠλίας ἄνθρωπος ἦν ὁμοιοπαθὴς ἡμῖν (v. 17a). Calvin encourages the reader "that if Elias was heard, so also we shall be heard when we rightly pray.... Lest anyone should object and say, that we are far distant from the dignity of Elias, he places him in our own rank, by saying, that he was a mortal *man* and *subject to the same passions* with ourselves."[33] Ralph P. Martin argues that James's focus is on "like us" and that this type of prayer, therefore, is attainable by any righteous person.[34]

This understanding of Elijah as ὁμοιοπαθής has variations. C. Leslie Mitton

---

Gehinnom, and the wars of Gog and Magog. 'The travails of the Messiah': 'day' is written here; whilst there it is written, *Behold, I will send you Elijah the prophet before the great and terrible day of the Lord comes*. The retribution of Gehinnom': 'day' is written here; whilst there it is written, *That* day *is a day of wrath*. 'The wars of Gog and Magog': 'day' is written here; whilst there it is written, *in that* day *when Gog shall come*."

[33] John Calvin, *Commentaries on the Catholic Epistles*, trans. John Owen (Edinburgh: Calvin Translation Society, 1855), 360 (emphasis original).

[34] Ralph P. Martin, *James*, WBC 48 (Waco, TX: Word, 1988), 212. Peter H. Davids comments, "Elijah was simply another human being like all those in the congregation reading the epistle" (*The Epistle of James*, NIGTC [Grand Rapids: Eerdmans, 1982], 197). See also Scot McKnight, *The Letter of James*, NICNT (Grand Rapids: Eerdmans, 2011), 450–51; and Dibelius (*James*, 257), who argues (as for all the exemplars in the epistle) that James draws upon the Jewish tradition rather than the biblical account (256), even though he then concedes that the emphasis on ὁμοιοπαθής contradicts the tradition (257). He sees no connection to verses 19–20.

notes that "the word [*homoiopathēs*] suggests that Elijah, no less than we ourselves, was sometimes unduly influenced by his feelings.... In this we realize that he is one of us. Since his frailties link him with us, his achievements should serve us as an example that we may emulate."[35] Likewise, Luke Timothy Johnson contends that the description of Elijah "avoids making Elijah a semidivine figure" and encourages a suffering community, because "Elijah did not pray out of a posture of ostensible strength; he was beleaguered and isolated when he prayed. *That* is the lesson to readers who see themselves as oppressed by the powerful."[36] Robert Foster comments, "It was as a mere man that Elijah achieved remarkable results.... He certainly felt alone as he faced the Mount Carmel challenge (cf. 1 Kings 18:22) and as he reflected on what he saw as a failed mission (1 Kings 19:10, 14)."[37] For these authors, James's use of the term ὁμοιοπαθής is grounded in Elijah's common humanity and frailty.[38]

Other commentators understand the illustration of Elijah in its context of prayer for healing. William R. Baker and Thomas D. Ellsworth, for example, understand Elijah's second prayer in terms of "divine restoration of the devastated land to its bountifulness," which "fits well with James's interest in extolling the power of intercessory prayer to restore an ailing person to health."[39] Robert W. Wall says, "Such prayers that agree with God's intentions to send rain and end droughts are similar to prayers that agree with God's will to heal people: in both situations God's will is to heal, whether nature or body."[40] Ironically, this ignores that it was covenantally also God's will for drought. Both Martin and Douglas J. Moo pick up on Peter Davids's explanation of the psychological power of the analogy of a restored

---

[35] C. Leslie Mitton, *The Epistle of James* (London: Marshall, Morgan & Scott, 1996), 207. See, similarly, Thomas Manton, *An Exposition on the Epistle of James* (1693; repr., London: Billing & Sons, 1962), 465; William F. Brosend comments that "it is God whose power and effectiveness is on display in the Elijah narrative, which may well be part of the point James is trying to make in saying that Elijah was like us" (*James and Jude*, NCBiC [Cambridge: Cambridge University Press, 2004], 155–56).

[36] Johnson, *Letter of James*, 344.

[37] Foster, *Significance of Exemplars*, 190–91.

[38] Some, like Patrick J. Hartin (*A Spirituality of Perfection: Faith in Action in the Letter of James* [Collegeville, MN: Liturgical Press, 1999], 123) simply find Elijah an example to be imitated. See D. Edmond Hiebert, *The Epistle of James: Tests of a Living Faith* (Chicago: Moody, 1979), 328; Dibelius, *James*, 242; R. Kent Hughes, *James: Faith That Works* (Wheaton, IL: Crossway, 1991), 268. David P. Nystrom concludes that "Elijah is singled out because his heart was sensitive to God. The point here is that sin hinders our ability to pray" (*James*, NIV Application Commentary [Grand Rapids: Zondervan, 1997], 316). Burchard opines that Elijah was "gerecht," as the audience should be (*Der Jakobusbrief*, 214).

[39] William R. Baker and Thomas D. Ellsworth, *Preaching James* (St. Louis: Chalice, 2004), 145. See also Burchard, *Der Jakobusbrief*, 214–15.

[40] Wall, *Community of the Wise*, 268.

land for prayer,[41] and Martin links the healing of a person and the "fruit" they might bear with the fruit the land bore, an echo of the wise person in 3:18.[42]

A second focus of interpretation understands Elijah's prayer as a prophetic call to repentance. Dan McCartney notes that "the occasion of Elijah's prayer that the drought would end was right after the Mount Carmel incident (1 Kings 18), which more than any other event in Elijah's life stands as a marker of God's judgment against idolatry and the restoration of righteousness in Israel."[43] Craig L. Blomberg and Mariam J. Kamell suggest that James uses this example because of the "sinfulness of ancient Israel, epitomized in King Ahab, whose overt rebellion and apparent repentance brought about Elijah's prayers," and "Elijah's prayers had the goal of bringing repentance and confession to the whole nation, thus restoring the people to a proper relationship with God."[44] Bottini concludes, "It could be said that the evocation of the closed sky or the drought-rain theme brought with it a series of other themes, such as sin, prayer, the invocation of the name of God, conversion, forgiveness of sins, the straight way, etc."[45] Kurt A. Richardson not only notes the eschatological emphasis of the Elijah narrative *and* the healing of the son of the Zarephath widow as an example of the form of healing prayer that James encouraged (although he goes no further with that second theme) but also points out that 1 Kgs 18 explicitly illustrates "double-mindedness,"[46] thus bringing him closest to my argument.

Many commentators highlight the awkwardness of the example of Elijah in its context of prayer for healing. For instance, Blomberg and Kamell ask:

> Why not the more dramatic encounter with the prophets of Baal (1 Ki 18:16–40) or the more directly relevant episode of the resurrection of the son of the Zarephath widow (17:17–24), given James's context of physical healing? Elijah's

---

[41] Davids, *Epistle of James*, 197; cf. Martin, *James*, 213; and Douglas J. Moo, *The Letter of James*, PilNTC (Grand Rapids: Eerdmans, 2000), 248, although Moo questions the tenuousness of the link.

[42] Martin, *James*, 213.

[43] Dan McCartney, *James*, BECNT (Grand Rapids: Baker Academic, 2009), 259. Burchard argues that "Elia betet gegen götzendienerische und für geständige Sünder.... An Elia konnte James die Doppelmacht des Gebets zu Heil und Unheil exemplarisch zeigen" (*Der Jakobusbrief*, 214). See also Manton, *Exposition on the Epistle of James*, 469.

[44] Craig L. Blomberg and Mariam J. Kamell, *James*, Zondervan Exegetical Commentary on the New Testament (Grand Rapids: Zondervan, 2008), 246–47.

[45] Bottini, *La Preghiera di Elia*, 172: "Si potrebbe dire che l'evocazione del cielo chiuso o del tema della siccità-pioggia portava con sé tutta una serie di altri temi come il peccato, la preghiera, l'invocazione del nome di Dio, la conversione, il perdono dei peccati, la retta via ecc." (my translation). See the critique in Darlack, "Pray for Reign," 17–21. Keith Warrington adds that suffering may be caused by sin, as it was in Israel's case of idolatry ("James 5:14–18: Healing Then and Now," *IRM* 93 [2004]: 346–67, here 365).

[46] Kurt A. Richardson, *James*, NAC 26 (Nashville: Broadman & Holman, 1997), 240.

prayer for drought is not as amazing as a prayer for resurrection, and in the original context (1 Ki 17:1) it is not even obvious that Elijah *does* pray.[47]

Laws finds the example surprising, "in particular that the appeal is not to that story of his miracles in which he is specifically described as praying and which might seem more appropriate to the context of James: the revival of the son of the widow of Zarephath."[48] Even Dale Allison falls into this speculation: "As to why our author thought of Elijah in this connection [to a righteous man praying] as opposed to Abraham, Moses, Samuel, or some other famed intercessor, or why he did not call to mind the even more dramatic encounter with the prophets of Baal, we do not know."[49]

These commentators cite stories encapsulated within the drought narrative in Kings but do not argue that this entire narrative might therefore be at work in James 5. Many seem constrained by the mention of drought and rain and therefore fail to pursue a broader use of the Kings narrative as part of the conclusion.[50]

If, however, we look briefly at scholarship regarding the example of Abraham in James, we find that many commentators include the entirety of Abraham's life in their purview.[51] For instance, Johnson follows R. B. Ward in seeing that "Abraham's deeds of hospitality [are included] among those 'works' that demonstrate his faith,"[52] not simply the Akedah. Davids concurs that Ward "correctly argues that the successful outcome of this event was seen as a reward for [Abraham's] *previous* righteous deeds of charity."[53] Most commentators follow, or at least give consideration to, Ward's thesis that the hospitable works of Abraham—while not alluded to in Jas 2:21–24—are included in James's discussion and therefore support the argument of James 2.[54] Ward warns that "when the author of James employs OT persons as examples, he sometimes elaborates his example explicitly, but sometimes he

---

[47] Blomberg and Kamell, *James*, 246. See also Moo, *James*, 248.

[48] Laws, *Commentary on the Epistle of James*, 235.

[49] Dale C. Allison, *A Critical and Exegetical Commentary on the Epistle of James*, ICC (London: Bloomsbury T&T Clark, 2013), 774.

[50] E.g., Joseph B. Mayor, *The Epistle of St. James*, 2nd ed. (London: Macmillan, 1897), 173; or Keith Warrington, "The Significance of Elijah in James 5:13–18," *EvQ* 66 (1994): 217–27; Warrington, "James 5:14–18," 346–67.

[51] Cf. Dibelius, *James*, 161–62, 168–74.

[52] Johnson, *Letter of James*, 249; R. B. Ward, "The Works of Abraham: James 2:14–26," *HTR* 61 (1968): 283–90.

[53] Davids, *James*, 130; so also Martin, *James*, 97.

[54] Ward, "Works of Abraham," 283–90. He comments that "the example of Rahab fits well the parable of 2:15, 16.... But the example of Abraham is somewhat more problematic" (285). Ward's thesis of Abraham as a historical model of hospitality has gained widespread acceptance. Yet Nicholas Ellis (*The Hermeneutics of Divine Testing: Cosmic Trials and Biblical Interpretation in the Epistle of James and Other Jewish Literature*, WUNT 2/396 [Tübingen: Mohr Siebeck, 2015], 199–210) and Foster (*Significance of Exemplars*, 59–103) have both challenged the hospitality thesis, arguing instead that Abraham and Rahab provide examples of endurance in trials.

presupposes his readers will know the reference."[55] A similar argument might be made for the examples of Rahab and Job, who together with Abraham and Elijah provide four powerful examples of Old Testament characters whose whole stories reveal their faithfulness to God in their actions.[56] Many already conclude that the allusion to the Akedah is the summation of Abraham's lifetime of faithfulness and that the "patience of Job" refers to his continued faithfulness in the entire book.[57] If James can allude to the whole of a story simply by giving its frame or a significant moment, it seems well worth asking whether the allusion to Elijah's rain narrative offers more than has been drawn out.

IV. A Narrative at Work

I propose that, by referencing Elijah's prayers against and for rain, the entire narrative of 1 Kgs 17:1–18:46 is in view in the Epistle of James. In positioning this example so close to the end of the letter, James brings together a number of important themes and thereby brings the epistle to its conclusion. James draws on the Jewish tradition as he has received it but focuses on the original narrative. Within the framework of 1 Kgs 17–18, there are at least five points where the narrative illustrates key themes in James. Not all of these connections bear the same weight; some serve rather as cumulative connections to bolster the argument.

1. James 1:27 asserts that "pure and faultless religion" looks after "orphans and widows in their distress," and 5:4 promises that God hears the cry of the oppressed. God begins by feeding Elijah in the ravine, a place of safety. But shortly thereafter, he is sent to stay with a widow, and through his presence God provides food and security for this widow and her son. Her desperate plan of eating one last meal before starvation is answered by Elijah's message—"don't be afraid." God could have fed Elijah in the wilderness throughout the entire drought, as God did Israel in the wilderness for forty years, but chose instead to work through the prophet's situation to answer the cries of at least one widow's family.[58] Further, in 1 Kgs 18:3–4 and 13,

---

[55] Ward, "Works of Abraham," 287.

[56] See here particularly Foster, who comments, "In naming an exemplar and citing an event an author (or speaker) cannot prevent an audience's collective mind reflecting on the wider story. Indeed, as we saw early Jewish exegetes did exactly that as they interpreted the Akedah as a summary of Abraham's life of faith and obedience rather than as a single event." He argues that all four examples work thus to provide models of faithfulness in trials.

[57] See particularly Christopher R. Seitz, "The Patience of Job in the Epistle of James," in *Konsequente Traditionsgeschichte: Festschrift für Klaus Balzer zum 65. Geburtstag*, OBO 126 (Freiburg, Schweiz: Universitätsverlag; Göttingen: Vandenhoeck & Ruprecht, 1993), 373–82.

[58] As is mentioned in Luke 4:25–26: "there were many widows in Israel in the time of Elijah … yet Elijah was sent to none of them except to a widow at Zarephath in Sidon." Luke seems intrigued that God worked to care for a non-Israelite widow.

God works through Obadiah as a leader and prophet who stands within the system to protect the persecuted prophets, illustrating a faith that worked for the protection of the oppressed.[59] Both Elijah and Obadiah risked their lives in various ways to stand against the oppressive regime of Ahab and Jezebel. The theme of protecting the oppressed, which is so important to the epistle, is thus highlighted again at the conclusion, illustrated by these chapters of 1 Kings.

2. James 5:10 further expands on the model of the prophets. Although endurance is often depicted as a passive act,[60] when faced with the sin and idolatry of Israel, Elijah challenges the king of Israel himself. In 1 Kgs 18:17–18, he confronts Ahab again: "*I have not troubled Israel; but you have, and your father's house, because you have forsaken the commandments of the* LORD *and followed the Baals.*" Elijah accuses the king and those with him of idolatry. Endurance like that of the prophets entailed confronting the powers that be. Elijah's deed is a reminder that to endure like the prophets is to take an active stance: to "maintain a belief or course of action in the face of opposition, *stand one's ground, hold out.*"[61]

3. Crucial for the context in James, Elijah provides an example of the effectiveness of the prayer *for healing*. While several commentators have noted that the story of the widow's son would have been a better example than that of prayer for drought/rain in this context, none argue that the healing narrative could be one reason why James highlights the whole passage. In 1 Kgs 17:17–24, the first time Elijah is explicitly said to pray, his prayer triumphs over death: "The LORD listened to the voice of Elijah; the life of the child came into him again, and he revived" (17:22). No illustration could better demonstrate how effective prayer can be, even in cases of extreme illness.

The widow in this story asks whether Elijah had "come to me to bring my sin to remembrance" (1 Kgs 17:18), a question remarkably apt when we consider that

---

[59] Elijah thought he alone survived, but Obadiah, described as one who "revered" the Lord (18:3), put his faith to work and saved one hundred prophets by hiding them from the wrath of the king.

[60] Because of this theme of endurance, many modern commentators suggest that the Testament of Job figures in the background of Jas 5:11. See, e.g., Cees Haas, "Job's Perseverance in the Testament of Job," in *Studies on the Testament of Job*, ed. Michael A. Knibb and Pieter W. van der Horst, SNTSMS 66 (Cambridge: Cambridge University Press, 1989), 117–54; Patrick Gray, "Points and Lines: Thematic Parallelism in the Letter of James and the *Testament of Job*," *NTS* 50 (2004): 406–24; David A. deSilva, *The Jewish Teachers of Jesus, James, and Jude: What Earliest Christianity Learned from the Apocrypha and Pseudepigrapha* (Oxford: Oxford University Press, 2012), 237–51. In contrast, see Seitz, "Patience of Job," 373–82.

[61] BDAG, s.v. "ὑπομένω." Ellis's work on the "Jobraham" narrative as it functioned in Jewish literature also moves the definition of "endurance" away from passivity and argues that both narratives are important for understanding the theology of James (*Hermeneutics of Divine Testing*, esp. 222–34). Like Job and Abraham, Elijah endures in the face of Ahab's oppression of the prophets and stands faithful before God in the trials he faces.

James also links some illnesses with sin and urges confession for healing (Jas 5:16). Elijah does not answer her charge, but, by restoring the boy, frees the woman from the wrongful belief that her son's life was taken to account for her own sin.[62] James affirms that confession can bring absolution, forgiveness, and healing, but also that not all illness is due to sin.[63] The freedom Elijah gives the widow fits with James's vision of mercy (e.g., 1:17–21, 2:8–13, 5:20).

4. First Kings 17–18 portrays other lessons regarding prayer. The example of Elijah praying at the end of chapter 18 coheres with Jas 1:5 and the "prayer of faith" that does not waver or doubt. Elijah faced a cloudless sky, "bowed himself down upon the earth and put his face between his knees" (1 Kgs 18:42). Seven times he sends his servant to examine the sky and only the last time does the servant report a cloud the size of a fist. Hearing of the tiny cloud on the horizon, Elijah runs. His assurance to Ahab in 18:41 that "there is a sound of rushing rain" comes well before any sign of rain is present, a warning given in confidence of faith. His announcement of the end of the drought, his consistent checks of the horizon, and the speed with which he runs from a tiny cloud reveal his faith that the drought *would* end as a result of his prayer.[64]

When Elijah first appears before Ahab in this narrative, he simply announces "As the Lord the God of Israel lives, before whom I stand, there shall be neither dew nor rain these years, except by my word" (1 Kgs 17:1). Unlike James's description of Elijah as προσευχῇ προσηύξατο ("he prayed fervently," 5:17), the narrator in 1 Kings does not describe Elijah's prayer.[65] Elijah's prophetic pronouncement, however, comes as a word from the Lord, "whom [he] stands before" (עמדתי לפניו, 1 Kgs 17:1) showing the reader Elijah's relationship with God through the stance of the righteous in prayer.[66]

---

[62] This reflects the pledge that "parents shall not be put to death for their children, nor shall children be put to death for their parents; only for their own crimes may persons be put to death" (Deut 24:16).

[63] James 5:15b begins with the strong conditional κἂν ἁμαρτίας ᾖ πεποιηκώς, ἀφεθήσεται αὐτῷ.

[64] Foster takes Elijah's persistence as an example of faith working (cf. Jas 2) (*Significance of Exemplars*, 184–89).

[65] See Johnson, *Letter of James*, 336; Brosend, *James and Jude*, 155; Mayor, *Epistle of St. James*, 175; Mitton, *Epistle of James*, 207; Laws, *Commentary on the Epistle of James*, 235; Moo, *James*, 248; Simon J. Kistemaker, *Exposition of James, Epistles of John, Peter, and Jude*, New Testament Commentary (Grand Rapids: Baker, 1986), 181, all of whom question James's insertion in some way. See, however, 2 Esd 7:109, where Elijah is said to have prayed (verb from v. 106) "for those who received the rain, and for the one who was dead, that he might live."

[66] See also 1 Kgs 18:15, 2 Kgs 3:14, 5:16. William Barclay remarks that "the Jewish attitude to prayer was *standing before God*; and so in this phrase the Rabbis found what was to them an indication that the drought was the result of the prayers of Elijah" (*The Letters of James and Peter*, 2nd ed., Daily Study Bible [Edinburgh: St. Andrew, 1960], 156).

Likewise, as James argues in 4:15, prayer ought to be done ἐάν ὁ κύριος θελήσῃ ("if the Lord wishes").[67] Elijah's prayer for drought was within the realm of God's declared will regarding a disobedient Israel. One of the covenant curses for those who turn aside and worship other gods is drought and subsequent famine (Deut 28:23–24). Restoration is promised for those who repent and return (Deut 30:1–10). Thus, in announcing the drought, Elijah invokes God's covenant curse for a double-minded people, and in praying for the return of the rain, he intercedes for what God covenanted would happen when the people repented.[68]

5. Elijah's prayer for drought and rain exemplifies prophetic prayer for judgment and for redemption. This theme is well developed in the traditional story and in early Jewish literature but has not been fully explored by commentators.[69] The *purpose* of the drought was to bring the king and his people to repentance, following the Deuteronomic covenant. As Ahab troubled the people of Israel by following Jezebel into idolatry, Elijah enacted covenantal judgment on a sinful king. Moreover, James's reference to ἐνιαυτοὺς τρεῖς καὶ μῆνας ἕξ ("three years and six months," 5:17) "was symbolically charged because it is half of seven, and in Dan 7:25 and 12:1 it is the length of the apocalyptic period of distress."[70] Judgment for covenant unfaithfulness seems inherent in James's appropriation.

Additionally, in the grand confrontation scene in 1 Kgs 18:21, "Elijah then came near to all the people, and said, 'How long will you go limping with two different opinions?[71] If the LORD is God, follow him; but if Baal, then follow him.'" As J. Robinson observes, "What is being described through the clash of these two men is a deep and bitter conflict between two opposed ideals of religion and human

---

[67] Warrington argues that the importance of God's will in how we pray "provides the most likely reason for [James's] adaptation of the Old Testament account of Elijah" ("Significance of Elijah," 224; see also Warrington, "James 5:14–18," 366).

[68] This mention of rain, and the nature miracle more generally, fits with James's preference for using rural or nature imagery to make his points (e.g., 1:9–11, 17; 3:1–12; etc), teaching people how they ought to be from the model of the natural. Alicia Batten observes that this may well be an intentional preference in line with Greco-Roman writers who see urban as artificial and the natural world as pure ("The Urban and the Agrarian in the Letter of James," *JECH* 3 [2013]: 4–20).

[69] Indeed, Giovanni Claudio Bottini contends that there is no emphasis on judgment in the New Testament accounts: "La minaccia del giudizio non è esplicitamente rilevata né in Gc 5,17–18 né in Lc 4,25–26 nonostante la drammaticità del-l'evento" (*Giacomo e la sua Lettera: Una Introduzione*, SBFA 50 [Jerusalem: Franciscan Printing Press, 2000], 133).

[70] Allison, *Critical and Exegetical Commentary*, 778. See also Darlack, "Pray for Reign," 71–73, for a fuller exposition on how three and a half years stood as an apocalyptic symbol of judgment.

[71] Cf. the NIV "How long will you waver between two opinions?"; the LXX is quite vivid: Ἕως πότε ὑμεῖς χωλανεῖτε ἐπ' ἀμφοτέραις ταῖς ἰγνύαις, "How long will you go limping on both legs?" [NETS]; MT: עד־מתי אתם פסחים על־שתי הסעפים. See Richardson, *James*, 239–40, for the explicit link with the two "double-minded" audiences.

society, which were so basically in conflict with each other that the very existence of the one menaced the existence of the other."[72] Just as James allows for no accommodation with the κόσμος and permits nothing less than the complete repentance of his double-minded people who want to have both the κόσμος and their Christian faith (cf. 4:1–10),[73] so Elijah faces a people torn between following their double-minded king into worship of Baal and following their prophet into worship of YHWH. The drought narrative of Elijah perfectly illustrates James's repeated call to single-minded faithfulness to God, providing the link between a righteous person praying for healing and the final concluding call to restore those who wander.[74]

Elijah's prayer for drought was not punitive but restorative, calling the people back from the error of their way, from their double-mindedness. This coheres with James's warning at the beginning of the epistle to pray—in faith—for wisdom, not as a double-minded person to whom God will not even listen.[75] Here, when the people repent and reaffirm the Shema, God hears and restores his covenant blessing on his people through the coming rain. The judgment and restoration theme in Elijah also illustrates James's warnings in chapter 2 against a false, workless faith, his urgent call for repentance in 4:4–10, his flow of thought that illness leads to confession and restoration in 5:16, and the call that all believers share in restoring those wandering in 5:19–20.[76] Elijah's prophetic act of withholding rain serves as a biblical model for James of God's opposition to the double-minded, for the double-minded are covenantally unfaithful, hence the strong μοιχαλίδες ("Adulterers!") in 4:4.

IV. Conclusion

Elijah was a "person like us," but the point of this example in James goes beyond a common humanity. Many other themes in James are illustrated in the two chapters of 1 Kgs 17–18. Within the three-and-a-half-year period to which James

---

[72] Robinson, *First Book of Kings*, 189.

[73] See Darian R. Lockett, *Purity and Worldview in the Epistle of James*, LNTS 366 (London: T&T Clark, 2008).

[74] Dennis R. Edwards starts in this direction but then backs away: "The Israelites' shift away from idolatry, accompanied by expressions of repentance, is consistent with the message of Jas 4:4–10. It may be that the illustration of Elijah's prayer regarding the weather is meant, in part, to serve as an allusion to the spiritual condition of the people: drought indicates spiritual distance from God, and fruitful land depicts spiritual restoration. The main point, however, is that prayer can bring about the transformation" ("Reviving Faith: An Eschatological Understanding of James 5:13–20" [PhD diss., Catholic University of America, 2003], 143).

[75] See ibid., 62–66, for a clear overview of the substantial links between Jas 5:13–20 and 1:1–12. Allison posits a chiastic structure of the letter that parallels 1:2–8 with 5:12–20 (*Critical and Exegetical Commentary*, 80).

[76] Foster, *Significance of Exemplars*, 188–91.

alludes, Elijah enacts a prophetic denunciation of a wandering people, cares for a starving widow, raises a child from the dead, challenges the double-minded people of Israel and their king to purify their hearts and hands, and exemplifies the prayer of active faith in accordance with the will of God. Rather than a single reason for this exemplar, invoking Elijah also calls to mind a rich array of intertextual parallels.

The whole of 1 Kgs 17–18 is relevant to the context of Jas 5. In an epistle concerned with a new vision of mercy and freedom (see esp. 1:17–21, 2:8–13, 3:17–18), Elijah heals the widow's son despite her unnamed sin and restores Israel to its relationship with God. By refusing the dramatic elevation of Elijah common to the time, James repudiates a spiritual partiality, refusing to view Elijah's example as unattainable. Rather, Elijah is ὁμοιοπαθής, and his readers can pray just as vitally. James calls his audience to the same sorts of actions: praying in faith, confronting power, and calling wanderers to repentance. James 1:5–8 warns against double-mindedness, the cause of Israel's punishment in those three and a half years. James begins his epistle urging prayer but not as δίψυχοι ("double-minded"), and chapter 4 teaches that the righteous person prays and acts in accordance with the Lord's will (4:15). James gives the double-minded his strongest call for repentance in 4:1–12 and concludes the epistle with the example of the intercessory Elijah, who exemplifies bringing others to repentance.

The example of Elijah at the conclusion of the epistle offers a key to the theme of James: becoming people characterized by single-minded devotion to God. Hence, we might argue that the conclusion begins with its call to pure speech in 5:12. A person who reflects the character of God in unified faith will speak the truth in their worship and prayers (5:13–16), standing before God in community as Elijah did. Verses 19–20 show the task of a person who prays for the repentance of God's double-minded people. Far from a stray afterthought, these verses bring the reader back to the themes that began the epistle and make clear the reader's responsibility to pray in faith like Elijah as they seek to restore the double-minded to wholeness. Thus, the whole section of 5:12–20, with Elijah as the capstone exemplar, provides a fitting conclusion to the epistle, drawing together the diverse threads into a final summation of what it means to live out single-minded faith in God.

Annual Index
Volume 137 (2018)

Amihay, Aryeh, "Biblical Myths and the Inversion Principle: A Neostructuralist Approach," 555–79

Amzallag, Nissim, "The Authorship of Ezra and Nehemiah in Light of Differences in Their Ideological Background," 271–97

Backfish, Elizabeth, "Transformations in Translation: An Examination of the Septuagint Rendering of Hebrew Wordplay in the Fourth Book of the Psalter," 71–86

Baker, Robin, "Double Trouble: Counting the Cost of Jephthah," 29–50

Bertschmann, Dorothea, "Is There a Kenosis in This Text? Rereading Philippians 3:2–11 in the Light of the Christ Hymn," 235–54

Bloch-Smith, Elizabeth, "The Impact of Siege Warfare on Biblical Conceptualizations of YHWH," 19–28

Briggs, William, "Fluid Dynamics: The Interplay of Water and Gender in Nahum," 853–70

Brookins, Timothy, "A Tense Discussion: Rethinking the Grammaticalization of Time in Greek Indicative Verbs," 147–68

Bryan, Steven M., "The End of Exile: The Reception of Jeremiah's Prediction of a Seventy-Year Exile," 107–26

Burt, Sean, "'Your Torah Is My Delight': Repetition and the Poetics of Immanence in Psalm 119," 685–700

Douglas, Alex P., "A Call to Law: The Septuagint of Isaiah 8 and Gentile Law Observance," 87–104

Duff, Justin Harrison, "The Blood of Goats and Calves … and Bulls? An Allusion to Isaiah 1:11 LXX in Hebrews 10:4," 765–83

Edwards, James R., "The Rider on the White Horse, the Thigh Inscription, and Apollo: Revelation 19:16," 519–36

Elder, Nicholas, "'Wretch I Am!' Eve's Tragic Speech-in-Character in Romans 7:7–25," 743–63

Esler, Philip F., "'All That You Have Done … Has Been Fully Told to Me': The Power of Gossip and the Story of Ruth," 645–66

Ferguson, Anthony, "The Elijah Forerunner Concept as an Authentic Jewish Expectation," 127–45

Fewster, Gregory Peter, "Manuscript, Voice, and the Construction of Pseudepigraphal Identities: Composing a Mutable David in Some Qumran Psalms Scrolls," 893–914

Fox, Michael V. "The Meanings of the Book of Job," 3–18
Fredriksen, Paula, "How Jewish Is God? Divine Ethnicity in Paul's Theology," 193–212
Fried, Lisbeth S., "150 Men at Nehemiah's Table? The Role of the Governor's Meals in the Achaemenid Provincial Economy," 821–31
Garroway, Kristine, "2 Kings 6:24–30: A Case of Unintentional Elimination Killing," 53–70
Glanville, Mark, "The *Gēr* (Stranger) in Deuteronomy: Family for the Displaced," 599–623
Gulliver, Mike, and William John Lyons, "Conceptualizing the Place of Deaf People in Ancient Israel: Suggestions from Deaf Space," 537–53
Hamilton, Catherine Sider, "The Death of Judas in Matthew: Matthew 27:9 Reconsidered," 419–37
Haring, James W., "Romans 5:12, Once Again: Is It a Grammatical Comparison?," 733–41
Heilmann, Jan, "A Meal in the Background of John 6:51–58?," 481–500
Jones, Brice C., "A Greek Papyrus Fragment with a Citation of Matthew 1:20," 169–74
Knust, Jennifer W. *See* Wheeler-Reed, David
Kovalishyn, Mariam Kamell, "The Prayer of Elijah in James 5: An Example of Intertextuality," 1027–45
Lang, T. J., "Trouble with Insiders: The Social Profile of the ἄπιστοι in Paul's Corinthian Correspondence," 981–1001
Last, Richard, "*Ekklēsia* outside the Septuagint and the *Dēmos*: The Titles of Greco-Roman Associations and Christ-Followers' Groups," 959–80
Leonard-Fleckman, Mahri, "Utterance of David, the Anointed of the God of Jacob (2 Samuel 23:1–7)," 667–83
Lyons, William John. *See* Gulliver, Mike
Martin, Dale B. *See* Wheeler-Reed, David
Martin, Troy W., "Concluding the Book of Job and YHWH: Reading Job from the End to the Beginning," 299–318
Massey, Preston T., "Veiling among Men in Roman Corinth: 1 Corinthians 11:4 and the Potential Problem of East Meeting West," 501–17
Matson, David Lertis, "Double-Edged: The Meaning of the Two Swords in Luke 22:35–38," 463–80
McClellan, Daniel, "The Gods-Complaint: Psalm 82 as a Psalm of Complaint," 833–51
Méndez, Hugo, "Mixed Metaphors: Resolving the 'Eschatological Headache' of John 5," 711–32
Miller, Shem, "The Role of Performance and the Performance of Role: Cultural Memory in the Hodayot," 359–82

Milstein, Sara J., "Separating the Wheat from the Chaff: The Independent Logic of Deuteronomy 22:25–27," 625–43

Nässelqvist, Dan, "The Question of Punctuation in John 1:3–4: Arguments from Ancient Colometry," 175–91

Pope, Michael, "Gabriel's Entrance and Biblical Violence in Luke's Annunciation Narrative," 701–10

Quine, Cat, "Reading 'House of Jacob' in Isaiah 48:1–11 in Light of Benjamin," 339–57

Reinhartz, Adele, "Passing the Torch," 785–88

Schellenberg, Ryan S., "Subsistence, Swapping, and Paul's Rhetoric of Generosity," 215–34

Screnock, John, "The Syntax of Complex Adding Numerals and Hebrew Diachrony," 789–819

Shinall, Myrick C., Jr., "The Social Condition of Lepers in the Gospels," 915–34

Smith, Geoffrey, "The Willoughby Papyrus: A New Fragment of John 1:49–2:1 (P134) and an Unidentified Christian Text," 935–58

Stevens, Daniel, "Is It Valid? A Case for the Repunctuation of Hebrews 9:17," 1019–25

Van Ee, Joshua J., "Wolf and Lamb as Hyperbolic Blessing: Reassessing Creational Connections in Isaiah 11:6–8," 319–37

Van Tine, R. Jarrett, "Castration for the Kingdom and Avoiding the αἰτία of Adultery (Matthew 19:10–12)," 399–418

Wasserman, Tommy, "Bringing Sisters Back Together: Another Look at Luke 10:41–42," 439–61

Weingart, Kristin, "'My Father, My Father! Chariot of Israel and Its Horses!' (2 Kings 2:12 // 13:14): Elisha's or Elijah's Title?," 257–70

Wheeler-Reed, David, Jennifer W. Knust, and Dale B. Martin, "Can a Man Commit πορνεία with His Wife?," 383–98

White, Justin J., "Image in Text: Interpreting the Ephah Vision of Zechariah 5:5–11," 871–91

Woodington, J. David, "A Precedented Approach: Paul's Use of the Law of Witnesses in 2 Corinthians 13:1," 1003–18

Yoo, Philip Y., "Once Again: The *Yam Sûp* of the Exodus," 581–97

New in 2018!

Wisdom Literature
Samuel E. Balentine

Wisdom literature is foundational to our life and learning, and its end is the shaping of a moral self and community attuned to the character of God. For the wisdom writings of the Old Testament, the pursuit of wisdom calls for the ongoing attainment of instruction, insight, shrewdness, knowledge, prudence, learning, and skill. This pursuit of wisdom is an ongoing journey, never a simple arrival.

Samuel E. Balentine is Professor of Old Testament at Union Presbyterian Seminary.

Introduction to the Hebrew Prophets
James D. Nogalski

Modern readers are invited to hear the ancient scrolls anew. Dr. Nogalski offers a basic introduction, which includes critical issues such as authorship, unity, dates of composition and revision, and structure. Drawing upon current scholarship, he shows how these issues are relevant to the theological themes and movements that help characterize the text and hold meaning for us.

James D. Nogalski is Professor and Director of Graduate Studies in Religion at Baylor University.

70 Hebrew Words Every Christian Should Know
Matthew Richard Schlimm

Studying basic Biblical Hebrew can add meaning to and enliven Christianity. Learning a language is like learning a worldview. Those who learn Biblical Hebrew can better understand not only what biblical authors wrote, but also how they thought. This usually requires years of study; however, this book is about getting right to the important, exciting insights.

Matthew Richard Schlimm is Professor of Old Testament at the University of Dubuque Theological Seminary in Iowa.

Jesus Darkly
Rafael Rodriguez

New Testament students have not always been well served by study of the historical Jesus, which tends to segregate Jesus from his significance vis-à-vis Israel's scriptures and God's agenda as this is developed among the New Testament writers in the living context of a faith community's memory. The witness of scripture does in fact help us remember Jesus well.

Rafael Rodriguez is Professor of New Testament in the School of Bible and Theology at Johnson University in Knoxville, TN.

See all current and forthcoming titles at
AbingdonAcademic.com

www.ingramcontent.com/pod-product-compliance
Lightning Source LLC
Chambersburg PA
CBHW021822300426
44114CB00009BA/287